Teaching Mathematics to Students with Learning Disabilities

Teaching Mathematics to Students with Learning Disabilities

Fourth Edition

Nancy S. Bley
Carol A. Thornton

pro·ed
An International Publisher

8700 Shoal Creek Boulevard
Austin, Texas 78757-6897
800/897-3202   Fax 800/397-7633
www.proedinc.com

An International Publisher

© 2001, 1995, 1989 by PRO-ED, Inc.
8700 Shoal Creek Boulevard
Austin, Texas 78757-6897
800/897-3202   Fax 800/397-7633
www.proedinc.com

Library of Congress Cataloging-in-Publication Data

Bley, Nancy S.
    Teaching mathematics to students with learning disabilities /
Nancy S. Bley, Carol A. Thornton.—4th ed.
      p. cm.
    Rev. ed. of: Teaching mathematics to the learning disabled.
    Includes bibliographical references and index.
    ISBN 0-89079-857-5 (alk. paper)
    1. Mathematics—Study and teaching (Elementary). 2. Learning
disabled children—Education—Mathematics. I. Thornton, Carol A.
II. Bley, Nancy S. Teaching mathematics to the learning disabled.
III. Title.
QA135.5.B56 2001
371.9'0447—dc21

                                 00-037457
                                    CIP

This book is designed in New Century Schoolbook, Formal BT, and Frutiger.

Printed in the United States of America

     7 8 9 10 11 12 13 14   17 16 15 14 13 12

To our husbands, Michael and Dennis,
our children,
Chris, Stephanie, and Jennifer,
and to
Gail and Genny,
for their ongoing, patient understanding and support
throughout the years.

Contents

♦ ♦ ♦ ♦ ♦ ♦ ♦ ♦ ♦ ♦ ♦ ♦ ♦ ♦ ♦ ♦ ♦ ♦ ♦

Chapter 6

Concepts and Computation of Whole Numbers ♦ *203*

Chapter 7

Rational Numbers: Early Concept Work with Fractions and Decimals ♦ *281*

Chapter 8

Extending Understanding and Application of Fractions and Decimals ♦ *323*

Preface

◆ ◆

Teaching Mathematics to Students with Learning Disabilities is a professional resource for teachers at the elementary and middle school levels who teach students with learning disabilities. Now in its fourth edition, this resource has been written with the belief that, though they learn differently, most students with learning disabilities can master important mathematical concepts and skills, can apply them in their day-to-day lives, and will use them to advantage in their future careers. This belief has evolved out of our personal experiences with students having learning disabilities that affect mathematics learning and achievement, and has molded the way in which our ideas for mathematics instruction have been developed and refined.

It has been said that to help students grow we must allow them to grapple with concepts and ideas that are *just beyond* their reach. Interactions with teachers who have used earlier editions of this book suggest that alternative approaches and sequences like those in this book are very useful for helping students learn important mathematical concepts and skills—even those that are seemingly *just beyond* their reach.

This fourth edition, consistent with recommendations in *Principles and Standards for School Mathematics* (National Council of Teachers of Mathematics, 2000), continues to emphasize problem solving, number sense, student decision making, and ways of effectively incorporating technology in mathematics instruction—from calculators and computer spreadsheets to the use of selected Web sites and computer software. Specifically, we explore strategies for helping students become more successful mathematical thinkers. A further reorganization of chapters in this edition and the presentation of alternative learning sequences accommodates a greater focus on concept development and applications. Also, the diagrams and figures have been updated and improved.

We recognize how critical it is in daily situations to be able to determine and use efficient methods of solving a quantitative or data-based problem and to recognize whether results are reasonable. These ideas underlie our analysis of instructional modifications that are sometimes necessary to meet and accommodate our students' special learning needs. Rather than treating all topics in the school mathematics curriculum comprehensively, we have chosen to focus on mathematics topics that can or do cause the most difficulty for students with learning disabilities.

For each major topic addressed, we provide background information that summarizes standard approaches and points out particular problems that students with learning disabilities may encounter with a given mathematics concept or application. Then we present at least one sample sequence of suggested learning activities to highlight the fact that instructional alternatives are often necessary to meet the needs of students with specific learning disabilities. The assumption is that teachers are familiar with standard approaches to handling the topics.

Previous editions have presented a variety of instructional adaptations that teachers can use or share with students to make them more successful in mathematics within the parameters of their specific limitations. Methods such as color coding, organizing file pages spatially, previewing, and getting students to restate or otherwise communicate their understanding of an important mathematical idea or procedure are among the many modifications used in the sample learning sequences in this book. Students with learning disabilities, like many other students, need to communicate their understanding actively—verbally, in writing, or by some form of demonstration—in order to internalize and remember. This idea is recognized as an important one and is interwoven consistently in the learning sequences presented in this edition.

Our overriding goal is to help students learn to compensate for their learning disabilities and to deal effectively with mathematics both in academic and everyday situations. Any inspiration we can provide toward accomplishing this goal comes primarily from the students with whom we have worked and from whom we have learned.

Chapter 1

❖ ❖ ❖ ❖ ❖ ❖ ❖ ❖ ❖ ❖ ❖ ❖ ❖ ❖ ❖ ❖ ❖ ❖ ❖

Planning Instruction
for Special Needs

Students with learning disabilities are able to learn . . . they just learn differently than most students (Hotz, 1999). For this reason, there characteristically is a discrepancy between their learning potential and their performance. Probably the single biggest obstacle to learning for these students is their inability to process and apply information at the same rate as their peers, making it appear that they are unable to work independently. (Although the authors are not aware of any specific research in the area of mathematics with regard to processing speed, information coming out in the field of language processing and reading should not be ignored when teaching students mathematics.) There are a variety of reasons for this, some of which are listed below:

- an inability to use critical thinking without direct instruction;
- visual perceptual difficulties that preclude accurately interpreting what is written on a page;
- poor retention;
- difficulty with auditory processing.

Most students who understand their learning disabilities and how they learn are highly motivated and willing to learn, and many have good study skills. Those students who do not understand their learning disabilities or are not able to use appropriate and necessary modifications are often the ones who begin to misbehave, withdraw, or simply not attend.

The problem may be compounded when these students are mainstreamed or taught in resource rooms along with children who have uniquely different learning styles, abilities, and interests. Mathematics teachers somehow must deal with each student's diverse learning needs. Too often the curricular goals may also seem unrealistic. How does one adequately teach the expected content and still help those students who have legitimate learning difficulties?

In regular mathematics classes, even the best attempts to handle the different learning needs of students with learning disabilities through individual assignments or cooperative learning schemes are sometimes thwarted. Although a teacher may be able to spend some time working individually with a child or a small group, overall the setting still demands the ability to process and apply information at a rate that may be more rapid than these students can successfully manage, thus preventing them from working independently. It cannot, however, be assumed that they will learn the needed skills on their own. They must learn to understand how they learn and then be taught what they need to do in order to participate in this type of environment.

A teacher may encounter additional problems in attempting to use textual material typically written for regular class students. Most commercial texts are visually confusing, causing students with learning disabilities to lose their place, have difficulty focusing on and copying problems, or be unable to accurately work in the space provided in workbooks. Lessons frequently are not sequenced to provide transition between topics, and there is often not enough review of important concepts. Students with language difficulties or those who have trouble reading may find the text hard to comprehend, while students who cannot readily transfer concepts from concrete to abstract may find the use of manipulatives confusing at best and perhaps even meaningless.

All of these issues are continually being addressed in the context of new thrusts in school mathematics. Students who enter kindergarten in 2001 can expect to graduate from high school in the year 2013. By then the world of mathematics will have changed significantly. Although computation will still be essential, the way students achieve results will be quite different. Students today and in the future must be able to (a) determine the most efficient way to arrive at an answer and (b) evaluate the need for an exact answer or an approximation. They must be competent to choose from and effectively use a variety of formats—mental calculation, estimation, a calculator, a computer, and/or paper and pencil. They must also be able to adjust to subtle differences between available tools, such as different types of calculators and different models of computers and software. The understanding and ability to clearly process language will be even more important. The language of computers and calculators has brought a whole new dimension to the world of mathematics.

Wise decision making and the ability to think critically are the keys to being a successful math student today and in the future. Practical problem solving rooted in a good sense of numbers and a good understanding of the relationships between numbers and operations is essential.

A word of caution is in order concerning the use of standardized tests. Recommendations based on the *Principles and Standards for School Mathematics* (National Council of Teachers of Mathematics, 2000) and *Assessment Standards for School Mathematics* (National Council of Teachers of Mathematics, 1995) have affected new versions of standardized tests. It is the authors' opinion that the effect on students with learning disabilities has been variable. The changes that are most noticeable include:

- more analysis of applied problem solving and critical thinking and reasoning in mathematics;

- allowing the use of calculators on the tests; and

- using a "portfolio" method of evaluating students' progress.

The latter two changes have probably had the most positive impact on learning disabled students, as they provide students with (a) alternative, and perhaps more relevant, ways of showing their understanding and ability to apply their knowledge and (b) an adaptation that takes into account the impact of their learning disabilities. In spite of these changes, however, many students still encounter enormous difficulty when faced with standardized tests due to language processing deficits. Although there is little research yet in this area, the research coming out in the area of phonological awareness should make mathematics teachers more aware of this issue. According to Dr. Kate Garnett of the Department of Special Education at Hunter College, "Some LD students are particularly hampered by the language aspects of math, resulting in confusion about terminology, difficulty following verbal explanations, and/or weak verbal skills for monitoring the steps of complex calculations."

Clearly, the emergence of a mathematics curriculum that emphasizes problem solving, critical thinking, language processing, and comprehension and computation has implications for planning educational programs in mathematics for students with learning disabilities. As in the past, the following "big ideas" must be incorporated but in such a way as to take into account students' learning strengths and weaknesses:

- Problem solving and conceptual understanding should be integrated at all levels and into all facets of a child's mathematics program.

- Students internalize mathematical concepts best by interacting with their environment through the use of realistic manipulatives and activities.

- An awareness of the language of mathematics must continually be taken into account. Written symbols, computational procedures, and vocabulary should be introduced and reviewed with exploratory work that focuses on providing meaning to what is written.

- Cooperative learning should be planned to take into account varying learning styles. Random selection of groupings does not benefit students with learning disabilities. Like all of us, these students have strengths and weaknesses, and, when working in a group, they should be allowed and encouraged to use their strengths.

- Students' feelings about themselves as learners and about their experiences with mathematics can greatly influence the level of their efforts and their eventual success. By providing an environment that is accepting, encouraging, stimulating, and relevant to how each student learns a program can foster a strong self-image and a positive attitude toward mathematics.

The following chapters will share techniques and ideas for incorporating these new theories into mathematics programs for students with learning disabilities in primary, intermediate, and middle and junior high schools. These chapters also will illustrate, for selected topics and for new thrusts related to those topics, how specialized techniques can be used within traditional sequences of instruction.

The overriding goal of this book is to present practical ideas for implementing instruction so that teachers can provide an environment in which all children will learn up to their potential. (Many of the ideas presented are just as helpful for students without learning disabilities and can be "invisibly" incorporated into the curriculum.) Sometimes, in order to do this, it is necessary to alter the standard mathematics sequence to meet the individual needs of students with learning disabilities. At other times, it is better to circumvent difficulties, using specialized methods, so these students:

- can use their strengths to compensate for their weaknesses, and

- will learn and independently develop more general compensatory techniques that will enable them to continue to learn and use mathematics.

We hope the ideas suggested will act as a springboard for teachers to develop their own ideas for teaching children with learning disabilities. No attempt has been made to deal with the content of the entire elementary school mathematics curriculum. It is assumed that teachers are familiar with standard sequences and approaches to presenting topics basic to that curriculum. Instead, the emphasis is on selected areas that commonly cause difficulties for students with learning disabilities. Instructional sequences that incorporate special techniques and adaptations for meeting special needs will be outlined. Most of these suggestions can be carried out in regular classrooms as well as in resource, clinical, or self-contained settings. The sample sequences and accompanying teaching ideas are meant to encourage teachers to be aware of learning differences, to develop and apply their own approaches, and to be comfortable using alternative, accurate sequences as the need arises. Based on this perspective, the remainder of this chapter is devoted to:

- providing the reader with an overview of learning disabilities as they relate to school mathematics through Grade 8, and

- suggesting general techniques that can aid classroom instruction and planning for students with learning disabilities.

LEARNING DISABILITIES AND THEIR EFFECT ON MATHEMATICS PERFORMANCE

Most mathematics teachers are familiar with at least some of the following situations:

- an assignment that is "wrong" because sloppy writing led to misreading or nonalignment of digits;

- the child who consistently receives high scores on quizzes of isolated basic facts yet has difficulty retrieving the same facts to solve word problems or longer computations;

- the child who never seems to pay attention during oral quizzes or explanations;

- the child whose work is correct but who cannot explain the reasons;

- children who mix up operations, skip steps in a multistep problem, or skip problems on a page;

- the older elementary student who has not memorized the basic facts;

- the child who cannot determine which of the four operations to use.

Every teacher probably can pinpoint at least one child who matches each of these descriptions and even add other examples to this list.

Such situations can be frustrating for both teacher and students. While these students may represent only a small percentage of students in a class, the nature and magnitude of the problems may be large enough to affect presentation of material and overall instruction.

Each case could involve a child with learning disabilities. Since such students typically have average or above average intelligence, teachers may mistakenly think that they are not trying, they are lazy, or they are not paying attention. Because these students frequently, and often rightly, feel that they understood something but are unable to show their understanding in a meaningful or perhaps acceptable way, many have mixed feelings about themselves. They do not look different, but they feel different. They often see themselves participating successfully in certain areas, such as sports, conversations, or even some academic areas. They try to work at least as hard as, and often work harder than, their classmates but still are not able to achieve in mathematics. They fail written tests, especially when there are time limits involved or perhaps a lot of reading. Even though there is evidence that cooperative learning can be effective, often students with learning disabilities do not study with peers for fear they will appear dumb. Outwardly they may profess to studying better alone but inwardly feel they are missing out on help and a lot of fun. Whether they are enrolled in a resource room or in a mainstreamed situation, they feel left out.

In order to help these students, both the teacher and the students themselves must understand the nature of learning disabilities. By understanding the interaction between learning theories and learning disabilities, teachers can plan instruction to:

- minimize frustration and social pressure, and
- increase awareness and acceptance of individual learning styles.

Toward that end, the following sections review common learning disabilities that influence success in mathematics. The major disabilities have been divided into several areas based on the related visual and/or auditory deficit. These areas include perceptual, memory, executive functioning, and language deficits (see Table 1.1). The area of nonverbal learning disabilities is also included (see Table 1.2 and related text on pp. 17–18).

Visual and Auditory Perceptual Disabilities

Figure-Ground Disabilities

Children with visual figure-ground difficulties may exhibit a variety of symptoms. They frequently lose their place on a page, skip parts of or entire problems, cannot locate relevant information on a page when they try to read a problem (even though they can locate relevant information when they hear a problem), or appear not to concentrate when copying problems from the book. Also, they tend to mix up parts of problems and often copy symbols incorrectly.

Table 1.1. Examples of How Learning Disabilities Affect Performance in Mathematics

Executive Functioning	• cannot draw conclusions; therefore, has trouble noticing and continuing patterns • cannot use prior knowledge to draw conclusions • has difficulty solving multistep word problems • has trouble continuing a counting pattern from within a sequence • has difficulty applying learned operations within a complex computation • has trouble applying generalizing information without a structured approach	
	Visual Disability	**Auditory Disability**
Perceptual		
Figure Ground	• may not finish all problems on a page • frequently loses place • has difficulty differentiating between operations in longer computations such as division • has difficulty chunking/visualizing groups	• has trouble discerning a counting pattern • has difficulty attending in the classroom
Closure	• has difficulty reading multidigit numbers • has difficulty perceiving a group as a whole • has difficulty continuing visual patterns • has difficulty reading algebraic equations, decimal numbers	• has difficulty counting on from within a sequence
Discrimination	• has difficulty differentiating coins and/or hands on a clock • has difficulty discriminating between or writing numbers • has difficulty discriminating between operation signs	• has trouble distinguishing between endings of numbers (e.g., 13 and 30) • has difficulty with decimal numbers • has difficulty discriminating between word parts (e.g., *addition* and *edition*)
Reversals	• reverses digits in a number (may also be a sequential memory problem) • has difficulty with regrouping	• has trouble remembering oral directions or sequences
Spatial/Temporal	• has trouble writing on lined paper • has difficulty with concepts such as *before–after; next to–above* • has trouble noticing size differences • has trouble aligning numbers	• has difficulty following directions using ordinal numbers • has difficulty with spatial adverbs (e.g., *first, next, last*)

(continues)

Table 1.1. *Continued.*

	Visual Disability	**Auditory Disability**
Spatial/Temporal (*continued*)		
	• has trouble writing fractions • has difficulty copying problems, setting up a page of work	
Memory		
Short-Term Memory	• has trouble retaining newly presented material • has difficulty copying numbers and problems from the board or paper • has trouble solving problems from a textbook	• has difficulty with oral drills • has difficulty with dictated assignments
Working Memory	• has difficulty solving word problems • has difficulty continuing a counting pattern from midpoint • has difficulty with simultaneous processing • has difficulty solving multi-operation computations	• has difficulty completing complex processes • has difficulty with simultaneous processing
Long-Term Memory	• cannot retain basic facts or processes over time • has trouble retrieving information at the needed time	• has trouble retaining orally presented information for extended periods of time
Sequential Memory	• has trouble with complex operations • has trouble accurately reading numbers • has difficulty solving longer number sentences and equations • has difficulty telling time • has difficulty solving multistep word problems	• misperceives numbers that are said (e.g., 32 becomes 23) • cannot retain story problems that are dictated
Language		
Expressive Language	• has difficulty with rapid oral drills • has difficulty counting on • has difficulty explaining why a problem is solved as it is	
Receptive Language	• has difficulty associating words with symbols • has difficulty with signs that have different meanings (e.g., fraction bar)	• has difficulty relating words to meanings • has difficulty with words that have multiple meanings • has difficulty writing numbers from dictation

Since most mathematics books present much information on a page, students with visual figure-ground disabilities may not differentiate between the problem number and the problem itself and may include neighboring digits in the computation. As a result their work appears carelessly done.

The worksheet shown in Figure 1.1 illustrates some of these difficulties. The computation in the first problem is almost accurate but includes the problem number in the final step. Problem 2 has been started correctly. The answer to 12 take away 6 is 6, but the answer is placed under problem 3. Since 7 take away 1 is also 6, the student proceeded with this computation, not realizing that an entire problem had been skipped. In problem 5, the child is still adding, possibly because of the similarity of numbers in problems 4 and 5. Problem 6 was begun but not finished, without the student being aware of it.

Visual figure-ground deficits also may interfere with the ability to accurately use a calculator or to read multidigit numbers. The proximity of the calculator keys, the size of the keys, and, particularly on some of the more advanced calculators, the size and amount on the keypad can be very confusing. These students often need calculators with color-coded keys and on which the addition and multiplication signs and the division and subtraction signs are not near one another. (Figure 1.2 shows a key pad that can be confusing to a child with visual figure-ground difficulties.) Reading multidigit numbers also is often confusing for students with figure-ground difficulties; they may confuse or skip digits within the number. It is not atypical for these students to misread the number 612 as 62, for example.

Auditory figure-ground difficulties can interfere with a student's ability to accurately perceive counting patterns. Although place-value ideas form the basis of our number system, most children learn to count by tuning into repetitive patterns they hear. Even 5 and 6 year olds learn to count by fives and tens, although they have no idea of the place-value concept. Learning to skip-count often does not come easily to children with this type of learning disability. They may be unable to discover the pattern (i.e., to localize the repetitive part and repeat it) without a much stronger oral emphasis than is generally used. Additionally, they may need a color-coded visual cue presented simultaneously.

Figure 1.1.

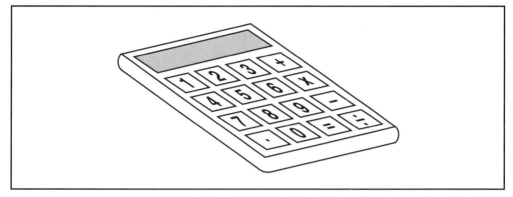

Figure 1.2.

Visual and Auditory Discrimination Disabilities

Visual discrimination errors may cause students to misread or incorrectly write numbers. Very young children often are not developmentally ready to discriminate one number from another. As a result, without even noticing the reversal, they tend to write numbers backwards, especially 2, 3, 5, 6, and 9. This difficulty is generally outgrown by the age of 7. Children with learning disabilities, however, may exhibit the problem more frequently, at a younger age, or beyond the normal developmental stage. Since they do not perceive the numbers correctly, the task of writing numbers, copying problems from the board, spontaneously writing them from dictation, or using a calculator can be extremely difficult. By the time they have written a number or keyed it into the calculator, they may have lost their place or be so far behind that the teacher is ready to erase the board, clear the computer screen, or change subjects.

Recognizing coins and telling time also can be very hard for children who are unable to discriminate subtle differences in size. The ability to recognize and differentiate between coins requires that a child notice discreet differences in size and in detail. As with the child who can read a word in isolation but not in context, some children can discriminate between isolated coins but cannot apply that knowledge to a practical situation. Similarly, telling time takes these students longer because they must consciously determine which is the minute (larger) hand on the clock while their peers locate it automatically.

As children encounter more and more symbols, visual perceptual problems become more prominent. Figure 1.3 illustrates several perceptually related errors made by children who, in fact, understood the concepts and knew how to handle the computation involved. In the first example, the computational process is right. The errors are due to interpreting the 6 as a 2. The second example shows what can happen when a child has trouble discriminating operation signs. At first, the sign was correctly seen as a plus sign and addition was performed. At the second step of the problem, however, the child perceived the sign as a multiplication sign and proceeded to use that operation. In the third example, the decimal point between the 5 and the 2 was not noticed, although the operational understanding is evident. What is important for the teacher of these students to realize is that for what was perceived, the work is accurate.

a)   46   b)   64   c)   5.2
     × 7   + 8   × .03
    294   492   1.56

Figure 1.3.

Auditory discrimination problems may be exemplified by the inability to accurately perceive number endings, for example, distinguishing between teen numbers and multiples of ten (e.g., sixteen and sixty). This, in turn, can affect a child's ability to sequence teen numbers and lead to a counting pattern such as the following: 9, 10, 11, 12, 30, 40, 50, 60, 70, 80, 90, 20. . . . The subtlety of this situation is that if asked to count aloud, the child may say the numbers correctly but incorrectly perceive what he or she hears. Depending on the severity of the problem, and the presence or absence of a visual discrimination deficit, these children may be able to correct the pattern if the symbols for 13 through 20 are placed before them.

Visual and Auditory Reversals

Another common perceptual difficulty results in reversals. Children who tend to make visual reversals not only make mirror images of individual digits, as noted in the section on discrimination, but might also reverse the digits of a two-digit number when reading or writing. The most common reversals occur in the teens: 21 for 12, 31 for 13, 41 for 14, and so on. This problem naturally leads to errors in computation. For example, children may carry the wrong number when regrouping. An example of how reversals can affect multiplication is illustrated in Figure 1.4. The child read 13 as 31 in the first problem and, consequently, multiplied 1 by 9. In the subsequent step, the 1 (of 13) was correctly located in the tens place and was multiplied next. Again, 9 was recorded in the product. In the second problem the digits were reversed when written down, thus accounting for the 7 in the ones place. The rest of the computation was accurate. This last example illustrates the importance of teaching all children, but especially those with learning disabilities, to first write the number that is to be regrouped. When using a calculator, students should be encouraged either (a) to write the problem down first and to check that what they wrote is what they meant to write or (b) to keep a clearly spaced hundreds chart in front of them so they can look at the number they mean to key into the calculator.

         13   58
       × 9   × 9
       99   477

Figure 1.4.

Auditory reversals may show up in a misuse of vocabulary. Students with this area of difficulty may accurately say or repeat a word that they have heard or read but use its antonym to solve a problem. In the authors' experience this seems to happen particularly with students who also have visual perceptual difficulties and/or language retrieval difficulties and are expending additional energy to determine what the symbol represents. These students seem to have an especially hard time understanding word problems and other practical situations as they are trying to accurately retrieve matching symbols, language, and operations.

Spatial and Temporal Disabilities

Temporal and spatial organization can greatly affect a child's mathematics performance and the ability to apply practical applications outside the classroom. Although children with temporal disabilities may be able to tell time by rote, their concept of time and, therefore, their general planning ability are often considerably impaired. A subtle, and sometimes unnoticed, result of a temporal deficit is related to the difficulty some children have with multistep computation or practical word problems. Since these students have trouble with the conceptual aspect of time, they often have trouble with the related language (vocabulary). Understanding and correctly applying temporal concepts such as *first, next,* and *then* can be quite difficult, and students may need visual cues to help them succeed with this type of problem.

Other problems characterize the child with spatial disabilities. For example, difficulty locating position in space—knowing right from left or up from down—can make the task of number alignment almost insurmountable. Renaming in computation becomes even more difficult. Children with this disability (a) need to understand *why* the regrouped number is placed above the tens digit and (b) need visual and kinesthetic clues to help them feel what various spatial terms mean.

Difficulties with spatial organization can prevent children from properly forming a number that they actually perceive accurately. They may reverse the position or invert it. Verbal cues such as "right" and "left" or "top" and "bottom" often carry little meaning and are, therefore, no help in recalling how to write the number. Specific training involving motor activities, color-coding, verbalization, and continual integration in daily, relevant experiences is essential.

At the upper grade levels, spatial and temporal difficulties may continue to interfere with the study of decimals, fractions, and multistep word problems. Even when conceptual understanding is strong, difficulties can arise. Locating where the decimal point belongs, determining the correct sequence of steps in a word problem, or properly placing the numbers in a fraction or a mixed number can be extremely laborious for a child with these deficits.

Motor Disabilities

For many children, the process of writing numbers may be so difficult that it greatly affects their ability to succeed in mathematics. Children with perceptual motor difficulties have trouble relating what they see to what they write. They cannot coordinate their eyes with the proper hand movements. As mathematical problems become longer and more involved, these children find it extremely difficult to complete written assignments because they expend so much time and energy retrieving and applying the necessary finger movements for number formation that they forget what they are doing. For these students, the increased availability of calculators and computers that are more visually clear than they have been in the past is invaluable and strongly encouraged.

Memory Difficulties

Efficiently using memory is a complex task involving the need for a strong working memory, short-term memory, long-term memory, and sequential memory (Denckla, 1994). Students with memory problems are often the ones who are accused of not listening, of doing careless work, or of copying a friend's work. After all, if they had been listening, they would have remembered the information. Students may have memory difficulties if they:

- are unable to execute a task immediately after accurately stating what to do;

- cannot accurately write down a homework assignment that is dictated or written on the board;

- are lost when the teacher continues a topic the next day after only a short review;

- are unable to use previously understood material as a basis for learning a new concept or skill.

Working Memory

Consider working memory to be the ability to smoothly and simultaneously process and apply information that continually bombards us. Working memory requires the ability to hold on to an image or an idea while simultaneously categorizing or classifying the information in order to provide an answer. For example, responding to oral drills takes efficient working memory. One must be able to remember (a) the number(s) that is (are) said and (b) the operation being stated while (c) retrieving the solution, possibly from long-term memory. (This process is compounded for students who have trouble with visual discrimination or visual memory and must expend energy also being sure that the number they are retrieving and perceiving is what was actually said.)

Students with working-memory deficits process only part of the information they hear. For example, they may complete only some of the problems or pages in a homework assignment because they could not remember all of the assignment that was dictated long enough to write it down. Similarly, the process of writing numbers independently or copying them from the board or from a textbook can be extremely difficult. The effort to retain what is to be copied and the accurate visual image while also processing correct finger movements can be quite laborious. Older students with working-memory deficits may be able to recognize the correct order of operations to solve a problem but find it hard to do so without the steps clearly listed for them.

Short-Term Memory

Short-term memory involves the ability to store information that might not be used for a short while but can be retrieved and used on (generalized) demand and perhaps without practice. Students with difficulty in this area may seem to understand what is presented in class and may even accurately complete related classroom assignments presented immediately after a discussion. However, if recess or lunch comes in between, by the time they begin to complete the assignment they have forgotten what to do or how to do it. Short-term memory deficits can also make writing or copying problems difficult for some. Unlike their peers who hold an entire problem in their minds (e.g., 48 + 63), these children must keep checking to see what they are to write or to key into the calculator.

Long-Term Memory

Storing information over longer periods of time so that it can be retrieved and efficiently applied requires good long-term memory. Students who are strong in this area respond well to the typical vertical mathematics curriculum; those who have memory difficulties, though, encounter problems, since generally there has not been enough time to overlearn material or sufficient review or previewing to provide them with the needed cues to make associations. These are the students who have trouble with unit tests or general review tests that cover several topics. They may do best on those topics most recently presented. Similarly, their performance on a test might indicate that they listened sporadically, retaining some concepts and facts but not others.

Sequential Memory

Many areas of mathematics, such as telling time, require considerable sequencing ability. Most children, for example, learn to tell time by the age of 7 or 8. But if they have trouble retaining a sequence, an otherwise simple task suddenly becomes difficult. Think for a moment of the basic steps involved in telling time:

- Which hand do I look at first?
- Which hand is smaller?
- What number does that hand refer to?
- What number does the other hand refer to?
- What number do I say first?
- How do I count by fives?

Assuming there is no spatial or temporal difficulty, the task of telling time requires that a considerable number of steps be sequenced properly. Ideally, and for most of us, these steps eventually make it into our long-term memory as a complete unit so that the process becomes automatic. In order to use each step as a transition to the next, children with sequential memory problems must learn each step to the point of overlearning.

Sequential memory also affects the ability to count money, to compute using the four operations, and to solve word problems. In addition, it affects a student's overall ability to process, understand, and apply what is taught to the class as a whole. Children with sequential memory deficits may retain only segments of information, which are therefore incorrectly used when working memory, short-term memory, and long-term memory are called into play.

Figure 1.5 shows the work of a student with possible memory difficulties. A close look will show that the child probably understands basic computation at the middle-grade level. The processes at that level are long and involved, placing great demands particularly on working memory, short-term memory, and sequential memory. This student is probably unaware that the problems are incomplete. Only so much could be held in the memory at one time.

Executive Functioning Disabilities

Martha Denckla, addressing the confusion inherent in understanding executive functioning, states, "It is generally agreed that the term *executive function* refers to mental control processes . . ." (Denckla, 1994), the components of which could be considered requirements for successfully using abstract reasoning. Some of the control processes involved are the ability to (a) retain, retrieve, process, and apply information and delay action while determining a response; (b) visualize a plan; (c) have a strong enough *sense* of time to plan a strategy that holds to a schedule; and (d) *automatically* use flexibility of thought.

Children with learning disabilities often have trouble with the learning requirements described above. They may be unable to pull information together to draw conclusions, to make associations, to use previously learned information as building blocks for learning new material, or to plan their time efficiently and effectively. Often students with executive functioning difficulties

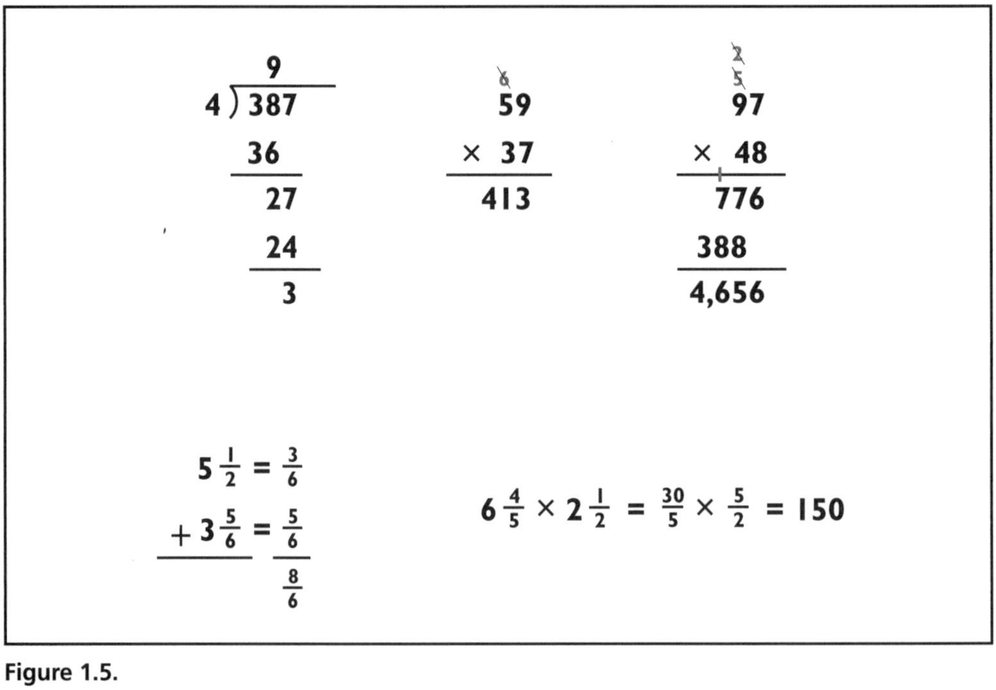

Figure 1.5.

begin to encounter problems in school only as they enter middle and/or high school, where material becomes more complex, requires more inferential thinking, and also requires more planning over longer periods of time. Prior to this time, much of the material they have learned has been provided in small enough chunks and with enough repetition that it may look like they have mastered the information, when in reality they have been able to use the structured and consistent approach that is so essential for early learning.

In math, executive functioning difficulties can be manifested in a variety of ways. Although students with such difficulties may be able to count by rote, continue a sequence of four or five numbers, and perhaps even "count on" when requested to do so, they may not recognize the need, for example, to count on when faced with a difficult or unfamiliar situation. For example, checking for the correct change or determining how much time is needed to get ready to go out might be difficult without specific instruction regarding a strategy. Counting on from within a sequence, especially when skip-counting is involved, as it often is when making change, is extremely difficult, and considerable drill and training are usually required to internalize the technique.

These same children have trouble with classification tasks. At a primary level, they have difficulty sorting shapes by one characteristic. Further, as they begin to use symbols, they may be unable to determine the similarity of numbers in a group (e.g., all even numbers). (Regardless of the specific disability, it is generally much harder for children with learning disabilities to find similarities than to find differences.) As they progress through school, the need to be able to classify continues but becomes more subtle. For example, learning to solve ratio and proportion problems requires the intuitive ability to see the relationship between this topic and finding equivalent fractions.

Word problems and other types of daily-life problem-solving situations can also be affected by difficulty with executive functioning. The ability to solve word problems greatly depends on developing an intuitive understanding of the different patterns that cause one to add, subtract, multiply, or divide. These students find it much more difficult to build up this background of problem-solving patterns; thus, they often need a "supply box" of examples as well as practice comparing words and symbols.

Abstract-Reasoning Disabilities

The ability to use abstract reasoning could be thought of as a subcategory of executive functioning, one that can be taught using concrete aids initially but becomes more automatic in most children as they develop their fund of learning strategies.

Children who have trouble with abstract reasoning may have trouble performing any of the components described below:

- verbalizing what has been learned or observed;
- associating what is happening with symbolic representations; or
- understanding what is being explained or shown.

These components could also be aspects of a language difficulty, but students with abstract-reasoning problems do not understand the process or concept, while children with language deficits can usually explain their understanding under appropriate circumstances (i.e., when provided with enough time or allowed to draw or build a description).

To develop and then exhibit their understanding, these children need the immediate and repeated association of numbers, operation signs, and other mathematical symbols that we substitute for words to understand the concept. Repetition and practice may help them feel comfortable with a given process or idea and allow for automaticity to develop. The confidence they gain from mastering the steps tends to allow them to focus their energy on understanding and applying the information. As a result, they can:

- begin to understand what it means to generalize;
- understand specific concepts;
- more easily reason and associate in general; and
- more readily apply executive functioning.

Language Disabilities

Expressive Language Problems

Children with expressive language difficulties, aside from articulation deficits, cannot verbalize clearly, if at all, what they may really understand. These are the students who have trouble with rapid oral drills. They may appear to be withdrawn or uncooperative because they do not participate in class. To avoid being embarrassed, they avoid these situations. They tend to do better in well-chosen cooperative groups where they can use a strength, perhaps being the note taker; on homework, where they have enough time to formulate and express their ideas; or when provided with visual cues. They cannot produce on demand; therefore, timed tests, whether oral or written, only make this disability more apparent.

Teachers commonly ask children to show that they understand a given concept by having them explain or apply it, either verbally or manually. This is especially true currently, when the emphasis is on clarifying understanding of procedures and using language to develop concepts. For children with expressive language deficits, this can be extremely frustrating. They need visual cues to help them retrieve words and then sequence the steps once the words are recalled. Often these students can more easily select a correct or incorrect process from a visual display or an orally presented list than they can verbalize an explanation. As a result, when a mistake occurs, they may recognize that something is not right but be unable to correct it spontaneously unless given alternatives.

Reading and writing decimals can be hard for children with expressive language difficulties. By comparison, fractions are easier. When one writes "$\frac{2}{100}$" or says "two one-hundredths," it is clear that a 2 and a 100 are included among the digits for the fraction. Decimals lack this cueing. Hearing "two one-hundredths" does not readily reveal the number of decimal digits in the number. Similarly, reading ".02" on a calculator does not automatically cue the response "two one-hundredths."

Receptive Language Difficulties

"What do you mean?" "Please repeat that." "Can I have a clue?" These questions, and many others, are frequently asked by children with receptive language deficits because they have difficulty associating meaning with words. On occasion, all of us hear common words, perhaps in context, and temporarily "blank out" on the meaning. Usually, the lapse is only temporary, a second or two. This is similar to what regularly happens to children with receptive language difficulties: they hear a word, recognize it as a unit, but fail to grasp the intended meaning.

In mathematics, this disability manifests itself in some or all of the following ways:

- difficulty following directions;
- difficulty understanding mathematical terms, especially those with multiple meanings such as *sum, times, difference,* and so on;
- difficulty solving a problem set up differently than originally presented;
- difficulty solving word problems.

Children with receptive language deficits often appear very literal. They may not understand simple jokes and generally find it hard to make sense of much of what they hear or read. Although they can repeat the exact words and may go through rote processes that are similar, they often are unable to repeat the same process if presented with the slightest variation.

Nonverbal Learning Disabilities

The child who has nonverbal learning disabilities (NLD) typically has a significantly higher Verbal than Performance IQ on the *Wechsler Intelligence Scale for Children–Third Edition,* though not all students with this discrepancy have nonverbal learning disabilities (Denckla, 1991). The child with nonverbal learning disabilities "is usually good at word recognition and spelling, but tends to be poor in arithmetic" (Badian, 1992, p. 160). These students misperceive social cues such as tone of voice and facial expression and have considerable difficulty with visual-spatial organization and understanding novel information. "Students with NLD also demonstrate marked deficits in subjects that involve complex problem solving and concept formation (such as science)" (Matte & Bolaski, 1998, p. 40). They have trouble with abstract reasoning, "lack understanding of mathematics concepts and do not readily solve problems in mathematics" (Foss, 1991, p. 129). They also may have visual motor difficulties that make writing laborious and their work sloppy. Organizational skills may be weak, and they tend to have trouble with visual imagery. They are, however, good rote learners. These students can learn to relate ideas and to apply their knowledge, but they generally require a highly structured, carefully sequenced program that provides them with a considerable amount of verbal mediation and small learning increments. "Interventions must be direct and explicit, and

Table 1.2. Nonverbal Learning Disabilities and Their Effects on Mathematics

Characteristics of Students with Nonverbal Learning Disabilities	Relationship to the Standards
Good at computation and use of formulas	Decreased use of formulas and algorithms
Poor at visual imagery	Increased use of concrete aids
Poor at abstract reasoning	Increased use of concrete aids; decreased attention to rote procedures
Need labels and have trouble retrieving vocabulary	Decreased use of key words and geometric names
Have difficulty writing	Decreased use of paper-and-pencil tasks
Describe "around" a word or situation	Increased mathematical discussions
Benefit from scanning for signal words	Decreased attention to key words

they must involve the student and consist largely of verbal communication and modeling (Matte & Bolaski, 1998).

Conclusion

Before we conclude this overview, it is important to address some areas that are not necessarily defined as learning disabilities but can sometimes look like learning disabilities and can have a strong effect on a student's progress, in any case.

Attention Deficit Disorder With and Without Hyperactivity

Many, but not all, children with learning disabilities also have Attention-Deficit/Hyperactivity Disorder (ADD), with or without hyperactivity. These children may be easily distracted either by external stimuli that most of us ignore or by internal stimuli of which we often are unaware. In general, they find it difficult to stay on task; they may seem to be in constant motion and appear not to be paying attention. In fact, they cannot sustain attention for a long period of time. They lose their place but may not even know that they have lost it. They may seem to be trying to avoid work. They may be inordinately attentive to marks on a page or to specks of dust. The slightest sound or sight distracts them.

In day-to-day situations they may also be the ones who have trouble making transitions from one topic to another. For example, turning the page of a book to begin a new topic may divert their attention from the introduction given by the teacher. They are usually quick to answer questions but often give irrelevant responses. Estimating answers is extremely difficult, and they tend to guess wildly. According to Zentall and Ferkis (1993):

> The mathematical instruction of youth with LD, ADD, and ADHD call for (a) mastery learning, which builds on prerequisite skills and understand-

ings, rather than spiral learning; (b) learning that involves active construction of meanings; (c) verbal teacher interactions with the child to assess and stimulate problem-solution strategies; (d) increased emphasis on assessment and teaching of mathematical concepts; (e) use of strategies, where appropriate, related to the requirements for reading comprehension and for memory in problem solving (e.g., for multiple-step problems); (f) attentional cues to help students prepare for changes in problem action, operation, and order of operation; and (g) novel instructional activities to facilitate overlearning basic calculations (i.e., to increase automatization). (p. 16)

A word of caution is in order. It is important to note that what we have described above relates to students who have had a careful differential diagnosis by a qualified and credentialed therapist. Without such an evaluation it is often difficult to know, for example, whether attentional problems are related to a true attention deficit, to difficulty with language processing, or perhaps to the frustration encountered by a child with visual perceptual difficulties.

Perseveration

Perseveration (the repetition of an activity even though a change is required) shows up in math in different ways. Children may perform the same operation throughout a page because they do not notice that the signs have changed. Or they may continue doing whatever was required in the first problem. Such behaviors can look careless. Careful, ongoing observation of such a child is needed to differentiate perseveration because of visual discrimination from perseveration because of figure-ground difficulties.

Figure 1.6 illustrates other ways that perseveration can affect a child's computational work. In the first step of the first problem, 17 – 9, the child continued counting backwards, unable to stop at 8. Similarly, in the second problem the count was extended farther than necessary for 6 + 5. By observing a child and requiring verbal clarification while the child is working, a teacher can tell whether the child is making conceptual errors or has no internalized means of stopping. (See Chapter 9 for a discussion of counting on.)

Once children have begun to attend, it may be extremely difficult for them to change activities unless they are reminded or physically drawn into doing so. Techniques such as handing children a clean sheet of paper on which to write or asking them to move from their seats to the board may help. Change from one academic subject to another, rather than to another topic in the same subject, may be necessary to prevent perseveration.

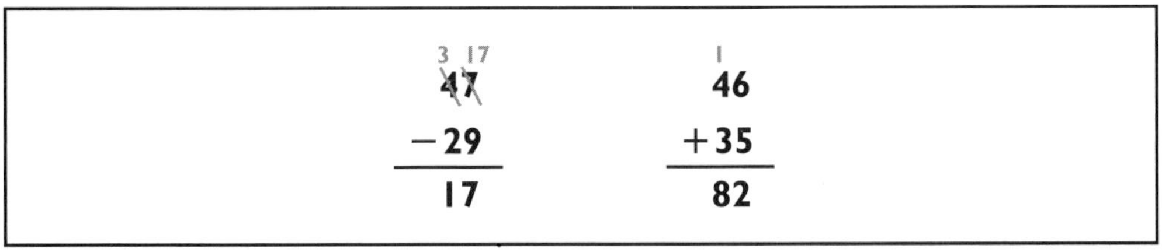

Figure 1.6.

Reading Problems

Many children with learning disabilities in math also have learning disabilities in reading, causing them to read below grade level. It is important that the teacher carefully determine whether a child is having trouble progressing in math because of difficulty reading. This is especially true for those students who have strong abstract-reasoning skills but difficulties in other areas. Since most mathematics textbooks involve a lot of reading and little ongoing, integrated review, teachers must be able to adjust learning expectations to allow these children to progress at an appropriate rate. Providing textbooks on tape and pairing a good reader with a strong math student who has difficulty reading are just two ways to address this issue. The important point to remember is that too often students look like they are having trouble with math when, in fact, they are having more trouble with reading.

For additional information regarding the relationship between reading and math, see Kulak (1993) and Russell and Dunlap (1977).

Learning Theory and Learning Disabilities

The nature and emphasis in mathematics education is changing, and there has been an increased interest in the constructivist approach in teaching and in the use of metacognition to help all students learn. Constructivist education emphasizes the child as an active learner who creates his or her own learning environment. Metacognition emphasizes awareness of how one approaches a task, in order to plan, evaluate, and monitor progress. These two approaches form an integral part of the current trend in mathematics education, in which students are encouraged to participate actively in their learning by creating "new mathematical knowledge by reflecting on their physical and mental actions" (Kamii & Lewis, 1990). The assumption is that they will be better able to understand and apply what they learn.

At the same time that we encourage and allow exploration as a means of learning and applying knowledge, it is necessary to remember the developmental issues of childhood. Most mathematics teachers, and primary school teachers in particular, are aware of the implications of Piaget's developmental theory of learning, which is based on the premise that children master mathematical concepts as they progress through certain developmental stages. Children with learning disabilities may need to have their instructional programs (even at the middle- and upper-elementary levels) geared toward these stages as new and more abstract and complex ideas are introduced, as such children do not always automatically or intuitively make associations.

One-to-one (or one-to-many) correspondence, classification, flexibility of thought, seriation, and conservation are all heavily emphasized in the early elementary years. Most students, even those with learning disabilities, often readily learn and apply those concepts at the concrete stage of instruction. As they progress to symbolic representation, they usually use the more concrete knowledge to accurately solve simple computation problems and to begin simple problem solving related to their life experience.

Students with learning disabilities who appear to be successful in math at younger ages may begin to encounter difficulties as the material becomes more "intuitive," complex, and abstract. Unlike their non–learning disabled peers, they have not internalized the above-described stages to the extent that they can apply their knowledge at a higher level and automatically. For example, although double-digit multiplication is carefully presented using concrete aids and verbal and pictorial descriptions, most children ultimately use one-to-many matching to be sure they have accurately solved a problem. (See Figure 1.7.)

A similar situation is presented in Figure 1.8, which shows the work of an 11-year-old boy who failed to exhibit true flexibility of thought. When questioned as to whether he noticed the signs, he replied, "Sure, but you always change the bottom number when they're written this way." This child had learned to multiply mixed numbers horizontally and to add them vertically. Although he recognized that the second problem involved multiplication, its vertical position confused him. In such a case, the teacher needs to "go back" to addressing flexibility of thought by some direct instruction—for example, "We can write addition and multiplication problems vertically or horizontally, but we still solve them the same way."

One last example: conservation and rational numbers. The ability to conserve implies understanding that the basic value or amount of something does not change, even though its shape or arrangement does. Children with learning disabilities tend to have difficulty applying the notion of conservation to advanced mathematical ideas, such as the topic of equivalent numbers. Figure 1.9 shows three types of numbers, all of which have equivalent value. A student who has trouble generalizing may need a direct approach to understand this example, even though the previous instruction involved a very concrete approach.

GENERAL INSTRUCTIONAL TECHNIQUES FOR DEALING WITH LEARNING DISABILITIES IN THE MATHEMATICS CLASSROOM

J. is very attentive in class, seems to follow most presentations, and usually is able to answer the teacher's questions. However, his work is always sloppily done; answers to problems run into each other, and the teacher generally is unable to match his work with the assignment.

A. regularly gets 100% on weekly basic fact tests, timed or untimed, but can never seem to give the correct answers to basic fact problems when called upon to do so in class. She consistently makes computation errors when solving application problems, although she obviously understands the concepts involved.

$$
\begin{array}{r}
58 \\
\times\ 9 \\
\hline
\end{array}
$$

Figure 1.7.

$$7\tfrac{3}{5} = 7\tfrac{6}{10}$$
$$+\,2\tfrac{1}{2} = 2\tfrac{5}{10}$$
$$9\tfrac{11}{10} = 10\tfrac{1}{10}$$

$$4\tfrac{1}{2} = 4\tfrac{2}{4}$$
$$\times\,2\tfrac{3}{4} = 2\tfrac{3}{4}$$
$$8\tfrac{6}{4} = 9\tfrac{2}{4} = 9\tfrac{1}{2}$$

Figure 1.8.

Then there is P., who never seems to complete his work—especially classroom assignments. When given time during class to copy problems, he asks to get a drink, breaks a pencil, or otherwise wastes time. When he does manage to copy and finish an assignment, he makes many errors—his method of solving may be correct, but his solutions are wrong.

These situations represent some of the problems a mathematics teacher might encounter and illustrate the demands placed on teachers to meet the needs of all students within a class. The children described, seemingly covered by the umbrella of carelessness, may all be exhibiting learning disabilities with which they are inefficiently trying to cope. An overriding goal of the mathematics teacher is to plan and implement instruction so that all students in the class will benefit. What can be done to avoid spending an inordinate amount of time with one child to the exclusion of others, or vice versa? The techniques described in the remainder of this section are intended to help teachers in this regard. Many of the ideas can be saved as a template on a computer so they can be easily adapted or retrieved and adapted.

Use Visuals and Manipulatives To Illustrate Important Ideas

Children with learning disabilities, like some of their peers in regular-class mathematics, often are concrete in their thinking. As a general rule, the use of simple or familiar objects to illustrate facts, ideas, and written symbols or processes promotes both understanding and retention.

Use Visual Cueing: Boxes, Circles, and Lines

In an earlier section we showed how children with figure-ground difficulties may find it hard to locate assigned problems in standard textbooks; that is, they

$$\tfrac{2}{5} = \tfrac{6}{15} = .4 = .40 = 40\%$$

Figure 1.9.

may not be able to visually separate the problems from each other. A useful, inexpensive tool for handling this difficulty is a geometric-shape template. The template can be used to box the problems in the book so they can readily be found. Separating problems from each other this way prevents a child from seeing all of them as one.

Homework, especially when it must be copied from the text, can be a mammoth undertaking for a child with fine-motor or figure-ground difficulties. Particularly at the intermediate and upper grade levels, it is not unusual for students to be assigned a page of 50 computation problems. Many children with learning disabilities are so overwhelmed by the magnitude of the task that they do not attempt the assignment at all. Those who try to complete the assignment may have so much trouble separating the problem number from the problem itself, for example, that their work will contain numerous errors that cannot always be explained easily. These are often the students who are accused of being lazy or irresponsible.

Consider for a moment what is involved in the seemingly easy task of copying problems from a book. One must be able to:

- distinguish the problem number from the problem itself;
- remember what one is copying and what the numbers look like;
- space the problems on the page so the numbers can be read and the problems solved later on without mixing one problem with another; and
- align the numbers properly while copying, to avoid errors in subsequent computation.

Due to this complexity, it may be necessary to shorten the task or split it into a 2-night assignment. One night the student circles the problem numbers and copies the problems. Rather than lined paper, teachers could provide centimeter-square graph paper, as shown in Figure 1.10, or help children to use a shape template to organize their papers, as shown in Figure 1.11.

NOTE: *With the increased emphasis on the use of mental calculation, estimation, and calculators, it is hoped that teachers are assigning fewer computation problems, both in class and for homework.*

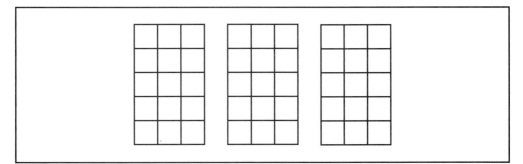

Figure 1.10.

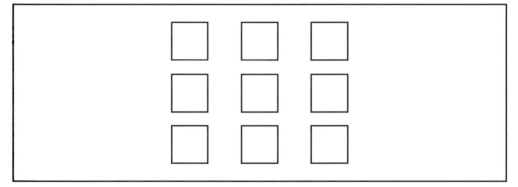

Figure 1.11.

For some children with learning disabilities, the use of lined paper, even as an aid for number alignment, only adds to the confusion. The added visual stimulus of the lines makes it hard for them to organize their work, especially if fine-motor deficits are involved. These students may have so much trouble staying on or within the lines and figuring out how to use them that their work becomes more illegible than ever. In these cases, teachers should insist that the children use unlined paper. (Figures 1.12 through 1.14 show sample sheets teachers can keep in a file or on a disk and draw upon as needed. Chapter 5 suggests more specific uses for pages of this type as an aid to computation.)

Before school starts each year, teachers could solicit the help of an aide, parent, or other volunteer to prepare textbook pages and different kinds of spatially formatted papers. The geometric-shape template could be used to organize the pages spatially in the first chapters of the textbook. Problem numbers also could be circled. Important directions or examples could be underlined with bright colors or heavy lines. A file drawer or computer template containing special worksheet formats for children with spatial or perceptual difficulties also could be stocked at that time.

Eventually, children should learn to perform some of these skills themselves. Early in the school year, therefore, it may be a good idea to set aside 5 to 10 minutes each day for children with learning problems to learn how to box, circle, and underline as needed. This exercise may be as important for a specific assignment as the computation itself. Activities such as these are of great value, since they teach the children acceptable ways of dealing with their disabilities. Compensatory techniques, such as boxing or otherwise delineating

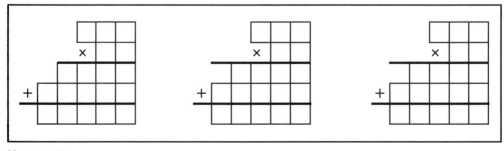

Figure 1.12.

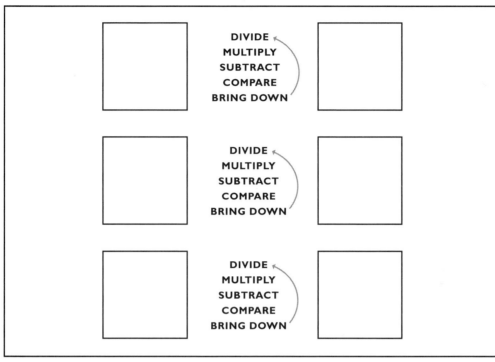

Figure 1.13.

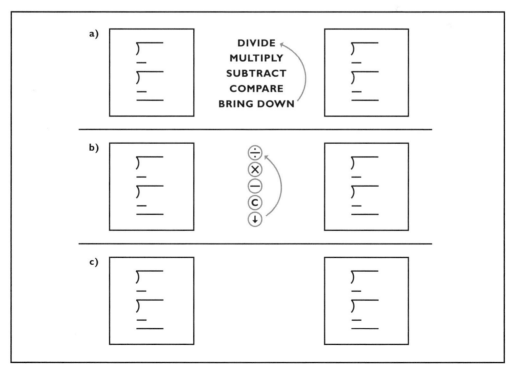

Figure 1.14.

the material, allow the children to keep up and be more a part of the mathematics class. These techniques also have carryover to other subjects.

Assign Fewer Problems and Minimize or Eliminate Copying from the Textbook or Board

It is important to remember the goal of a mathematics lesson. Suppose the purpose of a lesson is to review a computational procedure. Some students, especially those with spatial, motor, or perceptual disabilities, may make errors that seem to indicate that the students do not understand the procedure. Evaluating whether these students understand the concepts can best be done by minimizing the impact of the learning disabilities. This may mean employing techniques like those described previously, or it might mean:

- assigning only every fourth or fifth problem, rather than all the problems on a page;
- providing worksheets so children do not have to copy problems; or
- pairing students so that one acts as the "secretary" while they figure out the answers together.

If students are highly distractible or have figure-ground difficulties, it may be helpful to:

- teach them to place an X, a chip, or their fingers on the problem while computing so they do not lose their place;
- create several standard formats for worksheets and provide construction paper masks that blot out all but one fourth or one third of the page; or
- cut a worksheet into fourths or thirds and assign only one small section at a time.

Use Visual Cueing: Color-Code

Color-coding, although it can appear confusing to those of us without memory or perceptual difficulties, can be an effective way to teach many children with learning disabilities. It can provide them with any or all of the following:

- a way of focusing attention,
- a way of properly sequencing steps,
- increased ability to recall information,
- a way of identifying starting and stopping points,
- cues to the appropriate response, and
- increased ability to be independent.

It generally is advisable to color-code the first step in green and the last step in red. When using more than two colors, choose colors that are easily distinguished from each other. Do not make Step 2 orange and Step 3 red. For those few students who are color blind, use heavy lines instead of colors.

If students have auditory memory or perceptual difficulties, try to keep verbal directions and explanations short and to the point. Reinforce them with visual cues. In the case of children with reading or language interference problems, present concrete examples or illustrations that they can look at while explanations are being given. The use of color to focus, delineate, or cue in illustrations and other visuals also may help students with visual perception or memory problems. Teachers can use colored chalk or marking pens during teaching sessions for this purpose. (Figures 1.15 and 1.16 present ideas for color-coded pages that can be kept on file or on a disk and distributed as needed. Access to Math [Johnston, 1997], a software program, is especially useful for these types of pages. Structured pages can be made, color-coded, and saved as a template. They are easily retrieved and can be adjusted to match individual needs. Later, using the same colors, teachers can make special follow-up worksheets for individual students. Other ideas are included in subsequent chapters.)

Colors also can be used when boxing, circling, or underlining sections of a textbook. For example, directions might be underlined in green to remind students to "read these first." This simple technique will prevent children from spending an inordinate amount of time searching for the directions or trying to separate them from the problems.

Alter, Adjust, or Reinforce the Standard Text Sequence To Meet a Special Need

Most textbooks provide a standard sequence to be followed, but with some children that sequence may not be appropriate. For example, more and more texts introduce decimals and decimal computation before fractional computation. For children with auditory discrimination, spatial organization, or abstract-reasoning problems, a careful review of basic fraction concepts and symbolism along with simultaneous presentation of fractions and decimals may be necessary. Even in written form, fractions are more concrete than decimals—they trigger a better visual image of what they represent. The suggested review in

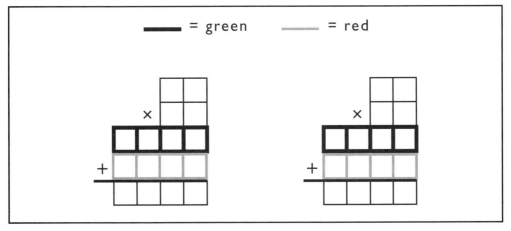

Figure 1.15.

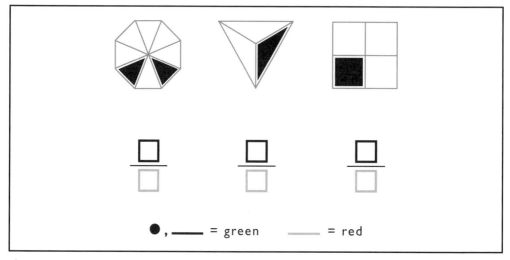

Figure 1.16.

Chapter 7 provides a basis for helping children learn decimal notation by associating it with fractions.

If students have memory difficulties and are familiar only with certain basic facts, use those facts when presenting a new procedure or concept. Make it a game. Let the class know that all the experimenting and work today will be with only a couple of facts. Controlling the lesson with known facts will allow those with learning disabilities to learn along with their classmates more readily. Additionally, this approach provides the overlearning that is so essential and allows children (even those who do not have learning disabilities) to circumvent their weaknesses while trying to learn something new.

NOTE: *Although overlearning is helpful for many students with learning disabilities, sometimes it can be an impediment to those with abstract-reasoning difficulties. The repetition of a process eliminates the need to make decisions. An entire page of word problems that require multiplication does not help one learn when* to multiply and *when not* to multiply. *If the goal is learning when to multiply but overlearning is needed, it may be sufficient for the child first to cross out all the problems that do not require multiplication and then solve the remaining multiplication problems.*

A final technique deals with homework assignments. Instead of assigning all problems on a given page, draw from several pages. Selectively list the problems and the order in which they should be completed. An assignment might look like this:

- page 235: problems 3, 7, 8, 5 (These problems may be three of one kind and a fourth that is slightly different.)

- page 182: problems 2 and 14

- page 203: problems 1 through 4, and 7

- page 182: problems 7 and 1

Insist that the children solve the problems in the order presented as a means of avoiding perseveration, developing sequencing skills, and improving reasoning. This approach can be used with an entire class.

Allow Children To Finger-Trace or Use Other Tactile Cues

In some cases, seeing or hearing is not enough. More involvement is required. Standard procedures parallel those often used in reading: finger-trace, say, then write. Sometimes children may be instructed to close their eyes while finger-tracing a textured example. For reversals, it is recommended that students finger-trace a textured numeral, then retrace the shape in midair or on paper before writing it.

Another technique can be used to reinforce retention of basic facts. Using the answer side of a flash card, children with visual memory problems might finger-trace both the problem and the answer. Upon turning the card over, they should try to give the answer immediately. If they forget, finger-tracing the problem again often triggers the correct response. Similarly, teachers can pair students and have one "write" on the other's back while that student says and writes the number on a piece of paper or on the blackboard.

Capitalize on Patterns and Other Associations To Promote Understanding or Retention

Many children with learning disabilities are helped by instruction that is based on using patterns or relevant associations. One technique is drawn from the area of basic facts. Often children can learn difficult facts by associating them with easier, known ones. The one-more-than idea is powerful in this regard (e.g., 5 + 5 = 10, so 5 + 6 is one more [11]). Three additional examples that employ associations are illustrated in Figure 1.17. Other suggestions are detailed throughout the following chapters.

Use Auditory Cueing

Children with visual, perceptual, or memory disabilities generally require a high degree of auditory reinforcement. At times, for example, it may be helpful for children to close their eyes to block out distracting visual stimuli and just listen. They might read a basic problem and its answer into a tape recorder and then listen to the playback for reinforcement. Examples of this basic approach are presented throughout the following chapters.

Make Samples for Students Who Need Them

Number Charts

In many classrooms wall charts stretch all the way around the room, often showing manuscript or cursive letters. Be sure to include a number chart as

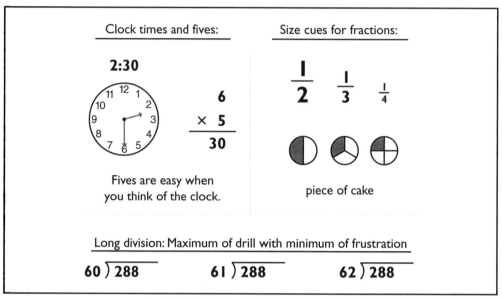

Figure 1.17.

well, even at the upper grade levels. It will help students who are capable of proceeding mathematically but lack visual memory or other capabilities to put the skills into practice. The chart will serve as an unobtrusive aid and reduce the chance that students with learning difficulties will be teased.

Charts for Special Ideas

Figure 1.18 presents a useful chart for children with receptive language deficits. Similarly, the technique pictured in Figure 1.19 has proven helpful to many students with sequential memory difficulties in mathematics. Charts like these are necessary references for many children with special problems, while also being helpful to the rest of the class.

Add = Plus = ⊕

Subtract = Take Away = ⊖

Multiply = Times = ⊗

Divide = Divided By = ⊘ ⟋‾

NOTE: A different color is used for each line of the chart.
Equal signs and circles are black.

Figure 1.18.

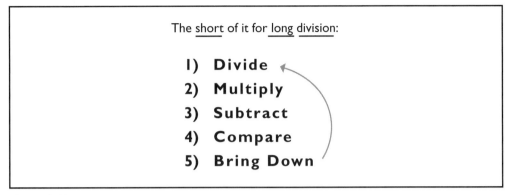

The <u>short</u> of it for <u>long</u> <u>division</u>:

1) **Divide**
2) **Multiply**
3) **Subtract**
4) **Compare**
5) **Bring Down**

Figure 1.19.

Other Techniques

To help children with nonverbal learning disabilities or those who confuse or forget the sequence of computation, techniques like the following, illustrated in Figure 1.20, might be employed:

- visual directional clues in a sample problem;
- flip charts for a sample problem, with a separate page for each step; and
- a sample problem, completed step by step, at the top of a worksheet.

Carefully Sequence Instruction in Small Steps, with Adequate Provision for Practice and Review

Proper sequencing of instruction is critical for students with learning disabilities, as is extra developmental and practice time for both understanding and retention of concepts and processes. In addition, breaking the learning process into small, meaningful segments makes understanding possible rather than overwhelming for these students. Specific suggestions for how to apply this technique are outlined for selected topics in each of the chapters that follow.

Sometimes teachers find it helpful to think of each of the following elements when planning a mathematics lesson:

Figure 1.20.

- daily review;

- "look ahead" activity (to teach or review a concept or skills embedded in an upcoming lesson);

- major thrust for the day; and

- minimath activities (connected with or separate from the lesson itself and focusing on concepts or skills that are best developed over time rather than in 2-week units; examples include problem solving, estimation, mental math, counting skills, calendar math, and time).

Sometimes, in conjunction with one or more of these aspects of a lesson, learning packets with special practice pages can be prepared in advance to satisfy the need for smaller increments and more review. A tape recorder can be used to provide extra practice for those requiring auditory learning. A tape recorder often is also helpful for students with visually based difficulties who are strong auditorially.

Many motivating games can be used to reinforce the learning of each small step. However, students must transfer from games to more applicable methods of showing understanding. Many students with learning disabilities cannot make this transfer independently. For example, some children can play basic-fact dice games very easily. They can recognize the groupings and may be able to give answers without counting. However, they may not be able to perform the same computations on paper or mentally. They simply do not make the associations independently. For these children, it may be necessary to use visuals such as those illustrated in Figure 1.21 to aid in the transition from games to other assignments.

It often is possible to make assignments or plan activities that build perception, auditory association, visual memory, or other processing skills. For example, allow students to use a computer to type in number sentences that are either dictated by the teacher or have been prerecorded. Some children may be assigned numbers or number sentences to copy, just as other children practice handwriting.

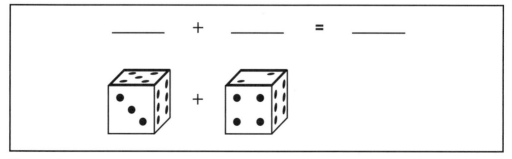

Figure 1.21.

Chapter 2

◆ ◆ ◆ ◆ ◆ ◆ ◆ ◆ ◆ ◆ ◆ ◆ ◆ ◆ ◆ ◆ ◆ ◆ ◆

Problem-Centered
Teaching and Learning

The National Council of Teachers of Mathematics (NCTM), in *Principles and Standards for School Mathematics* (2000), has continued its call for increased problem solving and real-life application in math education. As earlier NCTM documents have done, this one stresses the importance of including problem solving throughout the curriculum but also encourages the earlier introduction of what were previously thought to be higher-level thinking skills. Algebraic thinking and geometric understanding and estimation, topics that previously had not been introduced until middle school, are now being introduced in the primary grades. If these topics are approached in a consistent and clear manner, one that incorporates an understanding of child development and learning disabilities, this emphasis can be beneficial for students with learning disabilities. For younger students, the introduction of these topics can be a fun, creative way to develop reasoning skills, foster an appreciation for and curiosity about numbers, and develop a solid foundation for the later, more abstract but increasingly needed, algebraic and geometric understanding that today's world requires.

The need to use reasoning skills and to evaluate situations permeates one's life. Students must feel confident when they approach new or difficult tasks that they possess the necessary skills to make a reasonable attempt at accomplishing those tasks. Socialization skills, especially for middle and high school students, often depend on one's ability to continuously and accurately evaluate situations. "How much money will I need to go to the movies and out for lunch with my friends?" "I have to be at work at 5:00 P.M. Will I have enough time to go to a movie?" "I have a big project due in 2 weeks. How am I going to have enough time to get it done?" Situations like these involve many skills: the need to understand abstract vocabulary (e.g., "enough time" varies with the situation); a grasp of the "big picture" (e.g., being sure to take enough money when going out with friends); and the ability to retrieve and then apply previously learned skills in a reasonable amount of time (e.g., "How much can I order for lunch and be sure to have enough money left to go to the movies?").

In the past, problem solving in the mathematics curriculum placed heavy emphasis on reaching a final answer, rather than on the process of accurate reasoning. We live in a fast-changing world, and today the mathematics curriculum must emphasize: (a) determining what constitutes an acceptable solution (e.g., is the exact answer necessary or is "close" okay?); (b) evaluating various methods of reaching an answer; and (c) being willing to take a risk to attempt to solve novel problems. Teaching these skills involves a stronger emphasis on language. In daily life, we talk about going places with "some friends" or losing "a few" things. "Close enough" in one situation might not be the case in another. Students need to understand the multiple meanings of these terms. Even words like *half* and *quarter* have more than one meaning.

Strategies such as the following constitute an important component of any mathematics curriculum. They rely less on obtaining an exact answer than on determining which procedure is relevant and what type of final answer is needed:

- recognizing whether a problem contains enough information or extraneous information and then applying an efficient strategy;

- making an organized list;

- noticing patterns;

- analyzing a survey, graph, chart, or table;

- evaluating what type of procedure will be most effective;

- working a problem backwards;

- using reasonable guess-and-check tests;

- simulating a procedure; and

- retelling or demonstrating a problem in one's own words or using concrete aids or pictures.

When methods such as these are incorporated early on in the curriculum, students develop more comfort about taking risks, viewing mistakes as part of learning, and using different ways of thinking and approaching problems. They learn that sometimes there is more than one way to solve a problem and that there may be no "right" answer (e.g., "My friend and I got different answers, but they both make sense.").

Teachers must continually use and encourage a variety of ways to expand problem-solving skills. If the mathematics curriculum is approached developmentally, reasoning skills can be incorporated successfully even at an early age. Some effective approaches, which can be used at various levels, are summarized below:

• Young children and children with learning disabilities respond best when problem situations are within their experience. Even if the answer to "About how long until recess?" is "Two big dots on the clock" (as described by one child who looked at an analog clock), students will begin to develop a "feel" for time.

• Encourage and reinforce *all* estimates, even if the answers are way off or the approach is not efficient, before suggesting or asking for alternative approaches. *What is efficient for one person may not be efficient for another.* Developmental stages and confidence play major roles in successful estimation.

• Allow students to compare estimates. Leave for recess earlier on some days and later on others but return to class at the required time. Then ask, "How long did recess feel today?" "Did the amount of time feel different than yesterday?" Suggest to students, "While you are playing, think about how long you think you are playing today. Did you have more or less time to play today?"

• Pose problem situations orally and provide concrete, visual reinforcement appropriate to the age of the child. Doing this ensures that students with learning disabilities in the area of auditory processing or memory, abstract reasoning or working memory, can participate.

• Calculators and computers serve important functions in our society. At an early age encourage students to evaluate when to use these tools and also to understand that some people use them for different reasons than other people. Help students learn to recognize when they *really* offer a more efficient procedure than pencil-and-paper calculation.

• Begin early to encourage children to develop their mental calculation skills. For students with learning disabilities, mental calculation can be difficult, but it does not have to be impossible. Rapidly flash pictures, numbers, groups of objects, and the like to young students and those with learning disabilities. Initially, concentrate on helping them remember what they saw and accept even broad answers ("I saw lots of pencils."). Later, concentrate on what they saw first, second, and third. Incorporate words like *next, before, after.* ("Look for the pencils. What picture did I flash *after* I flashed the pencils?") Exercises like these provide a foundation for more efficient working memory later and may need to be practiced throughout the curriculum.

• Use concrete objects, drawings, and diagrams at all levels of instruction to clarify a problem, find a solution, and verify an answer. Have children act out problems.

• Encourage students to feel comfortable with open-ended problems and incorrect answers—"We learn from mistakes." When introduced to students at a young age, the process can become more of a game, similar to solving a puzzle or a mystery—"What's wrong with this problem? Let's see how many different ways we can make it make sense."

• Help students understand that something that is difficult for one student may be easy for another. Encourage students to help each other by having them talk about things that are easy for them and things that are hard. Provide opportunities for different students to solve the same problems but each in a different way.

NOTE: *This approach works well provided that pairings or groupings are carefully organized by the teacher, not randomly chosen.*

• Have children, even very young ones, write (match) mathematical sentences for (to) problems without computing the answers. Similar to the process of learning to read, early presentation enables "sound-symbol" relationships to be formed. At first, do not require (allow) answers to enable students to begin to understand that there may be a variety of accurate procedures. Accept all mathematical sentences, provided they are conceptually accurate.

• Provide opportunities for students to understand that we use math all the time and that most of the time the math we use does not require exact answers. For example, we need only to estimate how long it will take to go to the airport or how many CDs can be bought for $20.

Given the continual and rapid expansion of technology, learning to be comfortable with different types of problem solving is essential. This chapter will focus on what the authors view as the foundation for efficient problem solving. The ideas incorporate ways to help students develop confidence that they can (a) solve even novel problems; (b) retrieve and apply previously learned information in a variety of efficient ways; and (c) evaluate situations in order to be a productive member of a group.

PREREQUISITES FOR EFFICIENT PROBLEM SOLVING

Good problem solvers can estimate, predict, draw conclusions, evaluate, and use information effectively. These are skills commonly and regularly taught in the reading program. Too often they are not addressed as directly in the mathematics curriculum. It is important that mathematics teachers realize that children's abilities to handle these tasks greatly affect their confidence and success in the field of mathematics. These prerequisites are described in the following list; the emphasis is on developing a confidence in one's ability to approach and handle novel situations:

1. Problem solving involves the confidence and willingness to take a risk. Good problem solvers know that they will make mistakes and are willing and able to learn from their mistakes.
2. An understanding of the variability of the meaning of words and the ability to use flexible thought to apply this understanding affects one's reasoning skills. For example, what is "reasonable" in one situation might not be in another. A reasonable amount to spend on a movie before receiving one's allowance might be different than a reasonable amount to spend after receiving the allowance.
3. Effective problem solving involves predicting and evaluating what effect an outcome might have, as in the following example: "Mom said to buy enough apples so there will be some left over to take for lunch. That bag looks like an awful lot of apples, and I need lunch for only two days. If I buy too many, they might spoil. I wonder if the grocery clerk would let me buy a smaller bag?"
4. Having either good inner language or the ability to visualize is necessary for solving problems. Being able to talk one's way through a process or draw or visualize images enables one to evaluate whether one is heading in the right direction.

PROBLEM SOLVING AND THE STUDENT WITH LEARNING DISABILITIES

The suggestions in the first part of this section are important for *all* students, particularly with regard to developing a sense of confidence in their ability to be successful math students. To ensure that this feeling is developed and sustained in students with learning disabilities, however, instruction may need to include additional previewing, reviewing, altering the sequence of topic introduction, breaking instruction down into small units, and direct instruction.

Problem-solving situations call upon children to retrieve previously learned information and apply it in *new* or *varying* situations. Knowing the basic arithmetic skills, knowing when to incorporate them into new contexts, and then being able to do so are three distinct skills. Having all three skills makes problem solving easier, but inability in one does not mean that a student does not understand a problem. It may mean that that student's learning style has not been addressed. Similarly, because students can carry out the operations in isolation does not mean they know when to apply them or how to interpret the numbers involved.

As difficult as it may be for students with learning disabilities to master a particular skill, it generally is considerably more difficult for them to decide when and how to use that skill in new contexts and then to execute their knowledge in a meaningful sequence. This appears to be especially hard for students with nonverbal learning disabilities. According to Foss (1991), in discussing her research on people with nonverbal learning disabilities, "When academic demands shifted from rote learning of skills, facts, and procedures to more complex integrated learning and applications, these individuals began to fail, and to cease to try. . . . To be effective, interventions must address the problem areas directly and explicitly. They must also involve the student in planning to apply newly learned behaviors to similar tasks and situations beyond the training exercises." In general, students with learning disabilities will develop confidence in their ability to use the problem-solving process if they are provided specific help with:

- decision making,
- estimation,
- information use,
- language and vocabulary,
- sequencing,
- predicting, and
- patterning.

Because of their importance in the problem-solving process, each of these areas deserves special consideration in the mathematics program for students with learning disabilities.

Decision Making

The decision-making process is complex. It requires the ability to (a) use abstract reasoning; (b) understand and express understanding in a meaningful way; (c) retrieve appropriate, previously learned concepts and skills; (d) distinguish between those concepts and skills; (e) evaluate and choose the concepts and skills that are most appropriate in a given situation; and (f) continually self-monitor in order to determine the accuracy of the process.

Estimation

Although estimation could be considered a subcategory of decision making, because of its complexity the authors tend to view it separately. To successfully use estimation a student must have the confidence to make mistakes and then be able to evaluate those mistakes. For example, trusting that his or her pencil-and-paper answer is correct even though it is different from the answer on the calculator requires not only knowing that there is an error somewhere but being confident enough to decide whether (a) the calculation is wrong; (b) the numbers were typed in wrong; (c) the symbols on the calculator were misread; (d) one's pencil-and-paper or mental calculation really is wrong; or (e) the battery might be low on the calculator.

Information Use

In order to solve problems, students must be able to (a) interpret information accurately; (b) understand the stated or implied questions; (c) isolate information within a problem and sort out irrelevant from essential information; (d) determine what information is missing, if any; and (e) formulate a plan to solve the problem.

Language and Vocabulary

Dyslexia and learning disabilities in general are considered to be language based. This is extremely important to keep in mind when teaching math. Although the language involved in understanding and applying math is different from that involved in other areas of education, it is no less important. Word retrieval, receptive and expressive language, language processing, and clarity of expression are all required to explain and apply one's understanding (see Figure 2.1). Students must be able to:

- associate symbols with words and meaning;
- retrieve the word that matches a symbol;
- understand the word(s) in varying contexts (e.g., *backwards* means different directions in a horizontal and a vertical number line or hundreds chart);
- understand and apply subtle differences in meaning (e.g., "Mom said to be home in three quarters of an hour, but I thought hours had minutes, not quarters."). In isolation, or when given adequate time or proper cues, most students can process such differences, but, just as when teaching a foreign language, teachers must be aware of the subtleties of language involved in math.

Sequencing

Problem solving requires not only using information that has been learned previously but also choosing which previously learned information is needed and

> **Look at** ⊕
> **Think "add"**
> **Say "plus"**

Figure 2.1.

using it in a properly organized way. The sequences needed to handle real-life problems can vary from situation to situation. In one instance, it may be necessary to add first and then multiply; while in another, the reverse procedure might be required. Additionally, although a number of different sequences might result in the same accurate answer, one might be more efficient.

Predicting

Like the student who predicts in order to better comprehend what is read, the mathematical problem solver uses prediction to evaluate and solve a problem—for example: "What will happen if I try to solve this problem by just computing with the numbers I see?" "What am I trying to figure out? If I know that first, it might be easier to solve this problem."

Early on, extensive work with blocks, coins, and other real-life objects helps children think about "What might happen if I did this?" Teachers could spread some centimeter cubes out on a table and ask students to "predict what might happen if the cubes were all pushed together," (It's not too early to introduce important vocabulary.) encouraging different answers, such as: "They'd be closer together." "I'd be able to carry them easier." "I'd be able to count them more easily." All these answers (a) are acceptable, (b) involve predicting, (c) help children recognize different ways of thinking, and (d) develop self-confidence.

Patterning

Generally, when we think of patterning in mathematics, we think of numbers or shapes that follow a specific order, as in Figure 2.2. Patterning, however, is also an important part of solving common daily situations. For example, the processes of counting and determining the value of money both require patterning. To successfully compute monetary values one must recall individual patterns of counting by like coins and then be able to use those patterns in varying skip-counting ways. To count a group of three dimes, two quarters, and three pennies one must recognize and apply three different counting patterns—by quarters, dimes, and pennies. (See Chapter 4.) An extension of patterning underlies the ability to decide which of the four basic operations to apply in a given situation. Can students notice and retrieve the similarities and differences between a given problem and those previously worked using a particular operation? (See Figure 2.3.)

Some students with learning disabilities cannot visualize what is laid out from just the stated words—that the situation fits the pattern of addition or

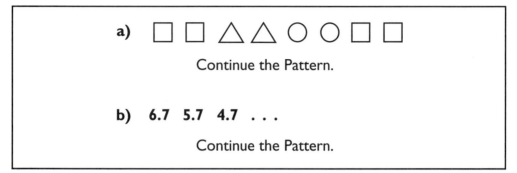

Figure 2.2.

division, for example. Since, in general, it is easier for students with learning disabilities to identify differences than similarities, work with patterning at all stages of instruction is essential. Those of us who do not have learning disabilities can intuitively associate the similarity between unstated patterns rather than the differences. We tend to ask students to point out differences only when they have mistakenly chosen the wrong operation.

LANGUAGE AND MATHEMATICS

The relationship between language and mathematics has been addressed in previous sections of this chapter and will continue to be addressed in other chapters. This section is meant to be a brief summary of the impact that language has on mathematics and an attempt to help teachers assist children to learn and progress in spite of language difficulties. Probably the most important tool a student can possess is what language therapists call "inner language." Inner language consists of the ability to monitor one's thoughts in a conscious (but silent) way. "I know I've seen that sign before, but I don't remember what it means. Where have I seen it? That's right—when I went to the grocery store, Mom said, 'Get apples plus pears,' but she wrote the + sign instead." How teachers help students develop this inner language is important. Generally, it works to consistently use the following steps:

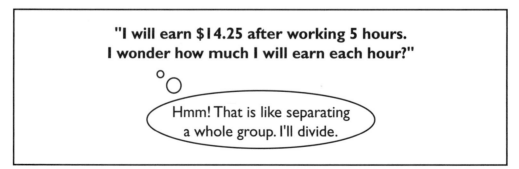

Figure 2.3.

1. Read the problem.

2. Picture or draw a picture of what is happening. (This step is similar to one used with advance organizers to help students organize their written expression.)

3. *Think:* What is the question? What do I want to know when I finish the problem? Is the information I have going to help me figure this out, or do I need something else?

4. Is an exact answer required?

5. What operation(s) is/are needed?

6. What is the best calculation method—calculator, mental calculation, or paper and pencil?

7. Check. Is the answer reasonable?

Using inner language helps students become efficient problem solvers *if language comes easily to them.* Students with expressive or receptive language and those with working-memory deficits may have trouble using inner language—or at least using it in a reasonable amount of time to keep up with the class. These students may require extra time, visual prompts, or perhaps an advance organizer, which the teacher or an aide has made, to look at while they are trying to solve a problem. Sometimes just being presented with the problem on tape or in a multiple choice format provides the language cues that might otherwise be missing and allows students to organize and plan ahead.

NOTE: *The authors recognize that in a regular classroom this may be very time consuming to do. An alternative, and one that can prove helpful to all students, is to assign this task to those students who use language to organize their thinking. This is an assignment that could be part of the math program or the written language program, with the added benefit of helping students to see the relationship between the two.*

In a previous section the importance of estimation was discussed. Successful estimation involves understanding the subtleties of language. When children are at an early age, teachers make sure they understand the difference in meaning of such expressions as "I *have* 7 crayons" and "I *have about* 7 crayons." Teachers can give students practice in different situations where students must describe a picture or an event, first using factual words such as *is* and *have* and then using estimation words like *about, nearly,* and *almost.*

In general, the mathematics program needs to include (a) an awareness of the impact of language on math, and (b) the flexibility for a student to progress in spite of difficulty in this area. If teachers teach students how to break problems into small steps, relate symbols to words *throughout the school experience,* and preview vocabulary when needed, students can become successful problem solvers. In many reading and writing programs students keep a vocabulary book, which they add to throughout the school year and from year to year. Students with learning disabilities can benefit from the use of such books even in their math program. A sample of "My Math Dictionary" used by a fifth grader is shown in Figure 2.4.

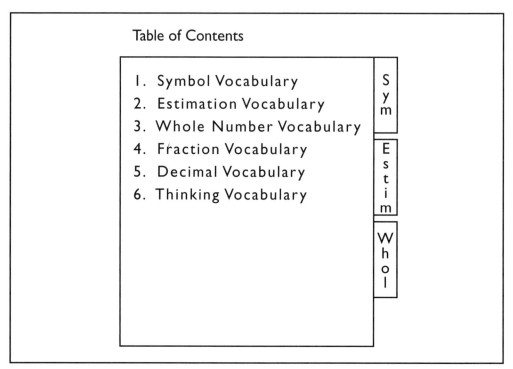

Figure 2.4a.

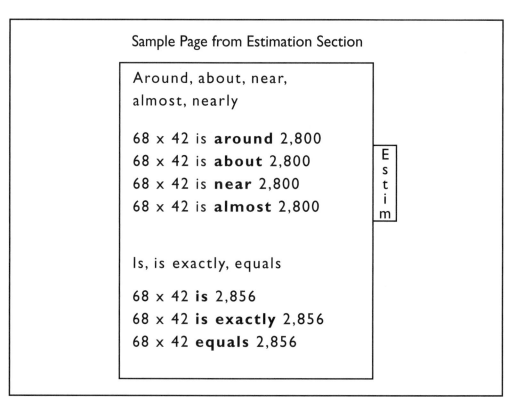

Figure 2.4b.

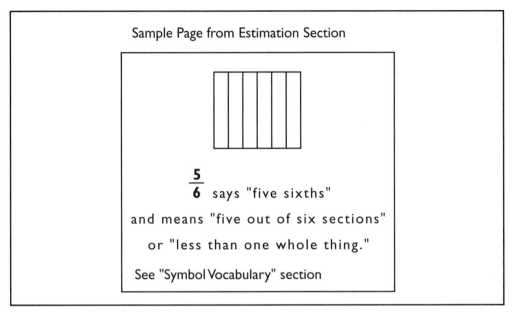

Figure 2.4c.

NOTE: *Part of developing vocabulary means expanding students' ability to make associations. By referring to pages in their dictionary, students can begin, unobtrusively, to develop not only associations and the ability to classify vocabulary, but also an understanding of the need to evaluate what they are doing. Figure 2.4c shows an example of how evaluating plays a part in understanding the language of fractions. The student must decide between various meanings that the fraction bar can have: "out of" in a fraction, "divided by" in division, as well as "and" in a mixed number."*

 ## Sample Sequence of Activities

1. **Number word to numeral.** Many children are unable to attach meaning to the verbal number names used in some problems. Practice pages like that shown in Figure 2.5 often are helpful. Initially, the student fills in the numerical representation. Later, the appropriate operation can be determined and the computation carried out.

☐ You work nine days ☐ and you work six hours a day. How long do you work in all?	9 You work nine days 6 and you work six hours a day. How long do you work in all?

Figure 2.5.

2. **Focus.** Help students associate words with numbers and symbols by presenting exercises like those shown in Figure 2.6. Figure 2.6a is used in conjunction with word problems that contain the troublesome terms *each* and *many*. The exercise helps students internalize the numerical meaning of the terms. In the first problem, *each* means 1, not 9, 3, or 7. *Many* may mean 8 or 43 but never 0 or 1. The exercise in Figure 2.6b focuses on developing meaning for the term *earn*. Similar exercises should be developed for other vocabulary terms that cause students difficulty.

3. **Key words.** Exercises like that in Figure 2.7 help children begin to associate mathematical meaning with words. Key words and their meanings are placed just before each problem and are highlighted within the problem.

NOTE: *Although it could be argued that teaching students to focus on key words can be misleading, if the ideas are taught in the context of multiple and implied meanings, the method can be extremely helpful for students with receptive language difficulties or nonverbal or abstract-reasoning difficulties. In the example shown in Figure 2.7, the same word* (return) *is used to reflect two different operations. The student should be encouraged to recognize the word as an "operation" word but to evaluate its meaning in the context of the sentence. Using concrete aids, pictures, and real-life situations is an essential part of this type of instruction, so that students have a mental image, and one to include in their dictionary, for future reference.*

The following pages are intended to encourage teachers to be continually aware of the problem-solving nature of mathematics and to expand their understanding of how language and math interact. It is far beyond the scope of this book to address all aspects of problem solving. The authors' goal is to address some of those areas that are at the root of math at any level of instruction.

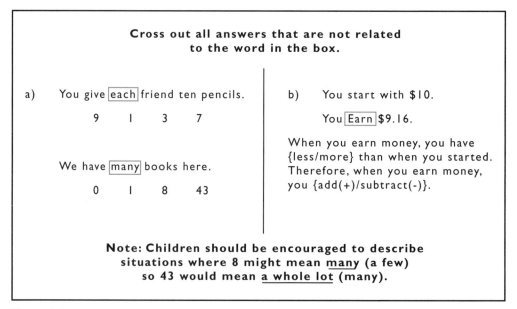

Figure 2.6.

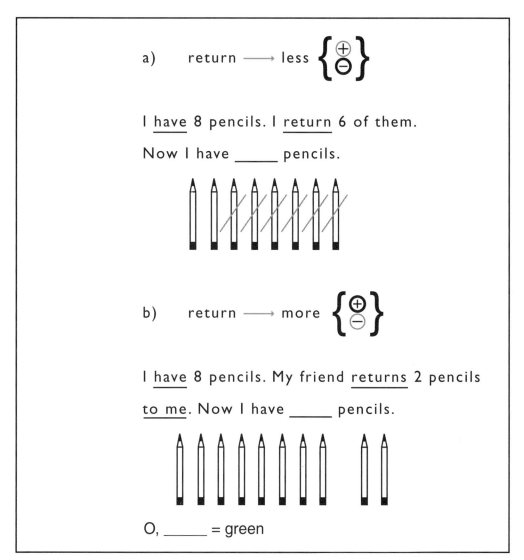

Figure 2.7.

COMPUTATION: CHOOSING
THE CALCULATION METHOD

Computation must be taught meaningfully and with careful attention to underlying concepts and relationships. A conceptual approach to computation often prevents many of the problems children otherwise experience when learning to compute. Part of this approach includes encouraging flexible thinking early on, as that is a prerequisite for making good decisions. (See "Prerequisites for Efficient Problem Solving" earlier in this chapter.)

Technology has drastically changed the methods by which we compute. To function in today's world, it is necessary to be able to compute in a variety of settings. Inexpensive calculators are readily available to perform routine computations accurately and quickly. Students should be encouraged to choose and use the method that is most appropriate in a given situation: estimation, a quick mental calculation, computing with paper and pencil, or using a calculator.

Students with learning disabilities may encounter difficulty using a calculator for perceptual reasons, but by choosing a calculator with a large display window and large numbers on the keys, they may be able to overcome that problem. Students with abstract-reasoning, short-term memory, or working-memory problems may encounter difficulty keying in a series of numbers and symbols. Teaching students to keep one finger on the problem and one on the calculator can help. There are also calculators available that display the entire operation as it is keyed in.

Some ideas that provide a basis for efficient problem solving follow. Remember: Foster a positive attitude. Children take a risk when they follow your direction to choose a calculation method. Decision making is required, and more than one response may be correct. Hold back from labeling a decision as *right* or *wrong*. Accept a broad range of answers and alternative solutions.

• *Provide good role modeling.* For example, in problem-solving situations, given a multiplication problem involving more than two digits in each number, tell students, "Let's use a calculator. It's not worth the time to crank this one out." Build into this process a reminder to "estimate your answer first, so you know if your calculator answer makes sense."

• *Use variation.* Assign computation problems with numbers of varying values. Make the assignment larger than usual and tell students to decide which ones are better done on the calculator. Have students explain their answers. (This could be enlightening. One possible response: "I don't know my facts. It's easier to do them all on the calculator." "It's too hard to write out all those problems.")

• *First do the easy mental-calculation problems.* Do the rest using paper and pencil. Provide specific exercises using a mix of problems—some that lend themselves to quick mental calculation and some that don't.

• *Let them evaluate.* Allow students to decide on the quickest method *for them* to solve a computation problem. Remind students that everyone's chart looks different—"What's easier for Maya might not be easier for Steven."

• *Emphasize situations where an estimate is good enough.* Many daily situations require only an estimate. Assign work where, instead of solving a problem, students must determine the best method to arrive at an answer. For example, if there will be 11 people at a party, is it good enough to say, "That's close to 10, so I'll ask for 10 party treats"? (Of course not!) On the other hand, when figuring whether $10 is enough to pay for 2 gallons of milk and a loaf of bread, an estimate will do.

DETERMINING THE CORRECT OPERATION

Typical Disabilities Affecting Progress: Difficulty with abstract reasoning, visual memory, receptive or expressive language, word retrieval, nonverbal learning disabilities.

Background: The need to decide whether to add, subtract, multiply, or divide enters many facets of daily life and involves intuitively understanding and applying patterns to a variety of situations. At the store we must decide whether the correct change has been given or how much money to give to the clerk. Purchasing school supplies involves recognizing when to apply the *pattern* of multiplication and when to apply the *pattern* of addition—for example: "I need two computer disks for each class and some extras for my homework. I have four classes. Each box of disks has ten disks—I'd better get an extra box of disks just to be safe."

The following activities describe some decision-making skills at the computation level. Teachers are encouraged to relate these ideas to meaningful situations so students understand the relationship between computation and problem solving and can apply their knowledge accordingly.

Sample Sequence of Activities

1. **Picture the operation.** Be sure children have a strong mental picture of each operation, especially as they begin to compute with rational numbers. For young children, use objects and color-coded pages, as in Figure 2.8, to help them associate, in this case, subtraction with the number sentence and the subtraction symbol. Relate this activity to their daily lives by having students describe (show, draw) what they do when they share their toys or take playing chips from a box so their friends each have the same amount.

2. **You tell.** In early work with simple number combinations, before the facts have been memorized, help students develop reasoning skills by presenting

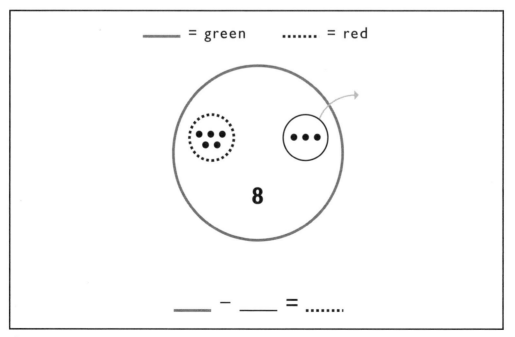

Figure 2.8.

What's the sign?

4	7	6
□ 9	□ 3	□ 4
13	10	2

Figure 2.9.

problems with answers but without signs, as in Figure 2.9. Have them supply the correct sign. As a preliminary exercise, discuss what the possibilities are by reviewing the outcome for different operations—"Remember, when we add, the answer is bigger than what we started with. When we subtract, the answer is smaller than what we started with."

NOTE: *However, once facts have been committed to memory, children tend to give answers spontaneously, often ignoring the sign and assuming they know what operation is required based on the configuration of numbers in the problem. For example, seeing the numbers 5, 6, and 30 in a problem, students may assume that multiplication is required because they know that 5 × 6 = 30. Emphasizing the meaning and importance of the sign early on helps counter that tendency.*

3. **Do it with big numbers.** As students begin to work with larger numbers, a similar exercise can be used (see Figure 2.10). When using larger numbers, keep the pace fairly quick so the children do not have time to compute the answer. Discuss the numbers involved. Make sure students can tell or show whether (and why) the answer will be larger or smaller than what they start with.

4. **Special help.** Students with visual memory or visual discrimination deficits, and those with word retrieval difficulties, may have trouble retrieving the correct sign without having a visual cue nearby. For those students, keep strips like the one shown in Figure 2.11 to be used at their desks. The strip will serve as a visual reminder of the association.

5. **Do the easy one first.** Older students who have learned when to use each of the four operations in situations involving whole numbers often have trouble with fractions and decimals when trying to:

463	834
□ 297	□ 129
760	705

Figure 2.10.

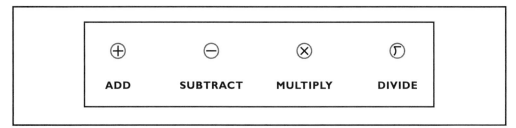

Figure 2.11.

- recognize which operation to use, and
- carry out the appropriate operation.

For these students, it is helpful to parallel two problems that are solved similarly but involve different types of numbers. Figure 2.12b shows an equation that gives many middle school and junior high students trouble. It is made much simpler when paralleled with that in Figure 2.12a.

NOTE: *The goal of this assignment is for students to understand how to solve equations with a variety of numbers. Rather than requiring paper and pencil, teachers should encourage use of the calculator, estimation, or mental calculation. If the ability to solve these computations accurately is in question, it may be wise to make this a two-part assignment.*

    6. **Tell what to do, then stop.** Follow through on these ideas in verbal problems by having students:

- read the problem;
- picture what is happening;
- use objects or drawing to picture the problem if that helps;
- think about what is being asked; and
- tell what to do (add, subtract, multiply, or divide).

At first, do not require that the children actually compute. After their papers are checked, the computation can be carried out and the result checked.

a) $9A = 73$

$$A = 72 \div 9$$

$$A = 9\overline{)73} = 8\tfrac{1}{9}$$
$$\underline{-72}$$
$$1$$

$$A = 8\tfrac{1}{9}$$

b) $4\tfrac{1}{2}A = 64$

$$A = 64 \div 4\tfrac{1}{2}$$

$$A = 64 \div \tfrac{9}{2}$$

$$64 \times \tfrac{2}{9} = \tfrac{128}{9} = 14\tfrac{2}{9}$$

$$A = 14\tfrac{2}{9}$$

Figure 2.12.

DETERMINING AND CHECKING FOR REASONABLE ANSWERS

Typical Disabilities Affecting Progress: Difficulty with abstract reasoning or expressive language.

Background: Problem solving involves not only knowing how to arrive at a relevant solution; it also involves evaluating the reasonableness of that solution with regard to both the numerical answer and the vocabulary word. As part of an ongoing problem-solving curriculum, continually do the following:

• Encourage students to predict results by estimating their answers with and without using computation—for example: "If I take a ten dollar bill to the grocery store and I'm only going to buy a bottle of water, I'll have *a lot* of bills and coins after I get change." "A bottle of water costs about $1.50. I'll probably get back *about* $7 in change."

• Present calculations that are already complete—some that are correct and others with answers that are way off; ask students to find and circle answers that do not make sense.

• Include mental calculation, estimation, and self-checking in all parts of the curriculum, not just in math class.

• Require complete sentences (either oral or written) for responses to problems, as in Figure 2.13.

NOTE: *Determining reasonable answers involves a good deal of expressive language, either aloud or internally. Be aware of those students for whom this might be difficult and provide them with visual cues, sequencing, and prompts that will help them demonstrate their understanding.*

MAKING GOOD USE OF INFORMATION

Typical Disabilities Affecting Progress: Difficulty with long-term memory, abstract reasoning, receptive and expressive language.

You work 8 hours a day for 6 days.

How many hours do you work in all?

I work _____ _____ .

(student fills blanks)

Figure 2.13.

Background: As noted earlier in this chapter, the ability to understand and retain information over the short and long term is an essential component to solving any kind of problem. Here we discuss the ability to make good use of information provided (or a lack of information). Daily life does not always present "neatly wrapped packages" that provide us with exactly what we need in order to successfully complete a problem. Sometimes there is more than we need; other times not enough; sometimes exactly the right amount. Taking the time to evaluate the given information needs to be an automatic part of the problem-solving situation.

Sample Sequence of Activities

1. **X what is not needed.** Present problems as illustrated in Figure 2.14 and have the students cross out any information that is not needed (in this case, the number of pages). Generally, this type of assignment is best spread over 2 days so responses can be checked and discussed before the students actually carry out the computation. For younger students or for initial presentation, highlight the needed items, as in Figure 2.15. As they become more proficient, have the children highlight the items in the question and in the statement part of the problem.

2. **Tell what's missing.** A similar procedure can be used to help students identify missing information. Initially, present problems in which the question asks for something that cannot be learned from the information given. Highlight the word in the question that calls for the missing information.

NOTE: *At the verbal level, when manipulatives are not used, this type of problem can be very difficult, especially for students with learning disabilities. Check the child's developmental level (see "Prerequisites for Efficient Problem Solving"*

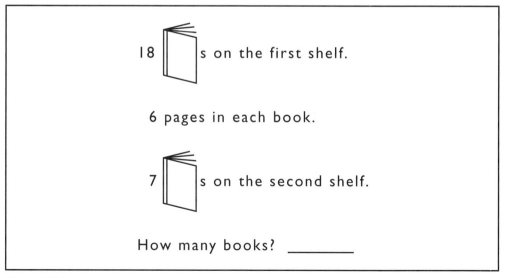

18 [book]s on the first shelf.

6 pages in each book.

7 [book]s on the second shelf.

How many books? _____

Figure 2.14.

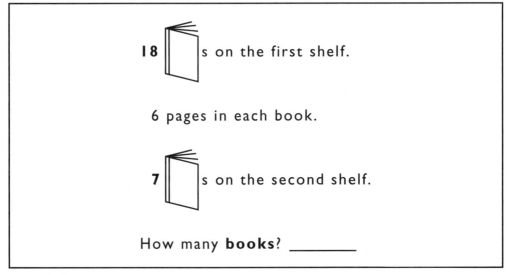

Figure 2.15.

earlier in this chapter) and provide a lot of practice using concrete aids. Make the transition to written and oral word problems very gradually.

3. **Just give the data.** Present short problems that do not ask a question but merely supply information. Have students determine what they know from this small amount of information. Figure 2.16 illustrates the format for an initial presentation that has proven effective, even with students who have retrieval or expressive language deficits. The goal, at this point, is to identify what information is supplied and what information will be useful in solving the problem.

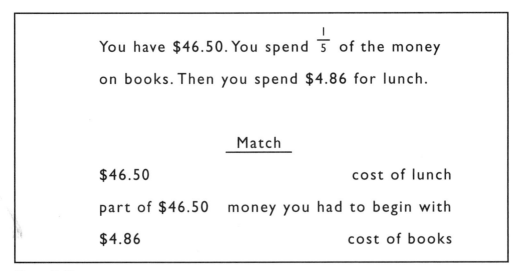

Figure 2.16.

NOTE: *This type of activity is especially helpful in preparing the ground for future work in geometry, where it is often necessary to look at a problem, go to the end, and know what the information presented means.*

4. **Two steps.** Problems involving two steps can be color-coded, as shown in Figure 2.17, to help associate the necessary information with the correct step. As before, do not require that students compute answers to the problems until they have checked to be sure the proper information for each step is available.

NOTE: *To develop independence, encourage students to do their own highlighting prior to solving the problem. This will make them more aware of the thought process and the task sequence involved.*

5. **Special help.** Even when the children are better able to identify, in context, numerals in written form, they may have trouble verbalizing, either aloud or to themselves, what they need to do to solve a problem. To help in such situations, present problems like that of Figure 2.18. Steps for solving the problem are shown in random order at the right. Seeing the information usually helps children verbalize what needs to be done. Then, step by step, in the spaces provided, they can write the computation in the correct order to solve the problem. As the children become more proficient, eliminate one or more of the completed steps.

6. **Picture choice.** For younger children, a variation of the preceding procedure consists of presenting a choice of pictures, as in Figure 2.19. Children choose the picture that best describes the problem. Encourage them to state the completed number sentence orally.

──── = green   .... = red

You earn $2.25 each hour.

You work 6 days, 8 hours each day.

1) How long do you work all together?

────── (days)
       (hours)

(student fills blanks and circles correct word)

2) How much do you earn? ────

Figure 2.17.

In the spaces at the bottom of the page,

copy the correct solution for each step and then solve.

You buy 14 pads of paper for 3¢ a pad.   14 x 5¢

You sell them for 5¢ a pad.   (14 x 5¢) – (14 x 3¢)

What is your profit?   14 x 3¢

    Step 1   Step 2   Step 3

Figure 2.18.

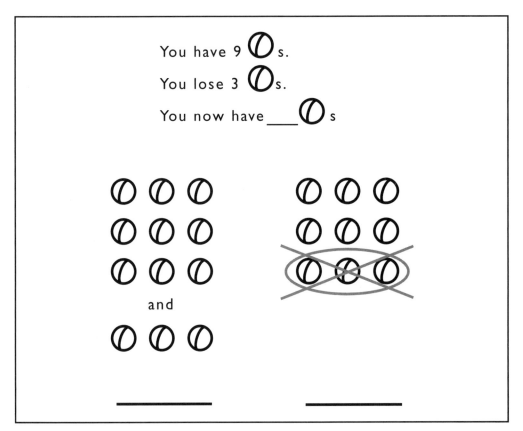

Figure 2.19.

RECOGNIZING THE PATTERN OF A PROBLEM

Typical Disabilities Affecting Progress: Difficulty with abstract reasoning, auditory processing, nonverbal learning disabilities.

Background: Typically, teachers address patterning at early stages of instruction and relate the concept to manipulatives and ultimately to counting sequences, such as counting by twos, fives, or tens. Most students are then able to intuitively generalize the idea to other situations, notably more complex computational procedures and word problems. Too often students with the learning disabilities described above do not automatically make this transition. By maintaining a structured, consistent approach throughout the mathematics curriculum, however, many of these students can become successful problem solvers. The ideas listed below are meant to provide suggestions and areas to consider; they are not all inclusive but should serve to highlight the importance of including patterning throughout the mathematics curriculum.

✎ Sample Sequence of Activities

1. **See the pattern.** Present simple visual problems, as in Figure 2.20, and have students circle the best solution.

2. **Word problems now.** As children become better at recognizing patterns for the operations, gradually introduce word problems. At first, present assignments in which students use only one operation. Help students manipulate concrete aids or draw a picture of the problem, as in Figure 2.20. Rather quickly move to pages with mixed operations and extra numbers. Continue to have students use manipulatives, draw pictures, and write the computation down as described above. Throughout, encourage students to look for patterns: by separating groups, finding the total number of equal-sized groups, and so on. Allow the children to use the concrete aids or to draw a picture of the problem as long as that seems helpful.

3. **Easy one first.** Sometimes working a parallel problem with whole numbers can help students solve a problem that contains fractions or decimals. A similar technique helps students solve problems in general. Some students go

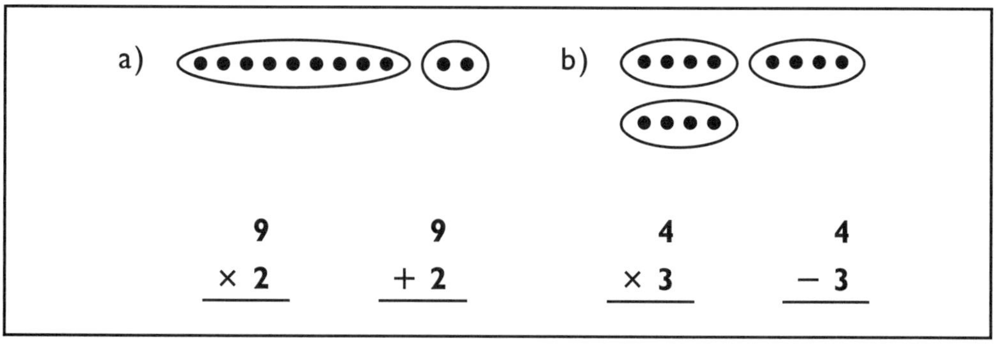

Figure 2.20.

blank when they notice that a word problem contains a fraction or a decimal. Giving these students a parallel problem with whole numbers often helps them recognize the general pattern to the solution, such as the sequence of operations, which they then can apply to the original problem with fractions or decimals. (See Figure 2.12.)

DETERMINING THE CORRECT SEQUENCE

Typical Disabilities Affecting Progress: Difficulty with expressive language, abstract reasoning, short-term memory, spatial or temporal organization, closure.

Background: In order for students to determine the correct sequence for a problem, they must possess a good understanding of the concepts *before* and *after,* regardless of whether the expected outcome is an exact number. Sometimes the best answer does not involve a number; rather, a decision must be made as to what sequence to follow. The correct sequence can vary depending on the situation, and children must feel comfortable with the ideas of *before* and *after* to make the necessary decisions.

Many students with learning disabilities need specific help with these concepts, even as they get older. Often this means reviewing the ideas prior to problem-solving situations. For example, asking a student with learning disabilities whether he or she wants to see a movie "before lunch" or "after lunch" may involve briefly reviewing temporal concepts first. The following activities propose some ways of helping students of all ages in this area. The suggestions are presented in the format of word problems so students can more easily transfer their learning to daily situations.

✎ Sample Sequence of Activities

1. **Before and after.** While most children learn to sequence steps as they mature, many students with learning disabilities must be taught a thought process to help them determine a given sequence of steps. To that end, it often helps to set up problems with the *before-after* concept clearly presented. This is especially true for situations involving two steps, one of which is not clearly stated (see Figure 2.21a). Provide worksheets as shown in Figure 2.21b. Ask students to cross out the wrong choice and then solve the problem.

■ *Variation 1:* Encourage children to predict what they would have to do in similar situations. Use coins or other manipulatives to assist.

■ *Variation 2:* Present two- and three-step problems along with the needed steps on individual strips or on the computer in a word-processing program. Talk with children, use manipulatives, and help them determine the correct sequence. Have them arrange the strips or use cut-and-paste functions on the computer to solve the

a)   You buy $3\frac{1}{2}$ lbs. of meat at $2.42 per lb.

How much change will you have left from $10?

b)   You buy $3\frac{1}{2}$ lbs. of meat at $2.42 per lb.

How much change will you have left from $10?

Before I can find the change, I need to know
(How much I spend)
(How much meat I buy)

c)   You buy $3\frac{1}{2}$ lbs. of meat at $2.42 per lb.

How much change will you have left from $10?

Before I can find the change, I need to know
(How much I spend)
(How much meat I buy)

Figure 2.21.

problem. For some students, especially those with memory problems, this task may be a two- or three-part assignment. Use the manipulatives one day; the next day, sequence the written words and encourage students to "picture what you did with the coins yesterday." Check the sequencing before they continue. Finally, have them solve the problem.

2. **Color cue.** Various activities in the previous pages have highlighted the effectiveness of color-coding as an aid to sequencing. Figure 2.22 shows another way to color-code a word problem so students begin to internalize the thought process and procedure for sequencing problems.

3. **Phase out.** As children develop sequencing skills, randomly list the necessary steps and have them number the steps in the correct order. If necessary, color-code either the word problem or the steps but not both (as in Figure 2.23). When checking the numbering, have the students note alternative sequences that their friends might have chosen. After the sequences have been checked, students can solve the problems.

NOTE: *The original version of the computer program* Math Blaster Mystery *(Davidson Software) is a good program to use in this area. It includes word problems and requires students to think about how to sequence problems. The teacher can enter problems and save them to a data disk, allowing the program to be individualized to meet the needs of most students. (See the appendix at the back of the book for addresses of software publishers.)*

_____ = green .... = red

You spend $1.28 per gallon on gasoline.

You travel 48 miles and use 18 gallons of gasoline per mile.

How much does gasoline cost?

step 1

I need _____ gallons.

step 2

I spend _____ in all.

Figure 2.22.

You earn $3.22 each hour.

You work 3 hours a day for 6 days.

Then you buy a book for $2.84.

How much do you have left? _____

_____ amount earned in all

_____ number of hours worked

_____ amount left after buying the book

sentence 1 = black
sentence 2 = green
sentence 3 = red

Figure 2.23.

PROBLEM SOLVING IN THE REAL WORLD

The activities in the preceding sections are of value only if students can apply and use the basic problem-solving skills in their daily lives. It is hoped that by considering a nonstandard topic (e.g., vocabulary building or decision making) as a specific skill and helping students learn ways to use the skill to approach problem-solving situations, teachers will make students more aware of how to use these skills in a variety of instances. The following list includes some activities to consider.

✎ Sample Sequence of Activities

1. **What works?** Give students opportunities to choose whatever method they want for solving a problem, even if their choice might not be the most efficient. Later, as a separate activity, help them identify more efficient methods.

2. **Each one different.** Present a problem to a small group of students and require that each student solve the problem in a different way. (If there are too many students, group them and require each group to come up with a different solution.) In order to follow these directions, students will have to find several different methods themselves in case someone else presents their solution first. Help students see why the various approaches resulted in the same, or different, solutions. Analyze why some approaches worked and some did not.

3. **Plan ahead.** Before going on a field trip, discuss with students the possible price of things they may want to do or buy. Include the actual cost of such things as entrance fees. Write the prices on the board and help students estimate a reasonable amount of money to bring on the trip.

4. **What's first?** Have students plan a segment of the morning schedule. Present alternatives that include required subjects as well as free-time activities. List the activities on the board along with the approximate times needed for each. Let the children decide on a sequence they think will work.

NOTE: *To help students see that not all sequences work out, let them choose whatever sequence they want. This may mean that not all work will be completed or that students will miss an activity. That's okay! Students will have learned a valuable lesson about planning ahead while they also learn about sequencing.*

- *Variation:* Some students, especially those with expressive language, short-term memory, or temporal difficulties, may be helped by having the activities written out on strips and the times of the activities noted on pie segments of an analog clock. They then can fill in the clock with the activities as shown in Figure 2.24.

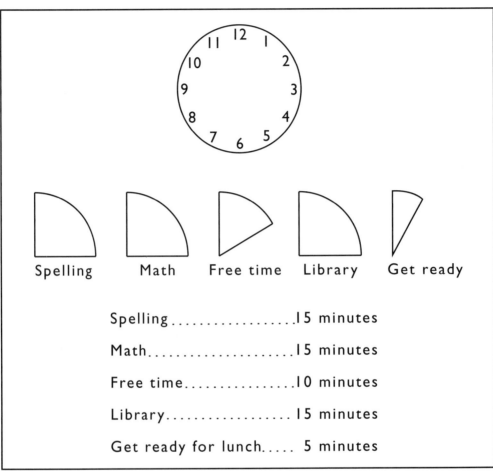

Figure 2.24.

Chapter 3

◆ ◆ ◆ ◆ ◆ ◆ ◆ ◆ ◆ ◆ ◆ ◆ ◆ ◆ ◆ ◆ ◆ ◆

Mathematics, Computers, and Students with Learning Disabilities

CURRENT TRENDS

As technology becomes more available and sophisticated, less expensive, easier to use, and more interchangeable across platforms, its application to education becomes even more important. In addition, with the continued emphasis on improving education so that it is more relevant to daily life, this increased availability takes on new meaning. Students now have an opportunity to develop a life skill from the beginning of their education, and teachers have an even broader range of resources from which to draw. In addition, the door has been opened to meeting the needs of all students by allowing for more individualization and a more dynamic curriculum. This is an exciting time, but it is also a critical time. Although technology has improved in all aspects, the authors recognize that there is still a lack of time and training available to teachers to allow them to implement technology in potentially important and beneficial ways. That is too broad a topic for this book and one that is best addressed in other arenas. With that understanding, though, it is the intent of this chapter to address not only some ways in which students with learning disabilities benefit from technology but also (a) to provide information and ideas that can easily be implemented and (b) to help teachers evaluate technology and software in light of different learning strengths and weaknesses. A "spectacular" piece of software or adaptation is only spectacular if it helps a student learn and become more confident and independent.

Planning and effective implementation of computers into the curriculum can seem overwhelming but need not be. If used properly, as a tool, by teachers who feel comfortable with it, the computer can provide simulated real-life experiences, practice at a pace that is slow and individualized enough for students to process material and overlearn where necessary, and opportunities for learning in a cooperative manner. For most students, the computer is highly motivating and often quite necessary. Those who are reluctant to join social situations involving a lot of conversation (e.g., students with expressive and receptive language difficulties or those with nonverbal learning disabilities) often can develop improved socialization skills by interacting with a peer at the computer. Additionally, a computer's response to mistakes can be less threatening than the personal response of a teacher, peer, or parent.

Mathematics teachers can effectively use computers in a variety of ways, such as to:

- increase students' logic, reasoning, and problem-solving skills through simulation and nonverbal understanding of relationships;
- improve retention of basic facts, computation procedures, and vocabulary relationships;
- remove the impact of fine-motor coordination and/or visual discrimination problems from affecting a student's ability to otherwise apply understanding of concepts;
- help students develop self-confidence through overlearning;
- foster cooperative learning and application of mathematics;
- improve understanding of the relationship of mathematical ideas to life skills through simulation and interactive tutorial presentations; and
- develop understanding of higher-level mathematical concepts through the use of databases and spreadsheets.

Although the computer can be of tremendous assistance in a variety of settings, teachers should understand how learning disabilities can affect the use of a computer. Some of the suggestions that follow involve direct monitoring by both the teacher and the student, a situation that is usually not fostered in the general use of a computer, when one tends to move quickly. Since the viewpoint taken in this chapter, and in the entire book, is that part of the learning process for all students, and especially those with learning disabilities, should be learning to use the computer as a tool and that it should be made to work for each student in an appropriate way, a different approach may be needed.

The following section focuses on students with learning disabilities in terms of their interaction with computers. The major disabilities have been subdivided similarly to the overview in Table 1.1 (see Chapter 1). Table 3.1 summarizes the discussion as it is presented in this chapter. At the end of each section, suggestions for general remediation techniques are provided and, where appropriate, divided into computer activities and off-computer activities. The authors are aware that some of the suggested activities are not yet available in programs, but the field has burgeoned so much that they may be available before long. Additionally, as teachers increase their comfort level with and knowledge of how to make adaptations, they will find ways of making adjustments that will work, based on their knowledge of learning disabilities, their own students, and the technology.

LEARNING DISABILITIES: THE IMPACT OF USING THE COMPUTER

Most teachers have encountered one or more of the following situations when students use a computer. A student:

- continues to hit a key or keys, randomly, until the screen changes.
- is unable to locate the correct response key even though the program only requires the use of, for example, numbers and the return key, or the return key and the space bar.

Table 3.1. Examples of How Learning Disabilities Affect Using the Computer

	Problem Area	Ways of Helping
Perceptual		
Figure-Ground		
Visual	• size of type • amount of material on the screen • tracking from screen to keyboard, keyboard to screen • locating keys on the keyboard	• use large type, colors • skip lines • allow enough time • use bold type, heavy cursor • use a touch screen
Auditory	• noisy environment • number of computers in room	• choose programs that reinforce without sound
Discrimination		
Visual	• noticing punctuation • too much on the screen • line spacing • type of screen reinforcement	• adjust screen placement (adjust, place to side of keyboard) • use a larger screen • use line tracker
Auditory	• misperception of endings	• highlight word or number as said • make tape to match lesson
Spatial/Temporal	• use of arrow keys	• provide small direction arrows on monitor • use I-J-K-M keys (or variation) for direction • set keystrokes in "Preferences"
	• difficulty with sense of time	• provide small on-screen clock
Memory		
Short and Long Term	• screen-to-screen retention	• ease of returning to previous screens • ability to access help screens
	• too much skill or subject isolation	• ability to input curriculum information
	• keyboard-to-screen retention	• use of a touch screen
Working and Visual Memory	• keyboard-to-screen retention • simultaneous processing • difficulty learning key location	• eliminate or reduce timing factors • on-screen keyboard • provide help screens
Language	• difficulty following directions	• preview screens off computer • eliminate timing • provide visual cues

(continues)

Table 3.1. *Continued.*

	Problem Area	Ways of Helping
Language (*continued*)		
	• difficulty with timed programs	• allow student to determine timing
Abstract Reasoning	• difficulty generalizing	• provide concrete aids • ensure skill or subject relationship to program • branching capabilities

- forgets why and how a particular screen was accessed and what the relevance of that screen is to what is being done.

- is able to play any available computer game successfully, even if use of the basic math facts is involved, but is unable to memorize the facts and accurately integrate their use into everyday experiences.

- is confused about the way symbols are represented on the keyboard compared to the screen. A particularly common confusion occurs in younger students who have not yet learned to discriminate between lower-case (on screen) and upper-case (on keyboard) letters. (See Figure 3.1.)

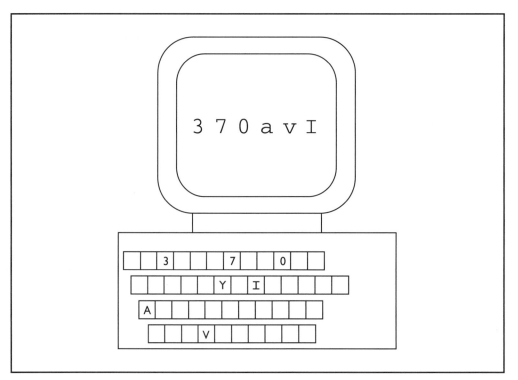

Figure 3.1.

VISUAL AND AUDITORY PERCEPTUAL PROBLEMS

Figure-Ground Difficulties

Background: Students with visual figure-ground deficits tend to have trouble keeping their place on the keyboard, especially if they need to look back and forth from it to the screen. Even those students who seem to know their way around a keyboard may have trouble because the keys are close together. Such students especially have trouble with the number keys and others that carry two symbols. Additionally, many programs use small print on the screen, making it still more difficult to sort out the information being presented.

Auditory figure-ground difficulties are compounded by the sound from other computers and computer users in the room. Even if no game is being played and the sound is turned off, the mere sound of typing can interfere with students' thought processes. If a sound factor is added, either to an individual student's program or to that of another child, even more confusion results.

Sample Sequence of Activities

1. **Cover it.** When only a few keys are needed, perhaps only the number keys and the space bar, it may be helpful to cover the remaining keys, as in Figure 3.2.* See Activity 2 under "Visual Discrimination Difficulties" later in this section for a variation of this activity.

2. **Time out.** When choosing commercially prepared programs or shareware or creating your own, be sure to choose or create programs that allow teachers and students to control the timing. Students with figure-ground deficits (and those with other deficits) will be relieved if they do not need to work within an arbitrary time frame as they search the keyboard.

---

*The key names used throughout this chapter refer to Macintosh computers. If your system uses different terms, adjust accordingly.

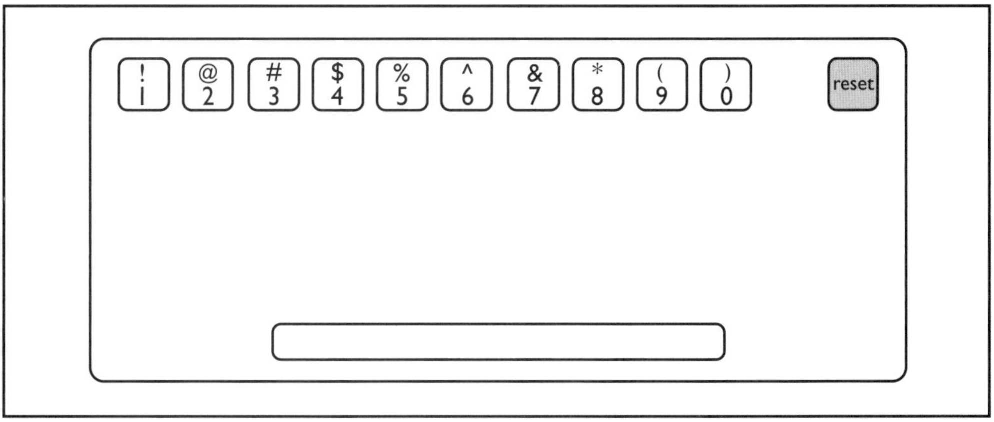

Figure 3.2.

3. **Hold still.** Select programs in which the location of the activity or computation remains reasonably consistent from screen to screen, so that students can practice finding information in a specific location and off-computer work is easier to arrange. (See Activity 1 under "Off-Computer Activities.")

NOTE: *Consistency of problem location can be even more important when students begin to use timed programs. There is less chance for them to lose their place if they know where to look ahead of time.*

4. **Block it.** Allow students to use headphones, even for games that depend on a bell or other sound. The sound of the other computers will not interfere as much, allowing students to attend more easily to what is required. Even when sounds such as beeps or bells are not part of a program, students with auditory figure-ground difficulties may benefit from using headphones simply to block out extraneous sounds in a room.

5. **Mouse it.** Choose programs that allow the use of a mouse. Even students with fine-motor problems are usually able to use a mouse, and the decreased need to look back and forth from keyboard to screen helps those with visual figure-ground problems.

When using laptop computers with track pads it may still be preferable to attach a standard mouse, which for some is easier to maneuver.

6. **Clear space please.** Students with figure-ground difficulties may have an easier time using a spreadsheet if the cell grid is removed on the display, leaving a solid background. (See Figure 3.3a.) Centering the numbers in each cell may help identify the column location more clearly. (See Figure 3.3b.)

NOTE: *This idea, and others presented in this chapter, show the importance of teaching students the numerous ways that computers can be adjusted and used to meet individual needs. Not all students, in fact probably most, will not need to make this adjustment. But those who do will be greatly relieved.*

▶ Off-Computer Activities

1. **Practice it.** Use a paper keyboard that matches the computer and highlight the keys in sections, as shown in Figure 3.4. Be sure to enlarge the keyboard so that fingers can fit easily on the keys. Prepare some tape-recorded and/or paper instructions and have students practice "typing" numbers and signs especially prior to using the computer.

2. **There it is.** Preview programs before students use them. If sample screens are not provided in the documentation, take screen shots of essential screens, print them, and preview important words and concepts needed for the screens.* These pictures can also be used with the keyboard practice described in Activity 1 above.

---

*On Macintosh computers screen shots are made by simultaneously depressing the shift key and the command (apple) and then either 3 or 4, depending on the model you are using. Using the "3" key will cause the computer to automatically take a picture, which you can later crop as desired. Using the "4" key will allow you to crop the picture before taking it. There are also shareware programs (such as SnapzPro from Ambrosia) that allow screen shots to be taken.

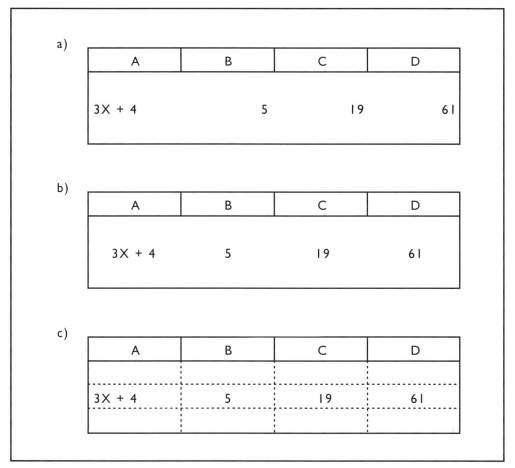

Figure 3.3.

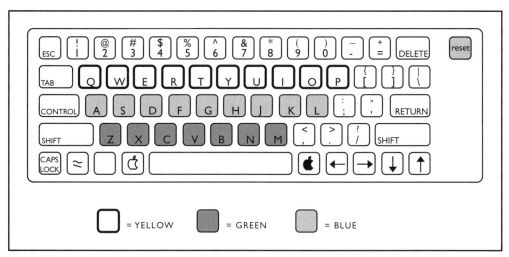

Figure 3.4.

NOTE: *To avoid extra work and to engage and expand all students' knowledge of how to use the computer as a tool, teach students how to take a screen shot and then have them make pictures as part of their computer work. Even students who need preview screens can be engaged in this activity if the teacher has previewed the program and gives them guidelines of what to look for (e.g., "Look for the picture with the cash register and take a screen shot of that.").*

Visual Discrimination Difficulties

Background: Students with visual discrimination difficulties who often misread numbers on written or typed pages tend to have similar problems when using a computer. The clarity of the print on the screen, the color of the monitor, and the size of the print all play a part in how well a child can discern the information on the screen. These children may have an especially difficult time reading decimal numbers, as it is often hard for them to discern the decimal point. Even using the arrow keys can be confusing, as these students try to figure out which way the arrows go. Frequently, there is too much on the screen, the text is too close together, the type is too small, and the clarity of the color or monochrome background interferes with a child's perception of the material. In addition, the graphics that accompany the text may be unclear in spite of continued improvements in this area.

✎ Sample Sequence of Activities

1. **Highlight it.** If possible, use programs with large type or fonts that can be sized and colored to meet individual needs. If a program with smaller print must be used, assist students by providing a tachistoscopic (slotted) card. It is easiest to use the card with a program that always places the numbers (the problem) in the same location. This allows the card to be attached to the monitor, as in Figure 3.5.

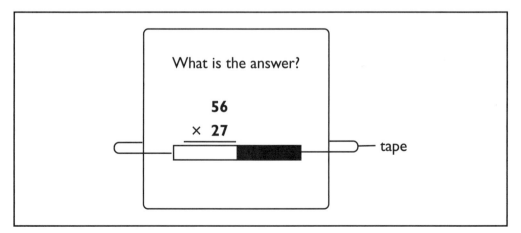

Figure 3.5.

2. **Hide it.** Some students have trouble using the number keys because there are two symbols on each. Due to the size of the symbols, students may spend unnecessary time (a) trying to separate the symbols and (b) trying to figure out which number they want. Since, generally, the goal is to locate the correct number, it often is helpful to cover the keys with removable stickers that have only numbers on them, as in Figure 3.6. Be sure the numbers on the stickers closely resemble the keyboard numbers. (See Activity 1 under "Figure-Ground Difficulties" earlier for a related idea.)

3. **Consistency please.** Use programs in which the screen format does not vary greatly from screen to screen. This enables students to focus their eyes more easily.

4. **Color-code it.** A computer provides wonderful opportunities to color-code work as needed. For example, students who might benefit from pages like those described in Figures 1.15 and 1.16, in Chapter 1, might do well using software programs such as Access to Math or Math Pad (see Don Johnston in the appendix), which allow for on-screen work in color-coded grids or printouts that can be customized by teacher or students. In addition, students who benefit from an on-screen calculator can access that while using these programs.

▶ **Off-Computer Activities**

1. **Look closely.** Preview the programs students will be using, to locate any oddly shaped words or letters. For example, sometimes an *m* may look something like that in Figure 3.7, or a + sign may be hard to read. Check the documentation for examples of the pictures used on the screen. Make copies (or take screen shots as described above) so students can become familiar with them before using the program. Play matching games, make flash cards, or devise other means of acquainting students with hard-to-read visuals.

2. **Find it.** Make flash cards of important computer words students need in order to load and/or run a program. If possible, make worksheets that

Figure 3.6.

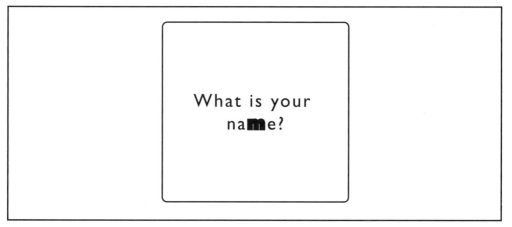

Figure 3.7.

involve those words and have students practice locating the words first on the worksheet and then on the monitor. Provide an acetate overlay that has a heavy line on it so students can place the card on the screen with the heavy line under the word.

3. **Consistency please.** When the screen format remains somewhat constant, off-computer activities can be developed to help students know what to expect.

Auditory Discrimination Difficulties

Background: Students with auditory discrimination problems may encounter difficulty using computers even when no voice synthesizer is involved. For example, those who misperceive endings on words or have trouble discriminating between ending sounds of numbers, such as *nineteen* and *ninety,* will likely encounter the same problems when using the computer—it may not be noticed if there is no teacher–student interaction at the time. Figure 3.8 shows an example of the problems such students may have in attempting to solve a com-

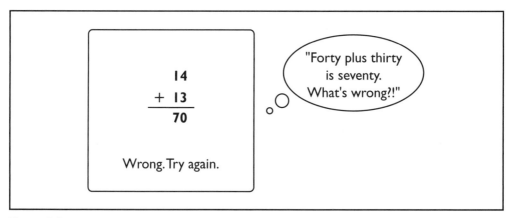

Figure 3.8.

putation problem. Depending on how friendly the computer feedback is when a mistake is made, frustration may occur.

Sometimes what might appear to be a careless error or a visual misperception is, in reality, trouble with auditory discrimination. Students with auditory discrimination may misperceive what they "hear" themselves say or think. For example, they may see the number 13, accurately say it as "13" (should someone be standing by who hears them verbalize what they see or repeat), but they may be simultaneously processing the number as 30 and therefore write it down or key it in as 30 or perform a calculation using 30. Depending on how well they proofread their work or monitor their activity on a screen or calculator, this type of error can go unnoticed. (This is where the need for good estimation skills becomes essential.)

✎ Sample Sequence of Activities

1. **Headphones help.** Sometimes simply using good headphones helps students with auditory discrimination problems. Although it may seem as if headphones would worsen discrimination difficulties, if the student can manually adjust the sound while listening, they can be of help by blocking out other sounds that might interfere.

NOTE: *As noted in the section on auditory figure ground, students with auditory discrimination difficulty may benefit from using headphones to simply block out extraneous sounds in the room.*

2. **Adjust the rate.** Check to see whether the rate of speech can be altered in the program or, depending on the needs of the program, if the sound be turned off entirely. (Many programs today allow for manual adjustment of the speech rate as well as the actual voice being used in the program, but not all do; it is valuable to check this out before purchasing a program or during the trial period.)

Strong visual learners and those with good generalization skills who have auditory processing difficulties may actually do quite well without any sound or by manually adding it in or adjusting it when verbal instructions are given.

▶ Off-Computer Activities

1. **Tape it.** Choose programs in which the sequence in which the problems are presented can be previewed. Have a volunteer or an aide list the problems in the order in which they will appear in the program, adding a "think bubble" containing the problem in words and color-coding the endings of any numbers that could be confused (e.g., thirteen). Before using the program, students should study the list and then keep it available, perhaps taped to the screen.

- ■ *Variation:* Provided it is easy to stop or pause a program, break computer use into two or three sessions. Initially, have students call up each problem and read the computation into a tape recorder. (Or they could write the information down if other issues do not interfere.) Students can then have that work checked by the teacher or an aide before proceeding.

2. **Preview it.** Particularly when students are solving problems involving teen numbers, it is usually helpful to preview the work. Choose programs in which the presentation order of problems can be previewed so students can be provided with practice ahead of time. Have students read the problems aloud and match or otherwise associate the individual numbers with the words. In this way, students are learning a method of checking themselves that can be helpful when they use the program independently.

Spatial and Temporal Disabilities

Background: The arrow keys are often used to move the cursor around the screen. The idea behind this is sound; however, the purpose may be defeated by the location of the arrow keys on the keyboard. Frequently, the placement of the arrow keys on the keyboard (e.g., all in a row, as in Figure 3.9) has no actual relationship to the direction of the arrows.

Concepts such as *up, down,* and *behind,* which already are difficult for some students to comprehend, become especially confusing on a computer monitor, where the orientation is different than it is on a piece of paper or any object that is parallel to the ground. (See Figure 3.10.) Moreover, the ability to involve children motorically is limited because their hands and the keyboard are on a different plane than the monitor, making it hard for them to feel the direction. This confusion can be compounded by the fact that accessing the next screen or the one before usually involves using the control (ctrl) key and some unrelated letter instead of, for example, N for *next* or B for *before.*

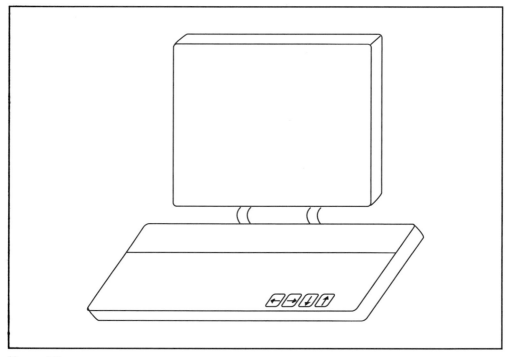

Figure 3.9.

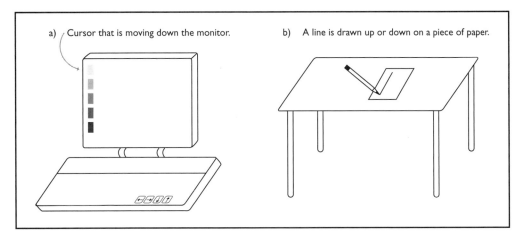

a) Cursor that is moving down the monitor.

b) A line is drawn up or down on a piece of paper.

Figure 3.10.

✎ Sample Sequence of Activities

1. **Stretch yourself.** In addition to the arrow keys, many programs also provide for cursor movement through use of the I, J, K, and M keys or some other combination in similar proximity. Such keys may be more helpful because they more closely replicate movement in space.

NOTE: *Some programs, especially some good shareware programs, allow the user to determine which keys will apply to movement. If you have such a program, evaluate your students carefully to determine whether an alternate set of keys, perhaps U and D for up and down would be preferable to the arrow keys or I, J, K, and M keys. On a Macintosh, for example, you may be able to go to Preferences from the Menu Bar and select the keys to be used for up, down, right, and left. (Color Fall, a shareware program that involves spatial orientation, is one such program.) Probably most students will find an alternate set awkward; some will not, however, especially those who rely on language association. See "Type of Learning Disability: Spatial or Temporal" at the end of this chapter for more information.*

2. **See it.** Place removable stickers on the monitor and on the arrow keys. The color of the stickers on the monitor should match the color of stickers on the keys. (See Figure 3.11.)

3. **Share the work.** Pair a student with good expressive language who may have trouble navigating the keyboard with another who is adept at using the keyboard. Working together on a program, the student with good language skills can state the action for the other to complete—for example: "Move the man up, right, and then down."

4. **Feel it/see it.** Prior to using a program that involves cursor movement involve students in some practice involving simultaneous visual and motor work on the computer. Using an integrated program (e.g., ClarisWorks) make a spreadsheet template that is formatted as shown in Figure 3.12. Students

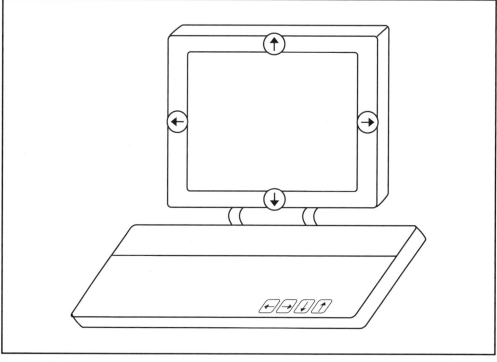

Figure 3.11.

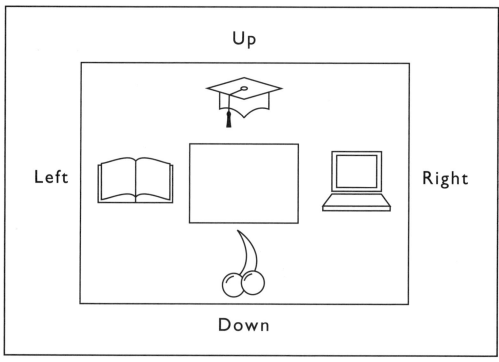

Figure 3.12.

can be paired for brief activities in which one gives the instructions (e.g., "up," "right," "left"), and the other places the cursor in the center box and follows the instructions.

Creative students who enjoy using the computer will like adjusting the template by inserting pictures of their choice. To preserve the needed format, lock the cells that should not be altered. (Just as disk information can be locked, so can spreadsheet information. Look in the Help menu of the spreadsheet or in the documentation to learn how to do this.)

5. **aMazing.** Some commercial programs involve mazes that are not too complex. Initially, students with spatial difficulties may be reluctant to use them, but with teacher assistance, reduced timing, and clearly defined lines on the screen, they usually begin to enjoy these games. While solving the maze, encourage them to verbalize the directions in which they are moving.

Using a drawing program, students can make their own mazes and practice solving them with a friend on screen or off. Tape the maze to the monitor and have students solve it there, rather than on a table.

6. **See the time.** Some programs have on-screen clocks or timing bars at either the top or the bottom of the screen. Have students start by using programs like this and help them notice the movement of the clock or the bar. In this way, they can begin to "feel" the time and use it to help pace themselves.

Figure 3.13 shows a screen shot of one such clock, a shareware program titled O'Clock (see "Type of Learning Disability: Spatial or Temporal" and the

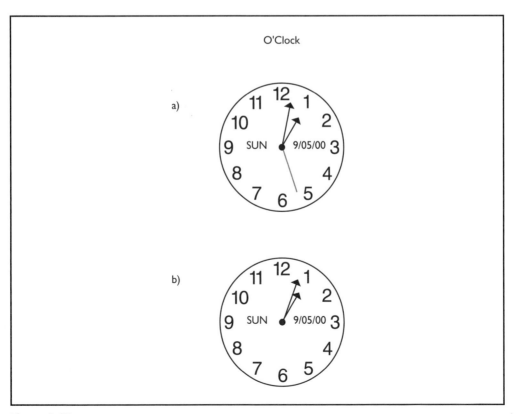

Figure 3.13.

appendix for more information). This is an actual clock that keeps time, with a second hand (Figure 3.13a) or without a second hand (Figure 3.13b), and can be adjusted for color, sound, size, and location. A word of caution though: Children with visual figure-ground problems may find these on-screen aids too confusing.

7. **Touch it.** Many programs can be used with a touch screen, which allows students to practice feeling the difference between directions on a monitor, on paper, and in a three-dimensional world.

MEMORY PROBLEMS

Short- and Long-Term Memory Problems

Background: The computer is patient and can provide the overlearning that is essential to students with memory problems. At the same time, however, as described in Chapter 1, students with memory problems can encounter unexpected difficulties because they are able to access only a certain amount of information at any one time. The screen holds relatively little information, and, even though previous screens may be accessed easily, students must continually flip between screens. If access to screens prior to the most recent screen is not (easily) available, the problem is compounded further.

The continual need to look back and forth between the screen and the keyboard often is problematic for students with short-term memory deficits, especially if they are unfamiliar with the keyboard or lose their place easily. They may forget what they are looking for while their eyes move back and forth between the screen and the keyboard. Worse, while they are searching the keyboard for the correct key, action may take place on the screen. Having missed it, by the time they look at the screen again, they no longer know what they are supposed to be looking for. The use of a mouse may alleviate these difficulties, especially for students who are good at simultaneous processing.

Commercial programs that do not allow for teacher or student entry of curriculum-related information may cause *skill-subject isolation*. Specifically, this occurs when students who have learned certain material in class following a planned sequence that meets their needs, use a computer to reinforce what they have been learning and are faced with a variety of information, only some of which is related to what they have been studying.

Visual and Sequential Memory Problems

Background: Some of the areas described above also apply to students with visual and sequential memory deficits. As a result, the need for visual aids to reinforce learning or to assist with recall is as important when students are using a computer as when they work out of a workbook or read a book. Realistic, clear pictures and graphics are essential. For example, a program designed to develop money skills should depict clear, simulated coins and bills but should also allow time for a student to use real coins while solving the problems.

Students with visual memory deficits may find it especially hard to become familiar with the keyboard since there is no visual (alphabetic) pattern to key locations and nothing concrete for them to use to help recall key placements. These students may benefit from learning keyboarding based on an alphabetic approach. If their fine-motor strength and coordination are good, they could use touch-typing finger placement but learn the keys in alphabetical order rather than following the standard "home-row" approach. For example, they could begin learning the keys by using the little finger of the left hand on the *a* key and the index finger of the right hand on the *b* key; letter drills would be based on those keys, rather than on the *f* and *j* keys. (To use this approach, select typing programs that allow you to edit the instructions.)

Working Memory

Background: Much of what is done on the computer requires strong working memory, the ability to hold information in the brain long enough to use it while performing another activity. To watch students play games on a computer, one could be led to think that this would not be an issue, and often it is not. However, students with learning disabilities who have no trouble with games may nevertheless encounter roadblocks when it comes to using the computer for academic tasks. To solve a basic computation problem (e.g., 34 + 25) requires the following tasks to be held in memory and performed in a seemingly simultaneous manner:

- accurate discrimination of the numbers involved;
- accurate discrimination of the operation sign;
- retrieving the correct procedure (e.g., addition) for the operation sign;
- retrieving the solution to the first step (e.g., 4 + 5);
- writing the answer on paper or locating the correct key and typing the number;
- retrieving the answer to the second step (3 + 2); and
- writing or typing the rest of the answer.

✎ Sample Sequence of Activities

1. **Help.** Many programs provide help screens that can easily be viewed on the monitor, should students need assistance remembering what to do. When possible, show students how to access those screens and how to position them to use while working. If text-to-speech software is installed, sometimes it can be set to read aloud the text of the help screen.

2. **Sequence it.** Ideally, choose computation programs that allow students to key in the regrouped number first, as in Figure 3.14a. (Unfortunately, such programs are not widely available.) If it is necessary to use a program in which the regrouped number is typed in second, choose one that at least asks the student to think about whether regrouping is needed.

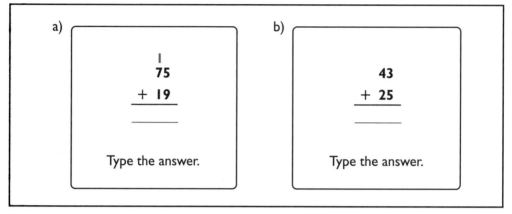

Figure 3.14.

NOTE: *Students with visual discrimination problems should not use programs that require the answer to be typed in from right to left.*

3. **Keep it there.** Activity 1 under "Abstract-Reasoning Difficulties" later in this chapter is also good for students with memory difficulties. The color coding helps them focus, and by having everything on the screen, they can recall and apply information more readily.

▶ Off-Computer Activities

1. **That's it.** Off-computer activities are helpful when students are trying to remember the key location for a specific program. Highlight worksheets as shown in Figure 3.15 to assist the student with recalling which keys are associated with which program. Words and corresponding keys should be highlighted in the same color. Make flash cards or concentration games for students to play with each other.

2. **I've seen that.** If possible, choose software programs that allow for entry of curriculum-related material. In that way, overlearning can be achieved, and ideas and sequences that have been addressed in class can be reinforced. Alternately, preview the programs ahead, make screen shots of some of the relevant pictures, and, using the screens, help students see relationships between instruction and the computer program. For example, if you are teaching students about percents and banking, preview the related screens with the students while discussing those topics. If there are worksheet exercises related to the computer program to be done, put balloon reminders on the assignment to trigger a visual image of the related part of the computer program.

EXPRESSIVE AND RECEPTIVE LANGUAGE DIFFICULTIES

Background: Much of the time spent using the computer involves responses that are elicited by the on-screen presentation. Often, to obtain credit for a cor-

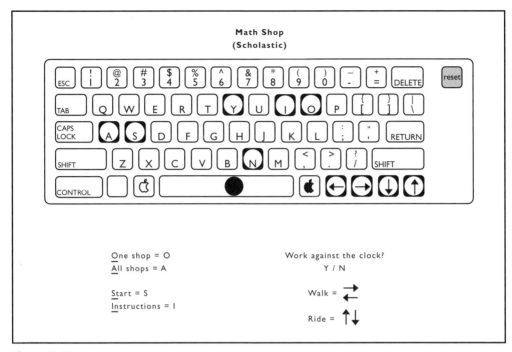

Figure 3.15.

rect response, the student must provide the answer with a minimum amount of cueing. If the information being presented is related to the student's experience, responding is easier. However, for students with language difficulties, the task can be confusing, especially if a time limit is involved. Time limits for such students make eliciting or comprehending information more difficult. Similarly, if the vocabulary and sentence structure used in the program are different from what has been used during class instruction or in books, students who have receptive language difficulties may have additional problems processing the material.

Sample Sequence of Activities

1. **Speak to me.** Some students with language difficulties may benefit from using commercial text-to-speech programs for computation. Access to Math (Don Johnston) and Math Pad (Intellitools) are two such programs. For younger students, or those working on learning their basic facts, an additional option is to use the program Let's Talk 2.0 (SCET Software) and type in simple computation problems to match a worksheet. The student can then click on the voice icon to hear the problem while looking at a page with the numerical representation.

▶ Off-Computer Activities

1. **Study it.** Many math programs require at least a small amount of reading, even if only to gain access to a particular section. Others, especially those

that work off of CDs, provide text to speech so that directions can be heard. Often, though, the directions are presented on a different screen, or overlaid on the current screen, which can cause difficulty for students who have language problems (or memory problems). Before a student uses such a program, preview it and make a list of essential words the student should be able to recognize, understand, and apply to use the program successfully. Put each word on a numbered 3×5 card *in the same order* as the words will appear when the program is running. (The numbers will indicate the order in case the cards get rearranged.) Make sure the child can read the words. Using these cards enables the child to focus on relevant material.

2. **Crossword puzzle.** At the beginning of the school year, have an aide, parent, or student make keyboard crossword puzzles as in Figure 3.16. (These can be made as templates in a spreadsheet program and then reused as needed. There are also commercial programs to make crossword puzzles.) Using a keyboard picture to match the computer keyboard, put labels on certain keys to match the puzzle clues, across and down. Students must fill in the boxes with the correct key names. (In Figure 3.16, the tab key is labeled 3a—"a" for "across." The word "tab" would be filled in the boxes for 3 across.) You can adapt this activity to match different computer programs as needed.

3. **Let's play a game.** A variation of Old Maid can be played by two or three children. Make pairs of cards like those in Figure 3.17. Each student starts with seven cards; the rest of the cards are placed face down in the middle of the table. Students take turns requesting cards based on the cards they are

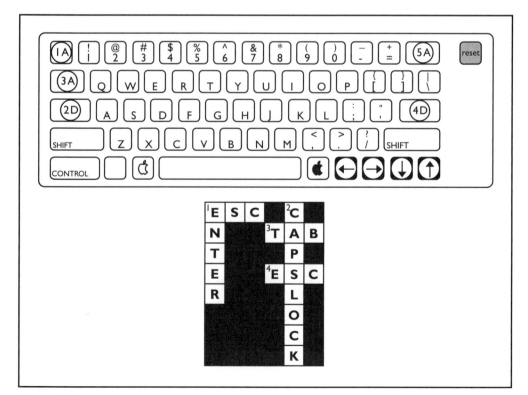

Figure 3.16.

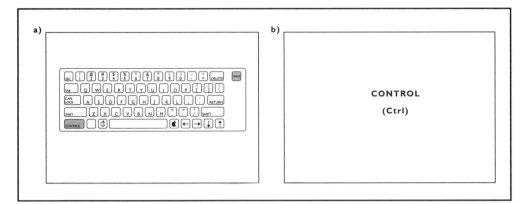

Figure 3.17.

holding. The child holding the card shown in Figure 3.17a, a keyboard with the return key highlighted, would ask for a card that has the corresponding word or key name on it. The child holding the card shown in Figure 3.17b would request a keyboard on which the control key is highlighted.

NOTE: *You may want to allow students to keep paper keyboards in front of them to assist with language requirements as needed.*

ABSTRACT-REASONING DIFFICULTIES

Background: The computer can serve as an effective tool for developing reasoning, logic, and problem-solving skills, yet many students find computers mystical because they are not concrete enough for children who have trouble drawing conclusions. "How does it remember so much?" "How does the disk know what to do?" "Why does *control* mean that it is the computer's turn?" These and many other questions are reasonable for any child, even adults, to ask. Much can be done to gain an understanding of these concepts. In reality, however, most teachers working with elementary school students have neither the expertise nor the time to explain what happens. They are concerned, though, that their students use the computer to good advantage.

Much software today involves more realistic application to real life, and the pictures and voices are much clearer than formerly. This is a great advantage to all students, especially those with learning disabilities, but careful choices need to be made. In general, when working with abstract ideas, try to provide as many visually realistic explanations as possible.

Sample Sequence of Activities

1. **Keep it there.** When spreadsheets are used to teach students about equations, it helps those with abstract-reasoning difficulties if the graph and

the spreadsheet are color-coded and kept on the screen at the same time, as shown by the shading in Figure 3.18. That way, they can watch what happens when they change the input values or change the grid size. (In Figure 3.18, for example, the information on the line with Equation 1 would be the same color as the line representing Equation 1 on the graph.)

NOTE: *Although spreadsheets can be wonderful tools for helping students of all ages begin to understand about equations at a more abstract and general level, it is the authors' belief that many students benefit from actually constructing their own graphs by plotting points on graph papers of different dimensions (e.g., four squares per inch, eight squares per inch, etc.). This is especially true for those who are not limited by visual perceptual difficulties and fine-motor problems but have trouble with abstract reasoning.*

2. **Real things, please.** As much as possible, encourage (require) the use of concrete aids and real-life objects along with a given program. In many instances, this may mean that the timing factors in a program will need to be adjusted.

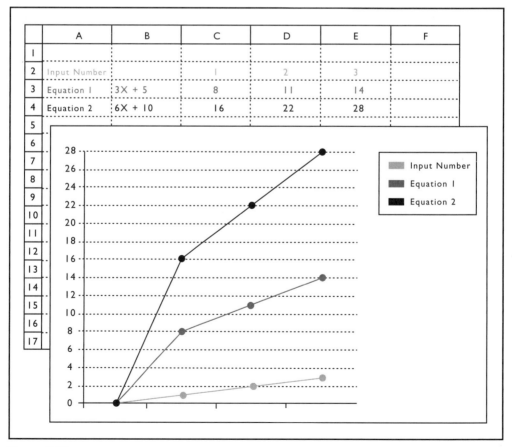

Figure 3.18.

EVALUATING SOFTWARE FOR USE BY STUDENTS WITH LEARNING DISABILITIES

General Considerations

Computers are becoming more available, but to successfully incorporate them into the daily classroom environment requires being able to effectively evaluate software in light of different learning styles and learning strengths and weaknesses. In addition, good incorporation involves an awareness of what type of software will work in different situations. As with the more traditional type of learning tools, such as textbooks and workbooks, a wide variety of needs must be considered when choosing or using software with students. No one piece of software can meet the needs of all students; moreover, specific guidelines may work with a learner for only a period of time and then not be as efficient. Before discussing the relationship of specific software to specific learning disabilities, some general areas should be addressed.

Choose programs that allow for the use of curriculum-related material. (Authoring systems, such as Hypercard [available from Apple Computer, Cupertino, California], which allow for complete curriculum integration, are not considered in this edition. Although they are ideal, if good, the authors recognize that most teachers do not have the time to implement them effectively. Instead, we have tried to emphasize ways in which teachers can use programs that are available on the market or on the Internet.) Computers can be of tremendous help in developing problem-solving skills, building retention, and extending abstract reasoning, but only if the material presented is relevant and sequenced according to the students' needs. Therefore, programs should allow for the following:

• Entry of teacher-made word problems that can follow a desired sequence and allow for proper reading level.

• The option of using either a clear on-screen calculator or a real calculator for students who need to work on problem solving and fact retention separately. (The shareware program Amos' Word Problems and the original Math Blaster Mystery are two such programs.)

• Basic facts to be entered according to the sequence described in Chapter 9. (Too many programs use the traditional, less appropriate method of "tables of.")

• Manual adjustment of the time needed to respond so that if help screens, on-screen calculators, or other tools are not available on the computer, such resources can be used off computer.

• The presentation of basic facts and computation in either a horizontal or a vertical format.

• Easy access to help screens and previous screens.

• Spelling errors or the ability to set preferences to recognize spelling variations. (Remember, language is an important and often neglected component in mathematics instruction.) For example, a game in which a student is required to type in the word *seventeen* in response to the question "How much is 1 ten and 7 ones?" should not penalize the student for misspelling 17—e.g., as *sevintene.*

• Automatic recording of student input, so that, if direct observation is not possible, the teacher can check the work at a later date. Ideally, a printout (paper or screen) should be available, similar to that shown in Figure 3.19. Too often students work independently at the computer while the teacher is occupied with other students, and there is no way for the teacher to evaluate their work later.

• Computer responses that are under the teacher's control. For example, a program involving basic facts might present the correct answer immediately following an error, while a program that is teaching fraction concepts might offer various types of help ("Do you want to see a picture?" "Shall I [the computer] help you?" "Did you mean to type that key?"). In the former case, correct rather than wrong answers are being reinforced. In the latter, problem solving is being reinforced.

• Fonts to be adjusted so that letters and numbers are clear and large enough for students to read easily.

• The opportunity for students to review incorrect or difficult problems.

• Fractions to be presented in a vertical format with a horizontal fraction bar rather than a slash.

• The option to branch (go) to another level—either to a more advanced one or to review—depending on the student's level. This should be under the control of the teacher and/or the student, rather than the computer.

Sequence

When selecting or developing programs, it is important to consider not only the relevance of the content to the ongoing curriculum but also the sequence of the content presentation. Students with learning disabilities often need the pre-

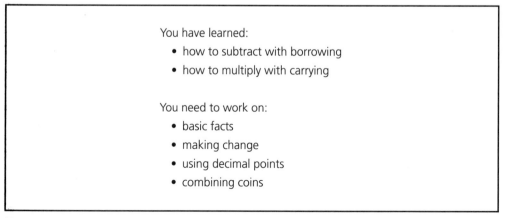

Figure 3.19.

sentation of instructional sequences altered from the traditional method in order to learn and retain information. For example, a child who requires a great deal of overlearning but tends to perseverate would not benefit from a computation program that presented only one type of problem at a time, such as adding without regrouping. Yet the same child might not be ready to solve problems with regrouping. Instead, an intermediate step might be helpful in which the child learns to differentiate between problems that require regrouping and those that do not. If the teacher could insert a decision-making section or option into a computation program, the student would have an opportunity to acquire the necessary skills without being impeded by a learning disability. (An example of one such idea is shown in Figure 3.20.)

Other content-related suggestions include:

1. allowing for teacher input at various points within the program so that a student can review as needed;

2. changing the format of programs so that the teacher is able to:

   a. determine the sequence of presentation and

   b. substitute numbers within the problems without changing the basic structure (i.e., the basic structure of not regrouping would remain, but the basic facts could be changed as a child learned various clusters according to the sequence suggested in Chapter 6);

3. allowing for curriculum-related information to be entered at selected points, depending on student needs;

4. providing help screens that can be used by the teacher (such as one based on the teacher's assessment of a student's work); and

5. using programs in which work can be saved on a separate disk. Then, if students need to stop before completing a program, they need not begin all over again unless that is preferable.

$$\begin{array}{r} 73 \\ +\ 19 \\ \hline \end{array} \qquad\qquad \begin{array}{r} 64 \\ +\ 21 \\ \hline \end{array}$$

Regroup? Y / N   Regroup? Y / N

(If regrouping is needed, the computer goes on to the next problem.)

Figure 3.20.

Response Format

Students with learning disabilities respond to information in various ways, depending on their specific disabilities. In order to instruct these students effectively, special education teachers must be able to clearly determine the goal of a particular assignment and then control the environment to the extent necessary. Only in this way will students learn the information without being held back due to learning deficits. For example, a student with expressive language difficulties might enjoy and benefit from using a computer if a multiple-choice format is available, while another student would do well if required to provide an answer without language cues. Programs with a format choice have the potential of not only being more individualized but also allowing two students with different learning disabilities to work together. Some further suggestions along these lines include the following:

1. Games that allow the teacher to choose whether a student must type in an entire answer (see Figure 3.21a) or only the number of the response selected (see Figure 3.21b) allow for broader use. Students with figure-ground, visual discrimination, or expressive language deficits might benefit from the second format because it involves less of the keyboard, whereas students strong in those areas who need to build up their memory might do better with the former.

2. Computer response to student input should involve some evaluation on the student's part. A student with figure-ground difficulties or perceptual deficits may type in the wrong answer unknowingly. Before the computer immediately responds to the input, it might ask a question such as, "Are you sure that is the answer you want?" At the very least, some time should elapse before the computer responds to the answer.

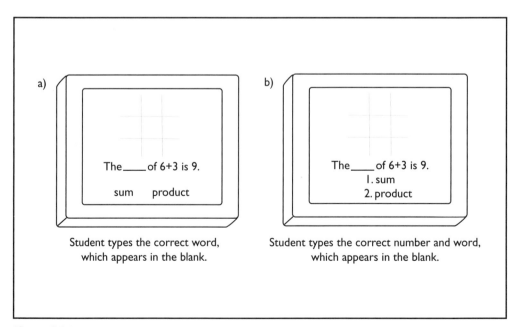

Figure 3.21.

Time Factors

For many students, time restrictions greatly inhibit progress. Students with language difficulties, for example, need time to process information. Students with figure-ground deficits may need more time to locate the keys on the keyboard. Memory problems affect students' speed. If there is no way to alter the built-in timing, many otherwise good programs lose their effectiveness. The following are additional considerations:

1. The teacher should be able to easily control the timing factor of any program. This means being able to set the timing before a student uses the program. In some cases, it also means allowing the student to control the timing, within certain parameters, as the material is mastered. For example, before a student begins a program, the teacher could set the timing to a certain speed and then establish parameters within which the student could increase or decrease the speed. While working on the program at different levels that have been predetermined by the teacher, the student could choose how to handle the timing at each level.

2. It should be possible to save timing changes for individual students so that the same time structure could be used during a subsequent session. This feature also would allow another student to begin or continue at a different speed without interfering with the work of other students.

Computation

When software programs are developed to teach either basic math facts or computation skills, the following factors must be considered. The presentation order of the facts is essential, to avoid having students feel as if they have to learn 100 (or 90) isolated facts for each of the four operations. The format in which the problem is presented (horizontal or vertical) and the method by which the student enters the digits in a computation problem also are important, both in terms of specific learning disabilities and in terms of understanding a concept. In addition, the location and size of the material on the screen are critical. Some suggestions follow:

1. When a student is required to solve computational problems on the monitor, the presentation should appear in a vertical position with input from right to left, except when regrouping is involved.

NOTE: *Chapter 6 describes a left-to-right sequence, which often is needed for students with severe reversal problems. Someday the left-to-right option for computation problems may also be available on computers.*

2. Those programs that do not allow for vertical presentation of problems should offer one of the following characteristics.

   a. The teacher should be able to preview the problems and the order in which they are presented so that the student has paper and pencil available to solve the problem, if needed.

b. If an on-screen calculator is not available within a program, the screen should be able to be sized so that a student can use an additional application with a calculator if needed. (See Figure 3.22.)

c. The program should allow for a well-spaced printout of the problems, so that the student has a worksheet.

3. If regrouping is involved, the student should be required to decide whether to regroup and to enter the answer so that the regrouped digit is entered first. If no regrouping is involved, a certain key can be designated to move the problem along.

4. Numbers should be sufficiently large and centered well enough on the screen that they can be read easily. This will keep the numbers from appearing to jump out at students with perceptual problems and will reduce the problems encountered by those students.

5. When solving division problems, even short division problems, the option of using either division sign ($\overline{)}$ or ÷) should be available, so that the teacher can determine ahead of time which one the student will use.

6. It is not always advisable to have students solve a page with mixed operations; however, that option should be available to the teacher ahead of time.

7. Fraction problems should use the horizontal bar instead of the slanted line, and computation should be presented vertically.

Branching Capabilities

Ideally, the computer should be an integral, related tool of the overall curriculum. As such, computers must enable users to retain the material presented without becoming bored or stagnating at a certain level. These are the same requirements that apply to any classroom instruction. To ensure that the computer meets these criteria, the following branching options must be available:

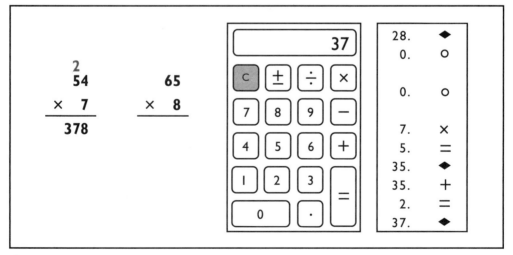

Figure 3.22.

1. The computer must perform ongoing evaluation so that, as a student either reaches mastery or continues to make errors, appropriate branching can occur.
2. The teacher should be able to exert some control over this branching by:

   a. accessing the student's input and noting the sequence in which questions were answered as well as the number of tries it took for the student to obtain a correct answer; and

   b. predetermining at what points the computer would decide when and where to branch.

3. The scope and sequence of the material presented in the software should be accessible, preferably in the printed documentation or at a help screen that can be used while the teacher navigates the program. This allows the teacher to:

   a. decide whether a particular program serves the purposes of the curriculum;

   b. decide how and when to have the computer branch to another part and when review is needed;

   c. develop off-computer activities that are related to the material used in the program; and

   d. develop materials that the student can use while working on the computer.

Reading Level

It is not possible to eliminate all reading demands from programs; however, the level and amount should be controlled to the extent possible. At a minimum, language typically is needed to give instructions. Software publishers should be encouraged to consider the following recommendations:

1. In addition to the intended age and/or grade level, it would help to give the reading level of the software program on the outside of the box. The age descriptions on the box frequently refer more to interest level than to actual reading level.
2. Directions should be made as simple as possible and should be written in clear, large print with generous space between the lines. An ongoing help line at the bottom of each screen would benefit students by reminding them of what to do in order to (a) return to the menu, (b) correct an error, and (c) receive help. If this feature is not possible, a simplified card containing the most basic user information should be included in the documentation. Such a card could be kept at the student's side while working.
3. To the extent possible, representative icons should be used to assist students in understanding the directions.
4. A glossary of words that the student needs to understand to use a program successfully should be included. This also would allow some off-computer activities to be developed prior to actual use of the program.

5. Programs aimed at developing problem-solving skills should specify both the interest and the reading level on the outside of the box and in the documentation.

6. On-screen help boxes with vocabulary and definitions or representative examples would assist students as they read the problems and possibly encounter words with which they are unfamiliar.

7. Software that is programmed to accept teacher-developed word problems is most helpful. The shell program could be written and published in such a way that the teacher could determine:

a. reading level and material;

b. number of steps in a problem;

c. types of problems presented;

d. what help would be given in solving problems, including:

- whether the steps would be listed in order, and
- things to consider prior to solving;

e. order in which problems are presented (sequential or random).

Teacher Utility

One of the important advantages of having computers in the classroom is their potential for individualizing instruction. It is especially important, therefore, that the classroom teacher have some control over the software and be aware of how students use the software without having to be present at all times.

Even though it is not realistic to expect teachers to watch students at the computer continuously, too often no monitoring takes place. In order to evaluate the usefulness of a given activity, teachers must take time to see how students are interacting with and responding to the computer. Otherwise, the computer simply becomes a source of busywork.

To enhance computer utility, teachers should consider the following suggestions:

1. The utility section must be easily accessible to the teacher but not to the student. In some instances, it is helpful for students to be able to access part of the utility section, but the record keeping and error analysis should be open to students only with the assistance of the teacher.

2. Automatic record keeping should start as soon as a student signs on to the computer by entering a name.

3. A paper printout showing the following information would help in assessing student progress:

a. number of problems attempted;

b. the problems attempted, the numbers keyed in to derive the answers, and the final answers; and

c. the percent correct.

4. If correct answers involve words rather than numbers, the program should allow the teacher to add a child's typical misspellings to the spell

checker, so that it will provide the correct spelling. Often, students with learning disabilities have trouble with spelling, and if the answer to a math problem depends on correctly spelled words, there is no way to measure math ability. At the very least, the program should accept spelling errors. Most teachers, however, are more familiar with the types of errors their students make than the software developers are, hence the advantage of flexibility in this area.

GENERAL RECOMMENDATIONS FOR SOFTWARE

As we become more and more sophisticated in our approach to teaching and to integrating computers into instruction, our knowledge of what makes software useful also has improved. The ideas in the preceding discussion apply to particular areas of learning and software. The following points are more general:

1. It is important for the student to be able to read what is on the screen. To that end, the font must be large. Just as some word processors offer a variation in the number of columns, math software should allow for varying the size of the type and perhaps even the boldness of the type.

2. When solving word problems, the student should be required to include a word answer along with the correct computation. If spelling is a problem, the student should be presented with choices from which one answer must be selected. Figure 3.23 presents one suggestion for younger students and those who have difficulty with the keyboard.

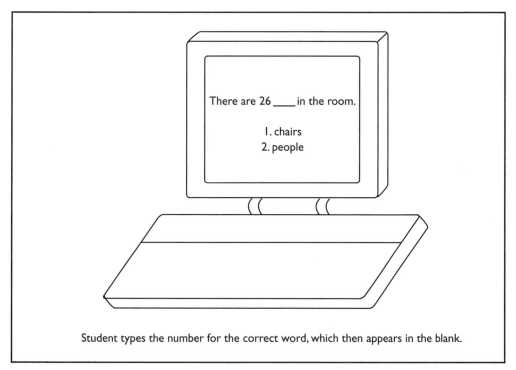

Student types the number for the correct word, which then appears in the blank.

Figure 3.23.

3. The spacing between numbers and between words should be clear. At the very least, double spacing between lines should be available to make it easier to read the material on the screen.

4. The use of underlining, arrows, and cursors to help focus attention is essential for many students. Screens change quickly, and many students with learning disabilities need help to refocus their attention to the correct place on the screen.

5. When graphics are included, many children, though enjoying and benefiting from them, nevertheless have trouble keeping their orientation. Therefore, these students need assistance, in terms of cursors and appropriate time limits, to locate the problem or the answer amid the graphics.

6. Much software benefits from and/or requires a color monitor. In such a case, it is important that the colors be very clear and the size of the numbers and letters large enough that the images are not blurred.

7. The area in which students solve problems should be located centrally on the screen. If more than one problem is presented or if an area is reserved for computation, the program should allow the teacher or student to organize the work space spatially.

8. Many programs provide off-computer activities. These should include activities that focus on the directions needed to work through material. This would enable the student to become familiar with the keyboard as it relates to a particular piece of software.

Specific Suggestions

The following is a short list of commercial and shareware programs that, in the authors' view, work well with students with various types of learning disabilities. (Except where noted, the shareware programs are for a Macintosh.) The software is listed by learning disability category. In no way is this list meant to be an endorsement for any one program, publisher, or Internet site, nor is it meant to be complete. The purpose of this section, rather, is to help teachers learn to evaluate the needs of the student in light of both learning disabilities and specific programs. Many of the programs listed have been highly publicized, but teachers still need to evaluate their appropriateness to a lesson or topic. Other programs that are not as well known are also worth evaluating, in the authors' opinion.

No one software program can meet all needs, and some are better suited than others to particular curriculum goals and specific learning disabilities. Even the most highly rated program in terms of ease of use, teacher utility, and content probably will not be equally useful to all students. Proper integration of computers in the ongoing instructional schedule requires an understanding of the relationship between curriculum goals and the effect of learning disabilities on successful use of computers. Additionally, teachers must evaluate the strengths and weaknesses of individual programs in light of student needs. (See the appendix at the end of the book for addresses of software publishers and Internet sites.)

NOTE: *A ▲ in front of a listing means that the program may be out of print. We have chosen to list them in spite of this situation because there are distributors* *and online sources that can be helpful in locating out-of-print software. To the best of our ability we have indicated possible places to find programs or at least search for help.*

Type of Learning Disability: Figure-Ground

Considerations for determining the effectiveness of software programs for students with figure-ground difficulties include:

- the amount and size of the print on the screen;

- the ability to track material on the screen by using a cursor within the program, teacher-made tachistoscopic materials, or a mouse;

- the amount of keyboard searching needed in order to work the program; the goal is to allow the student to focus more on the screen and less on going back and forth between the keyboard and the screen;

- whether the teacher or the student can adjust time factors;

- the consistency of the screen format; and

- whether sound is available but optional.

Commercial Programs	Publisher/Distributor	Platform
▲MathBlasterPlus*	KnowledgeAdventure	Mac/Apple
▲AlgeBlaster	KnowledgeAdventure	Mac/Apple
The Cruncher 2.0	KnowledgeAdventure	Mac/Windows
KidsTime	Great Wave	Mac/Windows
KidsMath	Great Wave	Mac/Windows
Access to Math	Don Johnston	Mac
Big Calc	Don Johnston	Mac
Math Pad	Intellitools	Mac/Windows
Robomath	Mindplay	Mac

Shareware Programs	Internet Address	Platform
Worksheet Maker	Little Fish Software http://members.aol.com/ weefishes	Mac
CalcWorksSE	Brochu Software http://sitelink.net/jbrochu	Mac

---

*This is the original MathBlasterPlus that was published by Davidson, now KnowledgeAdventure.

Type of Learning Disability: Discrimination

Considerations for determining the effectiveness of software programs for students with discrimination difficulties include:

- the size and spacing of numbers and words on the screen;
- the method used to focus students' attention on a task;
- the type of reinforcement used; and
- the clarity of the monitor, especially a color monitor.

Commercial Programs	Publisher/Distributor	Platform
Hands on Math	Ventura	Mac/Apple
Access to Math	Don Johnston	Mac
Math Pad	Intellitools	Mac/Windows
The Graph Club	Tom Snyder	Mac/Windows
Place Value 1s, 10s, 100s	Cambridge Development Laboratory	Mac/Windows/ Apple II
Penny Panda's Sticker Store	Micrograms	Mac/Windows
Dollars and Cents	Attainment Company	Mac/Windows
Big Calc	Don Johnston	Mac
The Cruncher	KnowledgeAdventure	Mac/Windows

Shareware Programs	Internet Address	Platform
O'Clock	AOL: Keyword is File Search; then search shareware for O'Clock	Mac
Worksheet Maker	Little Fish Software http://members.aol.com/ weefishes	Mac
SnapzPro	Ambrosia Software http://www.AmbrosiaSW. com/	Mac

Type of Learning Disability: Spatial or Temporal

Considerations for determining the effectiveness of software programs for students with spatial or temporal difficulties include:

- how the material on the screen deals with directionality;
- whether a minimal number of keys can be used to work the program and whether the keys are kinesthetically or visually related to the intended direction;

- how the program deals with movement in space—visual or temporal; and

- whether off-computer activities can be used to help the student understand the different orientations of a computer screen (vertical) and paper and pencil.

Commercial Programs	Publisher/Distributor	Platform
Hands on Math	Ventura	Mac/Windows
Access to Math	Don Johnston	Mac
Math Pad	Intellitools	Mac

Shareware Programs	Internet Address	Platform
Color Fall	John V. Holder Software http://www.cc.northcoast.com/~jvholder/	Mac
O'Clock	AOL: Keyword is File Search; then search shareware for O'Clock	Mac
Rommy Robot	Little Fish Software http://members.aol.com/weefishes	Mac
Tangrams	AOL: Keyword is File Search; then search shareware for Tangrams	Mac
Polyominoes 7.0	Kevin's Polyominoes Home Page http://kevingong.com/Polyominoes	Mac

Type of Learning Disability: Memory Difficulties

Considerations for determining the effectiveness of software programs for students with memory difficulties include:

- whether the teacher or the student has control of the time limits within the program;

- whether repetition of material is possible, if needed, especially after an error or at the end of the program for review;

- whether the presentation method of the material (i.e., random or sequential) can be controlled by the teacher;

- whether curriculum-related material can be entered into the program; and

- whether the teacher can preview some of the material so off-computer material can be used before or while students use the computer.

Commercial Programs	Publisher/Distributor	Platform
MathBlasterPlus*	KnowledgeAdventure	Mac/Windows
KidsTime: Match It Game	Great Wave	Mac/Windows
AlgeBlasterPlus*	KnowledgeAdventure	Mac/Apple/ Windows
Big Calc	Don Johnston	Mac/Windows
The Cruncher	KnowledgeAdventure	Mac/Windows

Shareware Programs	Internet Address	Platform
Follow Me	AOL: Keyword is File Search; then search shareware for Follow Me	Mac
CalcWorks	Brochu Software http://sitelink.net/jbrochu	Mac
Math Dittos2	Math Dittos2 http://www.mathdittos2. com/index.html	Mac/Windows
ScreenCloze	Little Fish Software http://members.aol.com/ weefishes	Mac
CopyPaste	Script Software http://www.scriptsoftware. com	Mac/Windows

Type of Learning Disability: Receptive and Expressive Language

Considerations for determining the effectiveness of software programs for students with receptive and expressive language difficulties include:

- ability to use a multiple-choice format;
- interactive ability with curriculum-related material;
- ability to control (or remove) the time limits with the program;
- ability to access previous screens;
- provisions for previewing vocabulary; and
- consistency of format.

---

*This is the original program, published by Davidson, now KnowledgeAdventure.

Commercial Programs	Publisher/Distributor	Platform
Access to Math	Don Johnston	Mac
Math Pad	Intellitools	Mac/Windows
Dollars and Cents	Attainment Company	Mac/Windows

Shareware Programs	Internet Address	Platform
ScreenCloze	Little Fish Software http://members.aol.com/ weefishes	Mac
Crossword Express	Crossword Express http://www.adam.com. au/johnstev/	Mac/Windows
Let's Talk 2.0	SCET Software http://www.scet.com; also at http://www. kidsdomain.com	Mac

Type of Learning Disability: Abstract Reasoning

Considerations for determining the effectiveness of software programs for students with abstract-reasoning difficulties include:

- ability to interact with the program using concrete aids;
- the use of representative visual cues on the screen;
- the ease of accessibility between screens;
- provisions for teacher preview of vocabulary; and
- ability to add help screens for curriculum-related material.

Commercial Programs	Publisher/Distributor	Platform
▲Math Blaster Mystery: Follow the Steps	KnowledgeAdventure	Mac/Apple
Stickybear Word Problems	Optimum Resources	Mac/Windows/ Apple II
Place Value 1s, 10s, 100s	Cambridge Development Laboratory	Mac/Windows/ Apple
Penny Panda's Sticker Store	Micrograms	Mac/Windows
Algebra Concepts	Ventura	Mac/Apple/ Windows
The Cruncher	KnowledgeAdventure	Mac/Windows

Shareware Programs	Internet Address	Platform
Amos' Word Problems	KidsDomain http://www.kidsdomain.com	Mac

Chapter 4

◆ ◆ ◆ ◆ ◆ ◆ ◆ ◆ ◆ ◆ ◆ ◆ ◆ ◆ ◆ ◆

Life Skills: Money and Time

Even before they enter school, many children can discriminate between a penny, a nickel, and a dime, and many can do simple computations using those coins. They may not always associate the correct coin with the correct name, but they usually use one of the three names when referring to a coin. Most preschoolers also develop some sense of time. If recess is later than usual, they "feel" it. If P.E. comes before lunch, instead of after, they feel that. Many even learn to tell time by the hour. For example, they may know that dinner is at 6:00, "when the little hand is on the six—if it's on the five, it's not dinner time."

Basic concepts and skills related to money and time are formally introduced, reinforced, and expanded during the primary school years. Thus, most mathematics programs gear early number work to the development of those skills. Usually by the end of first grade, children can tell time to the half hour, and most can recognize the difference between the five coins by name and value. Many can even find the value of coin groups to 25¢ and make change for amounts up to 10¢.

As children's experience and training base broadens, most continue to develop a feel for time that helps them sense how long they have to complete an activity or to wait for one to begin. Most youngsters also develop a general sense of how much money they need for particular items ("lots" or "a little"), what change is, and how long it will take to save enough money for something they want or need.

At the same time children are becoming more proficient with money and time, the vocabulary involved places greater demands on both receptive and expressive language skills. Children must now begin to deal with familiar words in new contexts. Expressions like "how much change," "ten minutes ago," "in a half hour," and "later," include words that may be part of their vocabulary but presented in less concrete ways. For example, children may have learned what *in* means by going *inside* a box or looking *inside* a book. There was a physical or pictorial representation to help them visualize if necessary. When these types of words start to be used with regard to money and time, they take on less concrete meaning. Helping children understand and use these expressions should entail more than merely having them parrot what others say. Care should be taken to ensure that they comprehend the underlying concepts.

As students progress through school, the demands increase to use money and time efficiently. By the time children reach the middle grades, they are expected to read time to the nearest minute and deal with large money amounts. Older students in middle school or junior high are expected to count out money amounts and make change without relying on paper-and-pencil calculations. These students need to be quite proficient with their sense of time as they navigate from class to class with only a limited amount of time in between. They also must learn to write checks and handle bank accounts—daily living skills of practical importance.

Children's success in mastering concepts of and skills with money and time can be greatly hindered by learning disabilities. If problems persist, they can affect social interactions; it's embarrassing for a teenager to go out with friends without knowing how much money to give for lunch or how to tell when to meet friends. Early work in this area is important but so is ongoing evaluation to ensure that developmental progress is occurring. Many of the tasks outlined in the preceding paragraphs require good visual and auditory memory, discrimination, and sequencing skills. Additionally, the language demands increase with regard to understanding idioms, associating new meaning with previously learned words, and processing more complex language.

This chapter addresses some of the common problems students with learning disabilities face as they try to master money and time skills. The first part of the chapter focuses on money. An introductory section suggests materials to keep in the classroom for use in teaching money; the remaining sections present ways to approach selected topics:

1. Coin discrimination
2. Counting money amounts
3. Paying for items and making change
4. Writing money amounts greater than one dollar

The last part of the chapter deals with teaching time. An introductory section describes helpful classroom materials; the remaining sections present ways to handle selected topics:

1. Reading clock times

2. Writing clock times

3. Naming the correct hour

4. Language and time: Understanding and using the various expressions for time

CLASSROOM MATERIALS FOR TEACHING MONEY

Concrete teaching aids and real-life applications help children build and develop confidence with new concepts and skills. This principle is particularly important when teaching children how to handle money. The following materials should be an essential part of the instruction:

- real money
- realistic coin and paper money stamps
- ink pads and bottles of colored ink
- laminated coin lines

- visually accurate play money, including color-coded coins
- dice games and other money activities
- adaptable practice pages (kept on a disk, in a file)
- empty items for a play store

Real money should be used whenever possible, particularly in early activities. Experience has shown that even very young children can learn to handle money with care and not lose it. A teacher might explain to them, "Money has *value*. We use it to buy what we need and want. People work hard to *earn* money. The coins in the bag belong to me, and I've worked hard to get them but I'm *loaning* them to you so you can learn about money." These are basic concepts that are part of the "money sense" for young learners.

As work progresses, continue to use real money whenever possible. At times, however, it is not practical, and money substitutes must be introduced. In such instances, it is essential that any play money and pictures resemble real money as closely as possible. Like many of their peers, students with learning disabilities find it difficult enough to relate money substitutes to real money without the added frustration of poor resemblance.

Coin stamps, both heads and tails, and paper money stamps can be purchased from many school supply companies. Keep several different colors of ink pads for money stamps. Color-coded coins can be useful when teaching and reinforcing coin discrimination and when dealing with children with figure-ground problems. Using these coins eliminates the interference of the learning deficit while strengthening retention and overlearning. Figure 4.1 provides an example of a color-coded coin line that is easy to make using either stamps and colored ink or colored paper. The sample can be laminated or covered with contact paper for durability.

Although it takes time, realistic simulated money can be made using coin stamps and either colored paper or crayons or software programs. Students

penny	nickel	dime	quarter		half dollar
1¢	5¢	10¢	25¢		50¢

Coin Line

penny = brown
nickel = black
dime = yellow
quarter = blue
half dollar = red

Figure 4.1.

with learning disabilities may benefit initially from coins that match the colors used on the coin line described in the previous paragraph. Once they have a strong visual image, students can gradually proceed to using more closely color-related paper coins.

The following sections suggest how to use the color-coded coins and coin line. Additionally, other money and many dice games can be played to reinforce money skills. A master for making two types of coin dice is provided in Figure 4.2. Ideas for using the dice are included in the sections that follow.

Throughout the chapter, various worksheet ideas will be described. These can be kept on file and be readily available for homework, learning centers, and extra reinforcement of specific skills.

COIN DISCRIMINATION

Problem Area: Inability to discriminate among coins.

Typical Disabilities Affecting Progress: Difficulty with visual discrimination, figure-ground, working memory, receptive or expressive language, word retrieval, understanding of words with multiple meanings.

Background: Very young children, preschool to about age 6, often have trouble discriminating fine differences in size while readily seeing gross differences such as that between the size of a dinner plate and the size of a quarter. Similarly, they find it hard to notice small differences in detail, especially when compounded by small size differences, as between a dime and a penny. Devel-

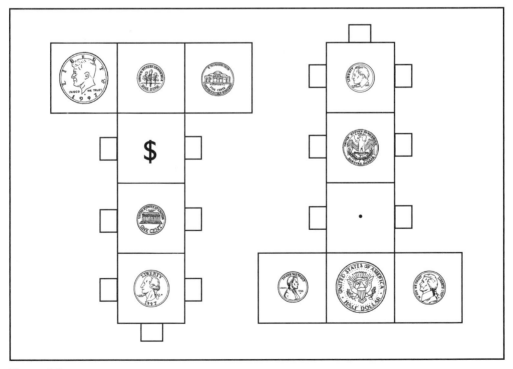

Figure 4.2.

opmentally, they may not be ready to do much more than order coins by size with the aid of finger tracing or by placing one on top of the other.

With continual exposure, most primary-grade children gradually learn to distinguish coins. They begin to look more closely at them, study them, and feel them. Their understanding of "bigger" and "smaller" may be weak, and, thus, it often is meaningless or even confusing to say, "The bigger one is a nickel." What does *bigger* mean? How can the nickel be bigger if the dime is worth 10¢ and the nickel is worth 5¢? Does *bigger* mean size or value? Through repeated experience, careful instruction, and developmental growth, children learn to associate the correct name with a given coin. By the time they are 6 or 7, most children can accurately match the coin with its name and often its value.

For children with disabilities like those listed at the beginning of this section, the discrete visual and spatial differences required to discriminate among coins preclude much chance of their doing that automatically. The following detailed analysis highlights the requirements involved in responding to the request "Give me the nickel, Peter":

- Receptively, the child must understand the meaning of the word *nickel*.

- The child must be able to perceive that coins are, in fact, different sizes.

- The child must be able to (a) revisualize a nickel or (b) tactually feel the difference in size between the nickel and other coins.

- Once the association has been made, the child must be able to retain it long enough to find the right coin.

For most children, these steps probably take 1 or 2 seconds to complete once the process has been mastered. However, for the child with learning disabilities, the effort to comply with such a request can end in total frustration, wild guesses, or refusal to answer. Therefore, more specialized instruction, such as that outlined below, is needed. The general approach that follows can be adapted to the child's current level.

✐ Sample Sequence of Activities

1. **Penny first.** The penny should be introduced first because it is more easily distinguished by its color and because there is a concrete one-to-one correspondence between the value and the amount of coins needed to represent the value. Let children pick it up, feel it, and compare its size, visually and tactually, with other small objects, including other coins. If they do not already know it, tell them its name (penny). Emphasize color, size, images on the coin, and whether its edge is rough or smooth.

2. **Penny line-up.** Give each child an envelope of real coins (pennies and silver coins). Have them sort out all the pennies and place them under the penny on the penny coin line.

3. **Penny match.** Give each child about 15 pennies, using real coins if possible. If the number of students makes this impractical, use a penny stamp on brown construction paper to make play coins. Provide an activity sheet like the

one in Figure 4.3 and instruct the children to cover each penny on the page with the ones given to them. Point out that although the penny pictures on the sheet are not colored, they have the same picture and are the same size as the pennies the children have. If the page is covered correctly, the pennies should form the letter *P*.

- *Variation:* Have children who learn best kinesthetically place tracing paper over the activity sheet of Figure 4.3. Then, using a penny or a stencil the shape and size of a penny, show them how to trace over each penny on the sheet.

4. **One penny is worth 1¢.** Discuss that money has value. We use it to buy things. Introduce the cent sign by writing the words "one cent" and the symbols "1¢" on the board. Explain that the words *one cent* can also be written as "1¢" and that a number with a cent sign (¢) next to it means that the number stands for an amount of money: "The value of a penny is one cent. One penny = 1¢." (If children do not understand the equal sign, use "One penny → 1¢.)

Have students put four pennies in a pile in front of them. To ensure understanding of vocabulary ask questions such as the following:

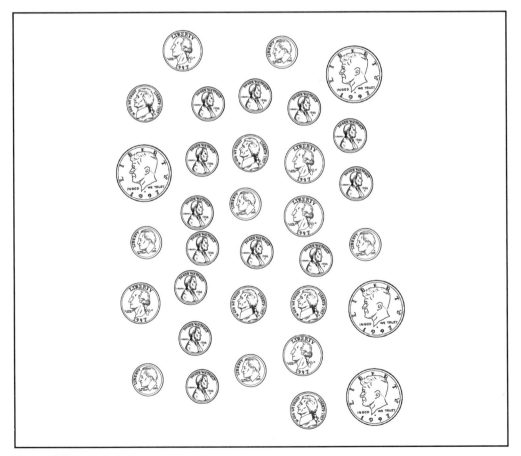

Figure 4.3.

- "How many *pennies* do you have?"
- "How many *cents* do you have?"
- "Do you have the same amount of *pennies* as *cents*?"
- "What is the *value* of the pennies?"
- "What is the *amount* of the pennies in the pile?"
- "Put 2¢ in a pile in front of you. How many pennies do you have now? How much is this pile of pennies worth?"
- "Suppose I wanted to trade with you. If I gave you three pennies, how many cents would you give me so we'd have a fair trade?"
- Put a pile of 5 pennies and 5 quarters in front of each child and say, "Pretend you are at a store and want to buy some gum. The price tag says 5¢. Show me how many pennies you would need to pay the cashier."

Continue until students recognize and understand the meaning of cents in relation to pennies.

5. **What coin next?** Use activities similar to those above to introduce other coins. The normal presentation of coins is: penny, nickel, dime, quarter, half dollar. If a child has difficulty with visual discrimination or size perception, use the sequence: penny, quarter, nickel, dime, half dollar. In our experience, this sequence is sometimes easier because of the greater difference in size between the penny and the quarter.

6. **Size it up.** As the coins are introduced, provide reinforcement pages, like that of Figure 4.4, that are color-coded to match the coin line. The purpose of such pages is to help children automatically differentiate coins by size and value. Children can match colored paper coins and/or real coins with the circles. Gradually, the color cues are eliminated. Children should be asked to name the coins they have placed on the sheet.

7. **Bingo.** For children with language deficits, a bingo game is a fun way to reduce weaknesses while using a possible strength—visual perception. The calling cards, the markers, the pictures on the bingo cards, and the space beneath each picture on the cards can be color-coded to match the coin line colors. In the space below each coin picture in Figure 4.5, a child would place the correct word or value when it is called. The calling cards list the name of the coin on one side

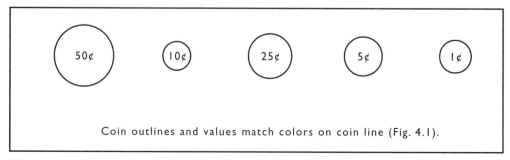

Coin outlines and values match colors on coin line (Fig. 4.1).

Figure 4.4.

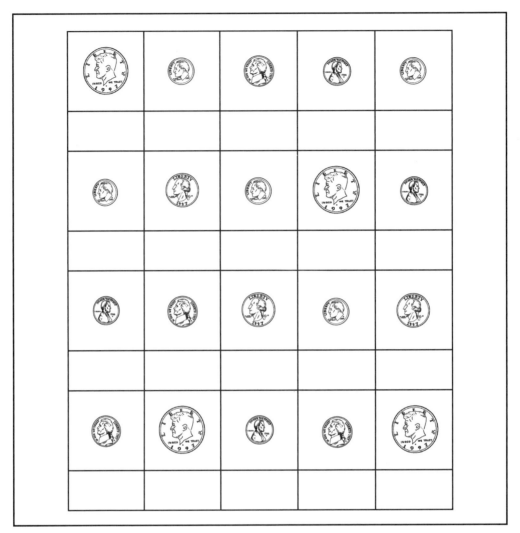

Figure 4.5.

and both the coin picture and the name on the other. The coin picture clue helps the student know what to call the coin.

■ *Variation:* Instead of writing the names of coins on the calling cards and/or markers, write coin values. Children then cover the coin that matches the value called.

COUNTING MONEY AMOUNTS

Problem Area: Inability to determine the value of a group of coins.

Typical Disabilities Affecting Progress: Difficulty with expressive language; sequential memory; visual perception, particularly figure-ground; working memory.

Background: Once coin recognition and basic values of coins have been established, most children learn to find the value of groups of coins. Early work starts with values up to 10¢ and gradually extends to counting money amounts to one dollar and beyond. At this point, it is helpful for children to begin to learn to automatically relate five pennies to a nickel and two nickels to a dime. The ability to do so makes handling money and coin groups much easier, particularly as groups of larger values are combined.

Two prerequisites to successfully finding the value of coin groups are: (a) the ability to count on from midpoint, and (b) a strong understanding that quantity (size) and value do not always match. There may be fewer coins than the actual cent value, and it is generally easier to recognize small, known groups within a larger group and to count on from that value. A child's ability to perform these tasks often depends upon being able to skip-count by 2s, 5s, and 10s and to count on by 2s, 5s, and 10s from various starting points.

Children having the difficulties identified at the beginning of this section may have trouble developing or applying skip-counting skills in this way. They may not recognize what pattern to use or when to switch from one pattern to another. Before describing activities intended to help children cope with these problems, it is assumed that students have mastered the following prerequisites:

• They can recognize a number pattern as one that involves skip-counting by 2s, 5s, and/or 10s.

• When dealing with numbers, apart from money, students can *continue* a skip-counting pattern that has been started.

• Students have been introduced to "switch" skip-counting (e.g., They start counting by 5s, then continue counting by 10s, or vice versa, as in the following pattern: 25 30 35 __ __ __ 60 70 __ __).

• Students can recognize, fairly automatically, the following substitutions: five pennies for a nickel, two nickels for a dime, two quarters for a half dollar, three quarters for other coins adding up to 75 cents, and four quarters for one dollar. An example of how to use "tailed" coins on a money line to reinforce coin equivalents is shown in Figure 4.6. (Coin "tails" are made from masking tape,

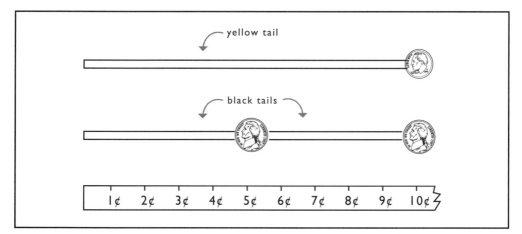

Figure 4.6.

attached to the coin, then folded in half lengthwise. Tails should be color-coded to match the colors of the coins in Figure 4.1.) Placed end to end, it takes two nickels to equal the *value* of one dime.

 ## Sample Sequence of Activities

1. **Count it out.** Keep pages or disk templates on hand, such as that illustrated in Figure 4.7. Give the child four crayons, each clearly different in color from the others and including a green and a red. Ask the child to underline each row of words with a different color, beginning with the green and ending with the red. Next, give the child a shape stencil like that shown in Figure 4.8. The four shapes should be outlined to match, respectively, the colors of the four rows in Figure 4.7. Given a group of coins, the children can place them inside the shapes in the appropriate sequence—greatest-valued coins first, pennies last. This step will initially require teacher assistance. After grouping the coins, the child fills in the blanks on the worksheet. As each blank is filled, instruct the child to read the entire sentence aloud before going on to the next blank. For children with closure difficulties who have trouble finding starting points and continuing patterns, the colors provide the needed cues. For those who have trouble expressing their thoughts or retaining a sequence, verbalizing the words "I have . . ." helps focus attention and initiate thought processes. The colors will help maintain the sequence.

2. **"Switch" skip-counting.** Using "switch" skip-counting to find the value of mixed coin groups can be difficult because it requires good word-finding skills, the ability to use working memory, and the ability to maintain a sequence. To help develop the needed counting skills, keep charts such as that presented in Figure 4.9.

Insert the charts into plastic holders and have the children write on the holders with dry-erase pencils. Instruct them to put a large X in any two squares in each row. In the empty box they write the money value obtained after they count the coins to the left and above. If fine-motor coordination is a problem, eliminate the writing. (Focus on the goal: developing switch counting, not writing.) Have the children place chips, with the correct value written on them, in the empty spaces. When the card is filled in, the children can use an answer key to correct it, or the teacher or another student can check it. Once it is correct, children can read the entire sequence aloud.

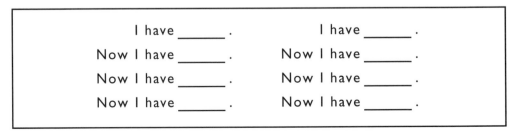

Figure 4.7.

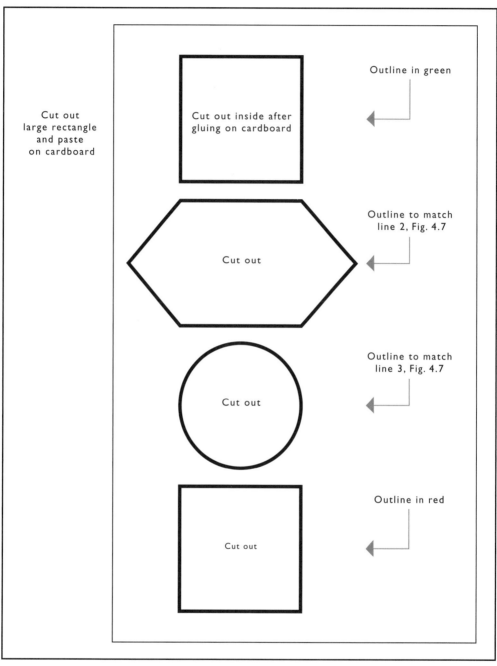

Figure 4.8.

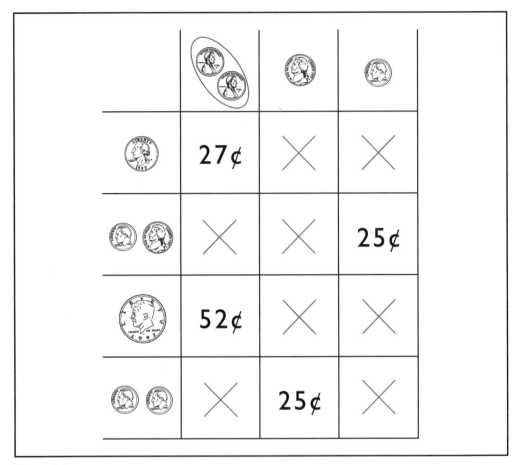

Figure 4.9.

■ *Example* (refer to Figure 4.9):

"Row 1: 25¢—27¢"
"Row 2: 10¢—15¢—25¢"

■ *Follow-up:* Counting money requires good auditory processing and visual, auditory, and sequential memory. Writing values down while counting aids learning, but eventually one should be able to add coin values mentally. Consequently, the next step in the preceding activity involves having children cover two squares with Xs in each row as before, but now instead of writing the total value obtained in the remaining box, they count the entire sequence aloud to the teacher or a friend or into a tape recorder.

3. **Money line.** Another approach to helping students determine the value of a group of coins consists of using tailed coins on a money line. In Figure 4.10a, for example, the child is given one quarter, one nickel, two dimes, and a penny to count. Tailed coins for each of these coins are chosen and placed end to end on the money line, greatest-valued coins first (Figure 4.10b). Figure 4.11 illus-

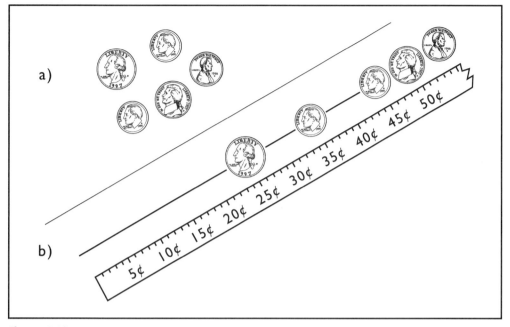

Figure 4.10.

trates the use of the money line to build or reinforce skills for "switch" skip-counting. The children can practice using tailed coins or refer to them, as necessary, until they master the technique using real coins. Once students can recognize coin equivalents with like coins (e.g., five nickels have the same value as a quarter), they can begin to develop an awareness of other common groups that do not involve like coins. The group of coins in Figure 4.12 is representative of a frequently used coin substitution. After a fair amount of experience counting coins, most children automatically recognize two dimes and one nickel as being worth 25¢. The child with learning disabilities may recognize this too but may not make an automatic transfer to the conclusion "a quarter—therefore, the value of this group is 50 cents because two quarters make 50 cents." The following activities help develop this skill.

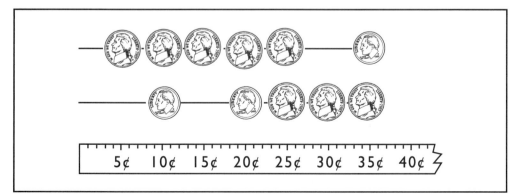

Figure 4.11.

Figure 4.12.

NOTE: *Teachers should be open to the possibility that some students may be better off using "switch" skip-counting that goes one coin at a time as shown in Figure 4.9. The goal is to determine the value of coins in an efficient way. What is efficient for one child may not be efficient for another.*

4. **The odd pieces.** Younger children enjoy puzzles. Those shown in Figure 4.13 can be cut out, pasted on 3×5 cards, and used for individual activities in a learning center. Note the circling to cue recognition of the three coins as one unit equivalent in value to a quarter. To encourage thinking, include one or two distracters in the puzzle set, like that shown in Figure 4.14. Children could be challenged to find the odd pieces (the distractors).

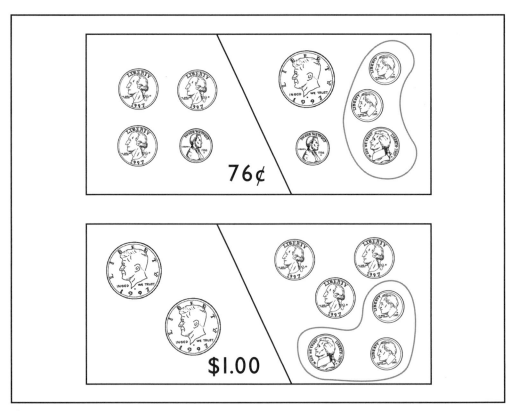

Figure 4.13.

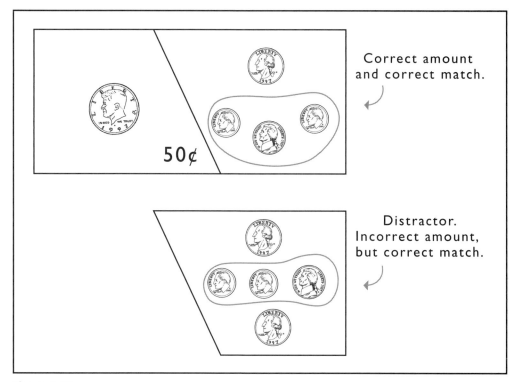

Figure 4.14.

5. **Bingo.** Make bingo cards, similar to those in Figure 4.5, except use coin values instead of coin pictures. The calling cards should have coins pictured on them like those on the right side of the Figure 4.13 puzzle pieces. The game is played like regular bingo.

6. **Fill in.** Students with expressive language difficulties often find it easier to fill in pages such as those in Figure 4.15a when they are accompanied by real coins. Gradually, the transition can be made to pages like that in Figure 4.15b, to be used without real coins.

NOTE: *The shareware program Let's Talk 2.0 can also be used for this type of exercise for students who need text-to-speech assistance.*

PAYING FOR ITEMS AND MAKING CHANGE

Problem Areas: Difficulty selecting money needed to pay for an item from a larger collection of coins; difficulty making change.

Typical Disabilities Affecting Progress: Difficulty with working memory, executive functioning, flexibility of thought, closure, sequential memory, visual figure-ground, visual discrimination.

Background: Being able to determine the value of a group of coins is a prerequisite to the more challenging skill of selecting those coins needed to make a given amount from a larger collection. This latter skill is needed in day-to-day

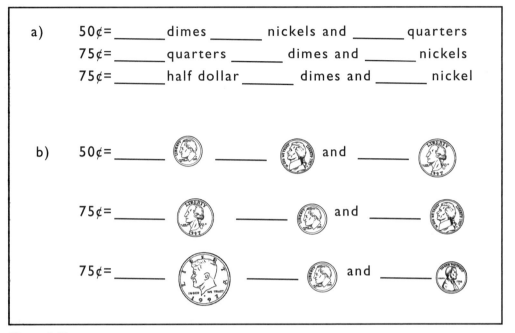

Figure 4.15.

situations as one examines the coins in a purse or pocket to see if there is enough to pay for an item or items. Some students with learning disabilities cannot apply the first skill to real-life situations. Children with figure-ground difficulties or visual discrimination difficulties may have problems finding the coins they want because they cannot sort them out from the group. Children who have trouble with executive functioning and/or inner language may become frustrated because the simplest (most familiar) way of making up a given amount is not possible with the coins they have.

Determining what coins are needed for a purchase involves more than just recognizing the correct group of coins and bills to use. It also means knowing (a) when one does not have the exact amount needed, (b) how much to give, and (c) how to check the change returned. In the workplace, if the cash register does not internally subtract and display the amount of change to be given, one must be able to count up from the cost until the amount paid is reached. To determine the amount of money to be given (or received) as change, a new counting process is required. It is now necessary to retain the purchase price in memory and count on from that cost using smaller valued coins first. Other coins are added until the amount paid is reached. Children with working-memory and sequential-memory problems usually find this very difficult. Those having the disabilities identified at the beginning of this section may fail to recognize the different skip-counting patterns involved or be unable to produce them automatically.

The first set of activities below suggests ways of determining needed coins from a group, assuming that a child has mastered the skills previously discussed in this chapter. Following these activities are other activities that deal with helping students accurately give and receive change.

Sample Sequence of Activities

▶ **Paying for an Item**

1. **You find.** Some students with figure-ground difficulties or visual discrimination difficulties may find it hard to identify, from a larger collection, the coins they need to pay for an item. For them, laminated cards with priced items and groups of coins such as those in Figure 4.16 are helpful. The cards show the coins needed to pay for a specific item. The child draws a card and takes from a bank of coins all the coins pictured on the card. Encourage the student to place the coins on top of those pictured until the card is full. These coins are then taken off the card and placed in a pile. Next, show the child a picture of an item to be purchased, such as the bat in Figure 4.16a. With a dry-erase marker have the child draw a circle around the coins on the card that are needed to pay for that item, at the same time naming the coins—e.g., "I need a dime and a nickel to buy the bat." Instruct the child to select coins from the pile to cover those circled on the card. Repeat, using different cards and items to be purchased. Children gradually learn to circle and name the needed coins independently. As they become more proficient, the circling can be eliminated and they can merely cover the correct coins on the cards. In our experience, this approach leads to independent recognition of needed coins.

2. **Let's go shopping.** Set up a "store" in the classroom and give each child a purse or an envelope of coins. (Alternatively, a container of coins could be

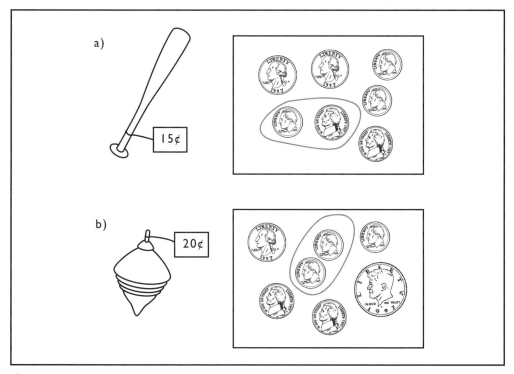

Figure 4.16.

placed on the "cashier's counter" for all the children to use.) At first, as students pay, accept any coins they give to pay for an item as long as the amount is correct. By observing a child's pattern of coin selection, the teacher can gradually suggest better choices in a manner that is logical to that student. For example, a child may choose a dime and five pennies to buy a 15¢ item. After complimenting the child ("Yes, a dime and five pennies equals 15¢. That's one way that works."), the teacher might then ask, "Did you notice that you can use one nickel in place of these five pennies?" Or, "You used six coins. Can you pay using only two coins?"

- *Follow-up:* Use worksheets such as the one illustrated in Figure 4.17. If necessary, use the coin colors in Figure 4.1 to outline the circles on the page. Gradually eliminate this prompt.

3. **Use what you have.** Point out that sometimes we do not have the proper coins to pay the way we would like. For example, we might want to buy ice cream that costs 25¢. If we do not have a quarter, then two dimes and a nickel, or five nickels, or even 25 pennies will do. Give the student several coins and ask for an amount of money that cannot be made in the "usual way" with the available coins. For example, give five nickels and ask for 20¢. As children become more proficient, give a quarter, five nickels, and four pennies for this task to force selection from a larger group of coins.

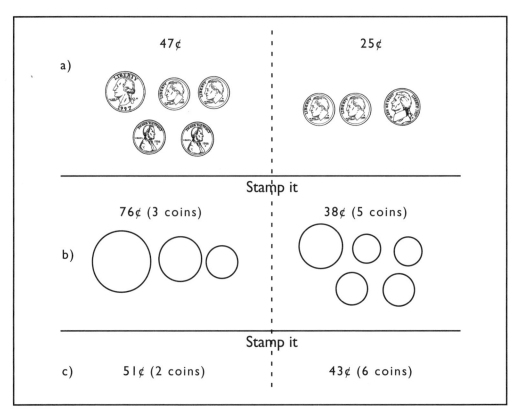

Figure 4.17.

■ *Follow-up:* Use worksheets like the one in Figure 4.18. For the example shown, the children can circle or place real coins on those pictured to show 20¢. If necessary, use coin line colors to outline the coins needed for the first few exercises.

▶ Making Change

1. **Count Up.** Use tailed coins on a money line, as in Figure 4.19, to introduce the idea of counting up to get from the cost to the amount paid. This approach concretizes the process of counting up and aids visual memory, working memory, and sequencing. A set of price-tag cards, like the one shown, is also needed. Children draw a card and place it on the line as illustrated to indicate where one starts the count. Tailed coins are then used to dramatize the counting on (in this case to 25¢). Children should be encouraged to "use as few coins as possible"—four pennies and one nickel rather than nine pennies in this example.

2. **Go and stop.** At this point, students with auditory-sequencing or memory deficits, as well as those with expressive language or executive functioning difficulties, usually find it easier to use worksheets such as that illustrated in Figure 4.20. The first example is for younger children, or any student who encounters reading problems; the second is its parallel for older students or those who read at the needed level. Students fill in the first four blanks. Then as they count up from the cost, they check each coin as if they were actually picking it up. Next they count and record the change—in this example, 9¢.

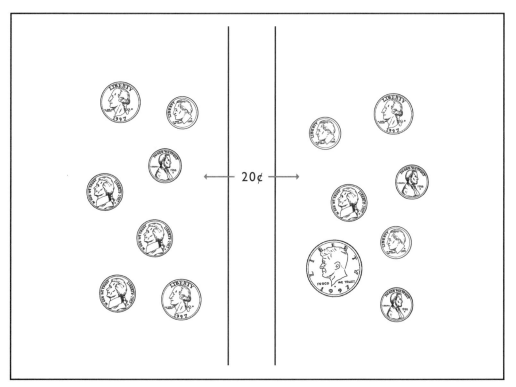

Figure 4.18.

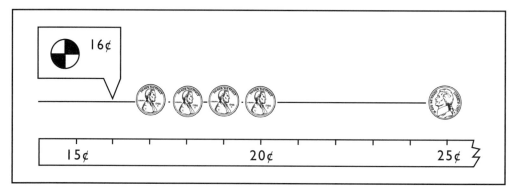

Figure 4.19.

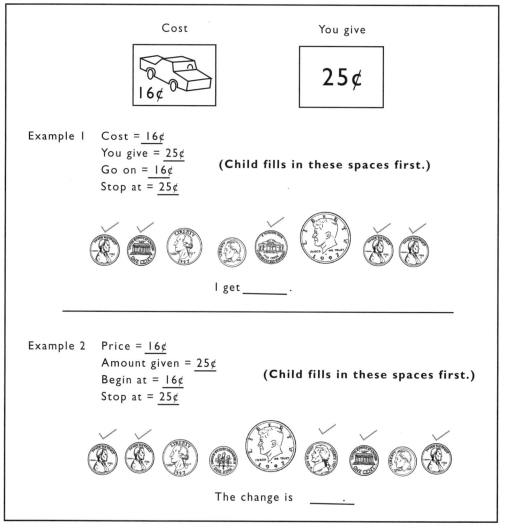

Figure 4.20.

To cue the meaning, the words *go on* (or *begin at*) could be written in green and *stop at* in red. For those in need of extra cueing, the word *cost* (or *price*) could also be coded in green and the words *you give* (or amount given) in red. Answer lines would be colored to match the words. Gradually, all colors and the amount of information to be personally recorded would be eliminated as the vocabulary, counting process, and thinking process become internalized. Recording the numbers to "go on" and "stop at" is dropped first. As short-term memory or counting skills improve, the price and the amount given may be eliminated.

- *Follow-up:* Provide real coins rather than stamped pictures of coins. At first it may be helpful to keep a worksheet showing the coin stamps as reference. If children tend to perseverate, do not be too quick to eliminate the writing while using real coins. It serves to break the counting and hence decreases perseveration.

NOTE: *Children with executive functioning deficits may have difficulty recognizing whether they have the correct coins to pay exactly or to make the needed change. They may try to ignore the problem, as illustrated in Figure 4.21. In this example, the first coin needed is a penny, which the child does not have. The value of the dimes, then, becomes meaningless and dimes are treated as pennies. To help, have the children first fill in the charts of Activity 2 above. Then have them compare the coins they checked with the coins they have.*

WRITING MONEY AMOUNTS GREATER THAN ONE DOLLAR

Problem Areas: Reversal tendencies or other difficulties when writing money amounts using the dollar sign and decimal point.

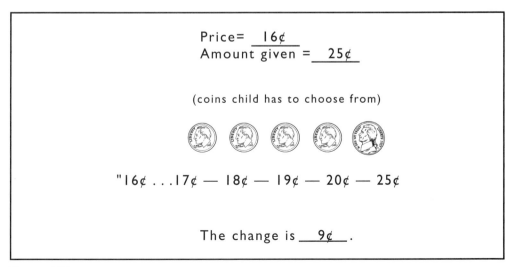

Price= __16¢__
Amount given = __25¢__

(coins child has to choose from)

"16¢ . . .17¢ — 18¢ — 19¢ — 20¢ — 25¢

The change is __9¢__ .

Figure 4.21.

Typical Disabilities Affecting Progress: Difficulty with spatial organization, visual perception, visual memory, language processing.

Background: Being able to accurately read and write numbers is important for check writing and other life skills. Children who are unable to organize their space due to visual or perceptual deficits, spatial disorganization, or poor language processing may have considerable difficulty writing down money values. For example, since we say, "Three dollars and sixteen cents," children may reverse the position of the dollar value and the dollar sign (see Figure 4.22). Or they may not associate all the words with the symbols. Specifically, they may not attend to the dollar sign and decimal point when reading or writing the numbers. The activities outlined below are directed toward helping students with those problems.

✎ Sample Sequence of Activities

1. **Dollar sign.** For those who have reversal tendencies or difficulty with simultaneous processing, it often helps to approach the problem in small steps. If children learn well through kinesthetic involvement, have them finger-trace numerals and symbols cut out of felt (or fine sandpaper), *dollar value first, then the sign.* Next have them rewrite the pattern traced—*dollar value first, then the sign.* Although this is an unusual order, it provides more immediate association between words and symbols. Each time a word is said, something is written. The more traditional way requires students to write one symbol ($) while saying or thinking an unrelated symbol (e.g., 4). Figure 4.23 shows a sample page that might be used as a follow-up exercise. First, in Step 1, the children finger-trace examples and write $4 as described above. In Step 2, the decimal point is introduced and associated with the word *and.* In Step 3, the number of cents is included. All three steps provide space (after the equals sign on the worksheet) for children to write the money amount independently.

2. **Greatest value.** This is a practice activity for two or three players. Provide the following five dice:

- Die 1: "$" written on each of the six sides
- Die 2: "." written on each of the six sides
- Die 3: 0,1,2,3,4,5
- Die 4: 0,5,6,7,8,9
- Die 5: 3,4,5,6,7,8

For each player, provide a five-space chart for the dice (Figure 4.24a) and a "Greatest Value" record sheet (Figure 4.24b). Children take turns throwing the

Three dollars and sixteen cents = 3$.16

Figure 4.22.

Step 1

$4 = ——— —— $8 = ——— ——
$3 = ——— —— $7 = ——— ——

Step 2

$4. = ——— —— $8. = ——— ——
$3. = ——— —— $7. = ——— ——

Step 3

$4.52 = ——— —— $8.91 = ——— ——
$3.67 = ——— —— $7.23 = ——— ——

Bold marks are green.
Gray marks are red.
The decimal point and dollar sign are black.

Figure 4.23.

dice and arranging them in the five spaces on the chart to show the greatest dollar value possible; in Figure 4.24a, that value is $9.40. If the amount is written and read aloud correctly, it can be entered on the player's record sheet for that round. The player with the greatest total after four rounds wins. (Keeping in mind the goal of this activity—writing money amounts correctly and determining the greatest value—consider allowing children to find the total using a calculator.)

NOTE 1: *This activity can be used unobtrusively in a mainstreamed classroom situation to aid a single child who may be having trouble in this area by allowing a social situation that can be adapted to a variety of students, not just the one with learning disabilities.*

NOTE 2: *Color coding is important in early work but can gradually be eliminated.*

   3. **Language follow-up.** For additional practice and to increase accurate language association, templates such as those in Figure 4.25 can be made on a computer and printed as needed. Children read, then write the given dollar value. If reading is a problem, the following options will help:

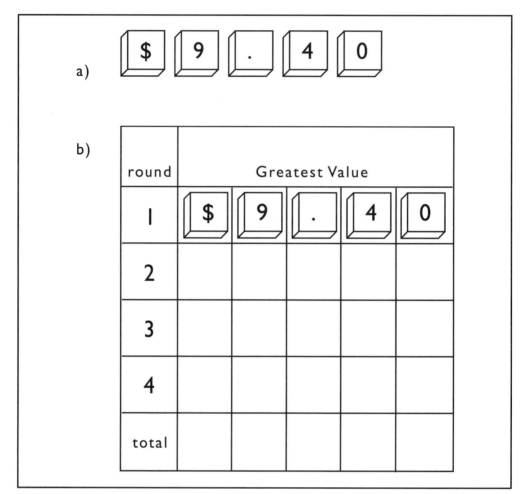

Figure 4.24.

- Prepare a tape recording for the left part of the page.

- Use a word processor with a text-to-speech feature and have students use that to follow along on the worksheet.

- Prepare Language Master cards to match the worksheet and have children run the cards through the machine while reading the worksheet.

■ *Variation:* It may be preferable to have some students write the dollar value first, then the sign, as explained in Activity 1.

CLASSROOM MATERIALS FOR TEACHING TIME

Most classrooms have a wall clock and perhaps a toy clock for students to use. However, except for workbook pages, little else in the room may be realistically

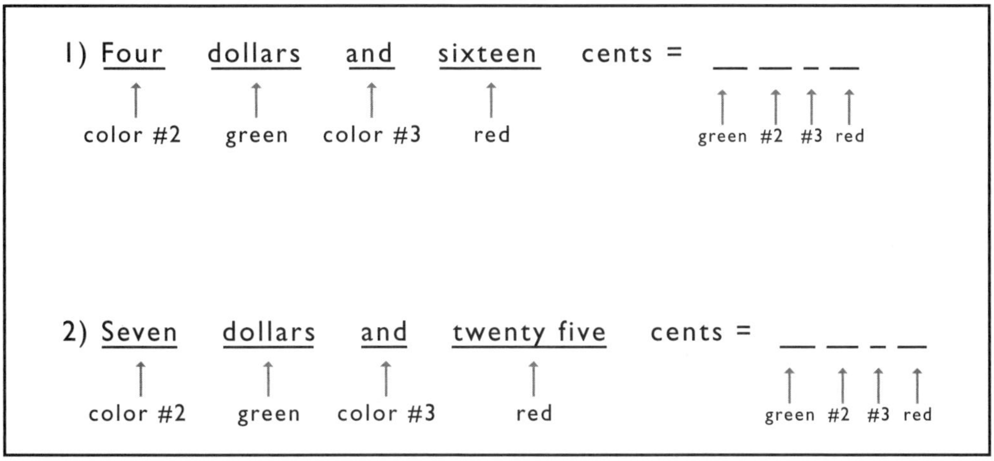

1) <u>Four</u>   **dollars**   <u>and</u>   <u>sixteen</u>   cents = __ __ _ _

  ↑   ↑   ↑   ↑   ↑ ↑ ↑ ↑

color #2   green   color #3   red   green #2 #3 red

2) <u>Seven</u>   **dollars**   <u>and</u>   <u>twenty five</u>   cents = __ __ _ _

  ↑   ↑   ↑   ↑   ↑ ↑ ↑ ↑

color #2   green   color #3   red   green #2 #3 red

Figure 4.25.

related to teaching time. Several items can greatly aid students in acquiring time concepts and skills:

- A small analog table clock, about 4 inches in diameter with clearly defined hour and minute hands, in different colors, if possible.

- A geared clock with a knob on the back to move the hands. (The hands should be distinctly different in size.)

- A digital clock that can be placed next to the analog clock.

- Clock stamps and ink pads (one red, one green).

The small clock is useful for children with visual discrimination or other perceptual problems. These students may have difficulty with a wall clock, which may be too far away for them to make any clear discriminations. Figure 4.26 gives an example of the size and face of a useful small table clock. The size of the hands is clearly different, and the minute intervals are spaced far enough apart for the child to point with a finger or a pencil. This type of clock provides the kinesthetic approach that is often necessary for children with visual-perceptual or spatial difficulties. It can be used to "feel" the time. Additionally, a large floor clock (made of poster board and covered with contact paper for protection) would be helpful in classrooms of younger children where gross-motor movements are often needed for the learning process (similar to rainbow writing practice to learn letter formation).

Since it is impractical to teach time only on a real clock, a geared clock provides the next best aid. Children can see how the hands move at different rates. They can actually "feel" the slowness of the hour-hand movement in contrast to that of the minute hand.

As digital clocks are so common, children must learn to read them. Most mathematics curricula now include a discussion of them within their chapters on time. Once children can read the numbers on a digital clock, they can be helped to make associations with the standard clock as an aid for "reading" its time.

Figure 4.26.

NOTE: *Before introducing children to analog clocks, be sure they*

- *can read two-digit numbers to 60 and*

- *can understand the relative position of numbers between 1 and 60 (e.g., 53 comes before 57).*

At this point, even though digital clocks are here to stay (and analog clocks appear to be on the way out), it still seems appropriate to give a word of caution regarding digital clocks. As convenient and useful as they are for teaching children to tell time, *they do not help develop a sense of time.* It is questionable whether that sense can be taught at all. The movement of time is mysterious, and digital clocks only reinforce the mystery. An analog clock at least provides a concrete way for children to develop a feel for how long an activity lasts. One can, for example, use an overlay as shown in Figure 4.27 to illustrate the time allotted to an activity by shading it in on the overlay. On a digital clock this is impossible.

Clock stamps are available commercially, and they should be standard materials for every classroom. They can be used easily by both teacher and student. When drawing in the hands, be careful to distinguish clearly between the lengths of the minute and the hour hands. Figure 4.28 illustrates the type of clock stamp we have found most useful.

The sections that follow suggest ways of using these materials to help students with learning disabilities develop important time concepts and skills. In addition, several pages and templates are illustrated that can easily be kept on file or disk and used for reinforcement or homework and other independent work.

READING CLOCK TIMES

Problem Area: Difficulty associating the correct hand on an analog clock with the spoken or written word.

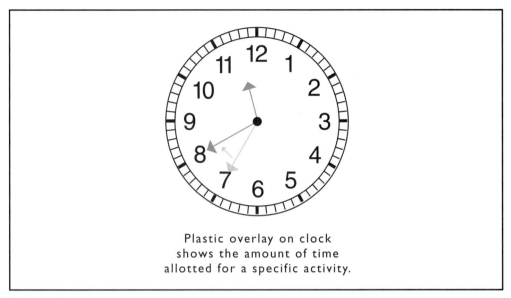

Plastic overlay on clock
shows the amount of time
allotted for a specific activity.

Figure 4.27.

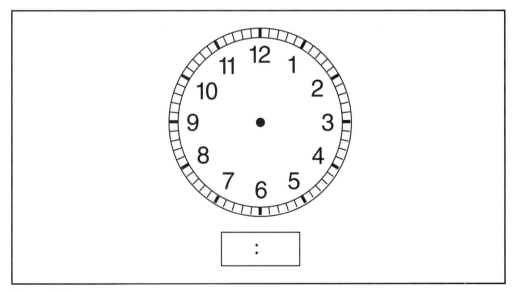

Figure 4.28.

Typical Disabilities Affecting Progress: Difficulty with visual discrimination, visual-sequential memory, short-term memory, expressive language, working memory.

Background: As mentioned earlier, many children develop some comprehension of time before they enter school. It is not uncommon for young children to be up earlier on school days than on weekends. Once the routine of going to school has been established, their internal clock begins to plan accordingly. They do not automatically begin dressing for school on Saturday. They may not know why they do not have to, but they have a sense that something is different.

Gradually, parents' words begin to have meaning, and on school days children understand that at 8:00 it is time to leave. They may not actually tell time, but if a parent says, "In 5 minutes it will be eight o'clock," the child understands that "soon we have to leave." Later the clock becomes more meaningful and the child thinks, "The little hand is on the 8. It must be time to go to school."

In the primary grades, intuitive understandings such as these are formally developed. While several sequences can be used to teach a child to read time from an analog clock, one of the more common, and one that works well for most children, is the following:

- time by the hour,
- time by the half hour,
- time by the quarter hour,
- time by 5-minute intervals, and finally
- time by minute intervals.

The above sequence works best with students with visual discrimination problems, as it progresses from gross differences in time to more visually discrete. Students with memory difficulties and those with sequencing difficulties may benefit from an alternate sequence, one that is more consistent and more language based. These students often benefit more from learning first to tell time by the hour and then by 5-minute increments (provided they have learned to "count on"). Emphasis is still on the meaning of the clock hands, but visual memory, sequencing, and language are reinforced because the student gradually moves around the clock in a consistent manner. Additionally, students with memory problems, who may not automatically remember to say 6:45, for example, have a way of helping themselves by counting by fives. Later, after the student has learned to tell time in this manner, and is therefore more ready to develop an automatic approach, emphasis can be put on recognizing fractional segments of half hour and quarter hour.

When teaching time to the hour, many teachers simplify the clock as in Figure 4.29a. Using a clock with only an hour hand makes it possible for most children to "tell time" as soon as they can read the numerals 1 to 12. Then the child can relate this one-handed clock to a spinner and "read time" by telling the number the hand is closest to. Once children can tell time to the nearest hour in this way, the teacher can point out the hour hand on a *two-handed clock*. The next step is to practice telling time on that type of clock by focusing on the hour hand, as in Figure 4.29b. If necessary in early work with the two-handed clock, children can be instructed to cover the minute hand.

After children can read and write 2-digit numbers (at least to 60), the spinner idea can be introduced for reading minutes (see Figure 4.29c). Now the child

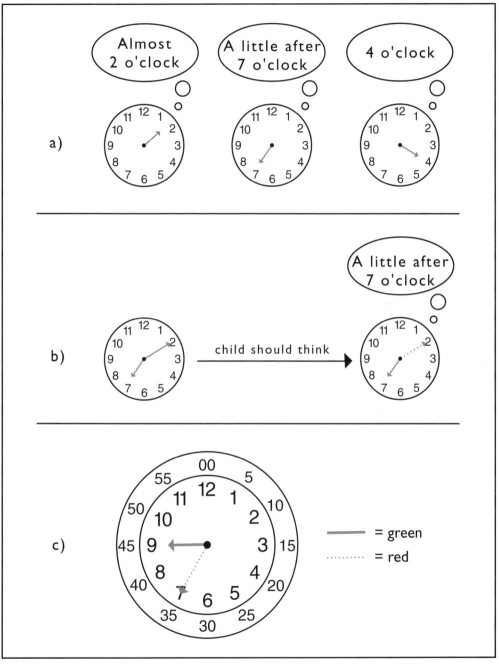

Figure 4.29.

tells time more precisely by reading the "hour" then the "minute" spinner (hand). Gradually, the association can be made between the minutes and the 12 clock digits. Additional experiences with a geared clock can help children see that as the hour hand moves from one hour to the next, the minute hand travels all the way around the clock. Children with good visual perception and long-term memory quickly learn what one says for given configurations of the hands. For example, "The little hand moves from one hour to the next while the big hand travels all around the clock.

Students using the "5-minute" approach described previously especially benefit from using the spinner depicted in Figure 4.29. The spinner provides a visual, logical framework for reading minutes and aids in recall when memory fails. In addition, as fractional segments are emphasized, most children can more easily learn to count on from these points.

Children with learning disabilities, particularly those with the disabilities described at the beginning of this section, may find even these simple approaches to telling time difficult. One common problem relates to correctly locating where the hands are pointing. Another involves correctly associating each hand with what one should say in order to read the time indicated by the hand. For example, some students with learning disabilities who can skip count by fives, fail, even after repeated use of the skip-counting technique, to make the necessary association. The following activities have proved successful in handling these difficulties. Since the goal is for children to read the hour first, followed by minutes, green color coding is used for hour times, red for minutes.

✏️ Sample Sequence of Activities

1. **Hour hand first.** On a large tag-board circle, glue or draw small circles at each of the 12 clock positions, as in Figure 4.30a. Make a deck of 52 cards, all containing circles, similar to those shown in Figure 4.30b. The circles should be the same size as those drawn in the clock positions of the larger circle. Write the numbers 1 through 12 on 48 of the circles (one number to a card; each number will be used four times) in the positions where they would appear on an analog clock; draw a small hour hand to point at each number. Write the numeral 13 on the remaining four circles. The numerals and the small arrow

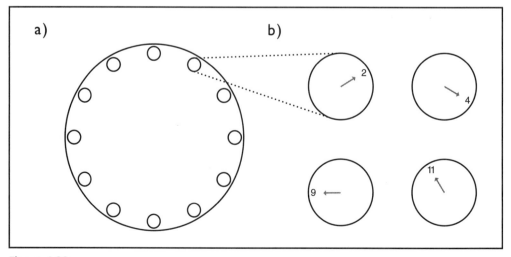

Figure 4.30.

that simulates the hour hand should be green. The child "deals," placing one card from the deck face down on each of the 12 clock positions of the large circle. A 13th card is placed in the center. This procedure continues until all 52 cards have been placed on the board (Figure 4.31). Then the child turns over the first card of the center pile and places it, face up, under the pile on the board that corresponds to the clock position drawn on that card. (See Figure 4.32.) The top card of that pile is then turned over and play continues. Every time 13 is turned over, it is placed face up under the four cards in the center. The child wins the game if all the cards are placed face up in the proper position on the board before the four cards with 13 are uncovered.

■ *Variation:* The child says the hour time whenever a card is properly placed.

2. **Five minutes.** A game similar to that of Activity 1 can be played to reinforce the skip-counting pattern of the minute hand. This time, make 52 cards beginning with 00 and counting by fives to 60 as if around a clock face. Make four cards for each number as before, but this time the arrow pointing to each number represents the minute hand and so should be noticeably longer than that described for Figure 4.30. (See Figure 4.33.) Use the large circle of Activity 1, but place a rim around the outside containing 12 circles for the 5-minute times. (See Figure 4.34.)

3. **Both hands.** Play the following bingo-type game. Make a set of calling cards picturing times on analog clocks. Use green for the hour hand and red for the minute hand. Provide 4×4" game boards for students with times written at the bottom of each square, as shown in Figure 4.35. Give each child 16 "clock" chips showing different times that fit into the space above the times. (See Figure 4.36.) These can be made by placing gummed labels on ordinary game board chips and drawing or stamping a clock face on each label. Do not color-code the hands on the clock chips. The children place the chips, face up, in front of them. To play, a caller (child or teacher) holds up a color-coded clock. Players decide whether the time shown by that clock is on their game board. If it is and

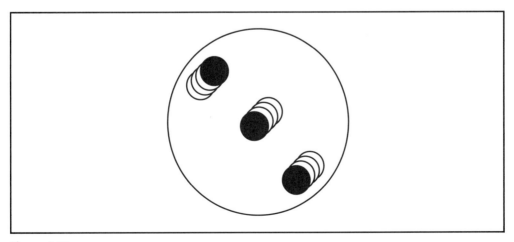

Figure 4.31.

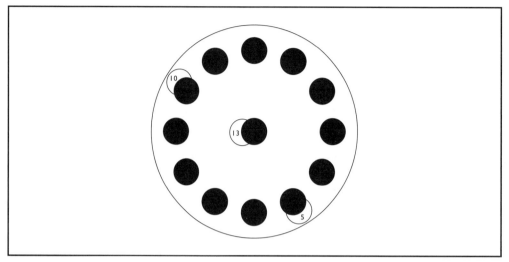

Figure 4.32.

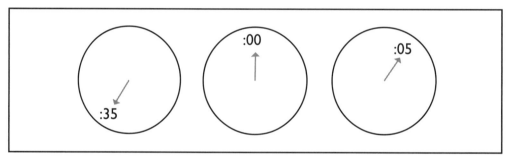

Figure 4.33.

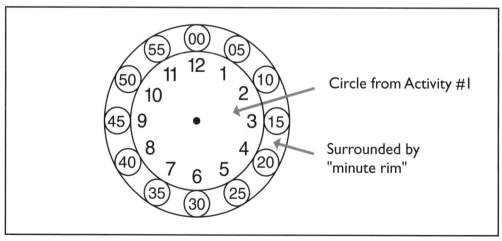

Figure 4.34.

4:30	3:10	6:55	8:40
9:20	2:15	7:30	10:50
5:40	6:05	12:45	9:10
8:00	2:30	1:25	4:35

Figure 4.35.

they have a clock chip that shows that time, they place that clock chip on the game board just above the written time. The winner is the first person to complete a row in any direction.

NOTE: *If game boards are covered with acetate or clear contact paper, color coding can be used when needed and wiped off afterward. Hour digits would be green, minute digits red.*

 4:30	3:10	6:55	8:40

9:20	2:15	7:30	10:50

5:40	6:05	11:45	9:10

8:00	2:30	1:25	4:35

Figure 4.36.

■ *Variation 1:* Alter the activity by placing clock faces on the game board and color-coded numbers on the calling cards. Game chips would also contain the written clock times. If necessary, those can also be color coded.

■ *Variation 2:* Place clock chips that match the clock times face down on the board. As a card is held up, the child decides whether that time is on his or her individual board. If it is, the chip is turned over. The first player to correctly complete a row in any direction wins.

WRITING CLOCK TIMES

Problem Area: Difficulty telling time on a real clock.

Typical Disabilities Affecting Progress: Difficulty with spatial organization, visual perception, visual-sequential memory, working memory, and expressive language.

Background: Many children with learning disabilities need a considerable amount of paper-and-pencil practice before they can use a real clock to tell time. The paper-and-pencil activities provide:

• overlearning;

• less interference from visual perception deficits because of the proximity of the paper;

• kinesthetic involvement for children who need it (they can run their fingers or pencils along the paper and feel the distance as they approach the correct number where the hand is); and

• sequencing cues.

The following ideas can be used to accomplish overlearning.

✎ Sample Sequence of Activities

1. **Color-coded pages.** Several types of pages can be filed for ready use. In Figure 4.37 the numerals 1 through 12 are green, while 00 through 55 are red. The boxes below the clock are also coded, the first green, the second red. The use of boxes rather than lines during early practice strengthens the relationship between digital and analog clocks, a relationship that must be directly reinforced for some children.

NOTE: *School supplies stores and catalogues make clock stamps with the numbers and boxes provided on the stamp.*

2. **Fade the cue.** Figure 4.38 illustrates one step of gradually fading the color cue. First, the red numbers are replaced with red dots, but when hands are drawn on the clock, they are still colored—green for the hour hand, red for

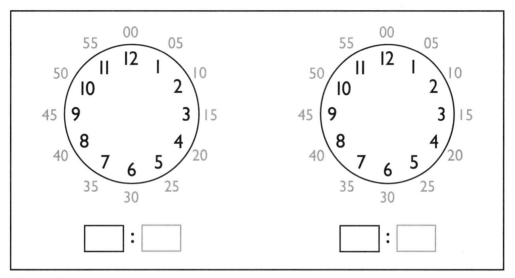

Figure 4.37.

the minute hand. The next step eliminates the colors on the clock hands. For some children, especially those with severe visual perception difficulties, the colors in the boxes may be eliminated first, followed by the colors on the hands. An alternative would be to keep pages such as those shown in Figure 4.39, with a color-coded example at the top, on file or disk. In Figure 4.39a, the clocks have green and red lines only for answers. Make the green line noticeably shorter than the red line. Provide auditory cueing by asking the child which hand on the clock looks most like the short green line. "Which hand do you 'go' on?"

NOTE: *The worksheets illustrated in this section, especially those with color-coding and numbers around the outside rim, make it possible to teach time even*

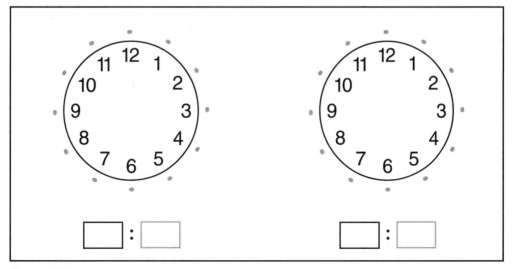

Figure 4.38.

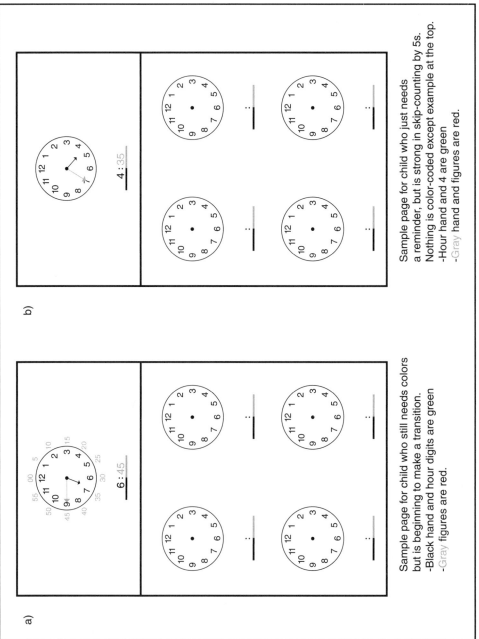

a)

6:45

Sample page for child who still needs colors
but is beginning to make a transition.
-Black hand and hour digits are green
-Gray figures are red.

b)

4:35

Sample page for child who just needs
a reminder, but is strong in skip-counting by 5s.
Nothing is color-coded except example at the top.
-Hour hand and 4 are green
-Gray hand and figures are red.

Figure 4.39.

to children who are weak on skip-counting by fives. For many, this approach pro-vides the way to overlearning.

3. **Card to help.** For students needing color reinforcement, especially as they make the transition to the real clock, keep a tag-board clock in the room. Cover it with acetate or contact paper so it can be color coded when needed. If color cueing is necessary, the child can use green and red markers or a dry-erase pencil to write over the numbers. (If this proves too difficult, motorically, the teacher should do it.) The child can use this card to help associate the clock hands and the sequence for reading clock times.

4. **Write and recall.** As children make the transition to a real clock, they may still need to write down what they see before they are able to express it. This is especially true for:

- students with memory problems that prevent them from retaining an entire sequence, and

- students with expressive language difficulties who have trouble learning if their flow of thought is interrupted.

The writing process is an intermediate step that allows students to focus on one part of the sequence at a time until overlearning has occurred. Keep pages available such as those shown in Figure 4.40. The children can work in pairs to complete them. Using the geared clock, one child sets the time shown on one of the clocks in Figure 4.40a. The other writes the time down on the page in Figure 4.40b. If necessary, the clocks shown can be color coded to help students express times correctly—hour first, then minutes. Make the hour hand green and the minute hand red.

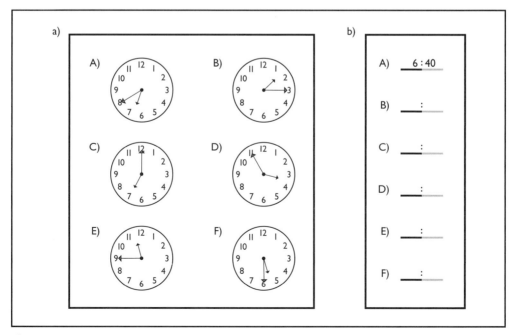

Figure 4.40.

NAMING THE CORRECT HOUR

Problem Area: Difficulty knowing which number is referred to when the hour hand is between two numbers.

Typical Disabilities Affecting Progress: Difficulty with spatial orientation, visual perception, memory, language association.

Background: Some children who know what words and numbers to associate with each hand and which hand to look at first may still be uncertain about which number to use when the hour hand is between two numbers. If their spatial abilities are weak, telling them to look at the number "in front of" or "before" the hand may be meaningless. Likewise, asking them to look at the lower number is confusing. What *is* the "lower number"? When the hour hand is between 12 and 1, there is no numeral underneath the 1. The following ideas should prove helpful in handling this problem.

✎ Sample Sequence of Activities

1. **Point the way.** Make a small green arrow, as in Figure 4.41a, that fits around the edge of the small desk clock. When the children are working with the clock, have them place the arrow at the hour hand so that it curves around and points to the correct number. A small hook could also be used on clock pages.

- *Variation:* If children have trouble manipulating the arrow, use a clear plastic overlay to cover the clock face. Using a marker or dry-erase pen, draw an arrow on the plastic. The child can then place the plastic over the clock and rotate it until the arrow is in place.

2. **Reinforce.** When providing children with clock pages for practice, include the arrows on the page. Have the children run a pencil, or preferably a

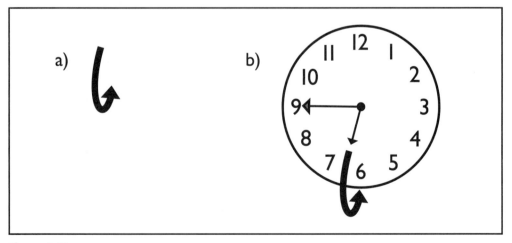

Figure 4.41.

finger, over an arrow and say the number it points to. In our experience, with continued kinesthetic reinforcement of this type, even young children are soon able to draw their own arrows well enough to use them as cues to determine which number to look at for the hour.

LANGUAGE AND TIME: UNDERSTANDING AND USING THE VARIOUS EXPRESSIONS FOR TIME

Problem Area: Understanding and using temporal expressions such as "in 5 minutes," "20 minutes ago," "half past three," "soon."

Typical Disabilities Affecting Progress: Difficulty with receptive language, abstract reasoning, spatial organization.

Background: Time can be expressed in different ways, but for some children with learning disabilities time signifies nothing more than looking at the clock and saying the numbers. While this knowledge may help them get where they have to be on time or know what time an activity is to begin, this skill alone does not enable them to predict or plan their time. When looking at the clock in Figure 4.42, consider that a child is likely to hear it described in any of the following ways:

- 6:40
- 20 minutes until 7
- 40 minutes after 6
- 20 minutes before 7
- 40 minutes past 6
- 20 of 7

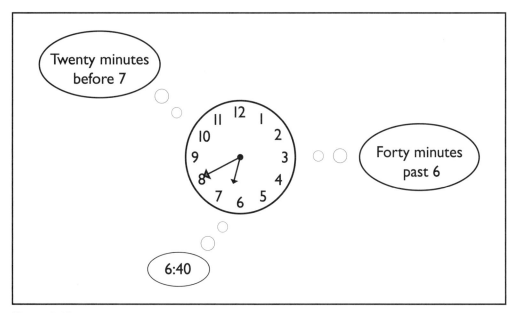

Figure 4.42.

With repeated exposure in their daily life most children gradually learn to understand these various expressions and later begin to use them in their own language. Students with learning disabilities, however, particularly those described above, may have a great deal of trouble doing that without special help. Those who have trouble with multiple meanings or synonyms may need to learn the different expressions one at a time, and it helps to have the coordinated effort of everyone who is working with the child. It may be difficult to use only one format consistently, but it is essential for such children to have an approach that is as carefully structured and consistent as possible. Since we recognize that it is not possible to maintain this consistency in all areas of life, teachers and parents should be aware of the language being addressed during instruction so that when other expressions are used they can determine whether a child understands the expression.

Initially, use only the numbers to give the time—e.g., "It is now 1:20, and it's time for math." Do not confuse children by saying, "It is 20 past 1" until you are sure they understand the meaning of "past." After children clearly understand that 5:20 and 20 minutes after 5 mean the same thing, the term *past* can be introduced. Similarly, when children understand 20 minutes before 6 to mean the same as 5:40, then *until* may be introduced.

Prerequisites to developing an understanding and use of temporal language include:

- skip counting by 5s to 60;

- counting on from within that counting sequence;

- understanding which hand moves faster and associating it with minutes; and

- identifying the minute hand on the clock and realizing that one counts on from that hand to determine "in 10 minutes" or "10 minutes ago."

The activities that follow address one aspect of the language related to developing a sense of time beyond reading clock numbers. The goal is to help students learn and meaningfully use and understand temporal expressions.

Sample Sequence of Activities

1. **Circular number line.** Once children are able to tell time using numbers only, review the concepts of *before* and *after* using a circular number line (a spinner, with the numbers written in sequence rather than in random order). Establish the idea that, on the circle (spinner), *after* still means that the numbers get larger, only now instead of going forward and backward, we are going around. To help establish eye movements when looking at the clock, present pages such as those shown in Figure 4.43.

2. **Geared clock.** Begin relating the concepts of *before* and *after* once the basic concept discussed in Activity 1 has been developed using a circular format. Use the geared clock and ask the children to turn the hands according to instructions such as "Set the clock to 8:10. Now set a new time that is *after*

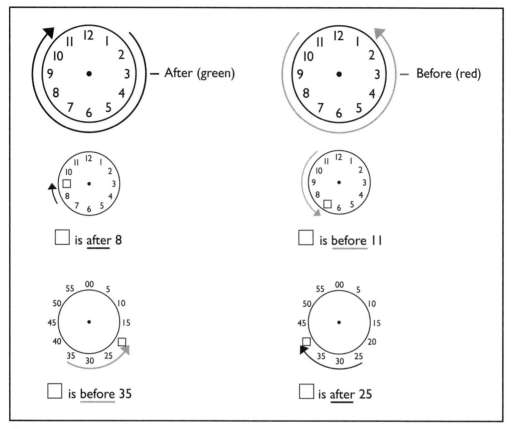

Figure 4.43.

8:10." At this point, the primary goal is to have the children "feel" how clock hands move in different directions.

    3. **Worksheets.** Practice pages of color-coded clocks, such as that shown in Figure 4.44, are often helpful. On such clocks, the numerals 1 through 5 should be green and 7 through 11 should be red. The child writes the time shown in two ways below the clock. The numerals 6 and 12 should be black.

NOTE: *A prerequisite at this point is knowing which hand represents minutes and which represents hours. The children will then know what hand to look to when deciding the number of minutes before or after an hour. Children should also know, for any given hour, what the next hour will be. That skill is necessary to help them determine the time before an hour. For example, 6:40 means 40 minutes after the hour of 6 or 20 minutes before (the next hour of) 7.*

    4. **Toward overlearning.** For students requiring overlearning, provide several practice pages using only one concept (e.g., *after* OR *before*). Very shortly, however, the pages should be mixed, using both *before* and *after*. Mixing the concepts will avoid perseveration and provide opportunities for reasoning and problem solving. Gradually include additional vocabulary such as *past, until,* and *of.*

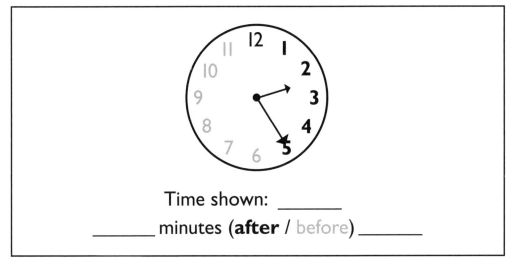

Figure 4.44.

5. **One step only.** Figure 4.45 shows a useful sequence for students who need help developing a one-step procedure for telling time. As shown in Figure 4.45a, students first write the time and then the equivalent expression using "minutes before" or "minutes after." Initially, decision making can be aided by color-coding the words *before* and *after.* Students who do not have fine-motor problems should be encouraged to write over the phrase as they say it. As students become more secure with this two-step process, begin to eliminate the first step, that of writing down the digital time, and extend the decision-making process as in Figure 4.45b.

NOTE: *For those students who do have fine-motor difficulties, an alternative approach is to write the expressions on a blank card for the Language Master. Keep blank, laminated clocks that can be clipped to the Language Master card.*

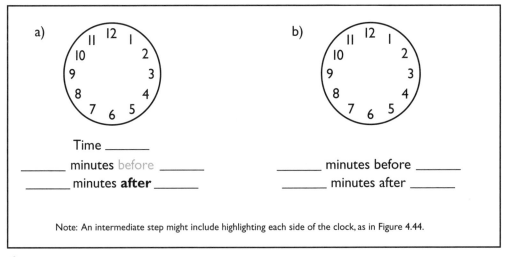

Note: An intermediate step might include highlighting each side of the clock, as in Figure 4.44.

Figure 4.45.

Using a dry-erase pen, fill in time on the clocks. The student then proceeds as above but, after writing in the information, slides the card through the Language Master and either hears it read or reads the words aloud. If the student reads the words, then he or she can run the card through again to listen. (The Language Master is a machine about the size of a small desk tape recorder. It comes with specially treated blank cards that are slid through the top of the machine, allowing the child to listen to what is said on the card. The teacher or a student can speak into the machine to record what should be heard as the card is passed through the slot.)

6. **Puzzle match.** For an independent activity, make puzzle cards like those shown in Figure 4.46. Whenever the word *before* is used, the clock is on the right. For the word *after,* the clock is on the left. Keep blank, laminated puzzles that do not have the times or the hands filled in. Fill in these puzzles, or have students fill them in, when more specialized learning is required. For example, if a student is working on telling time to the quarter hour and the half hour, the puzzles could be filled in using only those times.

7. **Special help.** For children with language deficits, pages like that in Figure 4.47 present a helpful way to build up comprehension. Initially, allow the children to keep an analog clock in front of them. Gradually eliminate the clock, since the use of the words *before* and *after* in time expressions requires comprehension even when no clock is visible. If the student has reading problems, provide a tape for use in conjunction with the page, place the page on a Language Master strip, or use the text-to-speech feature on a computer.

8. **Forward or backward.** Set a time on a geared or real analog clock. At first, use "5-minute" times like 2:15, 2:25, and 2:40. Have the children tell or write the time. Then ask, "What time will it be *in* 5 minutes?" As you say "in 5 minutes," emphasize the word *in* and move the hands of the clock. The children then say or write the new time. Do not change the hour during

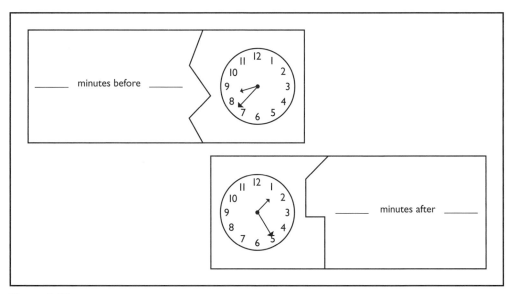

Figure 4.46.

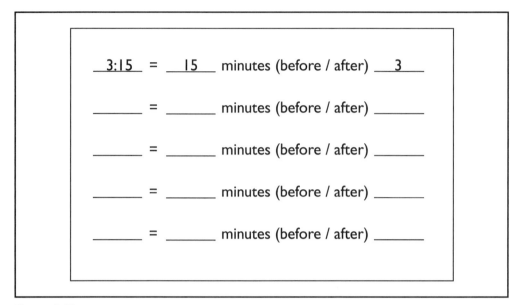

Figure 4.47.

the activity. Continue this procedure until the concept of *in* is firmly established. Use the same procedure to answer the question, "What time was it
5 minutes *ago?*"

Once the children readily recognize the difference between the two words,
mix the questions and have children practice moving the hands according to
the teacher's instructions. The major goal is for students to develop, kinesthetically, the feeling of the two expressions. Later, when they cannot move the
hands of a clock, the feeling will still be there. Many children actually move
their fingers as if turning the clock hands.

9. **Minute-hand card.** Give the child a clear plastic strip with a long
minute hand drawn on it and a hole at the end opposite the point of the minute
hand (Figure 4.48a). Also provide a page of clocks showing various times. First,
the child writes the time shown on a clock. Then the strip or card is placed over

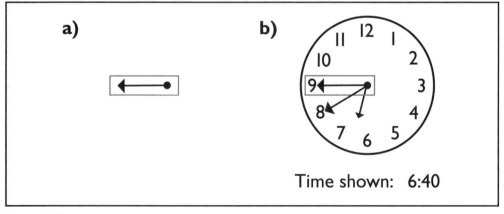

Figure 4.48.

the clock face so that its minute hand points to the number after the one the minute hand on the clock is pointing to, as in Figure 4.48b. Direct the child to point to the number indicated by the plastic card and say what time it would be then—for example, "In 5 minutes it will be 6:45." As proficiency is gained, use intervals of other than 5 minutes. Use the minute-hand card as long as it is needed.

10. **Follow-up.** Sample pages to reinforce this skill are shown in Figure 4.49a. As noted in the previous section, it is often necessary for the children to go through a two-step process: first writing the current time and then writing

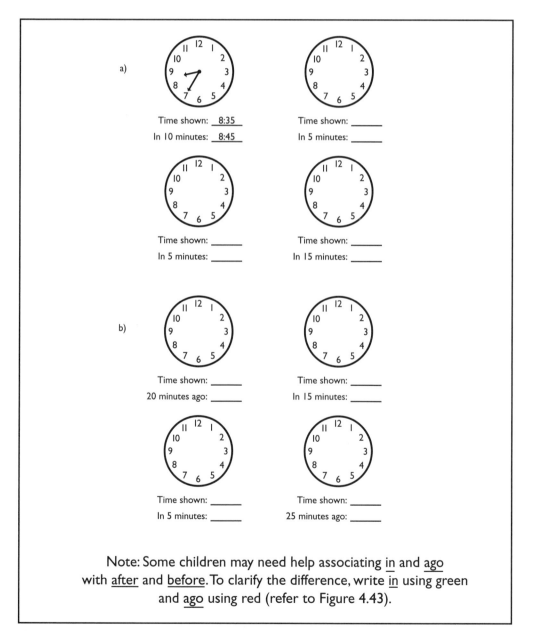

Note: Some children may need help associating <u>in</u> and <u>ago</u> with <u>after</u> and <u>before</u>. To clarify the difference, write <u>in</u> using green and <u>ago</u> using red (refer to Figure 4.43).

Figure 4.49.

the past or future time. Initially, the pages deal with only one concept, the time in the future or the time in the past. As students are ready, move to pages that mix those concepts, as in Figure 4.49b. When the child no longer needs to write down the current time, eliminate this step. For auditory cueing, remind the student: "Think: It is now _____, so in 10 minutes it will be _____."

11. **Card game** (for two or three players). A variation of the card game "Go Fish" can now be played. Make a deck of 20 cards with a clock face on each card (See Deck A in Figure 4.50a). Make a second set of 20 cards with a temporal expression on each (See Deck B in Figure 4.50b). Each child is dealt five cards from Deck A. The remainder of the cards are placed face down in the center. Deck B is placed face down next to them. Children take turns drawing a card from Deck B and choosing a card in their hand to play. Suppose a child draws the expression "in 15 minutes" from Deck B and chooses the clock 6:20 from the five Deck A cards in his or her hand. The student on the left is asked for a clock showing the time 6:35. If that student has that card, it is given to the child who asked, who lays down the pair of clocks. The child places the expression card in a discard pile, and the game moves on. If the child asking for a card makes a mistake or if the child to the left does not have the requested clock, the former draws from the fish pile until the correct clock is drawn or until five cards have been drawn, whichever occurs first. The winner is the one with the most pairs at the end. If necessary, the discard pile can be shuffled and reused.

12. **Compare.** For those children who need concrete associations for particular temporal expressions, make a game board such as that shown in Figure 4.51. Also provide a deck of cards with clock faces and some markers. Each space on the board counts for 5 minutes. Taking turns, each child draws two cards and places them, in the order drawn, at the bottom of the game board, as

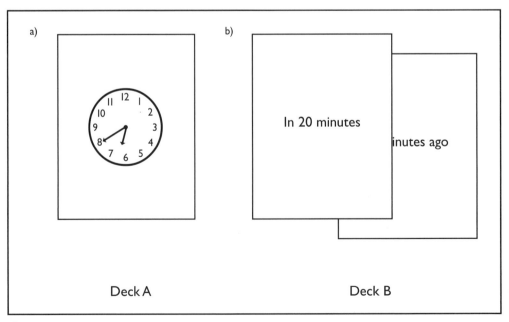

Figure 4.50.

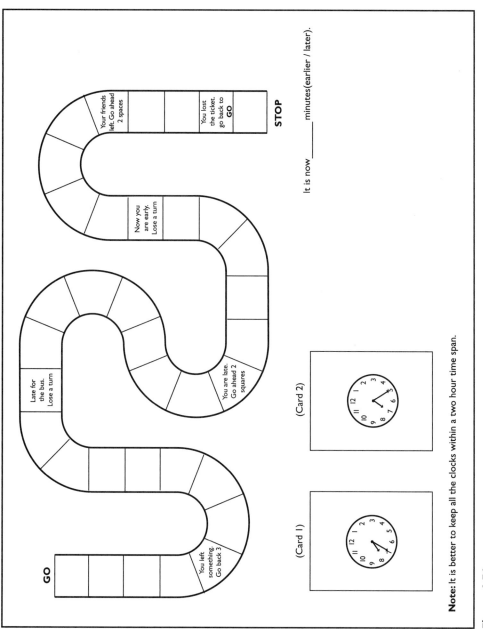

GO

Late for
the bus.
Lose a turn

You left
something.
Go back 3

You are late.
Go ahead 2
squares

Now you
are early.
Lose a turn

Your friends
left. Go ahead
2 spaces

You lost
the ticket.
go back to
GO

STOP

It is now _____ minutes(earlier / later).

(Card 1)

(Card 2)

Note: It is better to keep all the clocks within a two hour time span.

Figure 4.51.

shown. The child verbally fills in the blank and chooses the correct word (*earlier* or *later*). Since the second card drawn in Figure 4.51 shows a time that is 15 minutes earlier, the child moves backwards three spaces, counting by fives. Moving by fives dramatizes the difference between the two clock times. The winner is the first one to land on "stop."

Chapter 5

◆ ◆ ◆ ◆ ◆ ◆ ◆ ◆ ◆ ◆ ◆ ◆ ◆ ◆ ◆ ◆ ◆

Developing Number Sense: Number and Place Value

Number sense is an intuition about number relationships that helps us make judgments about whether a numerical response is reasonable. An overriding emphasis for numeric work involving students with learning disabilities is to provide carefully structured learning experiences that will gradually generate those number concepts, number relationships, and numeric skills that are foundational to the development of number sense. At first, children deal only with the numbers 1 to 10 or 12. They count groups of objects and record the number counted; they see and record clock times; they measure and record inch or centimeter measures; they use these numbers in early addition and subtraction work. Number sense grows as students develop understandings of larger numbers, and especially as they begin to identify unreasonable results during computation, to make predictions, and to estimate.

Numeric foundations are rooted in modeling the numbers and building accurate and efficient counting techniques. Then, when children can both read and write the associated numerals, number comparisons and sequencing tasks are introduced. Since number words are used in writing checks, those normally are dealt with as soon as a child's reading skills are developed well enough to handle them. Throughout, the overriding goal of developing "number sense" is nurtured by providing problem-solving and practical experiences that foster a "good feel" for the size of numbers, for operations on numbers, and for relationships between numbers.

It is assumed that teachers and educators using this book are familiar with standard sequences and techniques for developing these topics, as well as with the renewed emphasis on developing "number sense." From the perspective of the child with learning disabilities, however, standard approaches often fall short of reaching specific learning needs. This chapter focuses on the following areas within the early number and place value program that typically are troublesome to students with learning disabilities:

1. Developing number sense
2. Counting in early number work
3. Extending early counting skills
4. Reversals
5. Skip counting by tens and fives
6. Comparing numbers
7. Rounding and estimation
8. Reading and interpreting quantitative data from the printed word
9. Writing mathematics

For each of these sections, typical disabilities contributing to the problem are identified, and a carefully structured set of sample learning tasks and exercises is suggested. Special techniques, such as finger tracing and visual or auditory cueing, are also illustrated. A concluding section, "Using Technology," outlines further ideas to help students with learning disabilities understand number and place value.

DEVELOPING NUMBER SENSE

Problem Area: Inability to discern when a numeric response makes no sense.

Typical Disabilities Affecting Progress: Difficulties with abstract reasoning, visual or auditory association, and the ability to generalize information.

Background: Like problem solving, number sense is multifaceted and grows over time. Most students, but particularly those with learning disabilities, require carefully structured and ongoing learning opportunities that foster the development of number sense. Good modeling helps. A solid understanding of numbers and the ability to use number relationships are necessary. The goal in working with students who have specific learning disabilities is to help them gradually develop a mind-set for assessing the reasonableness of numeric results. This goal has broad implications if students are to make successful, independent use of quantitative data in daily situations.

Specific and repeated opportunities to examine or choose between answers that are "closest to" an exact computational result, repeated occasions to hear the reasonableness of numeric results evaluated in different ways by the teacher or capable peers, opportunities to make numeric estimates and then compare them to computed results—these and similar learning experiences should accompany a student's work in the area of number and place value. Ideas for implementing these strategies are outlined below. The types of tasks described in numbers 2 and 3, particularly, should be carried out frequently.

Sample Sequence of Activities

1. **More or less than 10?** Provide opportunities for children to think about and discover relationships.

- 8 + 4: Is this more than 10 or less than 10? Explain. (Students can self-check using a 10-frame card; 8 and 2 more fill the 10 frames, so 8 + 4 is more than 10.)

- What's 5 + 5? Is 5 + 9 more or less than that? How do you know? (Students can show 5 + 5 with counters and note that they need to put out *more* counters for 5 + 9.)

For each exercise, students should verbalize their reasoning, orally or in writing.

■ *Variations:*

More or less than $\frac{1}{2}$? Ask students to circle in green all fractions on a sheet that are more than $\frac{1}{2}$. (They should use fraction circles or bars to self-check.)

Closer to 50 or to 100? Have students circle in green those numbers that are closer (nearer) to 50 than to 100. If they have difficulty, try a kinesthetic or tactile approach: Ask the child to place a finger on, for example, 86 and say, "Close your eyes while I move your finger from 86 to 100. Then from 86 to 50. Which end 'feels' closer?"

Over or under? Provide repeated instances in which students are asked to decide which of two given estimates is better and to explain their reasoning. To aid their reasoning, provide a context, as in the following example:

$$652 - 298 = ? \quad \text{A. over 400} \quad \text{B. under 400}$$

"It's like there are 652 fish in the lake, and the fish company takes out 298. $652 - 200$ leaves 452. But it goes under 400 when they take out the extra 98."

2. **What can't it be?** Provide computational problems and a choice of two (or more) possible answers. Ask the child to predict: "What can't the answer be? Why?" (Teacher modeling of appropriate responses is important, so find opportunities to provide this.)

■ *Example:*

$$\begin{array}{r} 28 \\ + 37 \\ \hline 65 \end{array} \qquad \begin{array}{r} 28 \\ + 37 \\ \hline 515 \end{array}$$

"The answer can't be 515. It's not even 100, because $50 + 50$ is 100, and both numbers are less than 50."

3. **What's closest?** As described above, provide computational problems and a choice of two (or more) possible estimates. Ask the child to predict: "Which of the answer choices is *closest to* the exact answer? How do you know?" (As above, provide "think aloud" opportunities in which the student can hear—and perhaps rephrase in personal language—your reasoning or that of other students.

■ *Example:*

$$92 - 49 = ? \quad \text{A. 28} \quad \text{B. 48} \quad \text{C. 88}$$

"It's B. The problem is sort of like $100 - 50$, and the answer to that is 50—so 48 is closest."

COUNTING IN EARLY NUMBER WORK

Problem Area: Inability to accurately count a small group of (up to 10) objects even though the oral counting sequence for numbers to 10 is known.

Typical Disabilities Affecting Progress: Spatial organization difficulties, perseveration, impulsive learning approach, short-term auditory memory difficulties.

Background: Consider this scenario. Pedro "counted" the 6 chips on the table and announced that there were 10. He recounted them for the teacher in his characteristic manner, touching (most of) them as he went: "1–2, 3, 4–5–6, 7–8, 9–10. Ten chips."

Pedro does know the oral names and the correct counting sequence for numbers to 10. He has not, however, internalized the association of "one object—one number word," which is basic to accurate counting. Further, his general lack of spatial organization interferes with his counting, as he misses some objects in his count. Activities like the following have proved helpful to children like Pedro.

 ## Sample Sequence of Activities

1. **Ker-Plunk!** (Ideal for students with auditory learning strengths.) Provide a tin pan and metal washers or other objects that will make a noise when dropped into the pan. Take turns playing Ker-Plunk with Pedro. Going first, drop one washer in the pan and say, "One." Drop a second washer and say, "Two." Then give Pedro a few washers to drop and count as you did. Prompt him as needed: count with him; clap at each drop of the washer (standing near his dominant ear); or tap him on the shoulder or back to capitalize on any kinesthetic or tactile learning strengths. Make no special effort to have Pedro count beyond 4 or 5 in this activity. Repeat several times.

2. **All in a row.** Prepare a transparency showing 4 or 5 balloons in a row. Place a piece of paper over all but the first balloon in the row; flash the image on the wall at Pedro's height and have him touch and count each of the balloons as you uncover them, one by one.

NOTE: *Activities similar to these or the following might be used to help children who are strong auditory or kinesthetic-tactile learners. Notice that many of the following tasks require that each object be* moved *as it is counted—to help structure the counting so no object is missed or counted twice:*

- Count rubber bands as each is stretched and place them, one by one, around a door knob.

- Count blocks as they are taken from a box and place them, one by one, on a table.

- Count knots tied in a rope.

- Count pegs as they are pushed into a pegboard.

- Count beads as they are strung.

- Count unifix cubes as, one by one, each is repositioned.

EXTENDING EARLY COUNTING SKILLS

Problem Areas: Inability to count on or back two or three numbers; inability to visually recognize the number of objects in a 10-frame; inability to tell whether two or three numbers have been said in a vocal count.

Typical Disabilities Affecting Progress: Difficulties with visual or auditory association, closure, figure ground, expressive language, sustained attention, inner language, working memory.

Background: The early number program has its roots in counting. Children refine and rely heavily on counting as they begin their work in addition and subtraction. When the instructional goal shifts to memorizing basic facts, four extensions of counting contribute significantly to a child's success at quickly and accurately deriving answers to unknown facts:

- auditorally recognizing when two or three numbers have been said (11 – 9: "That's 9—10, 11." In this example, the child counted up *two* numbers. The answer is 2.);

- counting on (2 + 7: "That's 7—8, 9." Here the child starts with the greater addend and counts on two. The answer or sum is 9.);

- counting back (9 – 2: "That's 9—8, 7." Here the child starts with the total and counts back two numbers, to 7.);

- visual recognition of the 10-frame (6 and 4 fill the frame, as in Figure 5.1: 6 + 4 = 10). The 10-frame reference is useful for sums of 10 and related differences.

Each of these skills involves an extension of counting that can and should be developed in the early number program *prior to* any work with number facts. Otherwise, we ask children to learn two things at once: (a) the number facts; and (b) the counting skills for answering many of the easy number facts quickly. Rather, the goal should be to assure that the extended counting skills are intact before we ask children to apply them in early addition and subtraction. After children learn to count in sequence from one, we then turn to developing the following four useful extensions of counting. Until children develop these counting skills, it is useful to find 3 minutes in the daily routine to include activities like those outlined below.

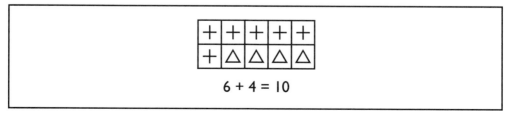

6 + 4 = 10

Figure 5.1.

Auditory Patterning

Is it necessary for children to finger count as they count on to add or count back to subtract 1, 2, or 3? Experience has shown that the following auditory patterning activities, started early, help students internalize these short counts, eliminate the need to finger-count, and assist in counting on and counting back. The activities sensitize children to the differences in the auditory patterns that accompany the beat of two claps and the beat of three claps. With repetition of these activities, they then develop the feeling of processing two vs. three numbers.

✎ Sample Sequence of Activities

1. **How many claps do you hear?** Clap one, two, or three times and ask students to tell how many claps they heard. When they become comfortable with this first activity, proceed to the following activity.

2. **How many numbers do you hear?** Say two or three numbers in sequence (forwards or backwards) and ask students to tell how many numbers they heard.

- *Examples:* "6, 7, 8." ("Three numbers.")
  "11, 10." ("Two numbers.")

Repeat this activity frequently. The payoff comes later in the addition-subtraction program. Given 5 + 3, for example, students tend to begin to recognize (without finger counting) when they have counted on for 3 more: "5—6, 7, 8." Or, for problems like 11 – 2, they tend to recognize (without finger counting) when they've counted back 2: "11—10, 9."

NOTE: *For children with auditory deficits, tap on the child's shoulder or back instead of clapping (Activity 1) or while saying the numbers (Activity 2).*

Counting On from Mid Sequence

The ability to count on from mid sequence is normally achieved around age 7. A child's natural development, however, can be "nurtured" by providing repeated opportunities to mimic a count that starts in mid sequence. Ideally, because this skill is so directly tied to mastery of nearly half (45) of the 100 basic number facts for addition, specific activities to foster counting on should be initiated a full year *before* any memory work with basic facts is introduced.

When counting on is applied to counting six or more objects, two skills that can be especially difficult for students with a learning disability are involved: (a) visualizing groups of objects as a whole; and (b) retrieving a number from mid sequence. To assist students, ensure that first activities include countable objects or dot cards to reinforce sight groups for small numbers. It may be necessary to work with students until they can immediately recognize by sight (without counting) one to four objects in any configuration and five or six objects arranged in the familiar dice arrangement. Later, a shift from total reliance on objects is recommended. The teacher's immediate goal should be to provide many opportunities in which the first vocal number in a count is *not* 1. These ideas are central to the following sample instructional sequence for children with learning deficits. The following activities involve body movement and further reinforce the auditory patterning for two and three.

✎ Sample Sequence of Activities

▶ Recognizing Sight Groups

1. **Is this two?** (For individuals or small groups; adapt to large-group instruction by using an overhead projector.) Place two small objects, in different configurations, under each of five boxes on a table. Give each child a number "2" card showing two spots. Lift a box briefly so that children can have a quick peek before it is put back. Then ask: "Is this two?" Do this with each box. Start this as a group activity, then call on individuals to respond. Children can check their answers by taking the pieces that are under each box and placing them on their "2" cards to see if they fit the number of spots. Repeat, but vary the arrangement and number of objects under the boxes, sometimes placing only one object under a box, sometimes three objects. In some cases, it may be necessary, at first, to use one color for all "2" clusters. Gradually, however, this cue can be eliminated.

- *Example:* Let green be the cueing color. At first use only green objects for the "2" clusters: for example, two green sticks under one box, two green beads under another, and so on. As a next step, use objects of different colors for the "2" clusters but place them inside a green loop, such as one drawn with crayon on paper. Gradually fade the loop out of the picture.

- *Follow-up:* Have children paste cloth scraps or construction paper pieces, by twos, on cards: "See how many different ways you can make two." Later use the cards, along with others that show one item or three items, in an "Is This Two?" flash card activity.

NOTE: *With some children, especially those who have expressive language deficits, it helps to associate the numeral 2 with the "2" clusters during early phases of the activity. The additional visual cueing helps students respond appropriately and promotes overlearning as well.*

- *Example:* After students have pasted the cloth scraps on cards, by twos, have them match each card with another card showing a green numeral 2. As the cards showing one item are added as distractors, the green "2" cards described above can still be used (see Figure 5.2). The color cue, then the numeral itself, can gradually be eliminated.

2. **Say what you see.** Use flash cards from the previous follow-up activity (cards showing one, two, or three objects). Flash the cards, asking students to

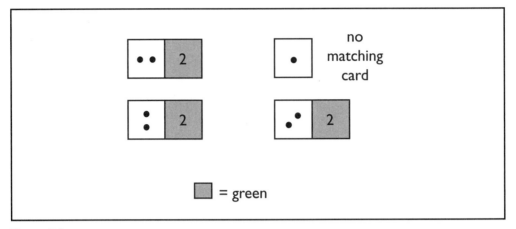

Figure 5.2.

tell how many objects they see. Use a thin underscore (e.g., green for two, black for three) *only* if necessary and plan systematically to fade any such prompt.

NOTE: *The previous activities can be adapted to nurture sight group recognition for groups of four.*

▶ **Counting On**

1. **Small handful.** Materials: 12 small counters in a box with a lid. Have a child take a small handful of counters (e.g., 5) from the box, count them, and place them in the lid of the box. Hold the box lid high, so no one can peek. "How many are in the lid?" ("Five.") "Let's put more counters in the lid. Count with me. Now" (as, one by one, three additional counters are dropped into the lid) "...there's 6, 7, 8." If it seems helpful, allow children to recount from 1 to check. Then return all counters to the box and repeat for other small handfuls. Each time, have children *count on aloud* from the number of counters in the lid as, one by one, 1, 2, or 3 additional counters are dropped into the lid.

2. **Act it out.** Use body movements that allow students to "feel" the pattern for counting on. For counting on two, model the activity while saying the following: "Sit, hands on knees. I will say a number (9). Count on two before you stand and say the last number in the count. 9—10, 11. Stand and say 11." Children repeat: 9—10, and then stand and say 11. Follow a similar procedure for counting on three: Have children stand, both hands down. Say one of the numbers, 4 to 9 (e.g., 8) and then say, "Count on three before you raise your hands above your head while saying the last number in the count. 8—9, 10, 11." Children repeat and raise their hands while saying 11.

3. **Show and count on.** Ask students to count with you as you place several dots (up to nine) on the chalkboard. Circle these dots and write the number for the dots, then invite students to *count on* with you as you continue to draw up to three additional dots (Figure 5.3).

4. **Say, unfold, and count on!** Materials: folded number or dot cards as shown in Figure 5.4. Use numbers 4–9 and one, two, or three dots on the cards. Children say the number, unfold the card, and count on.

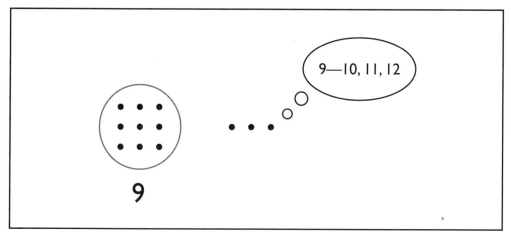

Figure 5.3.

NOTE: *As children become comfortable with the auditory patterning activities, the dot card can be replaced with a numeral card for 1, 2, and 3.*

5. **Turn over.** Line up large numeral cards along the chalk tray (Figure 5.5). Let children see you turn one card over (e.g., the 7 card). Point to the card in front of the 7 and say, "Read this card, [name of child]." ("Six.") "What comes after 6?" ("Seven.") Turn the card over to check.

NOTE: *It might help some children to say a number, finger-trace and say the next few numbers, then close their eyes while they repeat the sequence. From time to time, encourage children to recount from 1, emphasizing the last few numbers of the sequence.*

■ *Follow-up Activity 1:* As described before but using a large-scale ruler or number line, decide on a number and cover all numbers to the right of it with an arrow card (Figure 5.6). "What does the arrow point to?" ("Six.") Have children count on from the last number shown until you give a signal to stop.

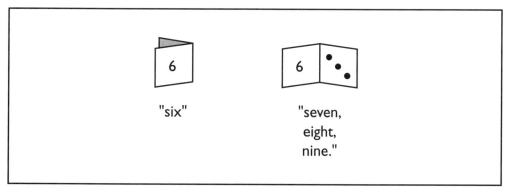

Figure 5.4.

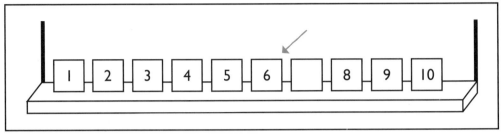

Figure 5.5.

- *Follow-up Activity 2:* As before, but this time encourage the children to study the ruler or card sequence so they can picture (or visualize) "in their heads" where the numbers are. Then have them close their eyes while you turn over a numeral card. Children who benefit from motor involvement might do well walking on a floor number line. "Look at the numbers while you walk. Stop on 14 and close your eyes. Think about what's next and take a step. Where are you?"

6. **Two more.** This activity prepares children to count on in addition problems with 2 as an addend (e.g., 6 + 2, 2 + 5, 7 + 2). Emphasis is on the auditory patterning involved and on developing inner language. Use the ruler and arrow card from Follow-up Activity 1 under "Turn Over." Point the arrow to a numeral (between 4 and 9) and have the children tell you that number plus 2 more. Orally emphasize the auditory pattern that makes this easy.

- *Example:* If the number pointed to is 6:

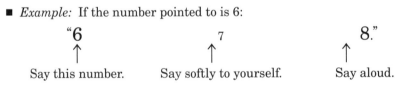

"6	7	8."
↑	↑	↑
Say this number.	Say softly to yourself.	Say aloud.

Repeat with other numbers, and later extend to addition problems that have 3 as an addend. Some children with auditory deficits or perseveration tendencies may have difficulty saying the middle number(s) softly. Such children might be taught to tap the table while speaking softly.

Counting Back

Children typically find it harder to count backward than forward, even for short counts. Students with poor working memory or difficulty sustaining

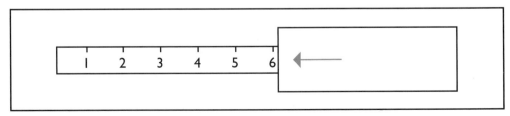

Figure 5.6.

attention find this skill especially difficult. Since about one-fourth of the subtraction basic facts can be quickly answered by counting backward, it is a skill deserving greater and *earlier* emphasis in work with numbers through 10 or 12. Too many school programs fail to develop this specific skill, leaving children to learn it while trying to apply it for answering subtraction problems like 9 – 2, 8 – 3, 11 – 2, and others. Children with learning deficits are among the first to be frustrated and fail in such a situation. To help a child acquire the skill level necessary for counting back two or three numbers in subtraction, ideas like the following have proven helpful.

  ## Sample Sequence of Activities

1. **Up and back.** Have children use two body motions: clap hands while counting up to a number; tap knees while counting back from that number. Later, count up (teacher only) and let the children count back.

- *Example:* Teacher says: "1, 2, 3, 4" (while all clap hands).
  Children respond (while all tap knees): "4, 3, 2, 1."

In a final phase, count forward "silently" and say just the last number (e.g., "4"). Children count backward, starting with that number ("4, 3, 2, 1"). *Be sure children can count back from 4 before extending the backward count pattern to 5. Then master that count pattern before extending further, and so on.*

2. **Break away!** Materials: 16 interlocking cubes. Taking turns, children make an interlocking cube train (e.g., a "9" train, a train of 9 cubes) and count backward as, one by one, they break cubes away from the train (Figure 5.7). For students with expressive language difficulties, it may help to have the numbers on each cube, initially. Once such students feel confident with the auditory pattern and have developed a visual image to assist them, the numbers can be removed.

3. **Say and sit.** Stand and say one of the numbers, 4 to 12 (e.g., 8). *Count back two* and then sit, simultaneously saying the final number: e.g., "8—7, 6," sitting on "6." Children repeat. Continue using other numbers.

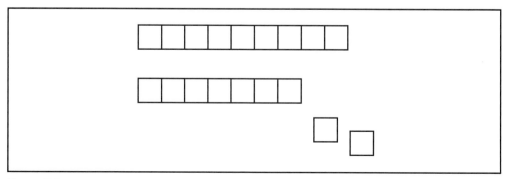

Figure 5.7.

4. **Knee touch.** Have children stand, both hands above their head. Say one of the numbers, 4 to 12 (e.g., 8). *Count back three* before you touch your knees: e.g., "8—7, 6, 5." Children repeat, using other numbers.

5. **Show—then strike and count back.** Ask students to count with you as you place several dots (up to 12) on the chalkboard. Circle these dots and write the number of dots; then invite students to *count back* with you as, one by one, you strike out three of the dots: 12, 11, 10.

Visual Patterning Based on the 10-Frame

Good visual imagery for the 10-frame is an important skill. One example of 10 things, or 6 or 7, is the number of objects "in the frame." (Refer to Figure 5.8.) The following two basic activities help build visual imagery for the 10-frame.

 ## Sample Sequence of Activities

▶ **Prerequisite skills:**

- Sight recognition of groups of fewer than five.
- Sight recognition of groups of five.
- Understanding of *top* and *bottom.*

1. **10-frame flash.** Materials: A set of 10-frame cards similar to those shown in Figure 5.9. Flash each card briefly, then remove it from sight. After flashing each card, ask, "How many stars did you see?" Repeat, emphasizing six–nine stars in the frame. It often is helpful to make comments like: "Nine stars—that must be *all but one* frame filled. Let's check." "Seven stars—that must be the top row and two more: 5—6, 7. Let's check."

NOTE: *Repeat in biweekly warm-ups until children are very successful with this task. Then move to the second basic activity below.*

2. **Frame fill.** Materials: 10-frame cards, as in Activity 1. Flash cards as above, then ask children to close their eyes. "Can you see the stars in the frame? How many would it take to fill the frame? . . . Let's check."

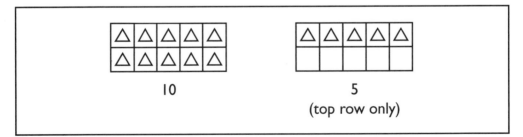

Figure 5.8.

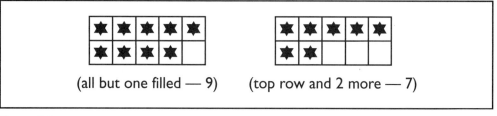

(all but one filled — 9)   (top row and 2 more — 7)

Figure 5.9.

NOTE: *Good mental imagery for the 10-frame paves the way for success later with 10 sums and for subtracting any number from 10. It also is basic to using 10 as a bridge for adding problems like 6 + 8 and 7 + 5, for subtracting problems like 13 – 8, 12 – 4, and for "harder" problems.*

Once children have been introduced to each of the types of activities described in this section, it is possible to provide a sample of each activity type (counting on, counting back, number of numbers heard [two or three], and 10-frame work) during a 3-minute "quick math" period sometime during the day. Until children have mastered the problems that rely on these skills, the recommendation is to review them in daily or at least biweekly mini-math sessions.

REVERSALS

Problem Areas: Number reversals (Ɛ for 3, 6 for 9, 23 for 32), disorientations (⅃ for 7), mirror images, and other disfigurations.

Typical Disabilities Affecting Progress: Difficulties with visual or auditory memory or visual discrimination, spatial organization, visual motor integration.

Background: Before children begin writing numerals, they should be able to count out the correct number of objects for each numeral being written. Further, those with severe visual-motor coordination difficulties should be provided with preliminary work at the gross-motor level. In extreme cases this may include movement exercises such as hopping, crawling, jumping, and ball catching. Gross-motor writing activities may also be necessary.

For example, children might form (or trace over) numerals in damp sand, or use a finger or wet sponge to trace over large numerals drawn on the chalkboard. Guide the child's hand and give verbal cues to prompt correct formation if necessary. For example, "Down, around, the 6 curls up; the 6 sleeps sound." It sometimes helps to have children close their eyes as you guide their formation of a numeral. "Feel the 6 go down, around. Now you make it" . . . first with eyes closed, then with eyes open. As children make the transition to paper-and-pencil writing, color and one-stroke patterns, suggested in the activities below, may be needed to address persistent reversal tendencies. Regularly throughout early writing activity, children should draw or display the appropriate number of objects for any numeral that is formed.

Whenever possible, early number and place-value work should be embedded in game, problem, or application settings to which children can relate. As larger numbers of objects are counted, children who can count by tens may independently note that grouping by tens makes it quick and easy for others to check their count. Developing efficient ways to count, record, and communicate to others about larger numbers of objects is the stepping stone to place-value understandings for multidigit numbers, which include grouping (by tens), partitioning numbers in different ways (e.g., 23 can be 2 tens and 3 ones or 1 ten and 13 ones), and comparing numbers.

Recent research emphasizes that place-value concepts are really learned when children are routinely challenged to solve and justify their solutions to numeric problems. The following two types of problems, focusing on groups of 10, should be used early in place-value work to engage students in using 10-trains (of interlocking cubes) and loose cubes to model and solve problems:

- The factory packed all the candies the man made. They filled 5 boxes, 10 candies to a box. How many candies did the man make? (Know the number of tens and ones. Find the total.)

- Yash had 54 stickers. His sticker book held 10 on each page. How many pages could he fill? How many extra stickers would there be? (Know the total. Find the number of tens and ones.)

Adults may link these two types of problems only to multiplication or division, but children will group and count by tens. A robust body of research stemming from the cognitively guided instruction projects out of the University of Wisconsin (Fennema, Carpenter, Levi, Franke, & Empson, 1997) emphasize that "the fundamental context for developing the notion of grouping by ten" is found in these types of problems. These researchers elaborate: "What is unique about problems to develop base-ten ideas is that objects are collected into groups of ten. That allows children to use principles of the base-ten number system to solve them" (p. 63).

The use of word problems to develop place-value understandings should ideally be extended to include addition and subtraction problems with multidigit numbers, as these provide an important forum for reinforcing place-value learning. At first these problems should be quite basic. All children—including those with learning disabilities—benefit from and develop their place-value understandings by engaging in extended problem-solving experiences like the following:

- Sami's sticker book holds 100 stickers. He has 17 dog stickers and 56 horse stickers in his book. Does he have room for 47 bird stickers?

In the past it was thought that such problems were too complicated for many students with learning disabilities. Teachers are now finding that past expectations, and hence results, were not high enough. Calculators can do the computing. The challenge is to nurture children's abilities to *think mathematically*. Experience has shown that children become better thinkers and better problem solvers when they are systematically involved in solving problems. Children also gain richer insights into numbers when they are allowed, even encouraged, to solve problems in *personally meaningful ways,* and when they can listen to and see *different solution approaches* used by other students.

In the sticker problem above, for example, one child, focusing on the tens digits, might think: "10 and 50—that's 60, and 40 more is already 100. So the book is too full to add in the extra stickers." Another child might do a paper-and-pencil computation and get 73 for the total number of stickers in the book, then count on by tens while finger tapping: 73—83, 93 (that's 20)—and 7 more to 100 makes 27. "There's only room for 27 more stickers, not 47."

A third student might use trains of 10 interlocking cubes and loose cubes to represent the 17, 56, and 47 stamps, push all the 10-trains together (to obtain 10 such trains) and count by tens to 100. This child might even combine loose cubes into as many 10-trains as possible and finally note that the total number of cubes is more than 100, so the stickers won't all fit—"In fact, 20 won't fit." Other solution approaches are possible, some using only paper-pencil computations, some using a hundreds chart, base-10 blocks, or other math aid. As the students work, they are likely to partition and regroup numbers in different ways, and hence reinforce or learn important place-value concepts. They may:

- group objects such as popsicle sticks or cubes by 10s and then *tell* or *write* the number of 10s and the number of extra sticks or cubes.

- count orally by 10s and use objects to show the count: "2 10s are twenty, 6 10s are 60," and so on.

- use the objects (10s and 1s) to help compare the number of stickers to 100.

If, as children work, consistent reversal tendencies are noted beyond the early primary level, then structured assistance, as suggested below, may be necessary. If the reversals mostly involve teen numbers, a reminder such as "Teens are different. They are back-to-front numbers—what you hear first you write last," often helps to correct the problem. Sometimes recounting from 1, following the page numbers of a book, and comparing with what has been written are helpful in highlighting and correcting the difficulty.

If a child has severe spatial organization problems, it is helpful to confine all writing activities to a horizontal plane. The down stroke on the 4 made by a child sitting at a desk, for example, has a different orientation to the body than that made while standing. It may be necessary in cases such as this to teach an alternate pattern for writing a 4 and a 5, a pattern that involves only one stroke (see Figure 5.10). These patterns have also helped children with severe reversal tendencies. If children still have difficulty with reversals, the following basic sequence may help.

✎ Sample Sequence of Activities

▶ One-Digit Reversals

1. **Stencil in.** Provide stencils that children can use to write given numerals. Place a green dot on the stencils to indicate the starting place. In Figure 5.11, the loop is outlined in red. This helps distinguish the 6 from the 9.

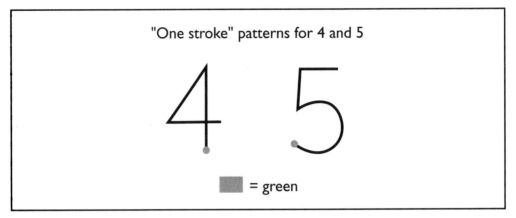

Figure 5.10.

When necessary, have children finger-trace before starting and use verbal cues to emphasize the correct formation of a numeral.

2. **Get the feel.**

> *Stacey saw six kites. Use counters for kites.*
> *Show what Stacey saw. Write the number.*

■ *Variation 1:* (For children who confuse two numerals, such as 6 and 9.) Have children use stencils to form both numerals. Use green dots to show the starting place on both numerals. Orally name both numerals, but for one use additional color and verbal cueing, as above, to emphasize its shape. Then tell the child, "Close your eyes. I'll move your hand. Am I making a 6?" (If the child says no, ask, "Am I making a 9?") If the child is not ticklish, write one of the numerals on the child's back. "Tell me what I'm writing. . . . Yes, 6. Go to the chalk tray and pick out a picture card showing six things."

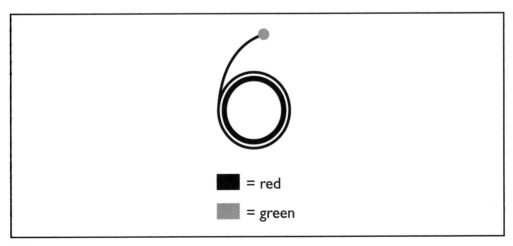

Figure 5.11.

NOTE: *It often helps to have textured numerals in front of the children while you finger-trace on their backs. Felt numbers are better than sandpaper because they are less abrasive. While you trace, have the children look at the numerals to help fix the association. When finished, have them trace over the numeral they think you made. If correct, and if they are able to write numerals, they can be requested immediately to do so on the chalkboard, on paper, or in sand.*

- *Variation 2:* (For children who make mirror images of given numerals [see Figure 5.12].) Move the child's hand or write on the child's back so the child can "feel" the numeral being written. Then have the child form the numeral in the air (or on the desk). This can also be done as you write the numeral on the child's back.

3. **Count and trace.**

- *Variation 1:* (For children who confuse two numerals, such as 6 for 9.) Have children count and complete the correct numeral to show how many, as in Figure 5.13. If necessary, use a green dot to show the starting place, and have children trace the numeral before writing it—"Does it feel like the 6? Does it circle round to sleep sound?" Use red outlining on the loop, as suggested above, if this helps.

- *Variation 2:* (For children who make mirror images of given numerals.) Have children count objects and write a row of the numeral showing "how many." Use color-coding to start the numeral. In Figure 5.14, the top curve is green. Solid, then dotted, lines are used. Children may need to finger-trace a few numerals before using pencil.

- *Follow-up:* It is typical for children to revert to former reversal patterns. The problem, though correctable, does take time to resolve. Worksheets

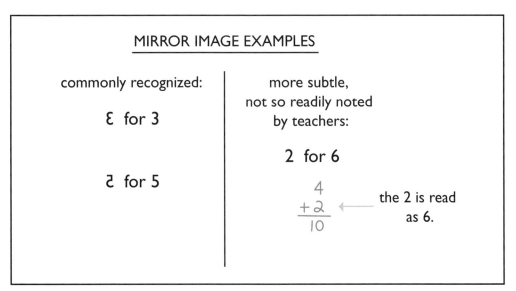

Figure 5.12.

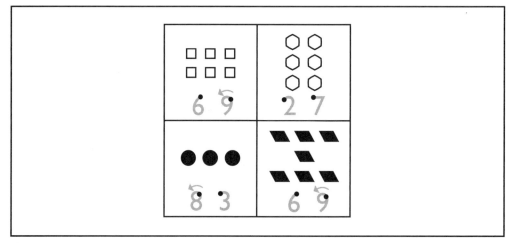

Figure 5.13.

like the one shown in Figure 5.15, that require only occasional independent writing of a numeral, provide self-correction when children forget the correct writing movement. As children trace over given samples, teachers might ask: "Do you feel you do it the same way when you write it?"

- *Optional Follow-up:* For children who have been introduced to addition (or other operations and related basic facts), it may be necessary to help transfer the numeral recognition skill to problem situations. Figure 5.16 suggests a way of doing this. Children are asked to complete the correct answer and to cross out the wrong one. Children can also be helped to transfer number recognition to printed numerals. Have them find and circle given numerals that appear in newspaper ads, for example.

4. **You do.** As children need less structured cues to write "problem" numbers on paper, use a green dot to show where to start (Figure 5.17a). Children count the objects, trace the solid numeral, and use it as a pattern for writing

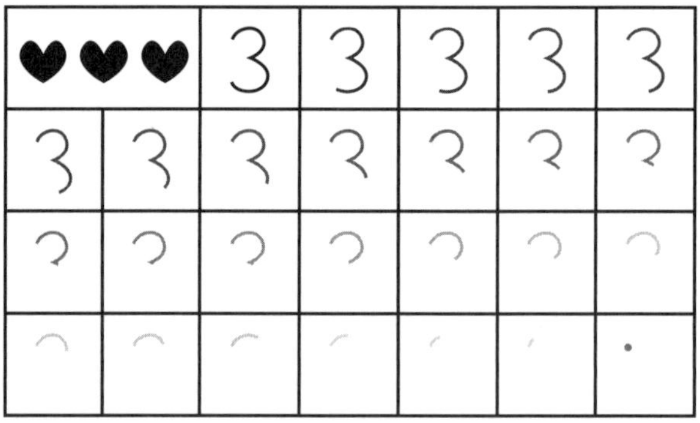

Figure 5.14.

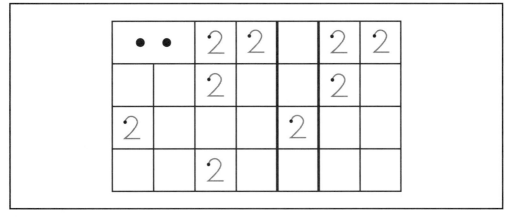

Figure 5.15.

other numerals in that row. If necessary, a yellow highlighter can be used instead of dotted lines to guide correct formation. Eventually, numeral patterns are given only at the top of the worksheet (Figure 5.17b). In these examples, color outlining of the 6 loop would be used if needed but would be eliminated gradually.

- ■ *Optional Follow-up:* Simple number combinations that involve the specific numerals being worked on would again be given. This time, however, the color-coded numerals of Figure 5.16 would not be shown. Figure 5.18 illustrates a way of making the activity self-checking. Write problems on the bottom part of a sheet of construction paper, as shown. Cover that part with contact paper so children can use a washable marker to answer. Write the answers to the problems on the other side of the top part of the sheet. Children can then fold the

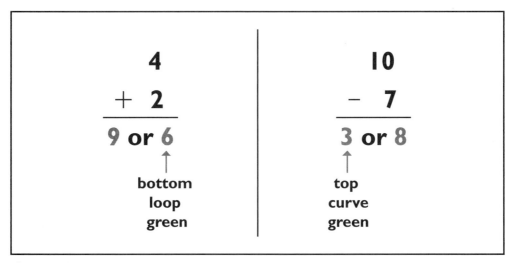

Figure 5.16.

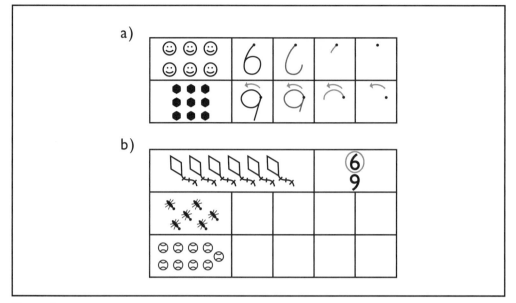

Figure 5.17.

top part down over the problems and compare their answers with those given.

5. **Hand numbers.** Children can be taught to use their right hand to check the shape of many numerals. The curves of the 2, 3, and 5 all coincide with the shape formed by cupping the right hand. The numerals 7 and 9 also can be "made" with the right hand and forearm, as in Figure 5.19. Left-handed children are at an advantage in this hand check. They don't even have to put their pencils down!

NOTE: *Activities and exercises similar to those in the preceding sequence can be used to help children who have other writing problems, including disorientation and misperception of numerals. Have model numbers available to which children can refer.*

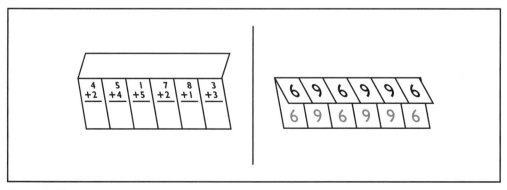

Figure 5.18.

Figure 5.19.

▶ **Two-Digit Reversals**

1. **Tens and ones.**

   Grandma made cookies. She filled 2 plates of cookies—10 cookies on each—and had 4 extra cookies. How many cookies did Grandma bake?

Use colored chips or graph paper pieces (see Figure 5.20a). Give the child 2 tens and 4 ones. Then ask: "How many stacks of 10?" ("Two.") Have the child place a green textured numeral beneath the 2 stacks of 10. Then ask: "How many ones?" ("Four.") Position these to the right of the 10-stacks, and have the child place a red numeral beneath the 4 ones (Figure 5.20b). Say to the child: "Two tens and 4, that's 24. Finger-trace the 24 so you get the feel of it. Start with tens." The child should say the number aloud as it is traced.

   ■ *Follow-up Discussion:* "Think of a traffic light. Suppose you want to walk across the street. When can you start walking?" ("When the light is green.") "Yes, green means start. Red means stop. Look at the numerals we used. When you read or write numbers like this [point], you *start* with tens, the green one, and *stop* with ones."

If the child has any difficulty relating 2 tens to 20, 4 tens to 40, and so on, take time out to reinforce this relationship. Use 10-stacks to dramatize the counting by tens. Capitalize on any phonetic similarities (e.g., *6* tens are *60; 5* tens are *50*). Repeat the activity with other numbers. Omit teens until later, when naming irregularities can again be pointed out.

   2. **Start with tens.** Give the child 2 tens and 4 ones, as in the preceding activity, and say: "Let's write how many chips you have. Where do we start?" ("Tens—2 tens.") "Write the 2 in green. How many ones?" ("Four.") "Write it in red (Figure 5.21a). What number did we write?" ("Twenty-four.") "Finger trace the number as you say it. . . . Now close your eyes and picture it while I say it. . . . Open your eyes. Is this what you saw?" (Refer again to Figure 5.21a.) Prompt the child as necessary throughout this dialogue.

   Now show the child Figure 5.21b. "Which of these say 24?" ("Last one.") "How do you know?" ("It starts with 2 tens.") Have the child finger-trace the number, as before.

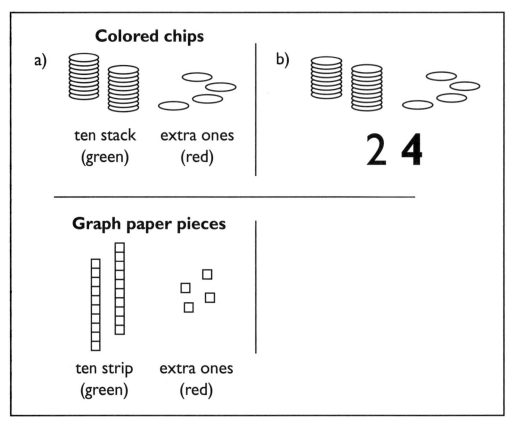

Figure 5.20.

Show the child Figure 5.21c. "This time there's no color. Can you remember which says 24?" ("Last one.") "How do you know?" ("It starts with 2 tens.")

Repeat with other two-digit numbers. A worksheet like that shown in Figure 5.22 can be used in conjunction with the activity. Boxes can be filled in during discussion with the child. Note that:

- It may be sufficient merely to underline the tens digit in green, the ones digit in red.

- The separation of tens and ones columns into individual boxes has been avoided. When that is done, some students, for closure reasons, do not see "24." They see a 2 and a 4. In our experience, these same students accept and profit from the color distinctions.

- *Follow-up:* Worksheets from commercial workbooks can be useful. It may sometimes be necessary, particularly for children with sequential memory deficits, to color-code their pages by underscoring the tens groups in green and the ones groups in red. Any response lines could be coded to match. It may be necessary to color-code only the first problem on a page as an example for completing others. Alternately, it may be sufficient to make cards available that show the coding, to which children can refer.

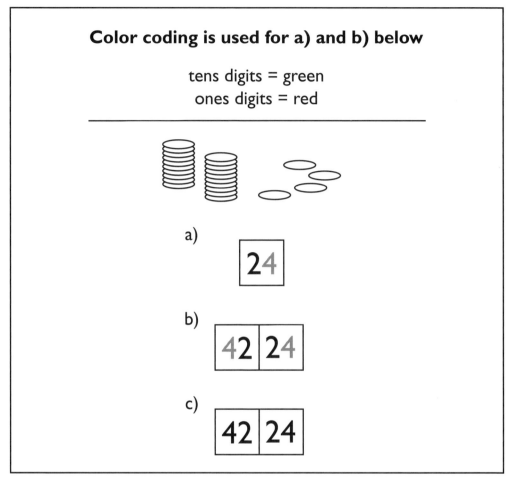

Figure 5.21.

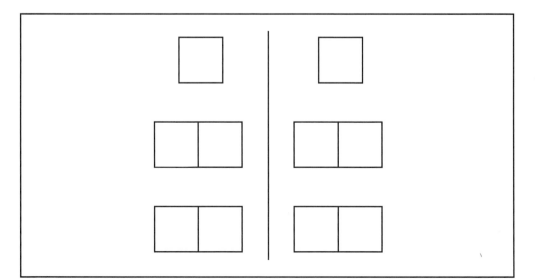

Figure 5.22.

3. **Write and show.** Prerecorded cassette tapes are excellent for practice activities. Use a storyline when possible. For example, "I'm going to tell some number stories that use two-digit numbers. Write any numbers you hear me say. Remember to start with tens. Here's the first story: Mom bought 24 cans of pop." (Turn off the tape while the child is writing.) "Now use tens and ones to show the number you wrote." (Turn off the tape while the child selects the 10-stacks and ones needed.) "How many tens and ones did you use? Listen again if you need to. Check by turning to page A of the answer book." (See Figure 5.23.)

Providing paper with predrawn boxes for children's responses will help avoid random placement of numbers. Also, if a child is highly distractible, setting up a definite workspace is beneficial. Use a plain sheet of paper, a plastic mat, or even a piece of smooth plastic tablecloth for this purpose. Use the workspace to focus the child's attention. "Use tens and ones to show me 24 in your workspace. . . . Good! Now clear your workspace."

- *Variation:* Provide a worksheet correlated to the tape. Have the child circle the correct number: 24 or 42. For the first part of the tape, the tens digit could be color-coded.

4. **Dot to dot.** Provide a prerecorded tape that dictates two-digit numbers, with a pause after each. (If necessary, the tape can be turned off between numbers.) Correlate a dot-to-dot pattern with the tape, so that a picture is formed if the child connects the dots between the numbers dictated. The tape could begin with a reminder to "start with tens." If necessary, the tens place of each two-digit numeral on the dot-to-dot sheet could be written or underlined in green.

5. **Secret message** (optional). Ask the child to number a paper 1 through 9. Now dictate a two-digit number to be written beside each (see Figure 5.24a).

Explain that the two-digit numbers are page numbers in a book. Provide the riddle book and instruct the child to find the penciled letter written beside each page number in order to solve a riddle you have selected from the book.

Figure 5.23.

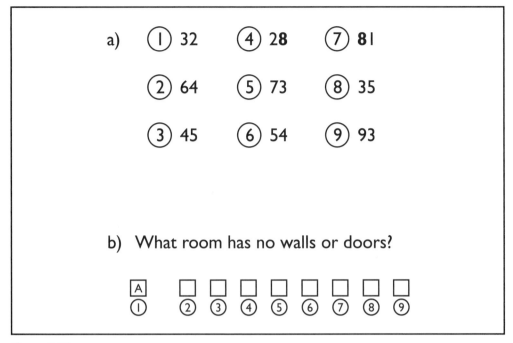

Figure 5.24.

"Look up the first number" (page 32 in Figure 5.24b). "Do you see an A? Write 'A' in the number 1 box on your worksheet. Then look up the other numbers and write down the letters that are next to them. See if you can answer the riddle. Remember to start with tens when looking for pages."

This has proven to be a very motivating activity for students with auditory memory problems, and it is one that can be constructed quickly. Use a riddle book from a public library to help.

NOTE: *For children with spatial or severe visual perception difficulties, the problem numbers may "run together" with other digits in a problem or answer. As a first step to the assignment, have students circle the problem number. Check their work before they proceed.*

Alternately, it may help to provide prenumbered sheets on which the problem numbers are written in a distinctly different color than that to be used by the child. If lined paper is used, skip a line between numbers. Or provide centimeter-grid paper (Figure 5.25) and have the children write dictated numbers in alternate squares. For students with working-memory difficulties it may be necessary to omit worksheets of this type.

6. **Terrible teens!** The naming irregularities of the teens should be pointed out to students:

- 2 tens and 4: "twenty-four" (24)
- 4 tens and 6: "forty-six" (46)
- But 1 ten and 7: "seventeen" (17)

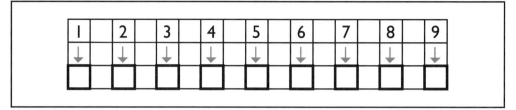

Figure 5.25.

We will start with tens to write teens. It is just that the verbal naming pattern does not hold. We must listen carefully to determine whether the ending is *teen* or *ty*. (The numerals 11 and 12 are in categories all their own.) Worksheets like those of Figure 5.26 can help children focus on the ending.

SKIP COUNTING BY TENS AND FIVES

Problem Area: Not understanding the patterning for continuing counting sequences (e.g., by fives and tens), even though basic place-value concepts are well established.

Typical Disabilities Affecting Progress: Difficulties with abstract reasoning, closure, visual or auditory association or discrimination, expressive language, visual or sequential memory.

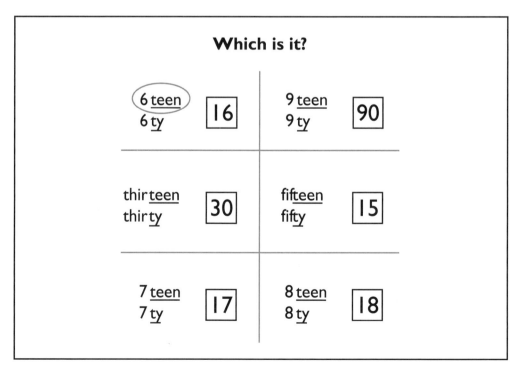

Figure 5.26.

Background: Counting on by fives or tens is useful for mental addition and subtraction, for early multiplication, and for daily situations involving time or money. Some children, however, such as those with any of the disabilities listed above, may be unable to continue even simple counting sequences involving those patterns. Suppose brownies should bake for 25 minutes. Such children may have difficulty counting on from the present time (by fives) to determine when the brownies should be taken from the oven. Likewise, such children may be unable to count or to count on by fives or tens to tell the value of given coins or to check change received. Shifting from counting by tens to counting by fives may also be troublesome. Applying counting skills for mentally computing even simple sums may be difficult.

These children typically fail to make associations and recognize patterns that ordinarily make counting on by skip counting a reasonably simple task. Therefore, special instruction, such as that outlined in the following activities, is required. Rather than basing an activity immediately on numbers, the sequence first involves the child in *patterning*—the root of the processing problem. At first, the child is given simple shapes and visual or auditory cues to help in recognizing and extending a pattern. Then, when the child is successful with number sequences (easily distinguishable numerals), color-coded counting charts are introduced.

✎ Sample Sequence of Activities

1. **Finish the pattern.** Use wood or construction paper circles and squares (circles one color, squares another) to lay out a simple repeating pattern. On slips of paper the same colors as the shapes, trace the dotted outlines of the next two blocks that would occur in the pattern (see Figure 5.27). Have

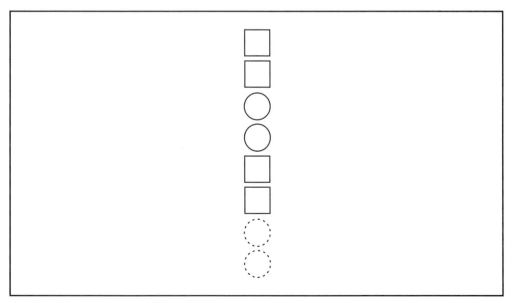

Figure 5.27.

the child name the shapes, in order, so that the child hears the "square, square, circle, circle" pattern. Then ask the child to find the missing blocks and finish the pattern. When all blocks are in place, have the child "read" the pattern (name all the shapes displayed, in order). Finally, ask the child to use the blocks to copy the completed pattern.

- *Follow-up:* Repeat with other patterns, gradually omitting the dotted cue.

2. **Draw it in.** Lay out a simple repeating pattern of squares and circles, as in "Finish the Pattern," but draw the repeating shape pattern on sheets of paper that have extra space. At first, use two different colors for the two shapes and include the dotted outlines. Ask the child to "read" or name the shapes and then complete the pattern. Next ask the child to read aloud the entire pattern. Finally, have the child copy (trace) the completed pattern in the extra space on the paper (using a template, if necessary). Gradually use more difficult patterns, fade the color cueing, and omit the dotted outlines. See if the child can add the next two or three shapes to the pattern without extra prompts. This is usually possible when pattern difficulty is gradually increased along with gradual fading of prompts.

3. **What's next?** Follow the same "read, complete, read again, copy" format of the two preceding activities, but this time use numerals that can be readily distinguished (e.g., see Figure 5.28). Similar cueing techniques can also be used if necessary.

4. **An easy one.** Show the child Figure 5.29 and say, "This is an easy one. Tell me what's alike in the numbers." ("All end in 0.") Then ask the child to read the numbers so that you can hear the auditory pattern. Ask, "What comes next?" ("Seventy.") "How do you know?" ("Seven comes after six.") Have the child finish the sequence and read it aloud. "Look at the numbers so you can visualize them in your head. . . . Now close your eyes and tell me the numbers." Prompt, as necessary, throughout this dialogue. Repeat parts of the dialogue as

7

7

4

4

7

7

Figure 5.28.

10

20

30

40

50

60

Figure 5.29.

necessary. If more patterning work is needed, adapt Activity 7 below to provide practice.

5. **Count on.** Provide dimes the child can use for counting by tens. If necessary, use a counting chart, as shown in Figure 5.30, on which the child lays the dimes while counting. (If a child's money concepts are too weak for this activity, refer to Chapter 4 for suggestions regarding counting coin groups.) Eventually, the child should be able to count by tens independently of the chart.

NOTE: *To prepare for mental math, for counting money amounts and checking change received: Place four dimes on the counting chart and have the child count on by tens from 40¢. Repeat, but vary the number of dimes initially placed on the chart.*

6. **To 100.** (Prerequisite: The child must be able to count meaningfully to 10. It is also assumed that the numeration instruction summarized in the "Reversals" section of this chapter has been carried out.) Show the color-coded counting chart of Figure 5.31. This chart is sequenced vertically rather than horizontally, as is commonly the case. Experience has shown that a vertical presentation makes it easier for children to see the patterning of the number sequence.

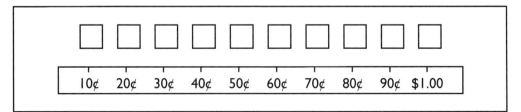

Figure 5.30.

0	10	20	30	40	50	60	70	80	90	100
1	11	21	31	41	51	61	71	81	91	
2	12	22	32	42	52	62	72	82		
3	13	23	33	43	53	63				
4	14	24	34	44						
5	15	25	35							
6	16									
7	17									
8	18									
9	19									

10s = green
1s = red

Figure 5.31.

Have the child count by tens *across* the columns. Now mask out all but the first column (0–9) and have the child read it aloud. Then slide the mask so that the first two columns show. Discuss how the second column is like the first. (The ones column in both is the standard counting sequence. This can be related to the idea of one more, as described earlier.) Have the child note that all numbers in the second column begin with 1—"This is the teen column." Count from 1 with the child, emphasizing the "teen" endings of the last numbers read. Slide the mask again to reveal the third column—"This is the twenties column." Have the child read the numbers in the incomplete column. Then ask, "What numbers come next?" Write down the numbers as the child orally continues the counting sequence to 29, prompting as necessary. For this, as for other columns of the chart, the child can be shown how the standard counting sequence of the ones digits will help.

Later, retrace the tens digits with green, recounting aloud with the child to emphasize the "20" part of each number named. Have the child finger-trace the first digits during an independent recount if that helps. Let the child, eyes closed, count the twenties aloud. Then ask the child to choose a number in a preceding column and count on from there—first using the chart, then looking away. Stress the 19–20 column shift. Repeat for other columns during this or follow-up sessions. Make the chart available to the child for reference. Use it as long as needed during review sessions in which the child either counts aloud or writes the numbers in sequence.

■ *Follow-up Activity 1:* Reinforce the tens transition with repeated oral work. First the teacher says a few patterns, emphasizing the switch. Then the student completes the patterns started by the teacher, as in the following examples:

- Teacher: "Nineteen—twenty . . . thirty-nine—forty . . . eighty-nine—ninety"

- Teacher: "Twenty-nine."
  Student: "Thirty."
  Teacher: "Sixty-nine."
  Student: "Seventy."

■ *Follow-up Activity 2:* When the auditory pattern for sequential count-ing is established, use objects (tens and ones) to dramatize and rein-force the meaning of the oral count. For example: Lay out 2 tens and one (to represent 21). Say to the student, "I will add chips, one at a time. Count aloud so we can keep track of the number of chips that are on the table at one time." (See Figure 5.32.) Repeat, varying the num-ber of tens and ones initially placed on the table.

NOTE: *It may now be necessary to review concepts and skills for comparing and ordering two-digit numbers. Suggestions from the following section, "Com-paring Numbers," can be adapted to this purpose.*

7. **By fives.** Use a worksheet similar to that shown in Figure 5.33 to lay the groundwork for the patterning involved in skip counting by fives. Following the sequence of patterns on the worksheet, first review the easier patterns with shapes, then turn to the numbers used when counting by fives.

Next show Figure 5.34 (the tens digits are coded green). Ask the child to read the column and then describe any patterns seen (the numbers end in 5 or 0; in the tens place there are two 1s, then two 2s). In order to see these patterns, some children may need to cover first the ones column and then the tens column with a card.

Ask the child, "What two numbers would come next?" Write them down as the child says them: 30, 35. Prompt if necessary. Discuss why those two num-bers were chosen. Then have the child say all the numbers aloud, continuing the count as far as possible (up to 100). Write down the numbers as the child gives the extended count. Underscore the tens digits in green if that helps

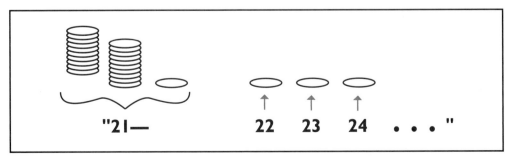

Figure 5.32.

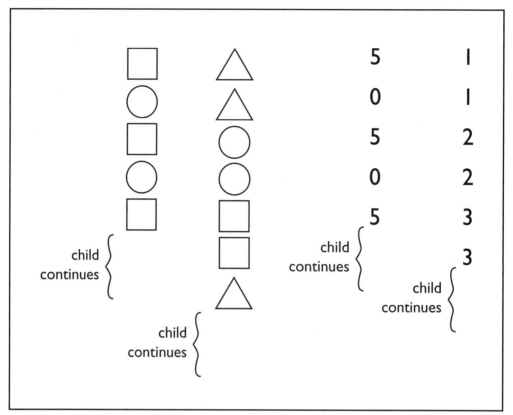

Figure 5.33.

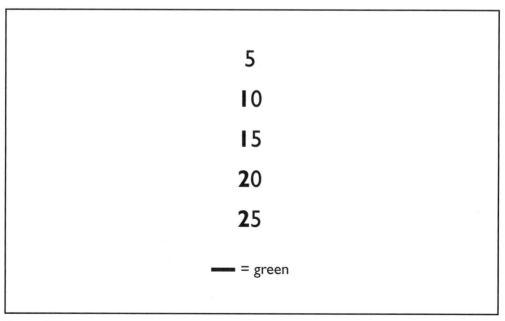

Figure 5.34.

to cue additional entries in the sequence. Then see if the child can repeat the counting pattern without looking at the chart. Make the chart available to the child for future reference and continue to use it as needed during review sessions.

8. **Nickel countdown.** Adapt "Count On" (Activity 5 above) to counting by fives with nickels. Note that the idea of counting by fives and tens can be extended to include (a) counting on from clock times, or (b) using nickels and dimes first to count by fives, then switching to counting by tens (and vice versa). The latter skill is often needed for counting money amounts or checking change received.

NOTE: *Follow-up activity 1 for "Turn Over" on page 155, as well as dot-to-dot patterns, can be used to reinforce most of the activities of this section.*

9. **Count on by tens, fives, and ones.** As confidence in counting by tens and fives is achieved, help students apply that learning to counting a mix of dimes, nickels, and pennies. The "Count On" activities (Activity 5) above can be extended for this purpose. It helps to take 3 minutes two to three times a week to develop this skill. Start a count and have children echo it—for example: "We'll count by tens, then shift to counting by fives: 30—40, 50, 60 (pause), 65, 70, 75."

NOTE: *Gradually extend to counting patterns that include tens, fives, and ones. Sometimes active hand movements help: spires for tens (up-down strokes), bumps for fives (left to right curved movements), and dots for ones.*

COMPARING NUMBERS

Problem Area: Difficulty recognizing the greater of two numbers or correctly using greater than (>) and less than (<) symbols. (The use of these symbols is not recommended for all children and should not be used in lower grades if it can be avoided.)

Typical Disabilities Affecting Progress: Difficulties with abstract reasoning, visual discrimination, visual association, spatial organization, visual memory.

Background: When comparing numbers less than 10, a standard approach is to examine the linear sequence of digits with children and note that: "When you count, the numbers that mean *more* come after others in the count." The first set of activities below suggests ways of prefacing this instruction to build a better conception of *more* (or *less*) for numbers up to 10.

When comparing numbers greater than 10, children typically may be asked to model the numbers with tens and ones aids and to match them one to one as in Figure 5.35. The focus is on starting big, with the tens (or hundreds) to compare. Many children with the disabilities identified above can understand comparison illustrated in this manner. Difficulties arise when materials are no longer used; when children are expected to use the less than and greater than symbols and fail to associate any meaning with them; or when children

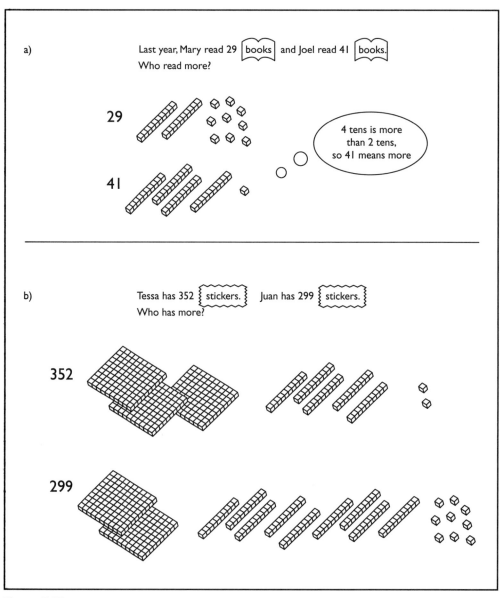

Figure 5.35.

incorrectly interpret the signs due to visual perceptual difficulties. Some reverse the symbols when writing them. Others forget which means which.

More important than the formal comparison symbols is the basic idea of which means more. As a daily living skill, this concept is a critical one. It enters into shopping—determining whether one has enough money to buy what is needed—and a myriad of other common situations. The important point of the second set of activities in the following sequence is to help students to compare larger numbers even when materials are no longer used. The use of symbols is secondary and in some individual cases would be omitted.

✎ Sample Sequence of Activities

▶ Comparing Numbers to 10

Prerequisite skill: Understanding the concepts *before* and *after* both orally and visually.

1. **Make Partners.** A first basic activity is to have children take two hand-fuls of objects or cubes (up to 10 in each hand) and lay them out or stack them up so that visual comparison is easy. Matching one to one, children can "make partners" with the counters and observe: "The side or stack with extras has more" (Figure 5.36). Consistently and repeatedly, this verbal observation should be stated—both by the teacher and by the child: "The side with extras has more." The child can write or circle the greater number each time.

2. **"Comes after" in the count.** After repeatedly matching and writing to record the comparison of two numbers as above, the link to the counting sequence can be made. Simply ask children to write the numbers 1 to 10 at the top of a sheet of paper, or to use their ruler. Call out two one-digit numbers and ask, "Which is greater?" If the child does not know, small counters can be used, as in Figure 5.36, to "match partners" to answer the question. If the child does respond correctly, it still is useful occasionally to "match partners," as shown, to reinforce correct thinking. Commentary to be repeated in this activity is: "Yes, and did you notice that the greater number comes *after* the others in the

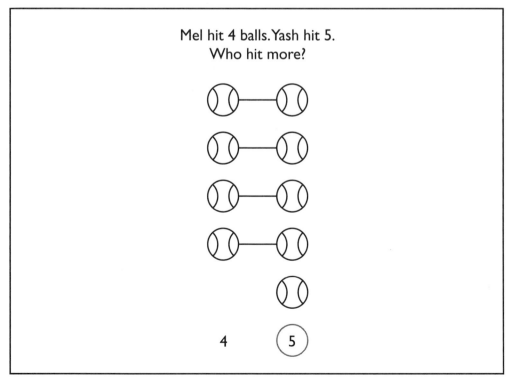

Figure 5.36.

count?" Relate this idea to the sequence of pages in a book. (See the note to Activity 1 in the following section.) *When children can comfortably identify the greater of two numbers, then parallel activities focusing on less or fewer than can be presented.*

▶ **Comparing Multidigit Numbers**

Prerequisite skills:

- Strong place-value understanding of the numbers involved, as suggested under "Background" in the "Reversals" section earlier in this chapter.

- Prior work with grouping aids, as in Figure 5.35, for comparing two- and three-digit numbers.

- Ability to use *more* and *less* to compare one-digit numbers.

- Understanding the concepts of *before* and *after.*

1. **See it.** Orally present two- or three-digit numbers with different first digits. Provide students with a measuring tape or number line paper, as in Figure 5.37. Have them write the numbers in the correct section of the number line. They can then fill in the sentence (Figure 5.37a) or use symbols (Figure 5.37b), whichever is appropriate.

NOTE: *This activity is a good starting point for students with spatial problems, as it allows them to see that the greater number always comes after the other one in the count. When the numbers are "far apart" in the counting sequence, it is not practical to rely on counting alone to determine a comparison. Instead, the more general tactic of comparing the greater-valued digits in the numbers (e.g., tens to tens, or hundreds to hundreds) is far more useful because: "The numbers compare the way the digits compare." Aligning numbers under each other, color-cueing, or finger-tracing lead digits in like positions is used throughout these activities to emphasize this approach. The link to the counting sequence is then made, often with the help of a library book or textbook.*

2. **More tens.** Present two two- or three-digit numbers with different first digits, as in Figure 5.38a. Have the children use materials (tens and ones chips) to represent each number (Figure 5.38b). Underscore the first digit of each number in green and discuss how you always "start big" to compare. Be sure children recognize that the larger number has more tens than the smaller number. Using the example in Figure 5.38, you could say, "Yes, 3 tens is more than 2 tens, so 32 is more (greater) than 24. And, when you count, the number that is 'more' always comes after the other number." Repeat with other numbers.

3. **Feel it.** To reinforce the "more than" idea and to review the meaning of "less than," pose a situation where _____ and _____ (use names of people the children know) are reading the same book. Write two two- or three-digit numbers with different first digits on the board, representing the pages the two people are on, and ask students to compare their locations in the book (see Figure 5.39)—"Who has read more pages?" Underscore the first digit of the numbers in green and have students note the location of the numbers in the book.

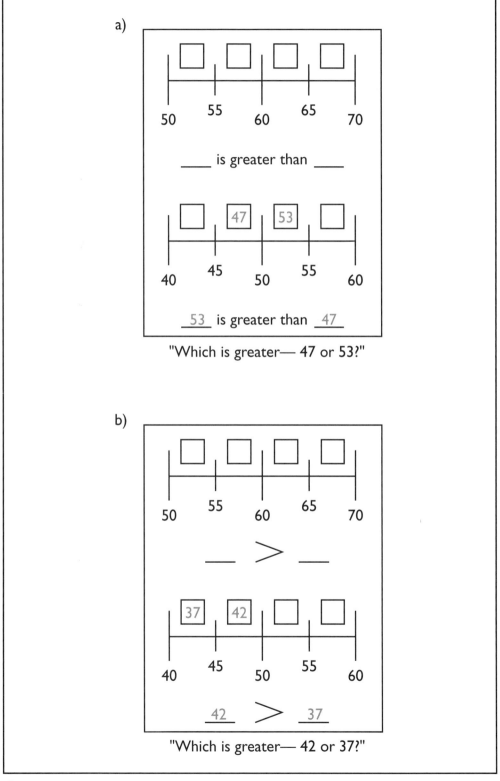

Figure 5.37.

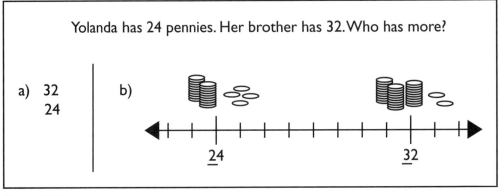

Figure 5.38.

Place markers at each page, close the book, and have students feel which number of pages is less. Repeat with other page numbers.

4. **Match and check.** Choose the approach from Activities 2 and 3 that seems to be the most effective. Use two- or three-digit numbers as in Activity 1.

• Write two numbers on the board. Have the children copy them onto a worksheet illustration where they "belong." For example, they are given 118 and 231, and they write those numbers on a drawing of book pages to show which means more and which means less, as in Figure 5.40. Discuss why 231 means more pages and have students feel the difference in thickness between the two groups of pages in an actual book.

• Cut out worksheet illustrations as described above and glue them onto cards (Figure 5.41). Write two numbers (in random order) on the other side of each card (the front). Underscore the first digit if necessary. Each child should also have a sheet of paper divided into two columns with the headings "Larger number" and "Smaller number." The children should then use each card in the following manner: (a) Study the numbers on the front; (b) close their eyes to imag-

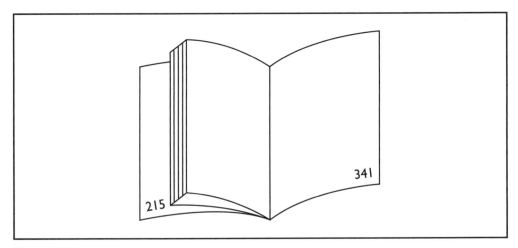

Figure 5.39.

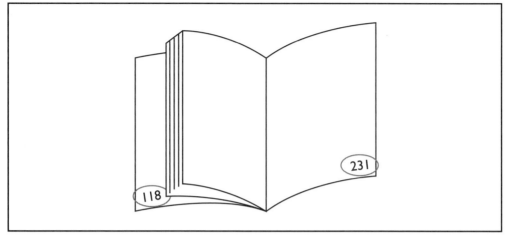

Figure 5.40.

ine what the numbers look like; (c) write the numbers in the correct columns on the sheet of paper; and (d) turn the card over to check the answer.

5. **Alligator Al.** Use auditory and tactile cues to help students attach meaning to the comparison symbols. For example, make an alligator hand puppet with its mouth clearly outlined, as illustrated in Figure 5.42a. Use two different colors and textures. Carry through the storyline that Alligator Al is always hungry and always reaches for the greatest number. Make a poster or file card miniature of Al's two views for students. Provide sandpaper and felt symbols to be placed between numbers as you show students how to position and read the symbols (Figure 5.42b).

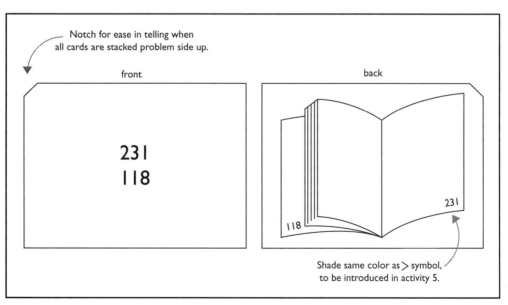

Figure 5.41.

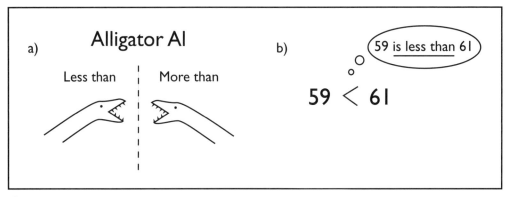

Figure 5.42.

Use two two- or three-digit numbers with different first digits. Invite the children to finger-trace the symbol while reading the comparison. For some number pairs, ask the children to retell Alligator Al's story (he always reaches for the greatest number). It is sometimes necessary to have children verbalize an association to make sure they grasp and retain it.

6. **More comparisons.**

- Dictate two numbers, a two- and a three-digit number, for children to write on dotted lines as in Figure 5.43. Discuss why the two-digit number is placed on the last two lines (no hundreds). Write a dotted zero in the hundreds place, if necessary, to help students with the comparison. Referring to Figure 5.43, you might note: "You always start big to compare. Here, 'big' means hundreds. *One* hundred is more than *no* hundreds, so *1*34 is more than 53." Repeat with other numbers. Use worksheet exercises to reinforce. At this point, the children could simply circle a number to indicate which number is more (or less).

- Adapt the above activity to focus on two two- or three-digit numbers that have the same first digits (e.g., 46, 49; 258, 262). Explain to the children, "You always start big to compare. If the digits are alike, you compare the next two" (Figure 5.44).

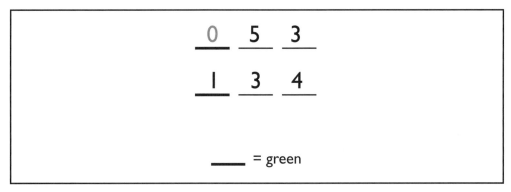

Figure 5.43.

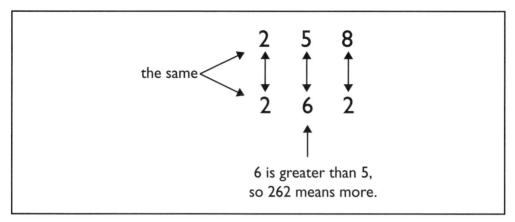

Figure 5.44.

- Provide mixed review exercises that require students to use symbols for comparing all types of two- and three-digit numbers.

ROUNDING AND ESTIMATION

Problem Area: Difficulty rounding two- and three-digit numbers to the nearest 10 or 100.

Typical Disabilities Affecting Progress: Difficulties with visual perception (figure-ground, visual discrimination), visual or sequential memory, abstract reasoning, or auditory processing.

Background: Most day-to-day work with numbers involves some sort of estimation, which generally means rounding numbers. Clearly, the ability to round numbers is a functional skill, often underestimated in importance. Since it is a difficult skill to teach, it is frequently avoided, especially with students who have trouble learning.

Mathematicians use one rounding "rule": look to the digit after. If it is 5 or more, round up; otherwise, round down. Social scientists sometimes use a different rule, one that is based on whether the number after is odd or even. In school, the mathematician guideline typically is adopted. Nonetheless, it is worthwhile discussing with students that the rule or procedure for rounding may differ across teachers.

✎ Sample Sequence of Activities

1. **Feel the line.** Have the students position the number to be rounded on a number line. (At first, do not use a number ending in 5.) For example, 53 would be placed on the line as shown in Figure 5.45a. Have students visually inspect the distance from the number to either end of the line and then slide a finger along the line to each end to feel the distance.

NOTE: *If students are strong tactual learners, make the number line longer to involve more gross-motor skill, or texturize the line. Have them close their eyes as they slide a finger to either end of the line.*

As students inspect and feel the line, relate the idea of nearest endpoint to the concept and vocabulary of rounding numbers. "Sometimes exact numbers are not needed. A close estimate will do. We often round numbers when we talk. For example, if 28 people came to a party, we might say: 'About 30 people were there.'"

Relate looking and sliding backward on the number line to rounding down; and looking and sliding forward to rounding up. In the party example, we rounded up. Later, extend to other number lines that involve other choices, as in Figure 5.45b.

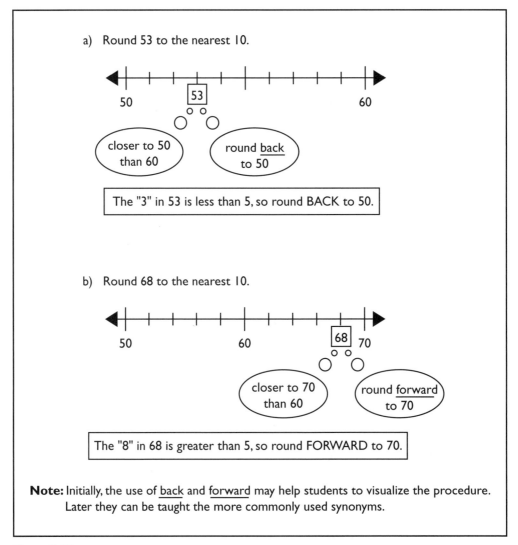

a) Round 53 to the nearest 10.

closer to 50 than 60

round back to 50

The "3" in 53 is less than 5, so round BACK to 50.

b) Round 68 to the nearest 10.

closer to 70 than 60

round forward to 70

The "8" in 68 is greater than 5, so round FORWARD to 70.

Note: Initially, the use of back and forward may help students to visualize the procedure. Later they can be taught the more commonly used synonyms.

Figure 5.45.

Gradually include numbers ending in 5 and introduce the convention of rounding used in mathematics: "To round, examine the digit after. If less than 5, round down (backward); if 5 or greater, round up (forward)."

NOTE: *It is sometimes helpful to use a series of undulating hills and a story line based on* The Little Engine That Could *instead of a flat number line. For the hill rising between 50 and 60, for example, 55 is at the top. Just like the Little Engine, until you get to the top (55), it's easy to slide back—to 50. Once at the top or beyond, you'd go forward—like the Little Engine—to 60.*

2. **A fast dime.** (Rounding to the nearest tenth. Small-group, teacher-led activity appropriate for students who cannot effectively use a number line.) Provide two decks of cards: a "banker's deck" and a "fast-dime" deck (see Figure 5.46). Place the banker's deck in a bank box along with extra dimes and pennies. This deck contains one card for each multiple of 10¢ (to 90¢). The fast-dime deck contains cards that list amounts between 11¢ and 89¢, but no multiples of 10¢ are included. Until the students understand the activity, also remove all money amounts ending in 5 from the fast-dime deck.

Shuffle the fast-dime deck and place it face down between the players. Students take turns drawing the top card from the deck and placing it face up in the playing area. They then use dimes (as many as possible) and extra pennies to show the amount on the card.

The banker selects the two cards from the banker's deck that are closest in value to that displayed (see Figure 5.47). The child must decide how a "fast dime" can be made. In the example from Figure 5.47, is 34¢ closer to 30¢ or to 40¢? The child must either add extra pennies to the 34¢ pile or take some away to indicate the choice made. Thus, either 6 pennies are added (to make 40¢) or 4 pennies are taken away (leaving 30¢). The latter decision earns the child one point, since it involves the least number of coins. When the students are comfortable handling these tasks, return the money amounts ending in 5 to the deck. Introduce the "banker's rule" that for these cards the "fast dime" is always the greater 10¢ value.

- *Follow-up 1:* Lay out cards from the fast-dime deck, one at a time, and have the students verbalize the fact that, for example, 34¢ is closer to

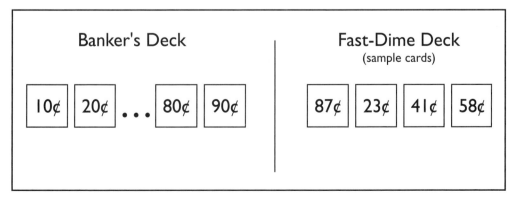

Figure 5.46.

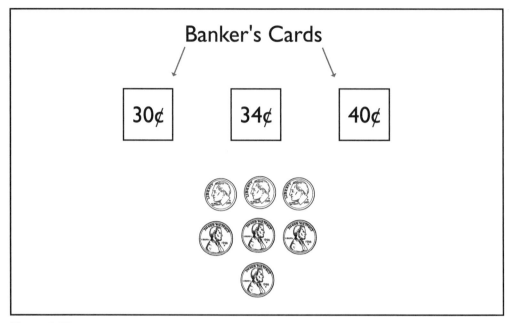

Figure 5.47.

30¢ than to 40¢. Allow the students to use dimes and pennies to verify this if necessary.

NOTE: *Be sure students understand what rounding means: when rounding, all digits beyond the digit one is rounding to will be zeros; when rounding to the nearest ten, for example, the ones digit will always be zero. Before rounding, the number after the digit one is rounding to is used to determine whether that digit will be changed to one higher (rounded up) or kept the same (rounded down). Use bills—hundreds, tens, and ones—to help students round three-digit numbers to the lead digit. Gradually eliminate cent or dollar signs on the cards as a transition to rounding any two- and three-digit numbers. If students hesitate during game play, provide practice, prior to another game, using matching money cards as in Figure 5.48, as that usually triggers the correct idea. Also allow students to use money to check as needed.*

3. **Color cue.** Help students focus attention on the "thinking digit" (the number after the digit one is rounding to) by color highlighting, as in Figure 5.49—the thinking digit (4) in green and the "changing digit" (6) in red.

4. **Nearer to.** Use number lines the length of a standard sheet of paper (Figure 5.50a) and premade worksheets that can be filled in (Figure 5.50b) to help students locate the nearer ten.

5. **Focus here.** Adapt the preceding sequence (Activities 1–4 above) to rounding larger numbers and to rounding within numbers. The following idea may help students who understand the concept but have figure-ground difficulties. Using problems like the one in Figure 5.51 help children focus on the correct digit by highlighting the thinking digit (8) in green, the changing digit (5), *and the corresponding word* (ten) in red.

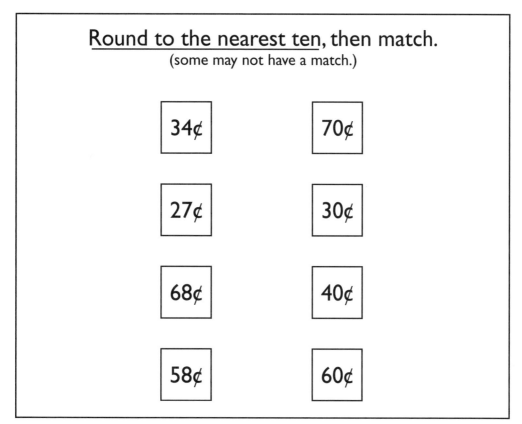

Figure 5.48.

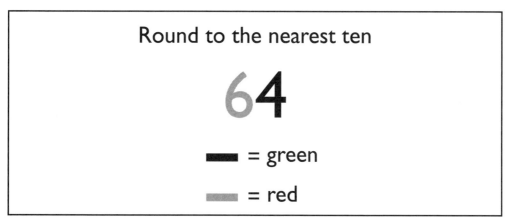

Figure 5.49.

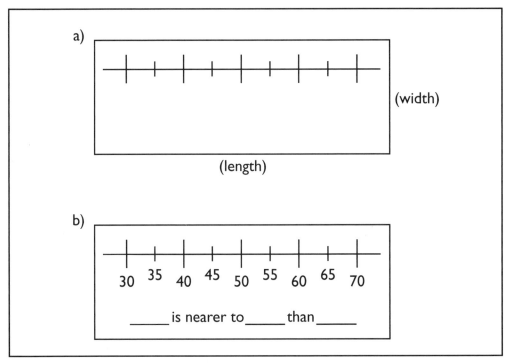

a)

(width)

(length)

b)

30 35 40 45 50 55 60 65 70

_____ is nearer to _____ than _____

Figure 5.50.

READING AND INTERPRETING QUANTITATIVE DATA FROM THE PRINTED WORD

Problem Area: Interpreting visually and orally presented numerical information.

Typical Disabilities Affecting Progress: Difficulty with abstract reasoning, auditory processing, the ability to generalize information, receptive and expressive language, visual memory, nonverbal learning disabilities.

Background: When they are still at a very early age, we help children begin to see the relationship between the spoken word and the written word. Often, however, we neglect to devote the same attention to helping them understand the relationship between numerical concepts and symbols, and oral and written language. Especially for students with visual memory or visual perceptual difficulties, nonverbal learning disabilities, and receptive or expressive

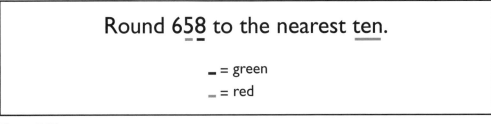

Round 6<u>5</u>8 to the nearest ten.

_ = green

_ = red

Figure 5.51.

language difficulties, confusion in this area can be problematic. Mathematics involves more than numbers; in fact, in today's technological world manipulating numbers can often be done much more rapidly and efficiently using calculators. Knowing when and how to use the available tools, however, involves language.

Many factors influence a child's success in reading and writing numbers. The ability to generalize is essential since, frequently, children hear familiar (mathematical) words. Even the individual numbers, 1 through 9, can have a variety of meanings depending on their use. Sometimes *4* means a quantity of items. At other times it identifies the place value in a larger number. Sometimes a word that sounds the same is used as a preposition and can also mean *pro*, as in "I am for vacations!" Interpreting quantitative data used in charts and diagrams involves a strong sense of language in order to visualize and understand the numerical representations. The following is just a brief list of ideas the authors have used to improve students' ability to use language successfully. They are meant to be stepping stones to other ideas and to an increased awareness on the teacher's part of the need to actively incorporate language into mathematics instruction.

Sample Sequence of Activities

1. **Associate.** Provide students with ample opportunity to associate numerical symbols with what they hear and see. Instead of using word problems in which the numbers are written as numerals, use problems in which everything is in words and have the students first "decode" the words by rewriting the problems using numerals.

NOTE: *Students with fine-motor difficulties might only be asked to cross out the word and write the number above the word. For others, however, the copying (or typing) provides extra reinforcement.*

2. **They're all around.** Encourage the students to "listen for all the math around us." Break a hundreds chart into groups of ten. Each student could be assigned one of the groups, with the goal of the day being to write down whatever is heard that is related to a number in his or her group. The numbers should be written across the top edge of a piece of lined paper that has been turned sideways, and whenever a child hears something related to that number, he or she can write the word or draw a picture in the column under the number; if writing is difficult, the child could use a tape recorder and dictate what has been heard.

3. **Explain it.** Using charts and tables from the newspaper, have the children make up stories about them. They could do this in groups or individually, depending on their interests, abilities and disabilities, and confidence. At first, and especially for younger students, omit the explanations and have students use their accurate narration skills to tell a story that goes along with the chart.

NOTE: *The goal of this assignment is to better understand the relationship between numbers and language. Some students may easily and willingly be able* *to write stories. Others may prefer to dictate or draw a picture. Accept whatever presentation method is the child's strong area.*

WRITING MATHEMATICS

Problem area: Difficulty writing multidigit numbers.

Typical Disabilities Affecting Progress: Difficulties with visual perception (figure-ground, visual discrimination, visual sequencing), visual association, closure, abstract reasoning, or auditory processing.

Background: Coupled with the need for understanding the language components in math is the need to be able to accurately associate what is heard and/ or seen with the ability to write a number. The opportunity to use materials such as those illustrated in Figure 5.52 to solve a wide variety of interesting problem situations is beneficial for helping students develop better intuitions

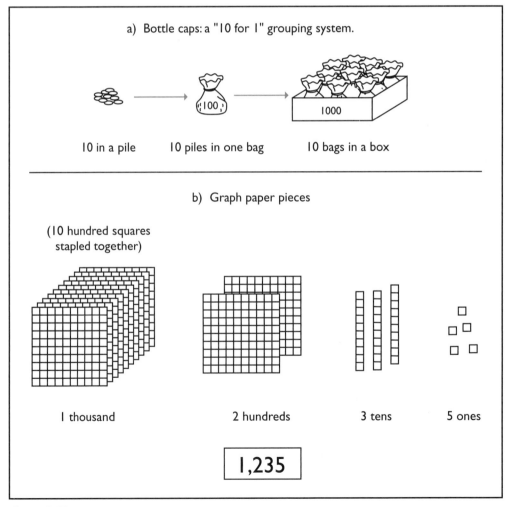

a) Bottle caps: a "10 for 1" grouping system.

10 in a pile   10 piles in one bag   10 bags in a box

b) Graph paper pieces

(10 hundred squares stapled together)

1 thousand   2 hundreds   3 tens   5 ones

1,235

Figure 5.52.

for large numbers. Using such materials often precludes common difficulties, such as writing "20038" for 238 or reading 415 as "forty-one five"—or at least establishes a basis for treatment when such difficulties do emerge.

To remedy the first problem, for example, ask a child to gather 2 hundreds, 3 tens, and 8 singles from a box of graph paper pieces. After the number of each kind of piece is recorded (Figure 5.53), the teacher might write the number in standard form and "model" the way it should be read. Teacher and child could then switch roles. As a follow-up, the procedure could be reversed: Start with a three-digit number card, read it, and show the number with graph paper pieces (Figure 5.54). In our experience it helps if students conclude that a three-digit number "talks about" *hundreds* and can be shown by three kinds of blocks. Stamps for hundreds, tens, and ones, available from many school supply companies, can also be used for this purpose. They should be among the teaching aids of every classroom in which mathematics is taught. (See Appendix at back of book.)

Correct teacher modeling may also be necessary to prevent children from reading 238 as "two hundred *and* thirty-eight." The *and* is properly reserved for the decimal point, as in $2.38 (two dollars and 38 cents) or 4.2 (four and two-tenths). Exception should be made, of course, for those few students who may need to use *and* as a pause for remembering how to group digits for reading a number. Using *and* in that manner is a crutch that should be discarded when it is no longer needed. (This situation parallels that of using "uh" or pausing to keep from stuttering.)

For students who read 415 as "forty-one five," underlining the hundreds digit sometimes helps, as in the following examples:

$$\underline{4}15 \longrightarrow \text{"4 hundred 15"}$$
$$\underline{2}13 \longrightarrow \text{"2 hundred 23"}$$

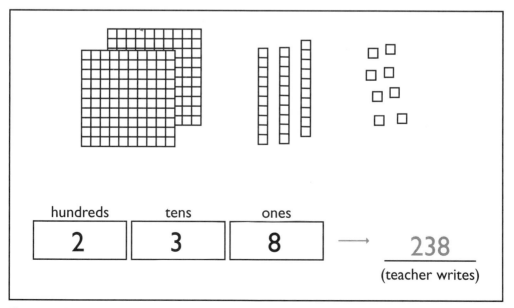

Figure 5.53.

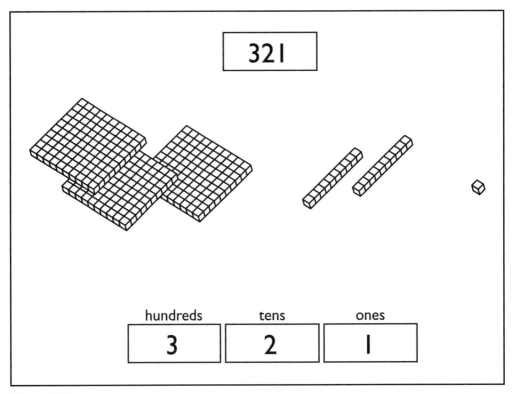

Figure 5.54.

Teachers might point out that the only new part is the first digit. Students already know how to read the rest. Provide a card for the child to move along, as in syllabicating, while reading the number.

Whenever possible, it is far better to embed number work and related problems in interesting or familiar contexts, rather than presenting them in isolation. Carefully selected applied or game settings tend to invite children's curiosity and interest and hence better nurture their place-value understanding and development of number sense. For example, as part of a unit on tropical rain forests, students might learn that, above the forest floor, the understory layer (smaller trees and bushes) might reach as high as 80 feet, the canopy (main tree) layer might reach 50 feet above that, and, finally, several giant trees in the emergent layer might be seen towering as high as 30 feet above everything else. Students might use materials (of their choice) to determine the height of some of the tallest trees in the rain forest. Or, using the fact that it rains almost every day of the year in a rain forest—or up to 400 inches each year—students might use materials to help provide information for a graph of the total amount of rain that might fall in a rain forest over 2 years (800 inches), 3 years (1,200 inches), and 4 years (1,600 inches).

If the students have difficulty as they begin to work with larger numbers or to interpret quantitative data in printed material, more specialized techniques may be necessary. Several helpful techniques are outlined in the suggestions that follow.

✎ Sample Sequence of Activities

▶ Reading and Writing Four- and Five-Digit Numbers

Prerequisite skills:

- Ability to read and write three-digit numbers. This includes a firm grasp of place-value ideas for three-digit numbers, including the understanding that when you hear the word *hundreds*, the number has three digits and that sometimes a zero is needed to show no tens or ones, as in 403 and 620.

- Prior work modeling four-digit numbers with graph paper pieces (refer to Figure 5.52b).

1. **Look!** As a first step, present number pairs visually (Figure 5.55). The thousands digit is green; all others are red. Explain that one comma in a number is read "thousand." The only new part comes before the comma—"You already know how to read the rest." Have children finger-trace the part that is the same within the pair, then read both numbers. Use no zeros in the hundreds place at this time.

NOTE: *Do not use colored digits with children having closure difficulties to avoid activating their tendency to treat multidigit numbers as a series of disjointed, unrelated digits. If some kind of highlighting is needed, underline the digits as in the example below:*

"*Read this: 423.*"

"*Now read this: 1,423.*"

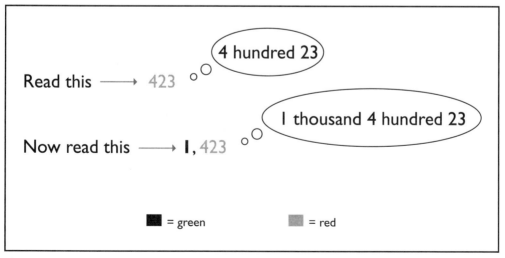

Figure 5.55.

Generally, this approach can be used any time and, except in severe cases, works as effectively as color-coded digits. As an alternative, use no colors. Have the child use a card as when learning to syllabicate (see Figure 5.56).

2. **Word match.** If the children can read number words, written practice exercises like those in Figure 5.57 can be given. The skill being reinforced is used in writing checks. In addition, the exercise prepares the child for the dictation in Activity 4 below ("Hear and Find"). The number of thousands is written in green to match the green underlining of the thousands place. The three-digit part, both underlining and words, is in red. The word *thousand* and the comma are the same color, so the children learn to associate the two. Later, when they need to learn to place the comma themselves, the format can be modified as in the second example of Figure 5.57.

3. **Find it.** Have children match color-coded words (as in Figure 5.57) to numbers that are not color-coded.

▪ *Follow-up:* Same type of match exercises but without any colors.

4. **Hear and find**. Call out four-digit numbers and have the children circle them from a group of numbers. Include three-digit distractors. At first, use color-coding as before.

5. **Zero holds the place.** Dictate "seventy-three," for example, and ask children to write the number on the dotted lines on their worksheet (Figure 5.58a). Discuss why the digits are placed in the last two spots. (No hundreds.) Explain that in larger numbers, zero in any place-value position is used to indicate that there are no groups of that place-value size. For example, 2,073 means "2 thousands, no hundreds, 7 tens, and 3 ones" (Figure 5.58b). Have the children then use base-10 blocks to verify the "match" between digits and blocks needed to represent the number. Present color-coded number pairs for children to read (the thousands digit green; the hundreds digit red). This time focus on four-digit numbers having zero in the hundreds place.

6. **More hear and find.** Adapt Activity 4 above to focus on four-digit numbers having a zero. Include numbers with zero in the tens place and the hundreds place, as well as numbers without any zeros. When the exercise is complete, have the children read aloud the four-digit numbers they circled.

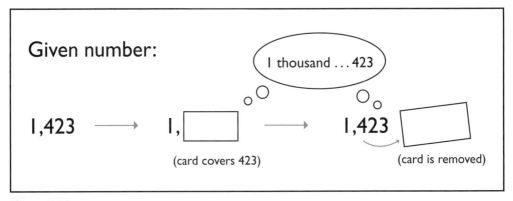

Given number:

I thousand . . . 423

1,423 ⟶ I,☐ ⟶ 1,423 ☐

(card covers 423)　　　　　(card is removed)

Figure 5.56.

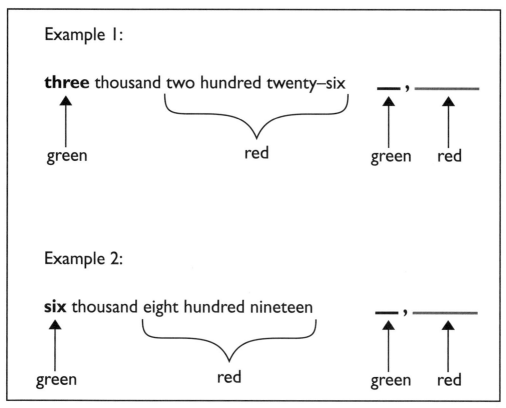

Figure 5.57.

7. **Tape it to me.** Dictate four-digit numbers and have the children write them. Alternatively, have the children play a prerecorded tape that dictates the numbers. Responses can be checked against an answer key.

NOTE: *Ideas from the preceding activities can be adapted to help students read and write larger numbers. A card chart such as that illustrated in Figure 5.59 is also useful. Within each period, the child reads the familiar one-, two-, or three-digit number and adds the "family" name (i.e., the name of the period). Except*

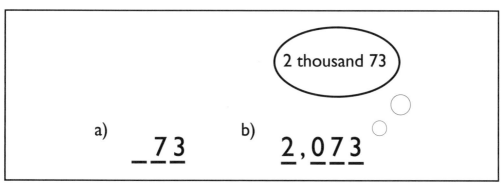

Figure 5.58.

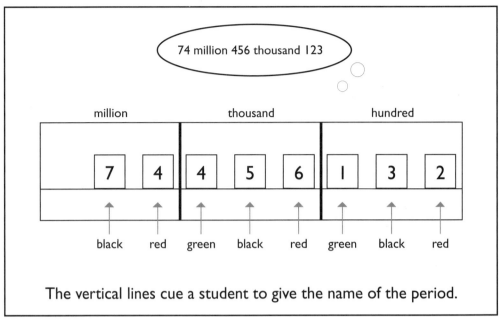

The vertical lines cue a student to give the name of the period.

Figure 5.59.

for students with closure difficulties, a green-black-red color-coding of digits within each period can be used to emphasize the idea. The chart can later be extended and used for reading decimals.

A pleated modification of the chart in Figure 5.59 is illustrated in Figure 5.60. Children enjoy "opening" a number at the comma to check that they are reading it correctly. Cover the writing surfaces with clear contact paper and use a wipe-off pen or pencil so that the digits can easily be changed.

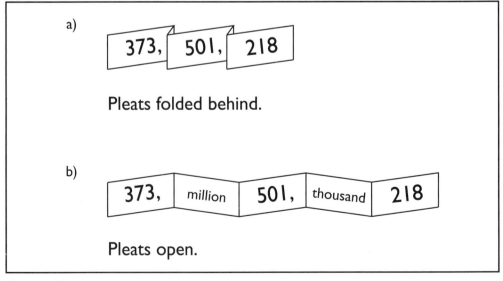

Figure 5.60.

USING TECHNOLOGY

Microcomputer and calculator tools have appropriate uses for enhancing foundational work in the areas of number sense, number, and place-value learnings. The suggestions of Chapter 3 have broad implications for this integration of technology with instruction.

Microcomputer software is readily accessible through educational supply companies. Some good shareware is also available on the Internet. Examples relevant to the topic of this chapter include:

Program	**Publisher/Distributor**
Math Tek	WBGU-TV
What Do You Do with a Broken Calculator	Sunburst
Number Connections	Sunburst/Wings for Learning
Grouping and Place Value	Sunburst
Math Keys: Whole Numbers	KnowledgeAdventure
Hands on Math	Ventura Educational Systems
Math Concepts in Motion: Number Sense	Gamco

Calculators can also be used to reinforce certain number learnings and to build visual and auditory memory skills. A large-key desk calculator may be helpful for students with motor difficulties. Those students and those with memory deficits may need to select a printing calculator so they can use a printed tape for reference when they lose their place or need to check for possible miskeying.

Since some students with learning disabilities have difficulty merely locating the numbers on a calculator, teachers must check for the following prerequisites before requiring calculator use:

- Students should be able to discriminate among the numerals and locate the numbers on the calculator. (Calculators with earphones and an auditory output may help.)

- Students should have sufficient eye-hand coordination to punch the correct keys. (The larger-key desk calculator with printing capabilities, mentioned above, may make calculator use possible.)

When these prerequisites are met, exercises such as the following can be carried out with a basic four-function calculator—one that has arithmetic logic and hence can complete the counting functions of example 5, below:

Example 1 (visual memory): Provide a list of numbers for the children to enter. For multidigit numbers, encourage them to look at, then punch, the *entire* number (or at least as many digits as they can) without looking back.

Example 2 (visual memory): Provide a list of number pairs. The children enter the greatest (or least) of each pair, then check against a key.

Example 3 (auditory memory): Dictate a number (or use a prerecorded tape). Have the children punch in the number, then compare it with a key. In early phases of the activity children with severe problems may be allowed to write the number before entering it.

Example 4 (auditory memory): Dictate a number (or use a prerecorded tape). Have the children enter the number that would follow it, then check with a key.

Example 5 (visual association): Show students how to skip count, count on, or count back using a calculator. For example, to skip count by tens on most calculators, the following sequence can be entered: 10 + = = = until the desired target number is reached. To count on *by* tens from a given start number (e.g., 40), children can enter the start number and proceed as before (e.g., 40 + 10 = = =) until the desired target or stop number is reached. To *count back* by ones from a given start number (e.g., 12), children can enter the start number, subtract 1, and press the equal key (e.g., 12 – 1 = = =) until the desired stop number is reached.

Chapter 6

◆　◆　◆　◆　◆　◆　◆　◆　◆　◆　◆　◆　◆　◆　◆　◆　◆

Concepts and Computation of Whole Numbers

It is essential for all students, including those with learning disabilities, to understand what it means to add, subtract, multiply, and divide—and to develop a good sense of when to use each of these basic operations in day-to-day settings. Solid understanding and "operation sense" enable students to reason in problem situations and provide a basis for developing computation skills carried out mentally, with paper and pencil, or with a calculator. Because our position is that students can move forward conceptually even though they have not yet memorized their basic facts, this chapter emphasizes foundational concept building for the four operations and being realistic about computation.

A major suggestion is to embed concept development in problem solving—with an emphasis on students understanding *when* to add, subtract, multiply, or divide. Whenever possible, computational examples should also be presented in the context of interesting or practical problems and applications so students develop a sense of purpose about computation. Regarding computation, some students with learning disabilities may benefit from alternative algorithms that are tailored to meet their specific learning needs; others may need to rely more on calculator computations. Within the bounds of their specific learning limitations, all students should be encouraged to develop estimation skills and "good sense" regarding the reasonableness of computed results.

In reviewing instructional program thrusts for whole-number computation and in writing IEPs, it is important to bring the focus on paper-and-pencil computation into perspective. There is very little need in today's technological society, for example, to add or subtract four-digit numbers outside the context of dollars and cents, to multiply by a three-digit number, or to do two-digit long division—so many teachers are appropriately reprioritizing where they ask students to expend their time and energies.

Some children, because of difficulty with abstract reasoning, receptive or expressive language, or auditory processing, lack or find it unusually difficult to develop important conceptual understandings necessary for success at the symbolic level. Other students with learning disabilities may, in fact, understand the concepts involved but still be unable to succeed with computation.

Children may lack the memory and association skills that normally allow one to incorporate previously learned skills and to arrive at correct answers. For example, associating the correct operation with a sign or symbol involves two skills:

1. the ability to differentiate among all the different symbols; and

2. the ability to associate the correct symbol with the correct process—addition, subtraction, multiplication, or division.

For many children, these steps are extremely difficult. Children with visual perceptual problems may have trouble because they incorrectly discriminate among the signs. Those with word-finding difficulties may be unable to retrieve the correct word for a given sign. Those with other types of receptive language deficits may be able to associate the sign with the correct word—add, subtract, multiply, or divide—but the word may carry no meaning for them. Another group of students, those with expressive language deficits, may not be able to elicit—either verbally or to themselves—the correct process without being cued visually or auditorially.

The students described above, and perhaps others as well, are the ones who often say, "Tell me what to do (or what the sign is), and then I can solve the problem." These statements do not mean that they have no conceptual understanding of the operation. They may be capable of showing what to do for each operation. However, at this stage they are not being asked to show what they know. Instead, they are being asked to determine the correct process based on a symbol for which they may not have the needed language. Once they identify the process, they are on their way.

After associating the correct symbol with the correct process, students must then usually determine the sequence that applies. Since most estimation and computation involve more than one step, confusion often arises. To further complicate the situation, many computations involve two or more operations, even though only one sign is used.

Consider the problem of Figure 6.1a. One common approach to the mental calculation is shown. Even though the operation sign is subtraction, the first step is addition: adding 1 to 19. Then, after the simple subtraction, 48 – 20, is carried out, it is necessary to add 1 to the answer to adjust the result back to the original problem. To carry out the paper-and-pencil computation of Figure 6.1b in sequence requires the following sequence: subtract, add, subtract, and subtract; yet the process is called subtraction.

Correct sequencing of steps is a difficult task for many students. Those with a memory sequencing deficit, whether visual or auditory, and those who have problems with working memory find sequencing especially difficult.

Further, the child with a visual discrimination difficulty, who confuses the + and × signs, may perceive the operation sign differently each time it is seen. Figure 6.2 illustrates how this disability can affect paper-and-pencil computation. At first glance, it would appear that this student needs more work, conceptually, on the process of multiplying a two-digit number by a one-digit number. However, listening to the student verbalize the procedure revealed that after carrying the 7, the student misperceived the sign and completed the computation using addition (7 + 4).

Alignment poses another difficulty. Consider the multiplication of two two-digit factors. Even with a good understanding of place value, basic facts, and multiplication by ones and tens, the ability to align numbers accurately can be tedious for some children. Figure 6.3 shows a step-by-step breakdown of the mental process involved.

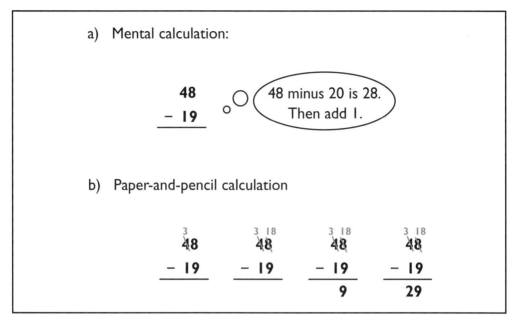

Figure 6.1.

For the child with poor fine-motor coordination or impaired spatial organization, the process of solving the problem becomes twice as long. Every time it is necessary to write a digit, this student must stop and look at the problem. The digits already present must be sorted out, and it is necessary to coordinate what is seen with what the hand does. Although this child may possess a solid understanding of place value and the steps involved, the sequence is interrupted, considerably and consistently, whenever it becomes necessary to write a number.

Visual figure-ground deficits and reversal tendencies also impede accuracy of paper-and-pencil computation. Consider Figure 6.4, in which a child is asked to perform a common subtraction problem. At first sight, it would appear that the difficulty might be inadequate mastery of facts (and, in many instances, it may well be). However, upon questioning this child, it became apparent that the difficulty lay in having to visually align the numbers in order to compute accurately. The first step was correct; the student thought, "6 take away 5," and wrote 1. Next, the numbers were correctly regrouped. But then the student lost the place and saw "6 take away 4." The last step, "8 take away 2," is accurate.

$$
\begin{array}{r}
\overset{\text{↗}}{48} \\
\times\ 9 \\
\hline
112
\end{array}
$$

Figure 6.2.

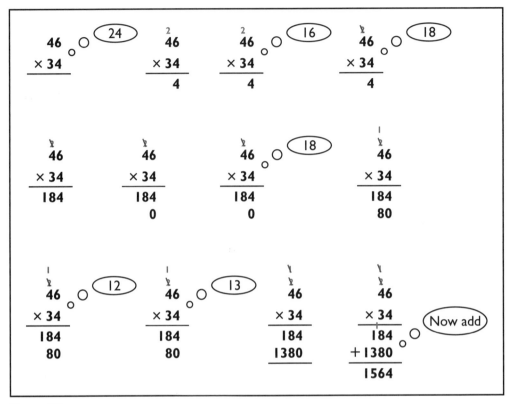

Figure 6.3.

For students with reversal and visual memory deficits, regrouping causes special problems. So does long division. Figure 6.5a shows how a child who tends to reverse might solve a division problem. In the first example, the 6 was perceived as a 2, but otherwise the computation and procedure are correct. Obviously, this student understands the steps for long division and knows the required facts for the problem.

Figure 6.5b shows the same division problem, but this time the way it would challenge somebody with reversal and discrimination difficulties. The student initially perceived the 6 as a 6 and wrote 1 in the quotient. However, at the multiplication step, the divisor was seen as a 2, thus, the product 2. In the subtraction step, the 2 was perceived as a 6, resulting in a difference of 2.

At first glance, this student might appear to be careless and unsure of the basic facts involved. However, in examples like this, careful questioning and

$$\begin{array}{r} {\scriptstyle 8\ \ 11} \\ 9\!\!\!/1\!\!\!/6 \\ -\ 245 \\ \hline 621 \end{array}$$

Figure 6.4.

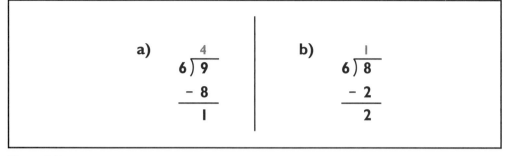

Figure 6.5.

evaluating a computation in light of a child's previous work may reveal that the child does know the needed facts and is familiar with the correct process. Specific learning disabilities may be at the root of the problem.

Computational accuracy often involves estimating to check whether an answer is reasonable. This is difficult for most students and especially for many children with learning disabilities. Although an essential part of learning how to estimate involves concrete presentations, actual application of the skill is abstract and requires a strong working memory and a considerable amount of reasoning and retention. Therefore, children who have any kind of processing deficit must learn to estimate through a highly structured approach. Many will not intuitively recognize when an answer is incorrect. Others may sense that something is wrong but be unable to figure out or express exactly what it is.

In the following pages we recommend sequences and techniques for helping students who have difficulties like those just described. Suggestions are clustered under the following headings:

1. Building concepts for the four operations
2. Computation: general difficulties
3. Mental computation and estimation
4. Addition of whole numbers
5. Subtraction of whole numbers
6. Multiplication of whole numbers
7. Division of whole numbers
8. Using technology

The first focus of this chapter is using children's intuitive understandings of "part-whole" as the basis for concept development for the four operations and emphasizing *when* to use each in a problem setting. Comparison situations are then addressed as an extension of basic concept work before reviewing general difficulties influencing students' success with computation. Ideas are also presented for handling computational difficulties for whole-number computation. Although calculator use is interwoven throughout the chapter, additional ideas are presented in a technology section that concludes the chapter.

Before addressing whole-number work, a final comment about instruction for decimal computation should be made. Because computational procedures for whole numbers and decimals are so similar, many teachers have been successfully emphasizing and relating these similarities during decimal instruction. Some students with memory, abstract-reasoning, or receptive language difficulties, however, find it easier to learn fractions first and then use fractions as the basis for decimal learning, including computation. From a language point of view it is easier for them to comprehend fractions than decimals, because the entire fraction is verbalized and—in written form—has a matching visual cue for each part said, whereas a decimal does not. For 0.3, for example, there is a visual stimulus to say "three" but not to say "tenths." However, the written fraction $\frac{3}{10}$ triggers saying both "three" *and* "tenths." For this reason, teachers sometimes base decimal computation on fractions. An analysis of learning strengths will help determine which path to take for particular students—whether to relate decimal instruction to whole numbers or to fractions. Ideas that address common misconceptions and errors related to decimals computation, addressed in Chapter 8 after fraction work, can in either case be adopted and used.

BUILDING CONCEPTS FOR THE FOUR OPERATIONS

Problem Area: Inability to know whether to add, subtract, multiply, or divide in a given situation.

Typical Disabilities Affecting Progress: Difficulty with abstract reasoning, visual or auditory association, expressive or receptive language, or executive functioning.

Background: Consider these situations:

- Mei put some coins in her pocket and walked to her grandmother's house. On the way she dropped 2 of the coins. She saw them fall into a storm drain, but she couldn't get them. When she got to her grandmother's house, she counted her coins—she had 5 left. How many coins did she have before she lost some?

- Yesterday Tammy Jo ate 5 cookies. Her little brother ate 3. How many more did Tammy Jo eat than her brother?

Students may use counters to "act out" and solve these problems or, if they have a good understanding of addition and subtraction, they will intuitively know to add to solve the first problem and to subtract to solve the second. Unfortunately, many students—including many of those with learning disabilities—may do just the opposite. They see or hear the word *left* in the first problem and subtract; they respond to the word *more* in the second by adding. Some may have no clue.

Students fail for many reasons, including identified learning disabilities. Many resort to "key words" with no appreciation of the "big *concept* idea" that addition and subtraction have a part-whole connection (Figure 6.6). They do not realize the following:

- You add to find the whole or total of two or more parts.
- You subtract from the whole to find a missing part.

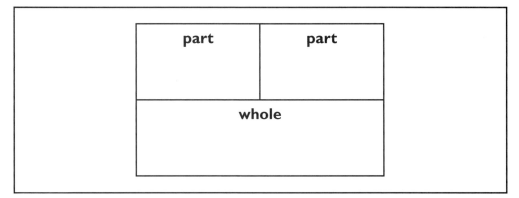

Figure 6.6.

In the coin problem, Mei lost *part* of her coins and had *part* of them left. She needed to find the *total* number of coins (*all* the coins, the *sum* of the parts, how many *all together*—words and phrases like these refer to the whole). Only when students recognize whether to add or subtract in a given situation do they understand the *concept of addition* and the *concept of subtraction*.

A first emphasis in concept development for any of the operations should be on "big" part-whole ideas, on using counters to act out problems and, finally, on recording what is done in number sentences using + or −:

- add (+) to find the whole (expressed in language to which a child can relate);

- subtract (−) to find a missing part.

Any emphasis on the multiple meanings of *key words* should be embedded in this context, as a way of sorting out whether the "whole" or "missing part" is needed. *Multiplication* and *division* are similarly related, but equal parts and equal groups are involved:

- When there are equal parts, multiply to find the total.
- Divide to find equal parts of a whole.

The following problems typify very simple types of number sentences for each operation: $4 + 2 = 6$, $7 − 3 = 4$, $2 \times 4 = 8$, $10 \div 5 = 2$. You *start* with some number, you use some operation to *change* it, and you have a *result*. To leave out one of the terms (start, change, or result) provides us with a framework for creating "problems" (see Figure 6.7) that form the basis for concept development.

Using the Operations: Comparison Situations

When children understand what *subtraction* or *multiplication* means, they then might consider the many uses or applications of those operations. Comparison situations are one such application. The Tammy Jo cookie problem in the opening paragraph of this section is an example in which subtraction is

Little Red Hen Stories
(part-whole problems)

Result Unknown	Change Unknown	Start Unknown
Join Situation	**Join Situation**	**Join Situation**
The Little Red Hen found 4 grains of wheat in the morning and 2 in the afternoon. How many did she find that day?	The Little Red Hen found 4 grains of wheat in the morning and more in the afternoon. How many did she find in the afternoon?	The Little Red Hen found some grains of wheat in the morning and 2 in the afternoon. How many did she find in the morning?
Whole thing is needed: 4 + 2 = 6 grains	**Just part is needed:** 6 - 2 = 4 grains	**Just part is needed:** 6 - 4 = 2 grains
Separate Situation	**Separate Situation**	**Separate Situation**
The Little Red Hen put 6 grains of wheat in her pocket but gave 2 to the birds on the way home. How many did she have then?	The Little Red Hen put some grains of wheat in her pocket, gave 2 to the birds, and still had 4 for herself. How many did she put in her pocket?	The Little Red Hen put 6 grains of wheat in her pocket, gave some to the birds and still had 4 left for herself. How many did she give to the birds?
Whole thing is needed: 6 - 2 = 4 grains	**Whole thing is needed:** 2 + 4 = 6 grains	**Just part is needed:** 6 - 4 = 2 grains
Join Equal Groups	**Separate into Equal Groups**	**Separate into Equal Groups**
The Little Red Hen put 4 grains of wheat in each of her 3 pockets to take home. How many did she take home?	The Little Red Hen had 12 grains of wheat and put 4 grains of wheat in each pocket. How many pockets did she fill?	The Little Red Hen had 12 grains of wheat and put the same number of wheat grains in each of her 3 pockets. How many did she put in each pocket?
Whole thing is needed: 4 x 3 = 12 grains	**Equal parts are involved:** 12 ÷ 4 = 3 grains	**Equal parts are needed:** 12 ÷ 3 = 4 grains

Figure 6.7.

applied. Success with comparison situations that apply multiplication or division is the foundation for understanding proportions, which, in turn, is related in an important way to algebraic reasoning. Examples follow:

- The giraffe in the zoo is 3 times taller than my sister Beth. Beth is 4 feet tall. How tall is the giraffe? *This situation compares height: the giraffe's and Beth's. Three Beths end to end would equal the giraffe's height: 3 × 4 feet = 12 feet.*

- The giraffe is 12 feet tall. My sister Beth is 4 feet tall. The giraffe is how many times taller than Beth? *12 ÷ 4 = 3 times taller.*

- The giraffe is 12 feet tall. It is 3 times taller than my sister Beth. How tall is my sister? *12 ÷ 3 = 4 feet.*

Ideas outlined below suggest ways of helping students with learning disabilities develop stronger concepts for the four operations and common applications to comparison situations.

✎ Sample Sequence of Activities

NOTE: *The essence of this work lies in children's repeated opportunities to retell oral stories, use counters to "act them out," and record number sentences to match (Figure 6.8). This work should be modified and embellished to meet special learning needs.*

▶ "Part-Whole" and Basic Concept Development

1. **Say it your way!** Children love a story. Start with a word problem based on the theme of a literature book children have recently read, or tell a story to which the children can relate.

> ■ *Example:* Mom had a plate of cookies on the table for us when we
> came home from school. There were 4 chocolate chip cookies and
> 2 peanut butter cookies. How many cookies were on the plate?

Now ask children to listen to the story again and say, "Try to remember the numbers you hear. Write them down when you hear them." Add a rebus—just enough of a hint to help a student retell the story in his or her own words. Notice that, in the example of Figure 6.9a, the total number of each cookie has not been drawn by the teacher, just enough of a rebus to remind the child. This is important so that the child, not just the teacher, thinks about the situation. Ask a child to retell the problem—what he or she knows and what he or she has to find out—using the rebus to help.

2. **Act it out.** Provide counters and ask students to act out the story and answer the question. Resist the temptation to tell them what to do with the

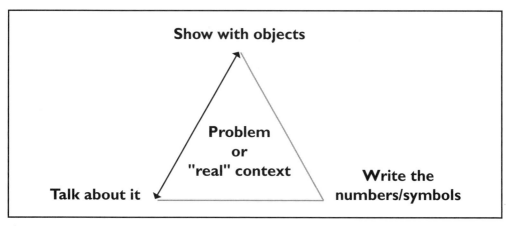

Figure 6.8.

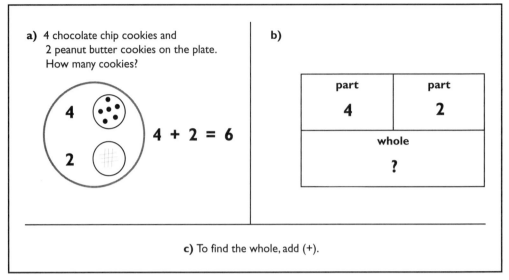

a) 4 chocolate chip cookies and
2 peanut butter cookies on the plate.
How many cookies?

4 + 2 = 6

b)

part	part
4	2
whole	
?	

c) To find the whole, add (+).

Figure 6.9.

counters. (Help as needed only *after* students have shown what they did to show and solve a problem.) Then have students *explain* what they did and *record a number sentence* to match their actions with the counters.

NOTE:

- *It is likely that students have seen + and − symbols before. If not, special care is needed when introducing these symbols and related vocabulary. A new symbol, for example, might be texturized (e.g., with school or glitter glue) and children can finger-trace as they read an expression or number sentence containing the symbol.*

- *Because it follows the left-right reading motion, many teachers emphasize the horizontal before the vertical format for number sentences. Eventually, children should become comfortable with both formats.*

3. **Analyze part-whole.** As students become comfortable with this routine, have them listen to a story problem and write the numbers, retell it using the teacher's rebus to help, act it out, explain, and record. Then introduce the chart of Figure 6.9b and think back on a problem just worked. "What about the 4 chocolate chip cookies, was that ALL the cookies, the whole thing—or just part?" (Just part, so write "4" on the chart under the first "Part.") "What about the 2 peanut butter cookies, was that the whole lot—ALL the cookies on the plate—or just part?" (Just part, so write "2" on the chart as shown.) Draw a question mark under "Whole": "We had to find how many cookies *all together,* and (pointing to the number sentence)—you found that was 6."

4. **Repeat.** Provide repeated opportunities for students to experience the routine outlined above, analyzing part-whole from time to time. If children have difficulty with a problem, model the action and then repeat immediately with a parallel problem. At first do only problems for which students write addition sentences (see Figure 6.7).

5. **Make a sentence strip.** Present three situations back to back for which students add to solve. Retain work on the board or on papers taped to wall space. Elicit from the child that *each time* you needed to find the WHOLE, and you ADDED. Write the child's words on a sentence strip (the child could read or finger-trace it if that is a good learning style; see Figure 6.9c) and post it.

■ *Example* (based on the coin problem at the beginning of this section):

TEACHER: What about the 2 coins Mei lost—were they ALL the coins she had or just part?

CHILDREN: Just part. ["2" is recorded under the first "Part" on the chart from Figure 6.9b.]

TEACHER: What about the 5 coins that Mei counted at her grandmother's house—were they ALL the coins she had that day or just part?

CHILDREN: Just part. ["5" is recorded under the second "Part" on the chart.]

TEACHER: [Placing a question mark under "Whole" on the chart] And what did we want to find?

CHILDREN: How many she had at the start.

TEACHER: Yes, the whole thing—and [pointing to the number sentence] you found that was 7.

6. **Look for and do.** Follow through by presenting a mix of addition and subtraction problems and ask students to do only those for which they would add to solve. In subsequent lessons provide time for students to write or tell their own addition problems. Reinforce, as appropriate, that each time the "whole" (the total, when the number is all . . .) is needed, then you add. If it helps, hang the different words for *whole* from the wall chart, making a mobile of it.

7. **Want just part? Subtract.** Parallel Activities 1 through 6, focusing on finding "just part." The goal is to gradually address the full range of addition and subtraction problem types illustrated by Figure 6.7.

8. **Color code.** On a wall chart, use a distinctly different color to code each operation symbol and its related vocabulary. In Figure 6.10, a diagram appears that illustrates the meaning of the subtraction symbol and everything that relates to subtraction is green.

9. **Have equal groups?** Use colored boxes and chips as in Figure 6.11 and a context like placing cookies on a baking sheet. Ask: "How many groups [baking sheets]?" "How many cookies in each group?" "How many cookies in all?" Repeat until the child is comfortable with the idea of these relationships.

10. **Calculator "x".** Now apply this concept to finding the total number of cookies for a situation such as that shown in Figure 6.12: "How many *times* do you see a group of 3 cookies?" ("Four.") Point out that you could count or even add to find the total cookies. But mathematicians have a special way to find the total for equal groups. They multiply. They write: "4×3 (4 *times* there's a group of 3)." Have the children finger-trace and write over the multiplication sign— then figure out the total and record it. Repeat for other contextual examples in

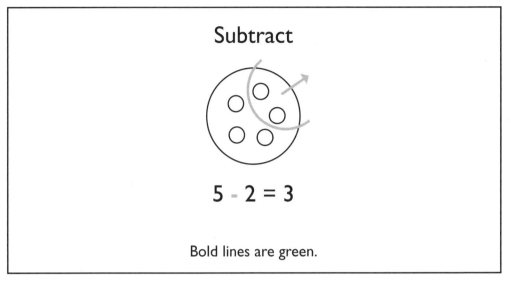

Figure 6.10.

which students write or punch into a calculator the matching multiplication sentence to find the total of equal groups.

NOTE: *If children have auditory or kinesthetic-tactile learning strengths, have them close their eyes and use sound or touch in association with the new vocabulary and symbol. Take the child's finger and tap it on the desk. "Let's tap out groups of 4. We'll do it 3 times:*

(tap-tap-tap-tap)   that's 4—1 time,
(tap-tap-tap-tap)   2 times,
(tap-tap-tap-tap)   3 times.

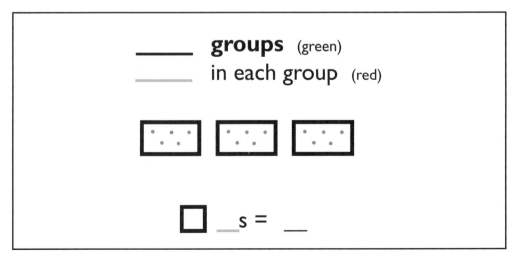

Figure 6.11.

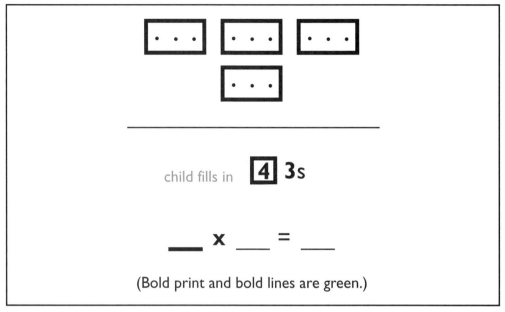

(Bold print and bold lines are green.)

Figure 6.12.

Three times *we tapped out a group of 4. Show me how to write this [3 × 4]. What's the total for 3 groups of 4?" ("Twelve.") Help students to see that they could count or add 4 + 4 + 4, but a shortcut to finding the total for equal groups is to multiply 3 × 4—in their head (when they know their basic facts), using a multiplication chart, or using a calculator—"How many total taps are there in 3 groups of 4 taps?"*

    11. **Want the total for equal groups? Multiply.** Parallel Activities 1 through 6 above, but focus on finding the total for "equal parts." Note how the part-whole chart has been modified in Figure 6.13 to fit the following sample multiplication situation:

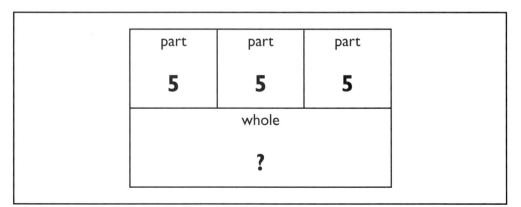

Figure 6.13.

■ *Example:* Joel put candy for party treats in 3 bags—5 candies in each. How many candies did he bag?

12. **Find equal parts of a whole? Divide.** Parallel Activities 1 through 6 above, using the last two problem types in Figure 6.7 to focus on finding equal parts of a whole. Involve students in creating their own multiplication and division stories.

Comparison Situations

This section considers two basic types of comparison situations: one readily solved by subtraction, the other by multiplication.

▶ **Comparison Subtraction**

1. **Cookie graphs.** Consider this situation:

> Maria ate 6 cookies. Her brother, Josh, ate 3.
> *How many more* cookies did Maria eat than Josh?

Children can count to determine "3 more." This and similar situations are represented as pictographs in Figure 6.14. (Note that the subtraction sign is missing—purposely!)

2. **See a pattern?** Students cannot detect a pattern from one example, but from three examples they may. To help, provide a calculator and ask a student

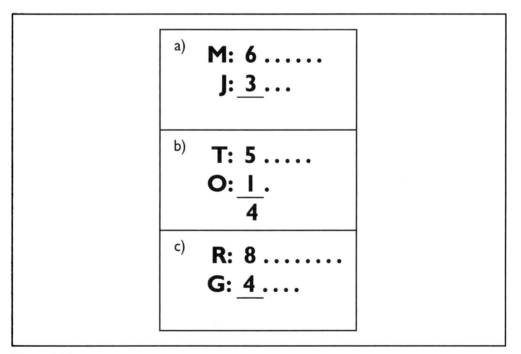

Figure 6.14.

to use the numbers in the problem in 6.14a to make the calculator show an answer of 3—"What did you punch?" ("6 minus 3 =") Ask the child to write in the "minus sign" that you forgot. As the child does so, comment that, "Yes, you subtract to compare. We compared here by finding *how many more.*" Repeat for b and c.

3. **Make a sentence strip.** Involve students in suggesting what to write on a sentence strip that tells what to do when you want to compare, or find *how many more.* (Subtract to compare.) At another time, revisit this idea but compare by asking *how many less* one has than another or by *finding the difference between* two given quantities. Write each concept on a sentence strip, perhaps making a mobile to hang in the classroom.

▶ **Comparison Multiplication**

1. **Show it.** Consider this comparison situation:

> Mark read 2 books over Christmas. His big brother read 3 times that many. How many did Mark's brother read?

Have students use counters to act out the situation (see Figure 6.15). Because they need the total of equal groups, students can relate to previous work and conclude that they can multiply 3 × 2 to get 6. Repeat for similar situations until children feel comfortable with the idea.

2. **Make a sentence strip.** As in previous work, elicit and write student observations for solving comparison multiplication problems on a sentence strip: "To find *how many times as many,* multiply (×)." Involve students in creating their own "times as many" stories.

COMPUTATION: GENERAL DIFFICULTIES

Controlling for Unknown Facts

Problem Area: Failure to succeed in estimation or mental or paper-and-pencil computation because of inadequate fact mastery.

Typical Disabilities Affecting Progress: Difficulty with visual, auditory, or long-term memory; visual or auditory discrimination; expressive language; simultaneous processing.

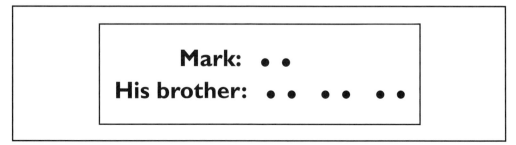

Figure 6.15.

Background: Computing involves using the basic facts. Students with learning disabilities, like their peers, become frustrated and often fail on computations involving facts they have not yet mastered. Many students are ready, developmentally, to learn more complicated computational procedures but have not yet committed the basic facts to memory. *To require them to learn the facts first may hold them back unnecessarily.* With these students, it is important to keep in mind, as noted in Chapter 1, the goal of a particular assignment. If the goal is to learn and use the various computational procedures, then memorizing the facts is a secondary and separate topic. Two approaches for dealing with this issue follow:

✎ Sample Sequence of Activities

1. **Controlled facts program.** One approach consists of controlling the entire math program around known facts. This very specialized approach involves considerable preparation and care. Specifically, it requires that one select or create problems and computational exercises so that only *known* facts are required for deriving answers. This approach is obviously not a practical one in mainstreamed or other instructional situations where teachers work with larger groups of students. However, it may be necessary in special cases.

NOTE: *Most children know at least some of the easier facts, such as doubles in addition or twos and fives in multiplication. Easy facts like these can be used to present or review computational procedures. In this way, children with learning disabilities can be a successful part of the class even though they may still be working on isolated facts.*

2. **Only known facts.** As shown in Figure 6.16, prominently display two basic facts that are being worked on. Review those facts at the beginning of the session, then select numbers for problems or exercises that involve only those facts and other known facts, in this case twos and fives.

3. **Cross out.** Give each child a sheet of facts such as that shown in Figure 6.17. Help students cross out (blacken completely) all the facts they have already mastered. Then allow them to refer to the sheet whenever necessary.

Figure 6.16.

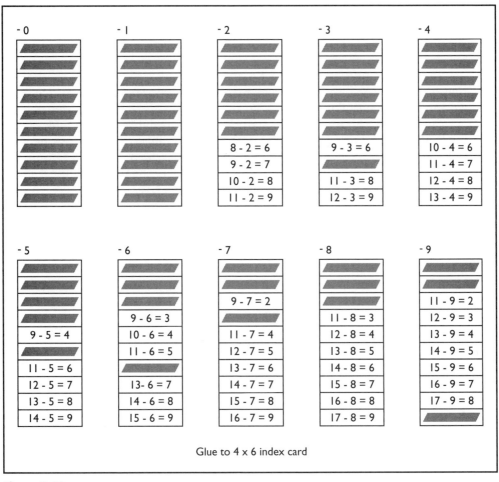

Glue to 4 x 6 index card

Figure 6.17.

In the meantime, challenge them to learn several unknown facts each week. Choose the facts carefully, following the suggestions from Chapter 9.

- *Example:* Select facts that are *one more than* some fact a child already knows. If a child knows 10 – 7 = 3, select 9 – 7 (1 less than 10 – 7). Make sure the children are aware of any relationships between new and known facts; suggest that they use those relationships to figure out answers if they become confused. Each day, provide tracking pages on the three or four facts being studied. Then, at the end of the week, test the new facts in a mixed review quiz that includes other known facts. Facts should be blackened out as they are mastered.

    To check for consistency over time, some teachers circle or highlight a fact the first time the student answers it correctly (and quickly) in an assessment setting. If the fact is also answered correctly (and quickly) in a second assessment setting, it is blackened completely as shown in Figure 6.17.

Basic Facts: Transfer to Larger Problems

Problem Area: Failure to answer correctly known facts embedded within larger computational problems.

Typical Disabilities Affecting Progress: Difficulty with visual discrimination or visual association, abstract reasoning, expressive language, memory, working or sequential memory.

Background: Many students with learning disabilities are unable, independently, to use basic facts within a computation until they have learned the procedure and feel comfortable with it. These are students who do reasonably well on fact tests. But they are unable to incorporate the facts into the computation until overlearning has occurred. It requires too much retention and sequencing for them to learn a new skill while trying to recall other isolated pieces of information. Hence they fail to transfer fact learning to computational situations. The suggestions that follow may help with this problem.

✏️ Sample Sequence of Activities

1. **Write it out.** If children get stuck within a larger computation because they cannot recall a known fact, suggest that they write the problem fact to one side. Seeing the fact in isolation often triggers recognition and allows children to proceed.

2. **Finger-trace.** If students are strong tactual learners, suggest that they finger-trace over the problem fact, quietly saying it to themselves. If they are strong auditory learners, on the other hand, simply saying the fact to themselves, or into a Language Master, may do.

NOTE: *Using the Language Master provides students the opportunity to check their answers by listening to what they said and matching it with the card they have in front of them.*

3. **Circle.** Have students circle the problem fact within a problem or write over it as a means of better focusing on it.

4. **Side by side.** Help train for the desired transfer to larger problems by providing practice sheets that place a basic fact beside a larger computational problem using that fact (Figure 6.18).

---

a)   7   47   b)   **7**   47
    + 8   + 68   **+ 8**   + 68
    ———   ————   ————   ————

(Bold digits are green.)

Figure 6.18.

5. **Color-code.** Provide extra visual reinforcement, if it is helpful, on the Activity 4 sheets, by color cueing, as suggested by Figure 6.18b.

6. **Look to the chart.** Allow children to use a multiplication chart, their cross-out sheet (a modification of the Figure 6.17 chart, with all facts visible), or a fact box. Experience has shown that as children feel comfortable with the computational procedure, the need for these aids will disappear.

MENTAL COMPUTATION AND ESTIMATION

Problem Area: Lack of confidence or difficulty with mentally computing and estimating sums, differences, products, and quotients.

Typical Disabilities Affecting Progress: Difficulty with abstract reasoning, short-term memory, sequential memory, working memory, distractibility.

Background: The ability to be successful with mental calculation and estimation rests on several important prerequisites. To mentally add, for example, children must be able to visualize two-digit numbers and either mentally count on or back by tens and ones or apply known facts. For any type of mental calculation or estimation, a firm understanding of place value and good number sense is required. Further, students must be able to retain information while simultaneously processing other information, a processing skill some students with learning disabilities lack. Using mental and estimation techniques for computation also involves risk taking and a certain flexibility in one's abilities to think about and manipulate numbers. Typically, for any given problem, a variety of different, correct options might be pursued for calculating an answer mentally or making a computational estimation. Many students with learning disabilities, partially due to their learning deficit(s) but also partially because of their history of failure with computation, lack the confidence to function well in situations that involve such flexibility and choice. Experience has shown that an early, consistent, structured emphasis on mental techniques, accompanied by expectations and opportunities to both explain one's solutions and listen to other different but correct approaches can help these students considerably.

In order to nurture personal confidence and a flexible mind-set for employing a variety of useful computational approaches, the development of appropriate mental calculation and estimation strategies should be addressed before paper-and-pencil computation is addressed within a school year. Otherwise, despite the fact that learning those strategies could be to their advantage, students tend to show greater reluctance to abandon paper-and-pencil methods at times when mental approaches would be more appropriate and, often, much easier. The suggestions that follow are offered in the spirit of early and continuing intervention. As in all instruction, a positive, supportive environment and good role modeling, including "think aloud" techniques, are essential.

Making Mental Calculations

Learning to compute mentally—that is, to calculate exact numerical answers without the aid of calculators or paper-and-pencil algorithms—is learning a useful skill. Many everyday problems can be solved mentally. For example, "It is now 2:30. I should bake the brownies for 35 minutes. When do I take them out?" Or, "I want to buy a tape that costs $9.95. I have $7.15. If I make $2.50 cutting grass for the neighbor, will that be enough?"

Within the school curriculum, some of the standard computational textbook exercises that historically have caused many children great anxiety, such as 302 – 163, can, in fact, be computed mentally more readily than by using paper and pencil and regrouping over zeros.

The premise pertinent to the focus of this section is that if students are eventually to select appropriately among computational alternatives, an effort must first be made to develop each individual's competence with each of those alternatives. This section aims toward that goal by focusing on specific, systematic instruction to develop mental computation skills.

The ability to compute mentally requires simultaneous processing, short-term memory and visual memory, receptive and expressive (inner) language skills, and reasoning skills, areas that some students find extremely difficult or lack entirely. In spite of their disabilities, other students can apply mental calculation procedures, as suggested below, when instruction is modified and approached in ways that accommodate their special learning needs.

One important aspect of teaching mental math is developing mental imagery to help students perform a computation "in their heads." Visual, auditory, and kinesthetic or tactile approaches may be used. For example, students might use their fingers to "write" a problem in the air or on the desk. For some mental algorithms, using teaching aids such as hundreds charts, money, base-10 blocks, or number lines during initial instruction may provide a frame of reference for later recall. Perhaps the key for students with learning disabilities is to help them explore what they are able to do, place greater emphasis on the use of the hundreds chart in early instruction, and help them develop "modified mental algorithms." These are algorithms that include writing some numbers as an aid to the mental thinking process. One approach that incorporates these aspects of instruction follows.

Sample Sequence of Activities

▶ Mentally Adding 10

1. **Calculator help.** If children possess the necessary skills, allow them to use a hand calculator to complete exercises such as those shown in Figure 6.19a. When a page is complete, have the student read across each row as follows: "26 plus 10 is 36; 48 plus 10 is 58." It often helps to give the child a card to uncover the numerals while reading (Figure 6.19b). Toward the end of the page, cover up the answer and have the child say the sentences and give the answers without visual reinforcement.

NOTE: *Students with receptive language difficulties may benefit from listening to such number sentences that have been taped by the teacher, a teaching assistant, parent, or someone else who can place emphasis on the pattern that should be addressed. To save time, use the Language Master or a computer with text-to-speech capabilities and emphasize the numbers when dictating.*

a)   26 + 10 = <u>36</u>   b)   26 ☐
            48 + 10 = <u>58</u>   26 + ☐
            37 + 10 = <u>47</u>   26 + 10 ☐

Figure 6.19.

    2. **Highlight the pattern.** In exercises of this type, some children are helped when a vertical format and colors are used, as in Figure 6.20. Highlighting the digits helps emphasize the pattern of change in the tens digits. The children could be instructed to complete the first part of a page with problems like those shown, leaving the last six or seven problems unsolved. When they have completed the first part, have the children analyze their work. Help them notice the pattern by pointing (a) first to the green tens digit in the problem and (b) then to the tens digit in the sum. While pointing, say each numeral: "two . . . three," "four . . . five." Continue this verbal patterning as the children fill in the green blanks of the unsolved problems. A similar procedure is used with the ones digits. When the page is complete, have the children read the problems as in Activity 1 above. Model the auditory emphasis of the tens digit pattern. For example, "Twenty-six plus ten is *thirty-six*."

    ■ *Follow-up:* To encourage mental calculation, follow up with similar worksheets in which children give answers orally (or dictate them into a tape recorder or the Language Master) before writing.

    3. **Practice.** To build up automatic addition of tens, present pages with color-coded horizontal problems, as in Figure 6.21. The colors are used for focusing and visual association with the vertical problems previously completed. The students read the problems as in Activity 1 above and fill in the blanks.

    4. **Toss up** (a practice activity for two players). Prepare a gameboard, as shown in Figure 6.22, and laminate the center strip. Using a grease pencil, write fifteen two-digit numbers in the center strip. Provide about 10 markers for each player and two dice, marked as follows:

Die 1: marked 4, 5, 6, 7, 8, 9
Die 2: marked 1, 2, 3, 4, 5, 6

26   26
+ 10   + 10
——   ——

▬ = green   ▬ = red

Figure 6.20.

$$\underline{5\underline{6}} + \underline{\underline{1}0} = \underline{\quad}$$

___ = green   ___ = red

Figure 6.21.

Taking turns, the players roll the dice and place the numbers that come up as a two-digit numeral on the left side of the gameboard above "+10." This number is added to 10. If the correct sum is on the board, a marker is placed above or below it as shown. If the correct sum is not on the board, the dice simply go to the next player. If players give an incorrect answer, they must remove one marker from their side of the board. The winner is the first player to place five markers in a row.

- *Variation:* To encourage mental calculation, give each player markers of two different colors and assign them different values (e.g., orange, worth 2 points; blue, worth 1 point). The game proceeds as described, but an orange marker is placed on the board when an answer is given after mental calculation; blue otherwise. The winner is the first to accumulate 6 points.

▶ **Mentally Adding Other Multiples of 10**

1. **Calculator help.** Proceed as in Activity 1 of the preceding section, but introduce multiples of 10 (20, 30 . . . 90) as the second addend.

2. **Relate to the basic fact.** To help develop the visual or auditory pattern needed and relate the addition to basic facts, exercises such as those shown in Figure 6.23 are helpful. Colors or bold print and underlining could be used to focus attention on the related basic facts. In Figure 6.23a, the child begins on the left and reads across, filling in the answers. Encourage auditory emphasis

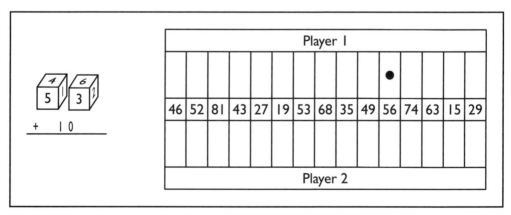

Figure 6.22.

a) **6 + 2 =** ___ **, so 6**0 **+ 2**0 **=**__

b)   **6**   **6**0   **6**3
   + 2   **+ 2**0   **+ 2**0

——— **= green** ——— **= red**

Figure 6.23.

to highlight the relationship: "Six *plus two* is eight, so *sixty plus twenty is eighty*." Examples of this type may later be extended to include adding a multiple of 10 to any two-digit number, as in Figure 6.23b. The vertical format of the second set of problems is more effective for some students. Whatever the format, finger-tracing like parts of related problems might be encouraged for a student who requires a high degree of tactile involvement.

- *Follow-up:* Encourage mental calculation. Use the exercises described above but ask students to give the answers orally before writing. Provide answer keys so that students who work independently can check their own work.

▶ Hundreds Chart: Stepping Stone to Mental Addition and Subtraction

NOTE: *Counting on by tens and ones is a prerequisite to hundreds chart use for adding or subtracting two-digit numbers. Use ideas from the Chapter 5 section, "Skip Counting by Tens and Fives" that emphasize counting on by tens and ones.*

1. **Count on.** Circle a two-digit number on a laminated hundreds chart with a washable green pen and circle the number beneath it in red. Provide students with small counters and explain: "Like the colors on a traffic light, green means go and red means stop, so we'll start at (the green number) and move from number to number until we stop at (the red number). Put your finger on (the green number). Every time I clap, think 10 more while you move along the path and cover that number." (Clap 10 times as students place a counter on each of the 10 numbers along the path to [the red number].) "How many counters did it take to go from (the green number) to (the red number)?" Clean the board and repeat with similar number pairs. Encourage students to predict how many counters will be needed each time until they recognize the pattern that, moving down one row is a shortcut for adding 10.

2. **Start with, end with.** Write two two-digit numbers (e.g., 29 and 54) on the board or on an overhead. Challenge students to find different ways to get

from one number to the other on the hundreds chart. In this example, starting with 29, one could count on by tens to 59, then count back by ones to 54 (29, 39, 49, 59—58, 57, 56, 55, 54). Or one could first go forward 5 to 34, then count on by tens to 54. Another strategy would be to move over one space to 30, move down two rows (adding 20) to 50, then count on 4 to 54. One also might start with 54 and count backward by tens and ones.

Whenever possible, provide opportunities for different students to explain their strategies (based on tens and ones moves) and *listen to the different strategies they suggest.* To foster the transition to mental addition and subtraction, summarize the counting moves in writing—and gradually let students take turns doing so. The first strategy above, for example, could be recorded as: $29 + 30 = 59$ or $59 - 4 = 54$.

3. **Apply to mental addition.** Initially allow children to use a hundreds chart (Figure 6.24) to add mentally. Students should be provided individual hundreds charts for this purpose. (For these, and other counting activities involving a hundreds chart, consider using a vertical chart, as illustrated in Figure 5.31. Some students will have an easier time with that kind of chart since the visual pattern is more regular.) Given a problem like $35 + 40$, for example, children might place a "peephole" card over the number for one addend and move the card down the column as they count on by tens: 35, 45, 55, 65, 75. Because the connection to the written number sentence is critical, the teacher or a partner might write the sum after it is obtained (e.g., $35 + 40 = 75$). Some teachers prefer writing these number sentences vertically, to relate to the vertical, paper-pencil algorithm. *Whenever possible, provide opportunities for students to listen to strategies others might suggest and to share their own approaches.*

Correct, *alternate solution paths* should be respected and encouraged. For problems like $35 + 40$, for example, some students may focus on the tens digits, use known facts, and immediately say, "75."

1	2	3	4	5	6	7	8	9	10
11	12	13	14	15	16	17	18	19	20
21	22	23	24	25	26	27	28	29	30
31	32	33	34	35	36	37	38	39	40
41	42	43	44	45	46	47	48	49	50
51	52	53	54	55	56	57	58	59	60
61	62	63	64	65	66	67	68	69	70
71	72	73	74	75	76	77	78	79	80
81	82	83	84	85	86	87	88	89	90
91	92	93	94	95	96	97	98	99	100

Hundreds chart

1	2	3	4	5	6	7	8	9	10
11	12	13				17	18	19	20
21	22	23				27	28	29	30
31	32	33		35		37	38	39	40
41	42	43				47	48	49	50
51	52	53				57	58	59	60
61	62	63	64	65	66	67	68	69	70
71	72	73	74	75	76	77	78	79	80
81	82	83	84	85	86	87	88	89	90
91	92	93	94	95	96	97	98	99	100

Chart with "peephole" card

Figure 6.24.

When children can comfortably add a two-digit number to a multiple of 10, the idea of adding to the nearest multiple of 10, then adjusting can be introduced for adding *any two two-digit numbers*. Initially, problems in which students *add* to adjust might be used (see Figure 6.25). Whenever possible, provide an interesting or practical context for the problems.

NOTE: *Children who are accustomed to the right-left, paper-pencil procedure of computing first with ones, then tens, and those with working-memory difficulties, may find it difficult to completely reverse their thinking and compute tens first, then ones. This latter approach generally is faster for mental calculation. Color-coding may help students make this shift. To help these students learn to visualize and retain the relevant part of the addition problem, present flash cards with the important digits highlighted, as in Figure 6.26a. Ask the student to state and solve the highlighted part of the problem. Later, these cards can be used without highlighting as in Figure 6.26b.*

• Next consider an alternative to 34 + 49 types. As in Figure 6.25, some students may find it easier to add 34 + 50 and then subtract 1 to compensate. Others may prefer to add 34 to 40 and count on 9! While the second approach may seem less efficient, it is more straightforward for some and should be allowed. Some students might prefer the second approach initially because they do not understand any other. Most teachers at least introduce the first (more efficient) method to see whether it is within a student's range of thinking.

NOTE 1: *If children have used the vertical hundreds chart of Figure 5.31, the above approaches can be easily adapted for use on that chart.*

NOTE: 2: *Students with short-term memory, sequential-memory or working-memory deficits may need to write what they are thinking, particularly when regrouping is involved—for example:*

> *"38 + 45 is 3 tens and 4 tens." (Student writes 70.)*
> *"8 + 5 is 8 ones and 5 ones, or 13." (Student writes 13.)*
> *"70 + 13 is 83."*

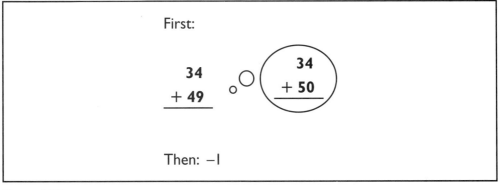

Figure 6.25.

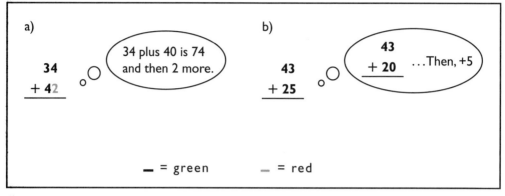

Figure 6.26.

4. **Apply to mental subtraction.** Similar procedures can be used to help students subtract two-digit numbers mentally. As with addition, respect students' choice of strategy and their need to write down their thought processes—a technique some students may have to use throughout life.

• As in addition, initially allow children to use a hundreds chart (Figure 6.24) to subtract mentally. Given a problem like 65 – 40, for example, children might place a peephole card over 65 and count backward by tens (moving back four rows) to 25. Other students may prefer to start with 40 and count on (40, 50, 60—and 5 more is 25). Still others may focus on the tens digits, use known facts, and immediately say, "25."

• Next introduce problems that require mental subtraction like 65 – 42, as in Figure 6.27, and emphasize subtracting the nearest multiple of ten, then adjusting. Using computation in a story context rather than in isolation helps students develop intuitions about the direction of the adjustment. For example, 65 – 42 might be accompanied by a story such as: "On Monday the park ranger stocked the lake with 65 fish and said 42 fish could be caught and taken. If only

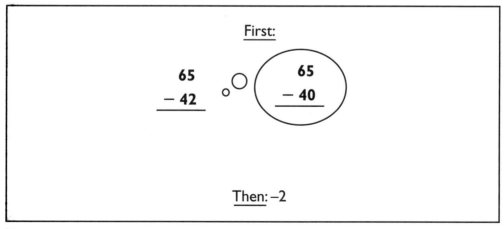

Figure 6.27.

40 have been caught, then fishing can continue until another 2 are taken from the lake (i.e., adjust by subtracting 2)."

• Finally introduce 65 – 49 types. As in Figure 6.28, some students may find it easier to subtract 65 – 50, then add 1 because they subtracted 1 too many. Again, a story context like the following may help students' intuitions about the direction of the adjustment: "On Tuesday the lake was restocked, so it started the day with 65 fish, and 49 could be taken. If a fisher catches 50 fish, 1 too many are taken, so 1 fish must be put back into the lake (i.e., adjust by adding 1)." As before, different correct approaches should be expected, respected, and supported.

Mentally Adding a One- and a Two-Digit Number

Addition involving a one- and a two-digit addend can be approached either as a paper-and-pencil computation (with or without regrouping) or mentally—as an extension of the basic facts. There are payoffs to handling problems of this type mentally:

  • The mental calculation approach may help children "add by endings" in column addition.

  • The mental calculation approach prepares children for multiplication with regrouping.

For students with visual perceptual or working-memory difficulty and those with abstract-reasoning difficulty, the single-digit addend can cause confusion. Students with auditory-processing or auditory figure-ground difficulties may not recognize the basic fact problem within the larger problem. If the problem is presented visually, the empty space in the tens place may be misleading, even for students who demonstrate a solid understanding of place value. For many, adding a "concrete" symbol to an empty space is more difficult than adding two two-digit numbers. The following ideas have helped.

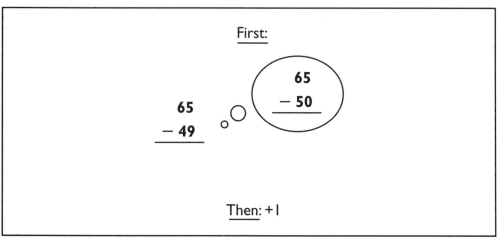

Figure 6.28.

1. **How does it end?** Figure 6.29a shows an exercise that has proven helpful for relating problems involving a one- and a two-digit addend to basic facts. At first, only problems that require no regrouping are presented. Blank file pages, computer templates, or Language Master cards using the format of Figure 6.29b, can be kept on hand and filled in as needed by the teacher. The color will:

- focus attention on the basic fact;
- develop reasoning and language skills;
- give visual reinforcement to students with auditory deficits; and
- give auditory reinforcement to children with poor visual memory.

As previously pointed out, it is necessary to check for intact color vision. In serious cases of color blindness, bold print and underscoring can be substituted to highlight and cue responses. In the example of 6.29a, the student begins on the left, reading silently or aloud, depending on preferred learning style. The horizontal part of the exercise follows the left-right reading sequence and reflects what a child should *think* while computing a problem of this type. The blanks are filled in as the student approaches them verbally.

NOTE: *These same pages can be used, if necessary, for textbook problems. Have the student copy out the problem, place it in the left-hand box, and then compute.*

2. **Flash! How does it end?** Once the student has internalized the thought process, flash a color-coded card like that of Figure 6.30. With the card as a cue, the child states the problem and completes the sentence, as in Figure 6.29.

3. **Side by side.** For children who have either internalized the preceding pattern or who can readily recognize visual patterns, present practice pages

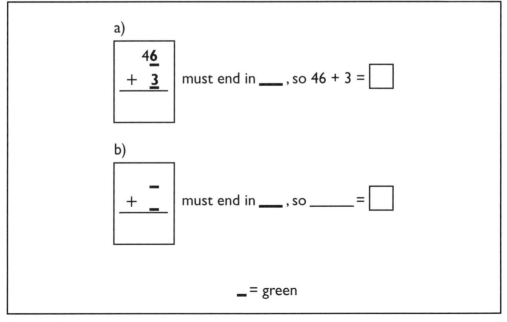

Figure 6.29.

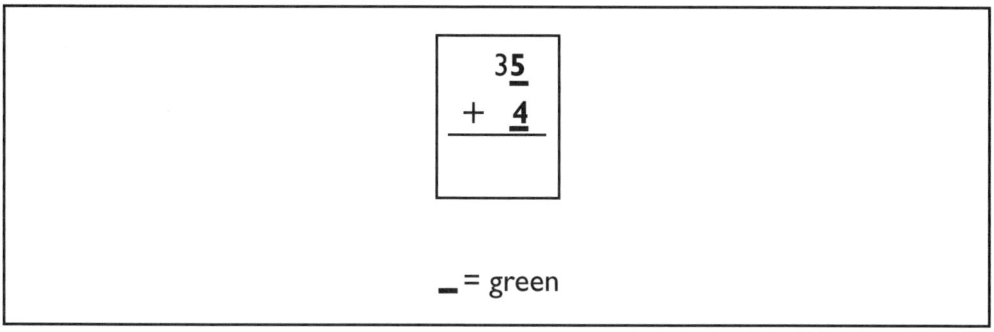

$$
\begin{array}{r}
3\underline{5} \\
+ \ \underline{4} \\
\hline
\end{array}
$$

_ = green

Figure 6.30.

containing exercises like that of Figure 6.31. The child is forced to focus on the pattern (visual and auditory) in each problem, thus eliminating the tendency to perseverate. By encouraging children to recognize and use a pattern, this approach fosters reasoning skills.

NOTE: *If color-coding is necessary, the original basic fact—in this case 4 + 5— should be written or outlined in green. In the remaining problems, that fact is underlined in green by the teacher or the students before the problem is solved. This type of exercise can be used with the controlled facts program described in Activity 1 of the "Computation: General Difficulties" section earlier in this chapter. The specific facts being worked on are immediately incorporated into actual problem situations.*

Mental Multiplication and Division

1. **Look ahead to mental multiplication and division.** Specifically work to extend children's counting and basic fact work in areas that provide necessary prerequisites for mental multiplication and division. In particular, reinforce, as needed, children's abilities to:

- skip-count by tens (see Chapter 5, "Skip Counting by Tens and Fives");

- skip-count by twenty-fives (link to work with money; see Chapter 4);

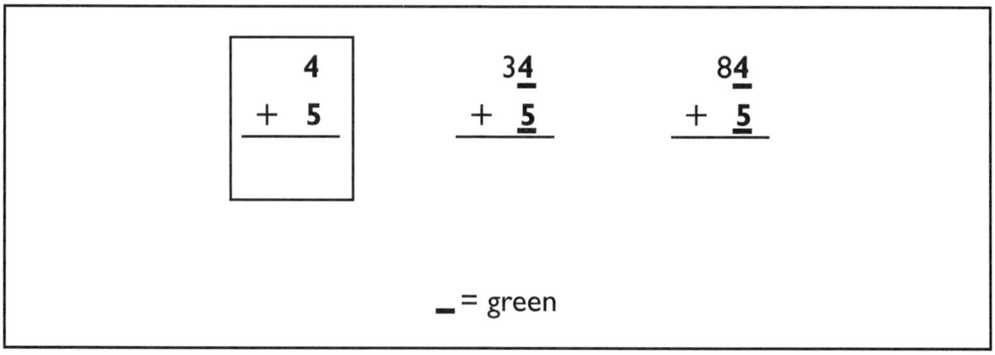

$$
\begin{array}{r}
4 \\
+ \ 5 \\
\hline
\end{array}
\qquad
\begin{array}{r}
3\underline{4} \\
+ \ \underline{5} \\
\hline
\end{array}
\qquad
\begin{array}{r}
8\underline{4} \\
+ \ \underline{5} \\
\hline
\end{array}
$$

_ = green

Figure 6.31.

- multiply multiples of 10 and 100. (Use color-coding and auditory or kinesthetic-tactile cues to help children to recognize and use the pattern of multiplying the non-zero numbers and adding the tail-end zeros.) Students should record calculator answers to any problem they do not immediately recognize, then analyze several clusters of facts to identify the pattern:

    Cluster 1: $3 \times 2 = 6$, so $30 \times 2 = 60$, $3 \times 20 = 60$, and $300 \times 2 = 600$.

    Cluster 2: $5 \times 3 = 15$, so $50 \times 3 = 150$, $50 \times 30 = 1,500$, and $500 \times 3 = 1,500$.

    Cluster 3: $2 \times 6 = 12$, so $20 \times 6 = 120$, $6 \times 20 = 120$, and $60 \times 20 = 1,200$.

2. **Apply to mental multiplication and division.** The major use of mental math involves multiplying multiples of 10 or 100 to check whether a given product or quotient is reasonable, as in Figure 6.32. Some students can learn to carry out simple one-digit multiplications like 12×3, 31×4, or $\$2.50 \times 2$ mentally. Unless the student is interested in doing so, further mental calculation of products may not be useful. The value of mentally computing simple quotients beyond division basic facts is limited.

Computational Estimation

Estimation applied to computation involves giving an answer that is "close to" the actual one. As such, it involves the ability to carry out some calculations mentally and assumes skills related to place value, rounding, and basic facts. Everyone estimates every day, in one form or another. "I think I can eat that much bread." "I think I have enough time to get to school." "I think I have enough money for what I'm taking to the check-out counter." Every day, newspaper headlines are full of estimates, and referring to them is a good way to

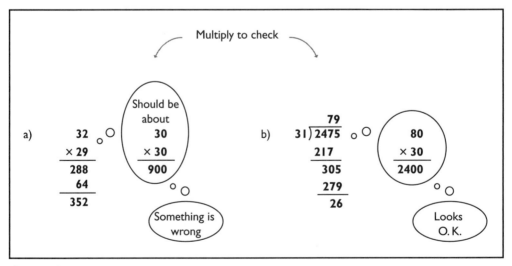

Figure 6.32.

acquaint students with the fact that in *most* everyday situations involving number, an estimate is "good enough."

Instructional emphasis focusing on the following steps is useful:

- developing an awareness of what estimation is about (an approximate rather than an exact answer, as one is used to giving in math);

- developing an awareness of how frequently an estimate is used in everyday numeric situations;

- developing an awareness of when an estimate is good enough and when one is not good enough;

- developing a range of estimation strategies;

- using estimation strategies in practical and other problem-solving situations;

- using estimation to judge whether results obtained are reasonable ones.

At times, exact answers are needed. If your neighbor agreed to pay you $2.10 an hour for a job, and you worked 2 hours, then "about $4" is *not* good enough. If there are 23 people at a party and the host thinks "about 20" when she brings out the party treats, that is *not* good enough.

On the other hand, there are times when an estimate might actually be better. Consider the following: You are going to meet some friends at 8:00. It usually takes about two and one half hours to drive there. You may want to allow a little more than that just in case something happens. An estimate is certainly good enough and probably better than relying on the exact time it took on previous drives.

When one estimates, a certain amount of mental calculation is involved. Exact answers, however, are not a goal. In fact, one typically computes with numbers that have been rounded off or otherwise simplified rather than with the actual numbers in the problem. The activities presented below first focus on helping students with learning disabilities learn and use the more important estimation strategies that are now a standard part of school mathematics curriculum. As in their work with mental calculation, these students may need to write out intermediate numbers as the basis for a final estimation. This may be especially true for children with difficulty with working memory, short-term memory, or sequential memory.

✎ Sample Sequence of Activities

1. **Focus on lead-digit or front-end addition.** Figure 6.33a suggests one way of helping students understand estimating by focusing on the "lead" digits of a problem. This approach is actually easier than rounding for many children. Instead of boxing lead digits, you might color-code them green during initial phases of instruction.

2. **Adjust the estimate.** In some situations, the rough estimate may be formed by calculating with lead digits. In other cases, a closer estimate may

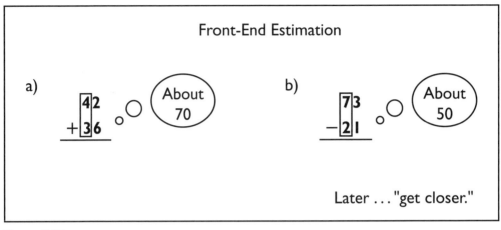

Figure 6.33.

be more desirable. When children have made an initial estimate by focusing on lead or front-end digits, then they might consider whether that estimate is good enough or they can "get closer."

In the example of Figure 6.33a, since there are 8 ones, that means that 70 is an underestimate. If the decision is to get a closer estimate, students need to note that there are almost enough ones to make another 10. A closer estimate is 80. Students might work a series of problems like that given in Figure 6.33a in steps. As a first step, they might make just the rough "lead-digit" estimate. As a second step, perhaps taking turns with the teacher or a partner, they might decide whether they are close to making another 10.

3. **Lead-digit or front-end subtraction.** Figure 6.33b suggests how similar work might be structured for subtraction. At first only a rough, "lead-digit" estimate is made. Later, children might be helped to determine at least whether the actual difference is "more" or "less."

In Figure 6.33b, for example, because 3 (in the ones place) is more than 1, the actual difference is a little *more* than 50 (for there would be extra ones after subtracting). In a problem like 73 – 29, where the 3 (in the ones place) is less than the 9, then the actual difference is a little less than 50 (for one would "take away" one of the tens in regrouping).

4. **Rounding.** Some students may prefer to use rounding techniques. In Figure 6.33a, one might think: "About 40 + 40, or 80." This is the estimation method typically emphasized in school textbooks. It involves applying rounding skills (developed in the "Rounding and Estimation" section of Chapter 5), retaining each rounded digit, and then mentally computing with those digits. As with other attempts at mental math, some students will need to *write* the digits they have rounded as an intermediate step and reference for completing the estimation.

5. **Use "nice numbers."** Introduce the idea of looking for "nice numbers" (easier numbers). In Figure 6.34a, there clearly is enough to pay for one tape, but not enough for two. In Figure 6.34b, if only one can is needed, it's easier to overestimate as shown.

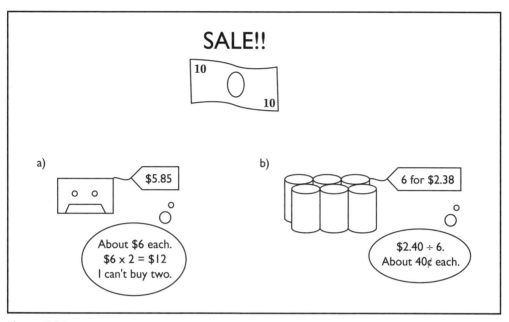

Figure 6.34.

6. **Use averaging.** Introduce the idea of averaging in order to get an estimate. When all numbers are "about the same"—as they may be in rainfall patterns in some areas, or in the individual meal costs for people sitting together in a restaurant—use the number that seems to be central. (For example: Four people are having lunch. The individual meals cost $12.50, $10.65, $15.35, and $13.75. The average will probably be somewhere around $13.00.) This number is sometimes called a "cluster point" or "average," though an average is not actually calculated.

7. **Just do those with answers of more than 40** (or any other assigned target number). Students must first develop estimation skill, as previously suggested. Then ask them to apply that skill in an interesting way. For example, ask them to estimate and then hand-compute just those problems for which they think the answer is above the target number.

It may be necessary to ask some students first to estimate and circle problems with an answer that is over the target number. When that step is checked, students could be directed to hand-solve the circled problems. Students working out of hardback books could place an acetate sheet over a page before circling. After that part of the assignment is checked, they could solve the circled problems on paper.

Each of the above activities requires students to decide between hand computation and some other calculation method. It also would be useful to systematically ask students to decide between estimation and mental calculation, estimation and using a calculator, and mental calculation and using a calculator. These types of activities involve viable alternatives and provide students with a background for deciding which computation method is "best" in a given situation in light of their abilities.

Determining Whether Results Are "Reasonable"

An important aspect of number sense is detecting whether a given estimate or other computational result is reasonable. This is a very difficult skill for many students with learning disabilities. Some of those students may be able to detect unreasonable answers only when results examined are "way off." We consider the achievement of this last skill to be of major importance and worth working toward. The suggestions that follow emphasize determining whether a stated result "makes sense." In implementing these suggestions care should be taken to make directions explicitly clear. Otherwise, students will tend to redo the computation rather than simply estimating, which is desired.

✏ Sample Sequence of Activities

1. **Select the most reasonable.** Students need opportunities to react to what is reasonable in a variety of contexts and situations. Noncomputational examples like those of Figure 6.35 may be used.

NOTE: *In order to estimate the answers to the problems in Figure 6.35, some students (not just small children) will need visual reminders. It may be helpful to provide real objects, have students weigh them (in the case of Figure 6.35a), and then decide. Alternatively, use pictures of common objects accompanied by approximate weights. In this way, especially students with expressive language or memory problems will have something to draw upon to help them estimate.*

2. **Predict the number of answer digits.** Having students identify the number of answer digits for specific computational examples helps them focus on the size of the answer. Later, they can examine the "size" of an answer to judge, rather quickly, whether it is unreasonable. One would expect the Figure 6.36 problem, for instance, to contain three digits. So something is wrong.

3. **One right on, one way off.** To start, it is easier for students to detect unreasonable answers when the same problem is presented twice: once with a correct answer; once with an answer that is "way off" as in Figure 6.37. Simi-

---

a) The telephone weighs about _____ pounds.

3   30   300

b) The number of books Tom carried to shool in his bag was about _____ .

4   40   400

Figure 6.35.

$$
\begin{array}{r}
\overset{\text{\tiny 2}}{3}4 \\
\times\ 5 \\
\hline
50
\end{array}
$$

Figure 6.36.

larly, many students find it easier to detect wrong answers when they are paired with correct ones or when they know that one of the pair is wrong. Each time, talk through the estimate(s) used to make the decision. This type of activity prepares for the recommendation in Activity 4 below.

4. **Does my answer make sense?** Give students calculations as in Activity 3 above, but mix the problems in with others. Gradually present random problems of the same general type—some that have correct answers and others with answers that are way off target. Ask students to identify those that make no sense. Talk through the estimates used to make the decision.

ADDITION OF WHOLE NUMBERS

Regrouping for Addition

Problem Area: Difficulty regrouping when adding two-digit numbers.

Typical Disabilities Affecting Progress: Difficulty with abstract reasoning, perseveration, visual figure-ground, reversals, and working memory.

Background: Many students are unable to retain a lot of information at one time. The many discrete steps involved in adding two-digit numbers are difficult enough for them, and they may not readily recognize when or know how to regroup. Automatic recognition becomes even more difficult as regrouping is extended to the hundreds place. The student must simultaneously make decisions while trying to recall correctly the sequence for carrying out the computation. In many cases, regrouping difficulty is a result of poor conceptual

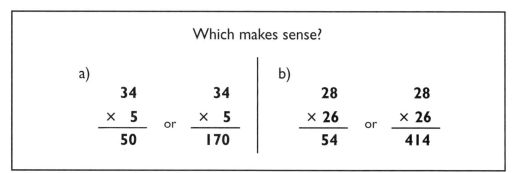

Figure 6.37.

understanding of place value. For the child with learning disabilities, however, all too often it is simply due to an inability to think without obvious, visual cues.

The following suggestions are helpful for children who have difficulty knowing when or how to regroup when adding two two-digit numbers. The suggestions assume that the children:

- possess adequate numeration understanding for two- and three-digit numbers (see Chapter 5); and

- understand, at least informally, that when adding two two-digit numbers, one adds like units and trades 10 ones for 1 ten whenever you have 10 or more ones.

The latter prerequisite assumes that the students have used grouping aids such as unifix cubes (10-trains and extra ones), popsicle sticks (10-bundles and extra sticks), chips (10-stacks and extra chips), or base-10 blocks or graph paper (tens and ones) to dramatize these ideas. Once this foundation is established and the child is ready to begin formally regrouping, activities like the following may be useful. Included in these activities are ideas for helping students with special perceptual, sequencing, memory, and abstract-reasoning difficulties.

✏️ Sample Sequence of Activities

1. **Readiness activity for two-digit addition.** Several months prior to formally introducing two-digit computation for both addition and subtraction, readiness activities should be carried out. Addition problems like the following should be presented to students:

- The baker baked 25 sugar donuts and 17 chocolate donuts. How many donuts did he bake?

- Yolanda counted 32 cookies that Grandma had already baked. Grandma said she still had 14 in the oven. All together, how many cookies did Grandma bake?

To foster readiness for formal computation with two-digit numbers, the opportunity to carry out the following tasks on repeated occasions are critical:

- Ask the child to write the numbers heard as the "story" problem is shared.

- Add a rebus as in Activity 1 (page 211) of "Part-Whole and Basic Concept Development" and invite a child to retell the story in his or her own words.

- Ask the child to use tens and ones (preferably unifix 10-trains and loose cubes) to solve the problem, explain what was done, and write the number sentence to match.

Note that *there is no formal regrouping at this point.* There should be two agreements between teacher and student as students use the tens and ones pieces:

- All cubes not needed for the problem are placed in a bag on the floor or in a designated area.

- So that the cubes can be quickly counted (by the teacher), make 10-trains whenever possible.

The readiness occurs as children repeatedly decide whether they have enough to group by tens. Readiness is further enhanced when students verbalize what they have done.

NOTE: *Similar readiness work should be carried out for subtraction. See the section "Two- and Three-Digit Subtraction with Regrouping," page 246.*

2. **What can't it be?** Present examples like those of Figure 6.38—"What can't the answer be? Why?"

Students will probably realize that 312 makes no sense. If they do not, have them use tens and ones to show 25 + 17—"Can't be 312—it doesn't come close. It's like—less than 2 quarters!" If students are at a loss to reason beyond counting, model good reasoning and repeat using similar examples—"Until you work with the loose ones you don't know if you have enough to make a 10-train. *That's why mathematicians have decided to 'work backwards'—to add ones first, then tens."* Have students use tens and ones to work out the problem, *combining ones first*—as you record step by step what happens. Then reverse roles: as you work out a similar problem, the student records. Repeat for several problems, some with regrouping, some without. *Ask the student* to summarize how to add two-digit numbers—verbally, by showing, or in writing (color-coding the ones digits green, to match the student's learning strength). Provide a basic fact chart or use other ideas in the section of this chapter called "Computation: General Difficulties" if basic facts have not been memorized.

3. **A few each day.** Repeat the following type of activity over a period of several days. Present a two-digit addition word problem. Have students write the numbers and then retell the "story" using your rebus for reference. Use tens and ones to solve, record step by step, and, finally, explain what was done. The goal is for students to independently record the solution or tell a partner what to record, step by step, to match what is done.

4. **Help for special difficulties.** If students forget to regroup as they record and write the sum as in Figure 6.38a, consider these ideas:

- **What can't it be?** Repeat Activity 2 above. Place the student's (incorrect) work and a correctly worked example side by side.

```
      a)                 b)
            25                  25
          + 17                + 17
          -----               -----
           312                  42
```

Figure 6.38.

- **A box cue.** Color-coded reminder boxes, such as those pictured in Figure 6.39 serve two needs, by providing:

  - help in the transition to the standard computational format for addition with regrouping; and

  - help for students with reversal tendencies.

In the example of Figure 6.39a, the children obtain 13 ones when they add. The normal pattern for writing 13 is "1" then "3"; so **urge children to follow this sequence when recording their answer.** *(Resist the tendency to follow tradition in arithmetic and tell students to "write the 3, carry the 1," as that only encourages reversals.)* The color scheme of Figure 6.39 encourages a more appropriate sequence for students with reversal tendencies: 1 first (in the *green* "go on" box), then 3 on the *red* "stop" line. Figure 6.39b suggests how to format pages in advance—to be filed and pulled as needed. When preparing the pages, include the boxes on all problems, even when regrouping is not needed. That forces students to determine whether regrouping is needed.

- **Doctor the text.** When using a text or workbook page, allow the students to draw dashes under each problem to match the columns (e.g., two columns, two dashes). This often serves as a reminder that only one digit is allowed per space. (If the textbook problems are too small for the students to mark, enlarge the textbook page, ask adult volunteers to help prepare texts in advance, or provide larger-sized problems on worksheets for the students to self-mark.)

- **Picture it: 10 ones for 1 ten.** Review the idea of exchanging 10 ones for 1 ten using chips (glued [green] 10-stacks and loose [red] ones) and color-coded tens and ones frames as in Figure 6.40a. The child fills in the spaces to describe the picture on the left and is then reminded that "something is not right. There are two digits in one of the spaces." The student trades 10 red chips for a green 10-stack, again filling in the blanks (Figure 6.40b), and then fills in the blanks in Figure 6.40c. Auditorially reinforce what is being done: "Yes, if there are 10 or more ones, trade 10 ones for a 10-stack."

NOTE: *For some students it may now be useful to switch to a frame that is designed to hold no more than 9 chips in the ones column.*

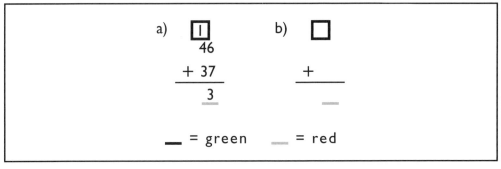

Figure 6.39.

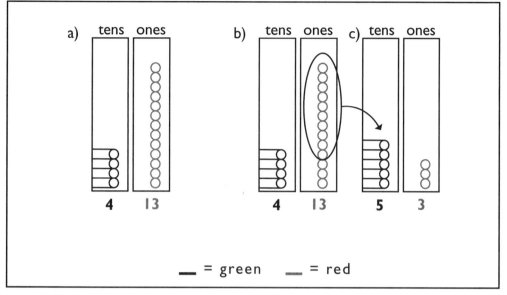

Figure 6.40.

• **Need to trade?** For students with sequencing or abstract-reasoning difficulties, exercises like that of Figure 6.41 may be helpful. "Are there 2 digits in one space?" To answer this question for each example, children may be asked to examine the right-hand boxes and circle those boxes that "are not right" and make them right—so the ones place is not overloaded.

NOTE: *It may be important for students with abstract-reasoning difficulties, particularly those who do not automatically employ flexible thinking—and also those with expressive language difficulties who may need a visual prompt to elicit related language, either silently or aloud—to have a card, or perhaps a reference page in their dictionary (see Chapter 2, "Language and Mathematics") such as that in Figure 6.42.*

• **Now add.** Directly follow through with exercises like those shown in Figure 6.43. *Note that part of the page is visually similar to previous work. This may take some pressure off the student.* If the student overloads the ones place when adding, the visual (color-coded) stimulus of the previous exercise will trigger the need to "make things right."

Column Addition

Problem Area: Inability to complete the sequence in column addition.

Typical Disabilities Affecting Progress: Difficulty with short-term, sequential, or working memory and/or visual figure-ground.

Background: Although a student may understand column addition conceptually, perceptually it can be extremely difficult, especially when "ragged

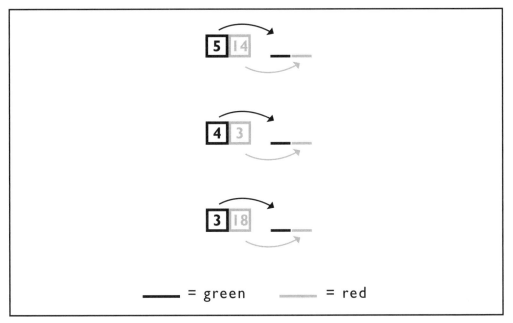

Figure 6.41.

columns" or regrouping is involved, as in Figure 6.44. Children with figure-ground difficulties find it especially hard to "keep the place" while copying or computing problems of this type. To complicate matters, the three-addend problem is really a four-addend problem because of the regrouping. The child who worked the example of Figure 6.44 handled the ones column addition correctly, even the regrouping, but forgot the 1 while adding the tens column.

For some students, using a hand calculator for column addition is a viable alternative to paper-and-pencil computation. Indeed, sometimes calculator use or estimation should take precedence over hand calculations. However, most

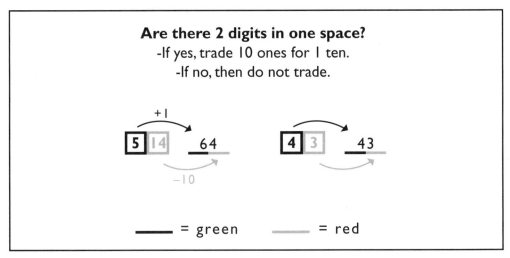

Figure 6.42.

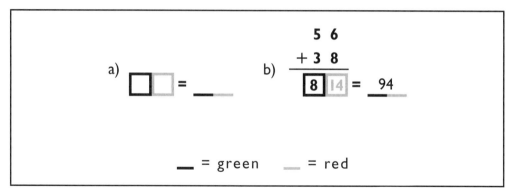

Figure 6.43.

students with learning disabilities can learn to add a sequence of three or four numbers. Compensatory techniques such as the following have proven effective in helping students acquire this skill.

✎ Sample Sequence of Activities

1. **One step at a time.** Approach column addition one step at a time. Prepare practice pages containing problems like that shown in Figure 6.45a. Before writing the final sum, the student fills in the blank line to the right of the problem with the sum of the first two addends. Use green for the first two addends and their answer line, red for the arrow and the last addend.

NOTE: *Pages using the problem format of Figure 6.45b can be kept on file and used as needed. The teacher fills in specific numbers if a controlled-fact program is used. Students can also copy problems from the text onto these pages. Alternatively, if textbook space is not too confining, the students can color-code text problems before solving. If difficulty with column addition is anticipated, textbooks could be coded in advance (perhaps at the beginning of the school year) by adult volunteers.*

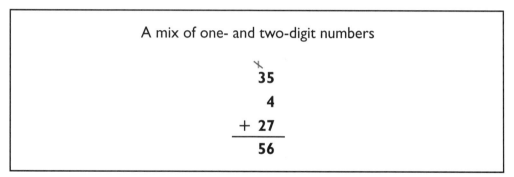

Figure 6.44.

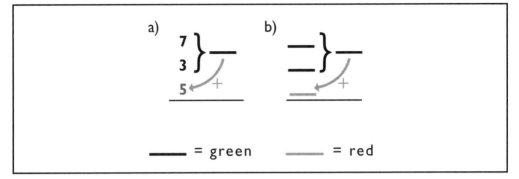

Figure 6.45.

2. **Cross out means 10.** For children with good visual but poor sequential memory, the approach of Figure 6.46 has proven helpful. The child adds down the column until a two-digit answer ($8 + 9 = 17$) is reached. The last digit that was added, in this case 9, is crossed out to represent the 10 in the sum. The student retains the 7 mentally and combines it with the next number to be added, in this case 6. The 6 is crossed out to indicate the 10 in 13, and the child writes down the 3. The number carried is the same as the number of digits crossed out, in this case 2. The same approach is used for remaining columns.

3. **Write the ones.** If visual memory or reversal deficits require that a child write subsums, the procedure suggested in Figure 6.47 can be used. The student adds the first two addends. Since the sum (16) is a two-digit number, the second 8 is crossed out and the 6 is written down, in that order. $6 + 9 = 15$, so the 9 is crossed out and the 5 is written below the line. As before, the number of crossed digits represents what should be carried.

4. **Visual helps.** For students having visual figure-ground or other perceptual deficits, any of the following techniques may be used.

- Teach the children to color-highlight a column before adding it (Figure 6.48a).

- Provide square centimeter paper and instruct the students to write one digit per square (Figure 6.48b).

- Provide vertically lined paper and instruct the students to write every digit on a line (Figure 6.48c).

$$
\begin{array}{r}
\overset{2}{68} \\
\cancel{49} \\
+\ 3\cancel{6} \\
\hline
153
\end{array}
$$

Figure 6.46.

$$\begin{array}{r} \overset{2}{58} \\ \overset{0}{3}\overset{6}{8} \\ +\ 4\overset{5}{9} \\ \hline 145 \end{array}$$

Figure 6.47.

- Provide a tachistoscopic card for covering columns not being added. The card should cover only the problem, with room to write the carried number at the top and the answer in the proper place. As the student works, the card is moved along so that only the numbers being added show through the slot. Figure 6.48d shows a step-by-step approach for using the card to solve an addition problem with three three-digit addends.

NOTE: *The entire card can be covered with acetate and children could be allowed to use a grease pencil to write the ones digit of subsums directly on it (see Activity 3 above). The acetate is wiped clean before another column is added.*

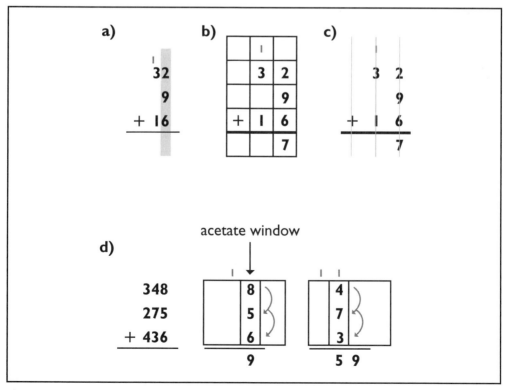

Figure 6.48.

SUBTRACTION OF WHOLE NUMBERS

When children turn to subtraction, they meet difficulties similar to those encountered in whole-number addition. It is not uncommon for some students to have problems subtracting a single-digit from a two-digit number; others find it hard to subtract multiples of 10. Knowing when and how to regroup are major stumbling blocks in subtraction, as in addition, especially for children with learning difficulties. Many of the activities described in the previous sections can be adjusted and used to aid in handling parallel difficulties in subtraction. Since some problems with regrouping require slightly different techniques than previously discussed, the following two sections will give additional suggestions for this topic.

As with addition, be accepting of invented, accurate, algorithms that may be more meaningful for individual children than "standard" approaches. Continue to embed subtraction computation in interesting, relevant problem situations.

Two- and Three-Digit Subtraction with Regrouping

Problem Area: Difficulty knowing when and how to regroup in subtraction of two- and three-digit numbers.

Typical Disabilities Affecting Progress: Difficulty with abstract reasoning, perseveration, visual figure-ground, reversals, and sequencing.

Background: As with addition, knowing when to regroup in subtraction is difficult for many students. Many tend to subtract the smaller from the larger number, regardless of its position within the problem. Figure 6.49 illustrates this error, typical also of children who do not exhibit specific disabilities. Often this error stems from poor conceptual understanding of the process of subtracting with regrouping. Some children with learning disabilities have strong concepts but visually reverse the numbers.

Other factors contribute to the widespread difficulty in this area. Figure 6.1 illustrated, step by step, how subtraction with regrouping is really a combination of subtraction and addition. The process requires a tremendous amount of mental computation and constant switching from one operation to the next and then back again. Thus, children are continually having to make decisions—they must know not only when to regroup, but also how. That involves realizing what operation to use and then applying it at each discrete step.

Several approaches may be used to develop the proper procedure for two-digit and three-digit subtraction with regrouping. Generally, it is most helpful to use the simplest model, that of "take away," as the basis for subtraction com-

$$
\begin{array}{r}
64 \\
- \ 35 \\
\hline
31
\end{array}
$$

Figure 6.49.

putation. In the problem 68 – 49, for example, students can be cued to think: "8 take away 9. Since there are not enough ones, a trade must be made (1 ten for 10 ones)." The "take away" approach aptly dramatizes the "big ideas" underlying subtraction computation: subtract like units; if there are not enough, make a trade. This approach constitutes the basis for the suggestions that follow.

✎ Sample Sequence of Activities

1. **Readiness activity for two-digit subtraction.** As with addition, readiness for subtraction computation should be carried out well in advance of formal instruction. This readiness should be embedded in problem solving and include problems like the following:

- The baker baked 42 sugar donuts and sold 18. How many donuts did he have left?

- Grandma baked 36 cookies, but we ate 12 of them. How many cookies did Grandma have left?

To foster *readiness* for formal subtraction computation with two-digit numbers, students should be repeatedly engaged in tasks similar to those laid out in Activity 1 under "Regrouping for Addition," page 237.

- Ask the child to write the numbers heard as the "story" problem is shared.

- Add a rebus as in Activity 1 (page 211) of "Part-Whole and Basic Concept Development" and invite a child to retell the story in his or her own words.

- Ask the child to use tens and ones (preferably unifix 10-trains and loose cubes) to solve the problem, explain what was done, and write a number sentence to match.

Note that there is no formal regrouping at this point. As with addition, students should place all cubes not needed for the problem in a bag on the floor or in a designated area.

Students will need to "break a 10" if there is not enough to take what is needed. *The readiness occurs as children repeatedly decide and articulate whether they have enough to take what they need or they need to break a 10. Readiness is further enhanced when students verbalize what they did.*

2. **Fair trade** (to prepare for a natural, meaningful transition to two-digit subtraction with regrouping). Provide a deck of laminated cards like that pictured in Figure 6.50a and a "band" of 10-stacks and loose chips. Taking turns, the children draw one card at a time and use the chips to indicate the number on the card. The teacher leads the following discussion by saying: "The bank needs another 10-stack. Will you trade one of yours for loose chips? How many loose chips would make a fair trade? [10 loose chips for the 10-stack.] Write what you have now" (see Figure 6.50b). Repeat with other cards, making a record of the trade each time.

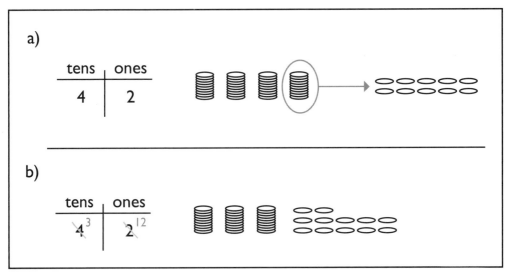

Figure 6.50.

3. **Take away.** Pose a problem like that of the baker with 42 donuts who sold 18. Relate the trade idea of Activity 1 above to two-digit subtraction with regrouping. In the example of Figure 6.51a, the children use 10-stacks and loose chips to show what the baker started with (42 donuts). The buyer wants 18. As in addition, we'll work with ones first, then tens—so the storyline has the buyer getting 8 loose donuts first, then a "box" of 10. Since there are only 2 loose ones to begin with, Figure 6.51b shows how a "box" of 10 is opened—so then there are 3 tens, 12 loose ones. The final result is in Figure 6.51c: after selling, there are 2 boxes of 10 and 4 loose ones, 24, left.

4. **Are there enough?** Some children—those with abstract-reasoning difficulties, those who are impulsive, and those who perseverate—may fall into the pattern of regroup, subtract, regroup, subtract. This pattern is continued whether regrouping is required or not. Force children to decide about regrouping. One suggestion is to present mixed problem types like those of Figure 6.52. Note that the ones digit of the minuend has been visually highlighted to focus attention on it. The children start with this digit each time and decide whether there are enough, so they can "take away" the number represented by the digit directly beneath it. (Use chips as in Activity 2 above, if necessary, to dramatize the first few problems.) Ask the children to circle the problem if there are not enough. Do not require that they complete the problems at this time.

5. **Help them decide.** Some students need more structured assistance before they can succeed with the task presented in Activity 4. Figure 6.53 shows one type of exercise that can be used. The underlining helps the children focus on the correct starting point in each problem. To force them to think more clearly about the relationship between the numbers, ask them to read across the line and fill in the blanks while doing so. Eventually, they internalize the sentence. As they do other problems, they are more likely to think about the way the exercise has prompted them.

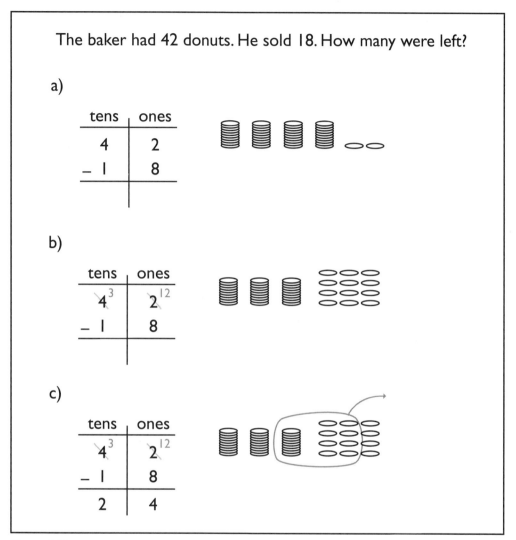

The baker had 42 donuts. He sold 18. How many were left?

a)

tens	ones
4	2
– 1	8

b)

tens	ones
4³	2¹²
– 1	8

c)

tens	ones
4³	2¹²
– 1	8
2	4

Figure 6.51.

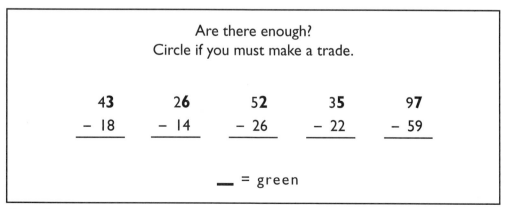

Are there enough?
Circle if you must make a trade.

43	26	52	35	97
– 18	– 14	– 26	– 22	– 59

___ = green

Figure 6.52.

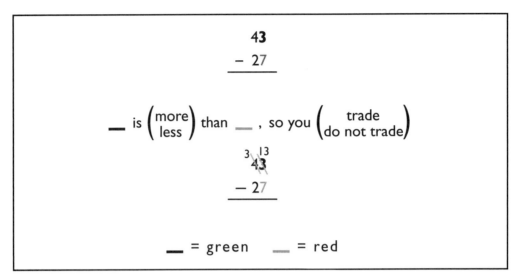

Figure 6.53.

NOTE: *The phrase "make a trade," used during work with 10-stacks and loose chips in previous activities, is used throughout the rest of this sequence. Some teachers may prefer to use the term "regroup." Whatever the students understand best should be adopted.*

6. **Cue box.** For children who have trouble sequencing or do not automatically associate written words with numbers, the cueing technique in Figure 6.54 has proven helpful. Pages of this type can be used to reinforce the last step of the sequence discussed in Activity 5 above.

7. **Block out.** As regrouping is extended to the tens and hundreds places, it is often necessary to remind students to continue thinking in the correct way. The "block out" card shown in Figure 6.55 is helpful in this regard. Used by the child as a marker while solving subtraction problems, the card serves to block out extraneous numbers, thereby allowing the child to focus on the pertinent numbers.

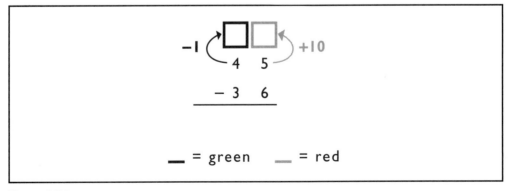

Figure 6.54.

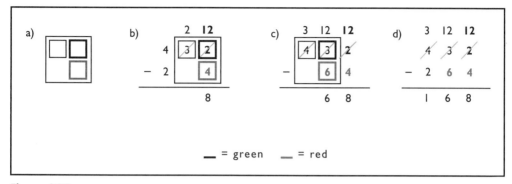

Figure 6.55.

8. **Different strokes.** Subtract like units—if there are not enough, make a trade. These are the "big ideas" behind subtraction. Some students apply these ideas, step by step, when computing: first ones, then tens, and so on. Others benefit by first going through an entire problem, noting all places where regrouping is necessary. Once this is done, they can backtrack and perform the computation. Children who benefit most from this latter method are those who have trouble sequencing or making switches in their thought process, and those who have difficulty with number alignment. Rather than forcing one procedural pattern on all students, note which method is easiest for an individual.

9. **Do it backwards!** Children with severe reversal problems often benefit from working problems left to right. In the example shown in Figure 6.56 the child begins with 9 – 2 = 7. Next, the student thinks, "5 take away 9." Recognizing the need to make a trade, the child crosses out the 7 and writes 6 beneath it. The 5 is crossed out and 15 is written above. The explanation is that, after the first subtraction, we still have 7 hundreds left, enough to trade, when necessary, for the 5. A similar procedure is used to complete the problem. (The approach is similar to the equal-additions methods illustrated in Figure 6.57, but it is easier for children with reversal tendencies to understand and follow.) For those who need help with number alignment, use graph paper or pages containing examples like that of Figure 6.58.

10. **Into the maze** (for two or three players). To reinforce the correct sequence, the need to regroup, and the skill of adding 10 to a number, prepare a game board as in Figure 6.59a. Also provide a grease pencil and wipe-off rag,

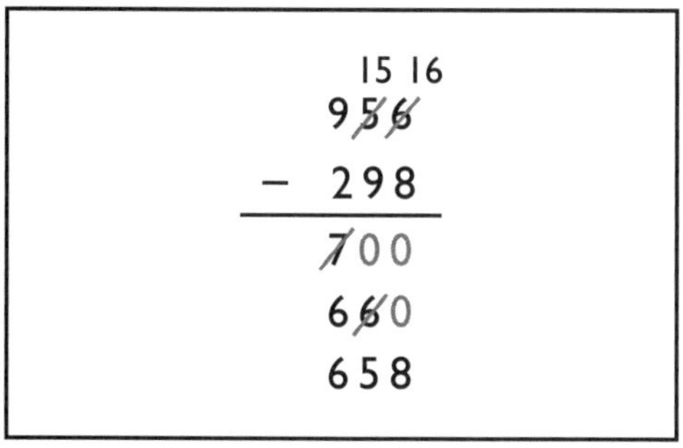

Figure 6.56.

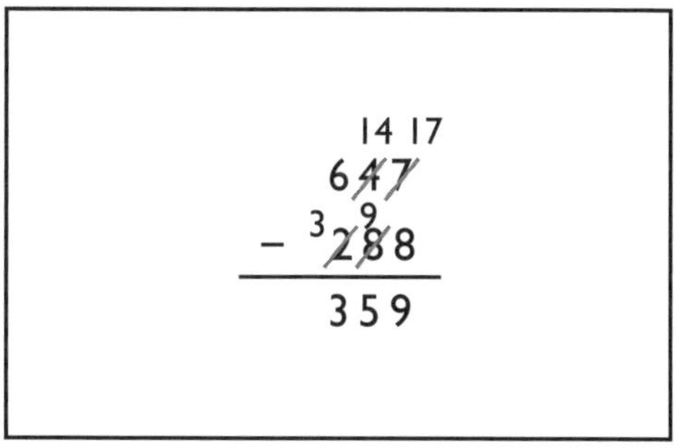

Figure 6.57.

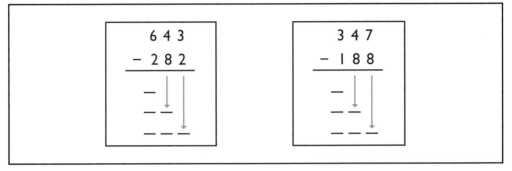

Figure 6.58.

a deck of laminated cards with subtraction problems like those of Figure 6.59b, an envelope for the cards, and a game marker for each player. To begin, cards are mixed and placed in the envelope. Taking turns, the players draw a card, state the problem, and decide whether a trade is necessary. If so, a grease pencil is used to show the trade. After the player adds 10 to the green number, he or she moves that many spaces on the board. If no trade is needed, the player simply subtracts the two numbers. The result is the number of spaces he or she may move. Answers can be checked by flipping to the back sides of cards. The first student to reach the garden in the middle of the maze wins.

Zero in Subtraction

Problem Area: Difficulty regrouping when zero appears in the minuend.
   Typical Disabilities Affecting Progress: Difficulty with sequencing, spatial organization, memory, reversals, and abstract reasoning.

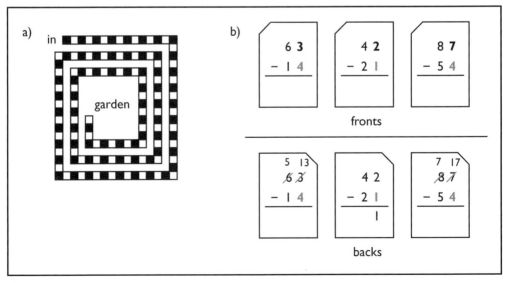

Figure 6.59.

Background: Zero difficulties are more prominent in subtraction than in addition. In subtraction of two-digit numbers with zero minuend digits, for example, the tendency to reverse is more dominant than when only nonzero digits appear (see Figure 6.60). Some children simply ignore the zero (Figure 6.61). Because of these and other erratic errors children often make, it is generally more beneficial to teach the concept and process of subtraction with regrouping before introducing zero in the problem. The specific lessons, incorporating ideas such as those that follow, could be carried out to help the children deal with zero in subtraction computations.

✎ Sample Sequence of Activities

1. **Act it out.** Use the "Fair Trade" and "Take Away" activities of the previous section to provide a physical frame of reference for two-digit subtraction with 0 in the minuend. Use multiples of 10 (20, 30 . . . 90) for the "fair trade" activity and include these same numbers in the minuend for the "take away" activity. (A sample problem for this latter activity is 60 – 13.)

2. **Think about it.** Prepare pages using the format of Figure 6.53, placing zero on the green line. If the child does not respond to the verbal association, adapt the "Cue Box" activity (Activity 6) of the previous section to work with zero.

3. **Circle.** Follow up with pages that mix zero and nonzero digits in the minuend for two-digit subtractions. Include both regrouping and nonregrouping. At first, just ask students to circle problems where a trade must be made. At a later time, they can complete the subtractions.

4. **Different names.** Use base-10 blocks (or graph paper models) or (if students' money concepts are strong enough) use bills—$100s, $10s, and $1s. In turn, model numbers like 203 and 304 and elicit that, for example, 203 can be shown using 2 hundreds, no tens, and 3 ones OR (after making fair trades) as 20 tens and 3 ones. Repeat until students are comfortable with this idea.

5. **One step.** Show the children how to make a trade (regroup) in one step, as in Figure 6.62. Initially, underline the 60 to focus attention—"We can think of this as 6 hundreds and no tens. We can also think of it as 60 tens. That's easier. When we borrow 1 ten, we have 59 tens left. Now we give that 1 ten to the 2."

6. **Hidden zero.** The method of Activity 4 above can also be used with a hidden zero, as shown in Figure 6.63. The student still views 71 as 71 tens, thus eliminating one regrouping step.

7. **Do it backwards.** An alternative to the "One Step" activity above is the method of subtraction explained in Activity 9 of the previous section ("Do It

Figure 6.60.

Figure 6.61.

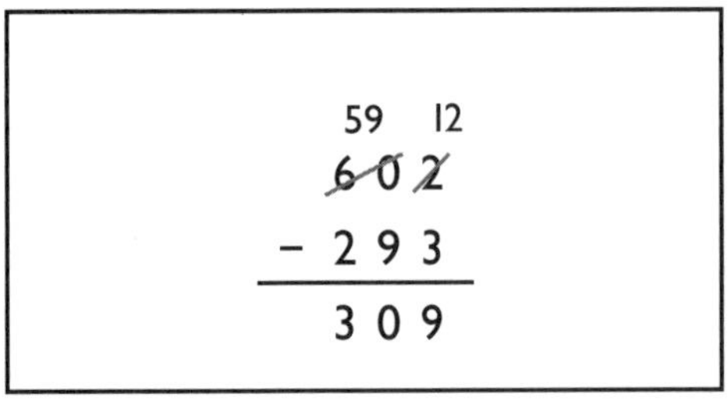

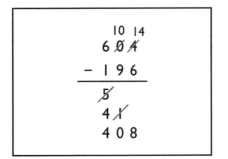

Figure 6.62.

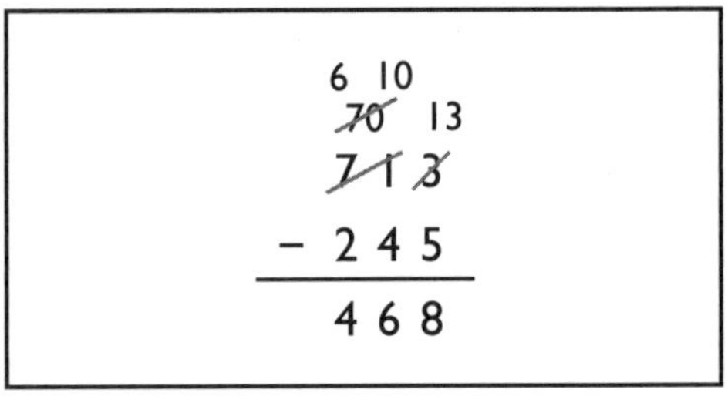

Figure 6.63.

Backwards"). This approach (as in Figure 6.64) has proven helpful to some students when a zero is in the tens place. Often children become confused when they reach the step shown in Figure 6.65. Continuity has been broken, and many, particularly those with short-term memory deficits, forget why they were doing what they were doing. The "backwards" left-right approach may help eliminate this problem.

MULTIPLICATION OF WHOLE NUMBERS

This section troubleshoots to meet targeted special needs that children experience with whole number multiplication. These problems may emerge as students work cooperatively or individually to solve problems in which multiplication is needed. Some teachers may choose to implement the suggestions presented here as a way of anticipating students' needs and thereby alleviating difficulties that might otherwise arise.

Though both one-digit and two-digit factors are treated, the need to be sensitive to individual needs and abilities is paramount. In favor of a *thinking* curriculum, written computation that is longer and more complex for any individual student might well be bypassed by employing a stronger program of calculator use, so that more important and mathematically significant aspects of the curriculum might be addressed. For all students, systematic review and integration of mental calculation and estimation strategies are important, as well as the expectation to continue to select the most appropriate computation method in any given problem situation.

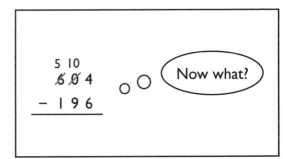

Figure 6.64.

Figure 6.65.

One-Digit Factors

Problem Area: Difficulty adding the regrouped digit or remembering the sequential steps of the algorithm; confusing the multiplication procedure with the more familiar addition procedure.

Typical Disabilities Affecting Progress: Problems related to short-term memory, visual memory, working memory, reversals, sequential memory, and figure-ground.

Background: Many students have trouble adding the regrouped digit when learning to multiply because they cannot perform the required mental computation. They may know the basic facts, but, if they cannot retrieve an accurate image of the two-digit number, they are bound to have trouble computing with it. Consider Figure 6.66. This student had no trouble with multiplication. Numbers were carried out properly and aligned properly, and the operations were sequenced correctly. What happened then? Notice the 85 in the product. After correctly recording first the tens and then the ones digit of 48, the student mentally reversed the digits for 18 (6×3). The child thought "81," and for that number the sum 85 ($81 + 4$) is correct. The digits of the product 48 were probably not reversed because they were recorded as said. There was no need to sort out a confused visual image.

We have noted how, as computational skills are expanded, the number of steps increases and accurate sequencing of the process becomes essential. Unless children have a clear conceptual understanding of the process and have overlearned each discrete procedure involved, it is often difficult for them to maintain the correct sequence and compute successfully at the symbolic level.

The activities that follow address conceptual foundations for multiplying with a one-digit factor and then focus on the one small step of the computational process for multiplication: adding the regrouped digit. The suggested exercises have proven effective in dealing with the problem highlighted in the example of Figure 6.66 as well as other related difficulties.

✎ Sample Sequence of Activities

1. **Act it out.** Use tens and ones to model a problem, as in Figure 6.67a. As with addition and subtraction, it's "first the ones, then the tens—so we know whether to regroup or not." As before, we also "make a 10" whenever we can. Elicit that multiplying (three 4s in Figure 6.67) then adding one extra ten has fewer steps (is faster than) any other way. The result of trading 10 ones for

```
        4
      3 8
    ×   6
    -------
    8 5 8
```

Figure 6.66.

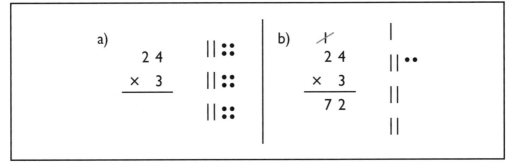

Figure 6.67.

1 ten, then carrying out the "multiply and add" step is shown in Figure 6.67b. Note how the "1" was crossed out when used in the calculation. This habit eliminates confusion with two-digit factors when more than one "carried digit" is shown.

2. **Relate.** If students have difficulty regrouping in multiplication, exercises like those of Figure 6.68 often prove helpful. These are an extension of the work begun in "Mentally Adding a One- and a Two-Digit Number" (page 229)

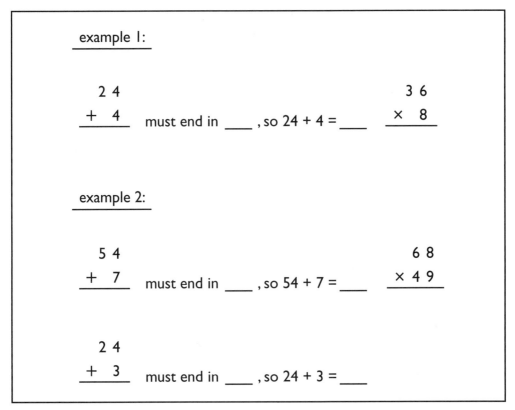

Figure 6.68.

and illustrated in Figure 6.29. Now an effort is made to relate the addition to its role in multiplication computation. In Figure 6.68 the student first solves an embedded addition problem and then a related multiplication problem. In example 1, students first find the sum of 24 and 4, filling in the spaces as they approach them verbally. The related multiplication is then carried out. When they reach the addition part of the problem, the children can look back at the answer. This eliminates the need to retain a reversed digit mentally. The speed with which the children can independently incorporate the addition procedure into multiplication will depend on how comfortable they are with the entire multiplication process. Allow them to use pages of this type so they can multiply with a minimum of interference from their learning deficits.

NOTE: *The second example illustrates how this idea can later be extended to work with two-digit factors.*

    3. **Color cue.** Figure 6.69 shows how to use color-coding to help students who have trouble sequencing even though visual discrimination presents little difficulty. The children are reminded to use the colors as a stoplight—multiplying first and then adding.

    4. **Different strokes.** The previous example can be adjusted as in Figure 6.70 for students who have trouble revisualizing the product in order to be able to combine it with the carried number. After multiplying the tens digit, the product (45) is written on the green line and added to the number carried.

    5. **Another alternative.** Students whose major difficulty is digit reversal when having to retain a number mentally should be encouraged to write the number down. Providing a box to the side of the problem, as in Figure 6.71, often is sufficient to avoid digit reversal. For left-handed students, place the box to the left of the problem.

Multiplying by Multiples of 10

This section focuses on developing understanding and skill when multiplying by multiples of 10. The specific link to "similar" one-digit multiplication problems is made through color-coding as a visual stimulus. The goal is for students to see the pattern of adding tail-end zeros, then completing problems using learned skills with one-digit factors.

Figure 6.69.

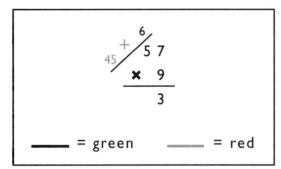

Figure 6.70.

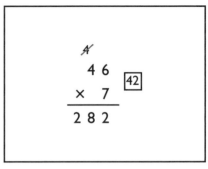

Figure 6.71.

Sample Sequence of Activities

1. **Look back.** Review multiplying one-digit numbers by multiples of 10 and 100 (Activity 1 under "Mental Multiplication and Division," page 231).

2. **Side by side.** Present multiplication problems like those shown in Figure 6.72. Children solve the first problem in each pair. Then, using a calculator, they arrive at the product for the second problem of the pair. (If there are not enough calculators for each student to have one, the children can take turns.) When the product is read to the class, it can be written on the board or an overhead. Use the colors as indicated to help the students notice the pattern. Gradually, extend the process to higher multiples of 10 and color-code them in the same manner.

3. **Relate.** A problem sequence like that of Figure 6.73 can be used effectively with students who, perceptually, cannot work the calculator. Remind the students of the relationship between multiplication and addition by initially setting up the problems as in Figure 6.73a. Most children who know their facts

Figure 6.72.

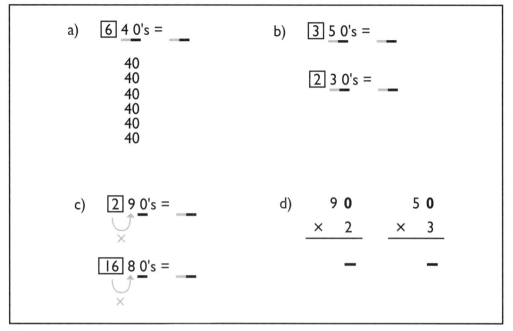

Figure 6.73.

and are strong conceptually will use multiplication to solve the problem, even in this form. Students who do not know the facts but understand the relationship between addition and multiplication can use a multiplication chart to solve the problems and cue them to the general pattern. The following narration, based on the problem of Figure 6.73a, suggests the type of discussion that might take place:

TEACHER: "Did you add the zeros each time?"

STUDENT: "No, they sort of tagged along each time."

TEACHER: "Right. What about the 4s? Did you add them?"

STUDENT: "No. 6×4 is 24, and that's easier."

By the time the students are working problems like those of Figure 6.73d, they generally note how "it's like multiplying by 2; since 90 ends in 0, so does the answer." A similar rationale can be used to support the multiplication of Figure 6.72. For 48×20, you write a zero in the product to show that you are multiplying by a multiple of 10. Otherwise, it is just like multiplying 2. Placing related pairs side by side on worksheets, as shown, reinforces this idea.

Two-Digit Factors

Problem Area: Difficulty multiplying two multidigit numbers.

Typical Disabilities Affecting Progress: Difficulty with spatial organization, working memory, sequencing, abstract reasoning, visual memory, and reversal.

Background: Many children have trouble multiplying two numbers when both factors contain two or more digits. The sequence is long and continually broken up by addition; a considerable amount of spatial organization is required, not only to place the numbers on the correct line, but also to align the digits properly; and visual memory and working memory are needed to retrieve the basic fact and regroup the correct number.

For many students, it is necessary to provide visual or auditory cues in early work involving two- or higher-digit multipliers even if they have a strong place-value comprehension and understand the use of the distributive idea for multiplication computation. The following activities suggest ways in which this can be done once the children are ready to begin this work at the symbolic level. It is assumed that the students can multiply two-digit numbers by one-digit factors and by multiples of 100.

Sample Sequence of Activities

1. **How many seats?** Consider this storyline to introduce two-digit factors in multiplication:

> The new playhouse has 23 seats in each row and has 25 rows. The first 5 rows are the reserve section—and have nicer seats than the rest. The other 20 rows are for general admission. How many reserve seats are there? How many general admission seats? How many seats does the playhouse have altogether?

Figure 6.74a illustrates the situation and the three tasks to be carried out:

- finding the number of reserved seats (5×23, a previously developed skill);

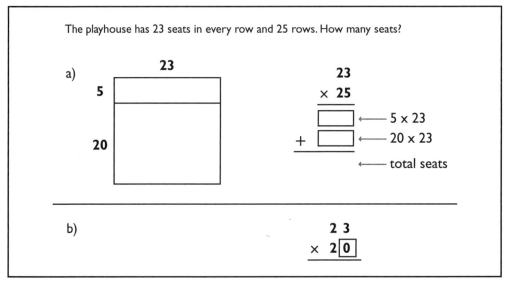

Figure 6.74.

- finding the number of general admission seats (20 × 23, a previously developed skill—using a post-it marked "0" as shown in Figure 6.74b helps to visually highlight this); and

- adding those two numbers to find the total seats in the playhouse.

The ideas that follow are helpful for developing these tasks with most students.

2. **Color cue.** Color-coded grid boxes, as in Figure 1.15, have been most effective in helping students organize the multiplication process, both spatially and sequentially. Figure 6.75 shows a sample problem completed by a child using the grid boxes. The student first multiplied by the green number (3). The digit to be carried was recorded in the green circle, and the units digit was placed in the appropriate green box. Next, the child multiplied 3 × 4, and added the 2 in the green circle. After crossing out the 2, the answer (4) was recorded in the second green box (the tens column). The student proceeded similarly with the multiplication by 20, this time using the red carrying circle and red boxes.

NOTE: *Students must be taught to write the carried digit first at all times and thereby avoid any tendency to reverse. Crossing out the carried digit should be a carryover of work with one-digit multipliers. When the colored circles are no longer used, the crossing-out technique will eliminate confusion over which digit to add whenever two or more carry digits appear.*

3. **Fade out.** As the students begin to feel comfortable with the process, the colors can gradually be eliminated, depending on the students' progress. Two suggestions follow.

- Children whose major difficulty appears to be spatial organization may be able to do without all the colors almost immediately. They will continue to need grid paper for a while, however, until they have overlearned the kinesthetic feeling and sequence. Gradually, the grid paper sheets can be replaced with pages using the format illustrated in Figure 6.76.

- Students having primarily sequencing difficulties may need to retain the color cue for the factor digits and carrying circles for quite some time.

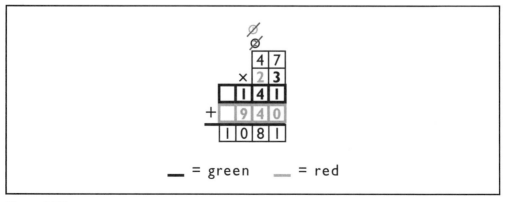

Figure 6.75.

$$
\begin{array}{r}
38 \\
\times\ 49 \\
\hline
----\\
+\ \underline{\quad\ -----}\\

\end{array}
$$

Figure 6.76.

4. **A zero card.** Children with figure-ground or abstract-reasoning deficits often benefit from being allowed to use a zero card or factor slide. Figure 6.77 shows, step by step, how a child uses a zero card. The student first uses the blank side of a card (Step 1) and covers the 6 (to block out extraneous numbers). After completing this multiplication, the card is flipped over and the 0 is placed over the 4. The idea being reinforced is that, to multiply by 64, you multiply first by 4 then by 60. Finally, you add the result. Figure 6.78 shows how a factor slide can be used in a similar way.

DIVISION OF WHOLE NUMBERS

The increased availability and lower cost of hand calculators, together with the infrequent need to use long division in day-to-day situations, has caused mathematics educators to question whether we should continue to teach the long-division algorithm. (The use of the calculator is an important component in teaching division, but it is essential that students have a clear understanding of decimal place value and its relation to fractions and remainders before using the calculator to solve division problems with remainders. In addition, care should be taken that the read-out on the screen is large enough for students with visual perceptual difficulties who may not otherwise see the decimal point.) In a real sense, the long division algorithm is as archaic as the square root algorithm. It clearly does not make much sense to spend 5 weeks on long division. In favor of emphasizing richer aspects of mathematics, this section

Problem:	Step 1:	Step 2:
48	$\overset{3}{4}8$	$\overset{4}{4}8$
× 64	×☐4	× 6⓪
	192	192
		+ 2880
		3072

Figure 6.77.

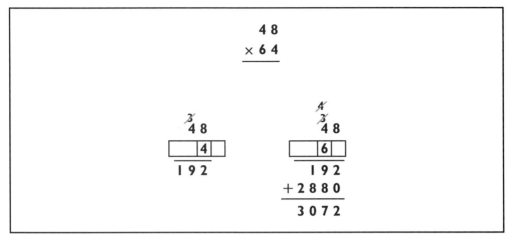

Figure 6.78.

will focus only on finding exact answers for division involving one-digit divisors as a way of reinforcing numeration understandings.

Instead of dealing with two-digit divisors for obtaining exact answers, this topic *is treated,* but from the perspective of nurturing number sense and estimation. The activity suggestions throughout this section are offered to provide ideas for working with individual students to meet targeted needs. While they do not refer to problem settings, it is assumed that this emphasis is a consistent one during instruction. As with other operations, the integration of other computation methods should be incorporated and encouraged, when appropriate. Further, the students themselves should be allowed, even encouraged, to use personally meaningful methods of recording their solutions to division situations.

If the standard algorithm is used, it is important to be sensitive to the fact that, aside from being sequentially difficult, it also requires good visual perception. Even with strong place-value comprehension, many students have difficulty aligning the digits in the quotient. Others, like the child who worked the problem in Figure 6.79a, are miscued perceptually by the problem itself. In this case, the child understood the long division process. He or she knew the remainder was too large but was confused because there appeared to be nothing more to bring down. When questioned regarding digit placement in the quotient, the child could only correct the error when a card was placed over the 26

a) 23 r6
   4)926
      8
     ――
     12
     12
     ――
      6

b) 23 r6
   4)9□
      8
     ――
     12
     12
     ――
      6

Figure 6.79.

(Figure 6.79b) to make the placement more obvious. This technique and others described below make it possible for students with learning disabilities to succeed with the standard algorithm for one-digit divisors, should this algorithm be used.

Beginning Long Division

Problem Area: Difficulty transferring from the concrete to the symbolic level for long division; inability to interpret meaningfully written long division problems.

Typical Disabilities Affecting Progress: Difficulty with visual memory, sequencing, abstract reasoning, retrieval, receptive language, figure-ground, inner language.

Background: For many children, the concept of division—using blocks, chips, money, and other concrete aids—is relatively easy to grasp. Thus, they soon learn to divide (separate) things into groups with the same number in each group. The difficulty arises when only symbols are used in the written problem. The functional division sign (⌐) tends to confuse students with reversal tendencies, whether visual or auditory. Yet the other division sign (÷) is not particularly useful, at this point. Generally, rather than confronting children with both symbols simultaneously, it is better to teach them to use the more functional one first, relating it as much as possible to concrete aids.

Because of the inherent reversal tendencies and involved sequencing in division, the process lends itself well to color coding. The colors provide the student with a starting point as well as a way of determining and maintaining the sequence. Suggestions along this line follow.

NOTE: *Students with severe reversal problems may do better using the division sign in reverse: 486⌐5. The procedure is the same, but the orientation of the division sign is more consistent with the needed language, eye tracking, and perceptual organization.*

✎ Sample Sequence of Activities

1. **Say it with chips.** As children make the transition to symbolic work for long division, it is often helpful to relate the work with materials directly to the written computational problems. Make puzzles available like those shown in Figure 6.80. Have the children cut the puzzles apart, as shown, before beginning, and then place the two pieces of each puzzle together, upside down, at the side of their desks. Each child should also have a supply of at least seven green chips. Using an overhead projector or felt board, display the division sign and go through the sequence described below with the children. For each puzzle, the presentation is similar to that indicated below.

TEACHER: "Start with seven chips." (After the seven chips are taken, the teacher tells the students to find the left piece of puzzle A.) "Write 7 on the green line to stand for the seven chips."

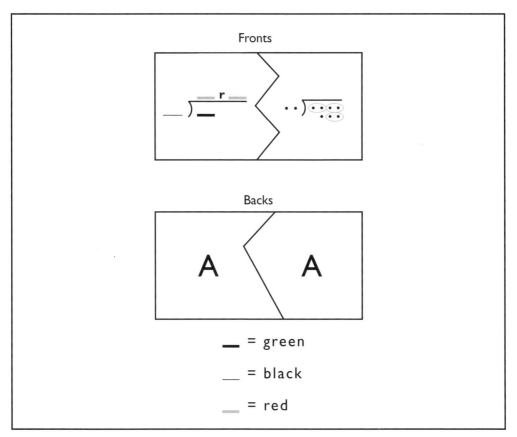

Figure 6.80.

TEACHER: "Use your chips again. Let's put the chips in groups of two. (Teacher uses the chips under the ⌐ to form groups of two.) Now let's write a 2 on the black line of the puzzle piece."

TEACHER: "How many groups did we make? Right. We made three and had one chip left over." (The children are instructed to put the numbers 3 and 1 in the appropriate places on their puzzle pieces to indicate this.)

This procedure continues until all left-hand puzzle pieces have been filled in. The children then put the puzzles back together to check their work.

2. **Puzzles alone.** Once students understand the previous work at the concrete level, show them the picture part of the puzzles and ask them to rewrite each problem on their own paper, using numbers rather than dots. To check, the children again match the puzzle pieces.

NOTE: *This method of presentation and reinforcement is effective even with upper–primary grade children. First, it offers the concrete aspect so essential to comprehension. Second, the direct teaching of the transition and the overlearning help build a strong base. Visual memory, sequencing, auditory memory, and abstract reasoning are all reinforced.*

3. **Follow-up.** After work with chips and puzzles, exercises like those of Figure 6.81 can be used by students with adequate reading skills. These pages are especially good for children who need to verbalize while learning but have trouble retrieving the words. Before the problem is solved using numbers, the left-hand section is completed. The teacher fills in divisor dots at the presentation. Then the children fill in the numbers at the right and solve the problems.

4. **Transition.** Figures 6.82 and 6.83 show transitional pages that can be used as the children develop better conceptual understandings and become able to sequence using symbols only. In Figures 6.82b and 6.82c the student can fill in numbers from textbook problems or the teacher can fill in numbers that are appropriate to the student's level. Figure 6.83a acts as an example that the teacher can fill in before the student begins copying textbook problems in the rest of the page.

Beginning Long Division: Special Help

Problem Area: Using only symbols to solve division problems.

Typical Disabilities Affecting Progress: Difficulty with auditory processing, perseveration, sequencing, visual memory, and closure.

Background: Even when the concept of division is established and the students can interpret the written long division problem, many children are still unable to proceed independently. For many, it is due to an inability to retrieve the needed facts. For others, the required sequencing and constant operation switch make it difficult to complete a problem accurately. Memory deficits may have prevented them from learning the basic facts and perseveration makes skip counting or the use of charts too difficult.

The following activities contain suggestions for how to help children deal with these problems. The assumption is that students' concept base is strong

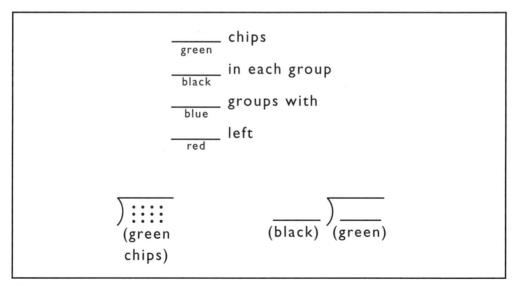

Figure 6.81.

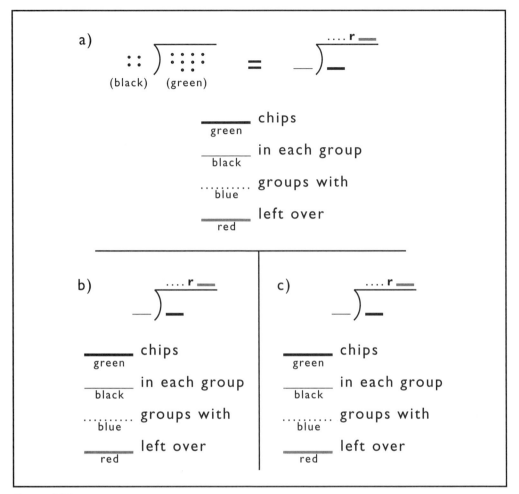

Figure 6.82.

and that the division problem difficulty is primarily due to individual learning difficulties.

Sample Sequence of Activities

1. **In the squares.** Many children need to see and feel what they are saying. Figure 6.84a illustrates a format idea for pages that can be kept in a file and used, as needed, to provide such reinforcement. The children place dots, lines, or chips (if necessary) in each square as they skip-count (Figure 6.84b). For those who need assistance with stopping, provide a stoplight above the last box needed or outline that box in red. Encourage the students to keep one finger on the dividend number and to compare it with the number of chips placed.

NOTE: *As overlearning occurs, the children independently place numbers rather than pictures or objects in the squares to show the skip count (Figure 6.84c).*

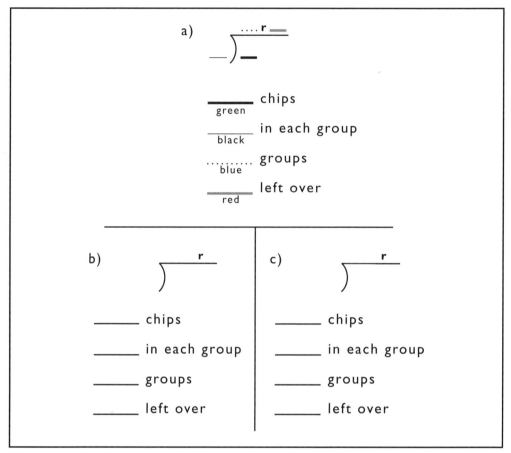

Figure 6.83.

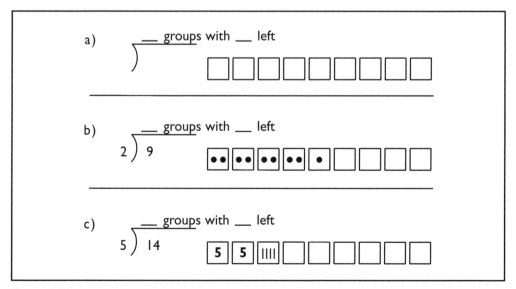

Figure 6.84.

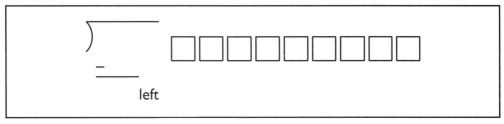

Figure 6.85.

2. **Transition.** As a transition to the long division procedure, Figure 6.85 illustrates a format for pages that can be filed and used. The teacher fills in dividend and divisor numbers at the time of presentation (Figure 6.86a). The student fills in the squares (Figure 6.86b) and determines the number of groups that have been made. Then a count is made to see how many objects have been "used up" (15 in this example). The child now subtracts to find the number left over.

NOTE: *For right-handed children the boxes should be to the right of the computation. For left-handed children they should be on the left.*

3. **Help for sequencing.** As students need the squares less but still require visual cues for sequencing, use pages containing problems like that of Figure 6.87. After filling in the quotient, the student is reminded to multiply by the box at the left. Figure 6.88 shows an alternative format designed to help with sequencing and provide the necessary language. Pages of this type are especially useful for students who have receptive language deficits. The pages can be color-coded if necessary. Assuming there is no perceptual or spatial organizational difficulty to bar copying, the student can fill in the blanks with problems from the text. Ideally, the problems should be copied as one assignment and solved as a second.

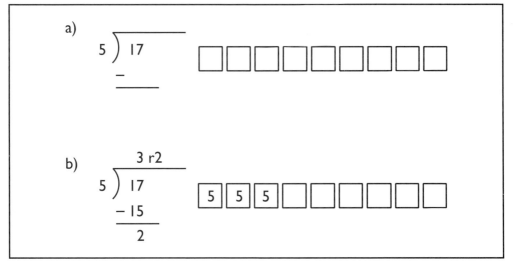

Figure 6.86.

$$2 \overline{)\,17\,}$$

☐ 2's = – _____

Figure 6.87.

4. **Relate.** The sequence suggested by Figure 6.89 can be used to help students more readily determine the correct quotient digit. An effort is made to relate division with remainders directly to basic facts. In the first set of problems (Figure 6.89a), the basic fact answer is given. The child is cued to use this to help solve the given division with a remainder. In Figure 6.89b, the students must answer the basic fact problem themselves before computing the long division example. The last problem set (c) requires that students write in the dividend closest to, but less than that of, the given long division problem. The idea of a left-hand basic fact problem can also be used in conjunction with the exercises suggested by Figures 6.87 and 6.88.

NOTE: *Throughout these explanations, the divisor has been used to describe the number of objects in each group. This interpretation has proven successful, given our approach, with LD students with whom we have worked. Obviously, the divisor can also mean the number of needed groups, with the quotient describing the number of objects in each group. This latter interpretation describes situations in which the children divide or share a given number of objects (see Figure 6.90). Because of research documenting the ease with which regular-class children relate to the idea of sharing, the concept is becoming increasingly popular in mathematics textbooks that present long division. Whatever the approach, it is important to be consistent until the process is learned. Once understanding and retention have been achieved, it is essential to also introduce the other interpretation. A suggestion for how to introduce the "sharing" idea is outlined in the storyline that follows.*

5. **Storyline for sharing money.** A money storyline can be used to provide auditory reinforcement for and give meaning to the procedure for long division. The problem of Figure 6.91a can be related to four students who find a bag of money containing 2 one hundred dollar bills, 3 ten dollar bills, and 5 one dollar bills. They cannot locate the owner. After turning the bag in to the police, the boys are allowed to keep the money and split it among themselves.

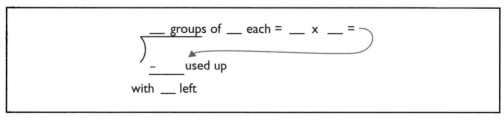

Figure 6.88.

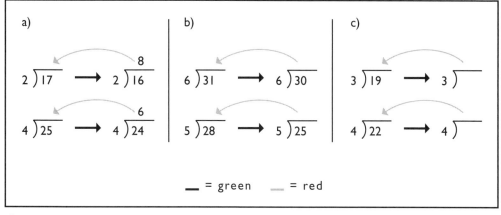

Figure 6.89.

How do they go about sharing the money? They are most excited about splitting the one hundred dollar bills first. (This fact reinforces the left-to-right procedure for computing long division problems.) With only 2 one hundred dollar bills and four people, what should they do? Tear the bills? No! They trade the 2 one hundred dollar bills in for 20 ten dollar bills. Now with 23 ten dollar bills, what's the *greatest* number of ten dollar bills each can receive? (Refer to Figure 6.91b.)

The story continues along these lines as the children divide what is left, thereby computing the long division problem. With one-digit divisors, play money can be used to dramatize the story. Eventually, the students should be asked to analyze the sequence suggested by the storyline, noting that there are *five basic steps* (Figure 6.92). Further ideas for focusing on the five basic steps of the long division process are contained in the following section.

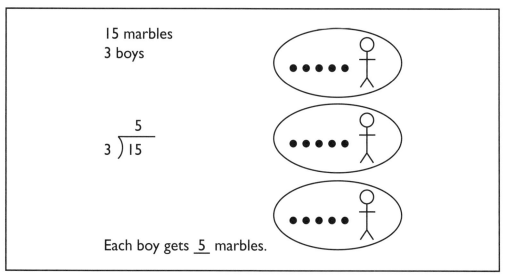

Figure 6.90.

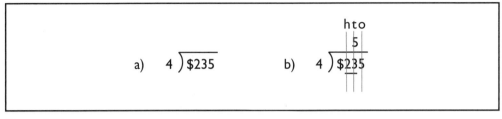

Figure 6.91.

Five Basic Steps

Problem Area: Difficulty retaining and sequencing steps in long division.

Typical Disabilities Affecting Progress: Difficulty with memory, sequencing, figure-ground, integrative processing, spatial organization.

Background: The long division process is cumbersome and often unnecessary, particularly for children with the learning deficits just noted. Although their conceptual understanding is adequate, these children may not be able to sequence the steps and place the numbers correctly to arrive at an answer. Sometimes the use of a calculator for long sequences is a viable and preferable alternative. However, if students are not able to use the calculator at this level (i.e., for division that involves remainders) or if their visual perceptual difficulties make using the calculator more complicated than using paper-and-pencil, then repeated drill, with the goal of overlearning the sequence, is recommended.

🖉 Sample Sequence of Activities

1. **Fill in.** Figure 6.93 shows a way of helping students organize their thoughts and build up a mental image of the sequence for long division. Before computing, the student fills in the blanks of the rectangle as a reminder of what the numbers represent. The student then continues, reading the words as they are approached to help with the sequencing and to give meaning to the numbers. If necessary, chips may be used to dramatize problems. Eventually,

---

Does McDonald's Sell CheeseBurgers?

1) **D**ivide ÷
2) **M**ultiply x
3) **S**ubtract –
4) **C**ompare
5) **B**ring down ↓

Figure 6.92.

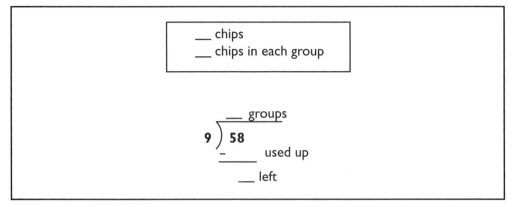

Figure 6.93.

the procedure should be related to the five basic steps of Figure 6.92. It is often helpful to display those steps on a wall chart or write them on cards the children can keep at their desks for ready reference.

NOTE: *If color-coding is necessary during early work with exercises of this type, colors should match those of Figure 6.81.*

2. **Longer problems.** As problems become longer and more involved, students typically encounter even greater difficulty in correctly placing digits. Figure 6.94 suggests one way of handling this situation. The words in the center column aid sequencing and eventually lead to overlearning. Encourage students to memorize them. The color-coding within the problem helps students organize the sequence and properly place the numbers while computing. When dividing by the green 3, for example, the student writes the quotient on the appropriate green line. When multiplying by a number on the green line, the product is recorded on the next appropriate green line.

NOTE: *Examples of pages similar to that of Figure 6.94 are shown in Figures 1.13 and 1.14. These can be prepared in advance, filed, and used as needed. Problems from the text can be copied directly into the boxes by students. If students*

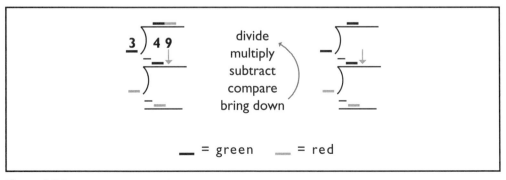

Figure 6.94.

need help with spatial organization, draw lines on some of the pages. This also helps those who have difficulty copying.

3. **Card slide.** For children who tend to reverse or for those with figure-ground deficits, provide a sliding card as in Figure 6.95. Instruct the children to cover up the digits not being used, as in the sequence shown.

4. **Problems within problems.**

• *Middle zero in the quotient.* In early work, avoid giving the students problem types for which you anticipate a high percentage of errors. For example, give students the chance to feel comfortable with the computational process for long division before introducing more difficult problems such as those with a middle zero in the quotient.

• *Think ahead.* The formatted pages of Figures 1.13, 1.14, and 6.94 can be prepared in advance, filed, and used to help students, as needed, with digit placement in long division.

• *Show where.* Many children find it necessary to determine the number of digits in the quotient before solving. To help, they can use a finger or a card and uncover the digits in the dividend one at a time, as in Figure 6.96. As the student determines where quotient digits should be placed, short lines are drawn to indicate the placement over the appropriate dividend figures.

• *Placing quotient digits.* Some children have trouble reasoning and, therefore, do not automatically notice if an answer does not make sense. (They will only notice if there is not enough room or if there is too much room for the digits.) For them it often helps merely to practice determining where quotient digits should be placed. Have the students place lines above the dividend numbers to show the correct placement, as in Figure 6.96. Do not require that they complete problems at this time. Gradually, through discussion and repetition, the student should begin to notice that when the divisor is larger than the first digit of the dividend, that space must be empty.

NOTE: *By determining the number of digits in the quotient first, they are then free to decide whether an answer is reasonable. Gradually, through discussion*

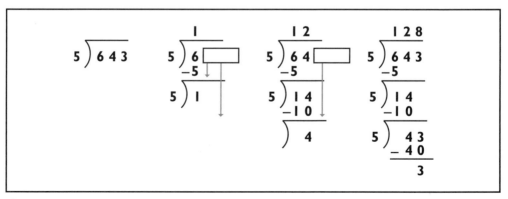

Figure 6.95.

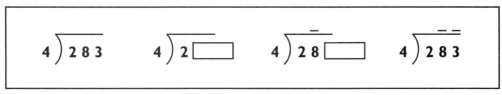

Figure 6.96.

and repetition, students should be encouraged to notice that when the divisor is larger than the first digit of the dividend the first space must be empty.

• *Graph paper.* As in multiplication, graph paper is helpful for aligning digits in long division. Keep some pages set up, as in Figure 6.97. Many children, especially those with severe figure-ground problems, cannot copy numbers onto the graph paper unless it is spatially organized as shown. However, once the initial organization is provided, the graph paper boxes help with alignment. Gradually, *as the child feels comfortable* determining the *number of digits* in a quotient, it also becomes easier to set up and compute the problem independently.

• *Block out.* Keep tachistoscopes, as in Figure 6.98, that can be used to block out all but the relevant part of a long division problem.

• *Transition.* As a transition to working the problems independently, have the child use the tachistoscope before solving. Figure 6.99a shows the original problem. The student decides where the first digit of the quotient will be, in this case over the 6, and places a line to mark that position. The tachistoscope is then placed as shown, and the student traces around the rectangle before removing the stencil (Figure 6.99b). The problem of Figure 6.99c is now ready for the child to compute.

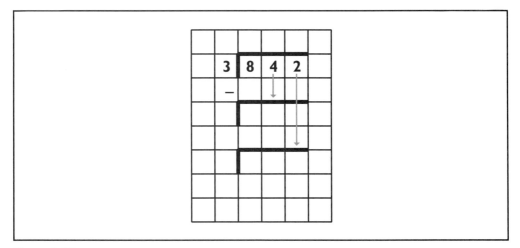

Figure 6.97.

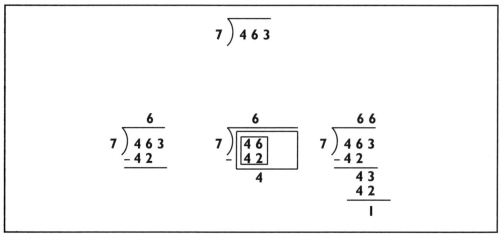

Figure 6.98.

• *Outline the sign.* Sometimes it is helpful to outline the division sign in a bright color. This helps the student distinguish the isolated parts of the problem.

• *Circle.* Provide practice pages of completed problems, as in Figure 6.100. Have the student circle each subtraction (or just the first one) within the division. This could be part of a 2-day assignment. On the first day, the student circles the subtraction problems. The next day, after the page is checked, the student receives a second sheet containing the same problems (not worked) to solve independently.

5. **Two-digit divisors.** In the introduction to the division section, we discussed our philosophy of the need to replace the time traditionally spent on paper-and-pencil computation of two-digit divisors with more significant mathematics. Instead of assigning children to actually hand-compute textbook exercises for two-digit divisors, use those exercises in a different way to nurture number sense. Four major types of activity thrusts are valuable:

• *Roughly identify the range of the quotient.* Ask students just to tell whether the quotient (division answer) will be a three-digit or a two-digit number. Rather than dealing with isolated numbers, placing the problem in a money storyline helps students gain intuitions about the range of the quotient and,

Figure 6.99.

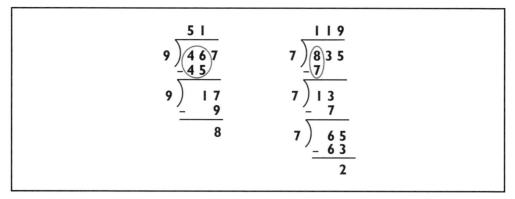

Figure 6.100.

therefore, places them in a position to be successful. The problem of Figure 6.101, for example, might be viewed as sharing $2,176 with 31 people. Using the card slide of Figure 6.95, we can help children realize that there are not enough thousand dollar or one hundred dollar bills to share among all the people. However, bank trades would give us enough ten dollar bills: a total of 217. Hence, we can share our ten dollar and one dollar bills, which means that the number of dollars each of the 31 people will get in the sharing is some two-digit number.

• *Get closer.* Relying on multiplying multiples of 10, as in Figure 6.102, students can get a little closer to the actual answer. Note the continued use of the storyline, at least initially, to place the numbers in a context that will nurture better intuitions.

• *Arrange low to high.* Make clear to students that there is no need to work any of the problems in a given row. Tell them to "just roughly identify the range of the quotient" and then "get closer" so you can rank the problems low to high, based on their quotients. Allow students to explain their thinking and (later) do a calculator check.

• *Create a problem.* Challenge students to copy the first problem in a row, then to:

- create a verbal problem that might use those numbers in its solution, and

- create a second problem whose answer is more than the first.

$$\begin{array}{cccc} \text{th} & \text{h} & \text{t} & \text{o} \\ \downarrow & \downarrow & \downarrow & \downarrow \end{array}$$

$$31\overline{)2176}$$

Figure 6.101.

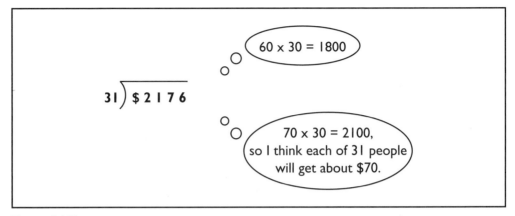

Figure 6.102.

Alternately, students might be challenged to create a second problem whose answer is *less than* the first; *about twice as much as* the first; *about half* the first; and so on.

NOTE: *Students can use a calculator to check whether the problems they create come close to meeting the requirements set.*

USING TECHNOLOGY

Most learning disabled students will readily turn to calculators as an alternative to paper-and-pencil computation because they can be used to get answers quickly. And when the calculators are in good working condition and are properly used and students have the needed conceptual background, they are accurate and can be invaluable. Ideas for integrating calculator use in instruction on the paper-and-pencil algorithms have been embedded throughout this chapter. This final section offers several practical suggestions for selecting among and using calculators.

Calculators with internal arithmetic logic can be used to carry out the counting activities outlined in the "Using Technology" section of Chapter 5. Other calculators have internal algebraic logic and automatically observe the conventional order of operations. That is, when processing an open sentence like $2 + 4 \times 5 =$, the calculator will internally process any *parentheses* and *exponents* first, then any *multiplications and divisions* and, finally, any *additions* and *subtractions*. The mnemonic some students use to remember what to do in manual calculations to observe order of operations is: *Please excuse my dear aunt Sally.* If a calculator does not "work right" when trying to do the Chapter 5 counting activities, then it has algebraic logic. It will observe order of operations and, for example, will provide the expected answer of 30. If the correct order of operations is addressed during instruction, then students do not have to *unlearn* the incorrect process of going from left to right, regardless of the signs.

Beyond basic calculator differences related to counting functions or order of operations, there are many different models from which to select, so students typically can find one that works well for them. For example, calculators that also have a printout can be used by students with motor or memory difficulties. The tape can be used for reference when input cannot be remembered. The tape also can be used to check whether digits were entered accurately.

Calculators with larger numbers on the printout, or that print out in different colors, can be used to accommodate students with visual deficits. "Talking calculators"—those with a voice synthesizer unit—are useful or may be necessary for others if the auditory output is very clear and consistent.

Some calculators display outputs in the thousands or greater with commas at the top of the number (e.g., 3'765). This type of display can be confusing and means that students must learn and then ignore (unlearn) a procedure. Such a calculator is not the best purchase.

In general, a calculator should be selected that carries out simple arithmetic functions like 3 + 4 in the typical linear sequence:

- enter the first addend;
- enter "+";
- enter the second addend;
- enter "=".

Some calculators would have students enter the two addends, then push the operation symbol "+". This style, of course, is more difficult for students to use. Some calculators display the entire "input," such as 6 + 4 = 10. Although difficult to find, they are not expensive and for students with memory and sequencing problems might be the best choice.

Some children work with calculators inefficiently because they do not know how to use the memory key. This is a particular skill that should be specifically addressed. Students with memory difficulties especially need to know how to use these keys. Calculators that provide four memory keys—MC (memory clear), MR (memory recall), M– (memory minus), and M+ (memory add)—are preferable to calculators that combine the MC and MR keys. Whatever the model, instruction in mathematics should include helping children to use calculators accurately and effectively, with all the power they possess, as a viable option to other forms of computation.

Microcomputer software related to problem solving with whole number operations and to whole number computation is increasingly accessible through educational supply companies. Examples include:

Program	Publisher/Distributor
MathTek	MathTek/WBGU-TV
Combining and Breaking Apart Numbers	Sunburst
What Do You Do with a Broken Calculator	Sunburst
Math Rabbit	KnowledgeAdventure
Stickybear's Math Town	Optimum Resource
Math Keys: Whole Numbers	KnowledgeAdventure
Math Word Problem Series	Optimum Resource
Access to Math	Don Johnston
Math Pad	Don Johnston

Chapter 7

◆ ◆

Rational Numbers: Early Concept Work with Fractions and Decimals

C hildren's early understanding about numbers pertains primarily to whole numbers. When they begin to extend whole number ideas, their first intuitions stem from day-to-day settings: half a glass of milk, part of a cracker, some of my blocks. As their education expands to include symbolic understanding of fractions and decimals, their mathematical power grows, enabling them to represent and solve a new variety of problems involving the more academic areas of measurement, graphing, and probability, as well as their applicability to real-life situations such as cooking, music, and shopping, to name just a few.

Acquiring a good sense for fractions and decimals involves having a solid understanding of and good intuitions about the relative size of whole numbers. Extending one's understanding of relative size to fractions and decimals, and later to percents, requires good abstract reasoning, the ability to infer and draw conclusions, strong receptive language, and the confidence to take risks in order to determine whether the results of a computation make sense.

In the typical school curriculum, early work with fractions precedes work with decimal numbers. Generally, however, beyond that introduction, most instruction addresses decimal topics before parallel fraction topics. The reason for this sequence is that:

- computation with decimals generally is easier and more closely related to whole-number computation than is computation with fractions, and

- calculators (until recently) and computers use decimal notation.

As pointed out in the following pages, however, for some students with learning disabilities the use of fractions in basic developmental work is more effective than other techniques. The rationale for this approach is that, particularly at the early stages of development, fractions allow for a more concrete approach. Once the foundation is laid, students can more easily apply their understanding to decimals and begin to more readily see the relationship between all types of numbers. This sequence provides the opportunity for instruction to focus on helping children (a) successfully compute with both fractions and decimals; (b) make decisions about which format is easier for a given situation or a given student; (c) select the correct operation; (d) decide on the most efficient method of arriving at a solution; (e) determine the need for an exact answer or an estimate; and (f) use a calculator efficiently and accurately.

When dealing with rational numbers, the choice of calculator can be extremely important for students with learning disabilities. There now are calculators that show the fraction form of a decimal using the horizontal bar, and it is strongly recommended that, at least for initial instruction, students use such calculators. Later on, when they need to use more complex calculators, which currently do not have the fraction read-out ability, they can make the transition.

The focus in this chapter is on following an instructional sequence for students with learning disabilities so that they can develop a basic understanding of rational numbers and can *read, write,* and *interpret* fractions and decimals in meaningful ways using good number sense. To prepare for this outcome, early work with rational numbers should include work with tenths, along with fractions having denominators of 2, 3, 4, 5, 6, 8, 9, 12 (for inch rulers), and 16. Five major sections provide a framework for discussion:

1. General areas of difficulty
2. Number sense for rational numbers
3. The language of rational numbers
4. Equivalent numbers
5. Selected real-life applications

GENERAL AREAS OF DIFFICULTY

Perceptual Skills

Perceptually, both fractions and decimals can be difficult. The mere act of correctly writing a fraction requires spatial organization that many children with learning disabilities lack. It is not unusual to see children writing fractions or mixed numbers as shown in Figure 7.1. This type of copying tends to appear careless, when, in fact, children may be perceiving the positions exactly as written.

Figure-ground deficits also can make it difficult for some students to sort out the relevant parts of a picture or to locate the decimal point in a decimal number. Textbook illustrations like that shown in Figure 7.2 can be visually confusing, making it impossible for students to use them effectively. These same children may have trouble computing because all the isolated digits of the fraction or the decimal number "run together."

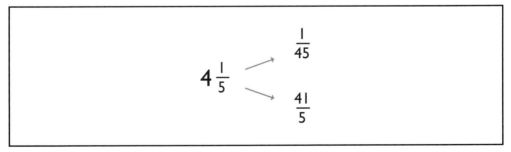

Figure 7.1.

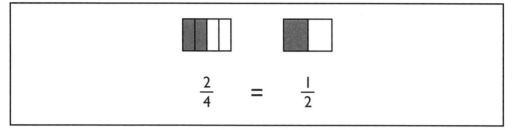

Figure 7.2.

Abstract Reasoning

Students with abstract-reasoning deficits often encounter difficulty with rational numbers regardless of how concrete the approach is. Using objects and pictures, we can actually show students that $\frac{1}{10}$ means 1 out of 10 equal parts. There are words and manipulatives to match each symbol in $\frac{1}{10}$. When faced with .1, however, even manipulatives do not always help; there are no words or manipulatives to match each symbol.

Similarly, consider Figure 7.3, in which both pictures represent the fraction $\frac{2}{5}$. Children who have trouble with multiple meanings find this idea extremely complex. While the concept of "two out of five equal parts" may be clear, the difficulty arises because the equal parts of the two shapes are different sizes. The unit, the "one whole," in each case is different.

Language and Vocabulary

Expressive and receptive language problems also commonly interfere with the ability to understand and use rational numbers. The language of fractions involves many familiar words used in a new context. Most children have heard the words *third, fourth, fifth,* and so on. By about second grade, it generally is expected that they can readily relate whole-number placement to them. However, now they must begin to apply new meanings to those words and make immediate decisions about how the words are being used. Students are

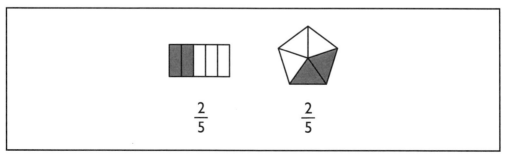

Figure 7.3.

accustomed to "hearing horizontally" and may have trouble associating the vertical fraction with the words. For example, suppose a teacher writes $\frac{3}{4}$ on the board and (a) instructs the student to shade three fourths of a rectangle or (b) asks how many people are in three fourths of the class. The child hears the fraction and may even be able to relate the words to the correct written form. However, when asked to apply the fraction in this new context, which is no longer horizontal (linear) in nature, the student becomes confused. ("What does 'three fourths of the class' mean? There are 20 people in here. I can't divide a person into fourths.")

These same children frequently experience difficulty when other vocabulary is introduced: for example, *equivalent, common, simplest, reduced, improper.* The words may be used over and over again—not necessarily in the same contexts—and many students find it difficult to retrieve and associate the proper meanings at the proper time. For example, each of the numbers in Figure 7.4 can be referred to using different words, yet they are all equivalent numbers.

Auditory Discrimination

Students with auditory discrimination difficulties may have trouble orally interpreting, reading, and understanding decimals. Distinguishing *tenths* and *hundredths* from *tens* and *hundreds* can be difficult and can slow down such students' ability to process and apply their knowledge.

NUMBER SENSE FOR RATIONAL NUMBERS

Problem Area: Poor intuition regarding the relative size of and relationship between fractions and decimals; difficulty making an appropriate estimate using fractions or decimals in practical settings.

Typical Disabilities Affecting Progress: Difficulty with abstract reasoning, receptive and expressive language, short-term and sequential memory, visual perception.

Background: Number sense for rational numbers develops slowly, even with the best role modeling and structured, ongoing experiences. Consistent efforts along the lines suggested in the following activities and exercises are critical. If we are to nurture a student's potential to develop good number sense for fractions and decimals, structured activities related to that goal belong as an ongoing, important thrust of both the fraction and the decimal programs.

$$\frac{8}{6} = 1\frac{2}{6} = 1\frac{1}{3}$$

Figure 7.4.

✎ Sample Sequence of Activities

1. **Sort fractions.** Use fraction cubes, fraction bars, and numerical representations to conclude that a fraction is close to:

- 0 when the numerator is very small in comparison to the denominator;
- $\frac{1}{2}$ when the numerator is about half the size of the denominator; and
- 1 when the numerator is very close in size to the denominator.

Ask students to sort fractions, as suggested by Figure 7.5.

2. **Sort decimals.** Similar activities can be carried out with decimals to determine whether a given decimal is closer to 0, .5, or 1. (See Figure 7.6.)

Approximating Fractions and Decimals

Problem Area: Difficulty noting relationships between fractions; difficulty noting relationships between decimals; good number sense.

Typical Disabilities Affecting Progress: Difficulty with abstract reasoning, sequential memory, expressive language.

Background: Number sense for fractions and decimals involves the ability to (a) demonstrate good conceptual understanding, (b) use relationships between numbers, and (c) think about and use rational numbers in meaningful ways. Mental activity, a degree of critical thinking, and the ability to use common sense and evaluative thinking are all important components for success in this area.

A classroom atmosphere in which the emphasis is on thinking rather than exact answers helps students become comfortable in any of these areas. Written work is an essential component but need not—in fact, should not—be the primary means of solving problems. Rather, written work should be a tool to assist the child with retention, sequencing, expressive language, and so on.

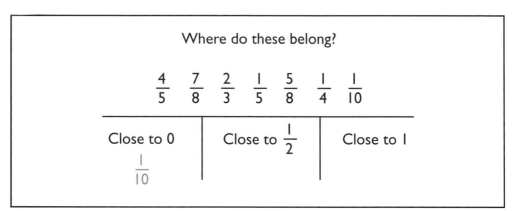

Figure 7.5.

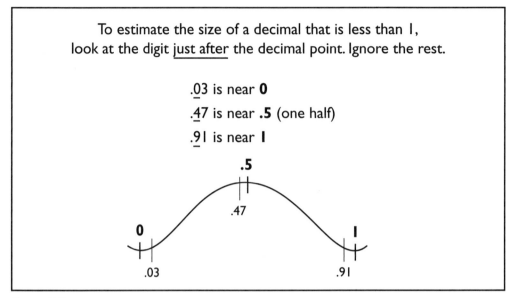

To estimate the size of a decimal that is less than 1,
look at the digit just after the decimal point. Ignore the rest.

<u>.</u>03 is near **0**
<u>.</u>47 is near **.5** (one half)
<u>.</u>91 is near **1**

Figure 7.6.

If common-sense thinking about fractions is an important goal, suggestions like the following may be in order.

✎ Sample Sequence of Activities

1. **Close to.** Ask students to study a list of fractions or answers to problems they have completed. Have them identify fractions and decimals that are
"close to" 0, $\frac{1}{2}$/.5, 1/1.00, 2/2.00, $2\frac{1}{2}$/2.5, or some other related target number.

NOTE: *Some students, such as those with short-term memory problems, may
need to have a number line in front of them to use as a reference point.*

- ■ *Variation:* Students can apply the knowledge developed in this activity
  to estimate answers to computation problems. For example, given
  1.75×2.3, a student might estimate the product as "close to 2×2, or
  about 4."

2. **Adjusting estimates.** In many cases, estimates may be adjusted. In Figure 7.7, for example, each addend is less than the number used in the estimate,
so the estimate given is an overestimate. Students should consider whether estimates they have given are over or under the actual figure. In many practical situations, as when buying material to make a dress or build a fence, it is better
to be over than under.

3. **Accept a range of estimates.** Knowing that any number of alternate
responses can be correct is helpful to timid students. This is especially important in early stages, when the goal is to develop students' confidence in taking

risks and making estimates. For the problem in Figure 7.7, for example, any of the following responses might be accepted as an estimate for the computation:

- about $1\frac{1}{2}$ or 1.5
- a little more than 1
- about 1
- a little less than $1\frac{1}{2}$
- less than 2

In early stages, accept a broader range of estimates and help students explain their thinking rather than concentrating on very close estimates.

4. **Does my answer make sense?** Present students with computations and ask them to round off and estimate the answers. These problems should not be in any particular context. Accept a wide range of answers, as described in Activity 3 above. Next, using the same computations but in different contexts, have students evaluate their estimates relative to the context. For example, if you need $1\frac{7}{8}$ cups of sugar for one recipe and $\frac{1}{4}$ cup for another, would you have enough sugar if you have just 1 cup? After all, $\frac{1}{4}$ is closer to 0 than to 1.

Ask students to identify those answers that make no sense. Talk through the estimate(s) used to make a decision. Given this background of experiences, students typically have a more positive attitude toward rational numbers and are often more likely to catch errors when they turn to a variety of forms of computation.

THE LANGUAGE OF RATIONAL NUMBERS

"As the complexity of mathematical symbolism increases, students become more dependent on their prior learning and their language to lend meaning to more technical mathematics language. Accordingly, we need to give students many opportunities to form connections to the language of mathematics" (Capps & Pickreign, 1993, p. 9). Students with learning disabilities, especially those with

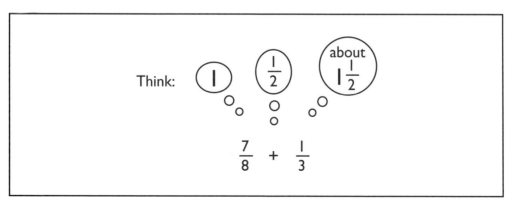

Figure 7.7.

nonverbal learning disabilities and those who have trouble with receptive language and/or spatial organization, may need some additional assistance understanding and applying the language of rational numbers in written form. Although it is often preferable simply to use a calculator and read the answer, or do the work mentally and state the answer, many of these students need the additional visual cue or motor involvement. Writing something down on paper helps them recall, focus, understand, and apply what they are learning.

Reading and Writing Fractions

Problem Area: Accurately writing fractions and mixed numbers.

Typical Disabilities Affecting Progress: Difficulty with spatial organization, eye-hand coordination, receptive language.

Background: Once fraction concepts have been established using physical materials, it generally is assumed that children will have little difficulty reading and writing the numbers. This is not always the case, however. Sequentially, students may know the order in which fraction digits should be read or written, but, spatially, they may be unable to place the digits properly (see Figure 7.8). Similarly, they may hear the correct sounds and associate them with the symbols, but retrieving and writing them properly may be an entirely different matter.

For younger students or for those who have learning difficulties, it often is necessary to provide specific practice in writing and reading fractions, much like what is done with handwriting. As students make the transition from concrete or pictorial representations to symbolic representations, it may be necessary for the teacher to review the goal of individual lessons. Is the goal to associate the correct fraction with its concrete or pictorial representation? Is it to write the correct fraction for a given model? Is it to write a fraction that is heard? Is it to read a fraction that has been written?

Too often we think of these steps as one and the same, but for many children with learning disabilities they are not. Often these students must internalize, for example, what it *feels like* to write the digits of a fraction in the proper spaces. Even older students often benefit from the gross-motor involvement of writing fractions on the blackboard. Until they begin to feel more comfortable with the spatial orientation needed to write fractions, most of their energy will be expended on number placement rather than on understanding.

The following activities suggest ways to help children write fractions correctly. The major assumption is that difficulties are not due to conceptual misunderstanding.

---

34 instead of $\frac{3}{4}$

Figure 7.8.

✎ Sample Sequence of Activities

1. **Trace.** Felt numbers, rainbow writing on the chalkboard, or a sand or salt tray often is helpful for students who need kinesthetic involvement and gross-motor activity while learning to write fractions. Children trace over a given fraction and then immediately write it, perhaps starting on large art-sized paper or on the blackboard and then moving progressively to smaller surfaces.

2. **Color cue.** When students are ready for paper-and-pencil work, start by using exercises like those in Figure 7.9. The goal is to develop the spatial organization, visually and kinesthetically, required to write fractions correctly. Colors are used to help with sequencing and number placement: "When you write, green goes first—on top." Coat the green shading and box outline of several examples with glue. When the glue is dry, the children can finger-trace over the raised surfaces. Eventually, they will write the number independently (at the end of the line following the equals sign).

3. **Choose.** If the goal of the assignment is to write fractions to describe a shaded region, see the example in Figure 7.10, which shows how to avoid difficulties due to spatial deficits. The children cross out the wrong answer and write over the correct one. The fraction then is written independently, immediately after tracing.

4. **Mixed numbers.** Writing mixed numbers presents even greater problems for children with spatial difficulties. Now a sense of midpoint is added, in addition to up and down movements. Figure 7.11 shows one type of exercise that can be prepared in advance and kept on file. The colors are used to help students:

- develop the correct sequence for writing numbers;
- locate the correct position for each digit; and
- associate the parts of the number with the related parts of the picture.

The goal of the assignment is to help students spatially organize their writing of mixed numbers.

5. **Stencil first.** For students with more severe deficits, keep stencils on hand (see Figure 7.12a). Instruct students first to use a stencil to write a fraction and then to write it again without the stencil. The two fractions—the

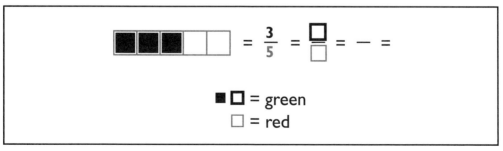

Figure 7.9.

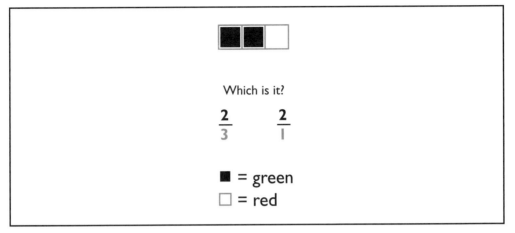

Figure 7.10.

stencil and the nonstencil copy—should be written side by side. In this way, the first serves as a pattern for writing the second.

6. **Tape it.** The stencils shown in Figure 7.12a can be used for students who have trouble writing fractions without a visual cue. Provide boxed paper as described in Chapter 1. Have students listen to a tape recorder and write down the dictated fractions. If color-coding is needed, put tape around the sides of the stencil as shown in Figure 7.12b. Students "go" on green and write the first digit of each proper fraction dictated on top (in the numerator) and the second digit dictated on the bottom (in the denominator).

7. **Words to numerals.** Many students have trouble associating number words with the correct position of the digits in a fraction. Color-coded exercises, as shown in Figure 7.13, often help with both spatial organization and language association. Note that the students rewrite the fraction independently as a last step of the exercise.

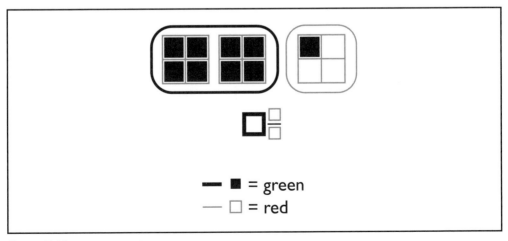

Figure 7.11.

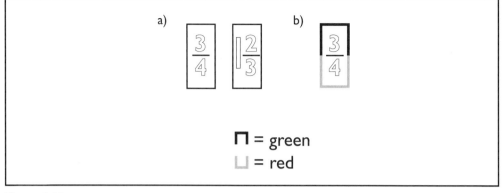

Figure 7.12.

- *Extension:* To develop the idea further, colors can be used, as in Figure 7.14. In the first two examples, children read the words, fill in the blanks, then write the fraction independently. The variation in the last example requires that students describe the picture verbally before proceeding.

NOTE: *Throughout these exercises, bold, dotted, or regular line drawings can be used instead of color cueing for students who are color blind.*

8. **Fringo.** A variation of bingo can be used to reinforce basic fraction concepts and provide practice writing fractions. Make a set of calling cards representing fractions, as in Figure 7.15a. Also make a set of game boards with fractions in each square (see Figure 7.15b). Instead of chips, provide the students with plastic overlays and grease pencils. Players take turns pulling a card and stating the fraction name. If the symbol is on the game board, the student writes over it with a pencil. The winning pattern should be determined before the game.

Writing Improper Fractions and Mixed Numbers

Problem Area: Difficulty writing a quotient as a mixed number; difficulty changing an improper fraction to a mixed number.

Typical Disabilities Affecting Progress: Difficulty with spatial organization, visual figure-ground, abstract reasoning, sequencing, auditory processing.

Background: Even with the increased use of calculators and the decreased emphasis on long division, students still must understand the relationships

$$\frac{\textbf{three}}{\text{fifths}} = \frac{3}{5} = \qquad \blacksquare = \text{green}$$
$$\blacksquare = \text{red}$$

Figure 7.13.

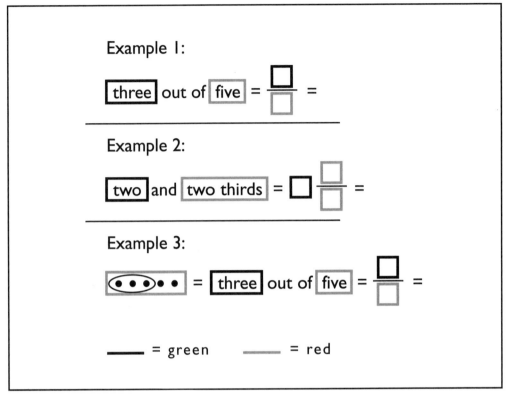

Figure 7.14.

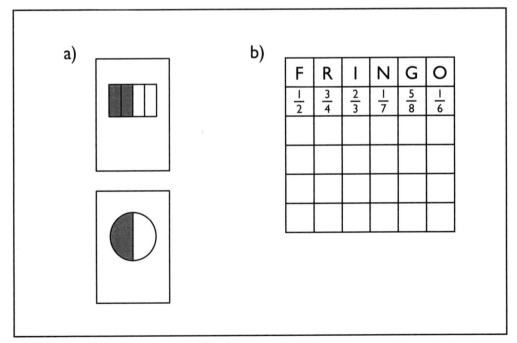

Figure 7.15.

between the decimal answer on the calculator, the quotient in a division problem that has been done using paper and pencil, and the solution to a problem. There are times when it is most expedient to use either mental calculation or paper and pencil, especially for problems involving small numbers. At these times, in order for the work to have meaning, students must be able to express the answer as a mixed number. However, spatially, writing and aligning the numbers can be demanding. Additionally, at the symbolic level, even when the division is simple, because there are many numbers to sort out, children may forget what the numbers mean. As a consequence, they lose track of the correct sequence for writing the digits. Certain techniques may be used to deal with such problems. The exercises that follow have proven effective in our own work with students with learning disabilities.

Sample Sequencing of Activities

1. **Color-code.** Color-coded pages for simple division problems with remainders, as shown in Figure 7.16, constitute the initial practice needed to help students spatially organize their work. First, they follow the color cueing and merely copy the numbers in the correct boxes. (The completed division example is given at this stage.) Then the mixed number is rewritten, independently, to provide extra reinforcement. The goal is to help students learn the correct placement of the digits. The color scheme controls for extraneous interferences by drawing students' attention only to relevant digits and their placement.

2. **Divide, too.** Once students feel more comfortable about transferring the quotient to a mixed number, have them do the division as well. Generally, it is a good idea to encourage students first to write the final answer in the form ___R___. This method tends to prevent them from losing the remainder in the mass of the other numbers; it also emphasizes the meaning of what they are doing.

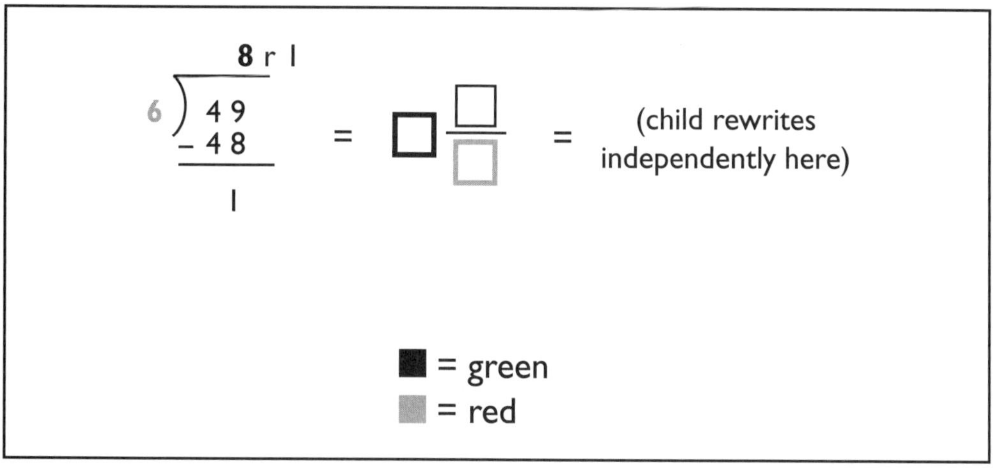

Figure 7.16.

■ *Variation:* For students with language difficulties, use the form ___ Remainder ___.

3. **Sample problems.** Pages with color-coded examples at the top can be used to help students make the transition from colors to no colors. Colors are not used for the other problems on the page. If children become stuck, they can refer to the coded examples at the top of the sheet.

4. **Relate.** Figure 7.17a shows a way to help students discover the relationship between a fraction and the division process. This exercise also paves the way for changing improper fractions to mixed numbers (see Activity 5 below). Students solve the division problems and fill in the blanks. Have them read aloud and, for selected examples, partition the objects into groups to dramatize what is said. As a follow-up, present exercises like those of Figure 7.17b.

The children could copy mixed numbers from previously worked division problems into the boxes and rewrite each in the form ___R___ (see Figure 7.17b). Ask them to verbalize how the quotient and the mixed-number expressions mean the same thing. Tie this in with the work of Figure 7.17a by allowing students to place small objects in groups to prove the equivalence. Sample file pages are shown in Figure 7.17c.

5. **Improper fractions to mixed numbers.** Figure 7.18a suggests a pre-formatted page that can be kept on file and used with teacher-made problems or with problems students copy from the text. As suggested by the example, colors often are essential at this point. Specifically, they reduce difficulties due to

a) $7\overline{)6\,4}$ $^{r}\underline{}$ = ___ whole groups with ___ out of ___ left.

$8\overline{)5\,9}$ $^{r}\underline{}$ = ___ whole groups with ___ out of ___ left.

$9\frac{1}{7}$ = ___ whole groups with ___ out of ___ left.

$7\frac{3}{8}$ = ___ whole groups with ___ out of ___ left.

b) $\boxed{9}\frac{1}{7}$ = ___ r ___

$\boxed{7}\frac{3}{8}$ = ___ r ___

c) $\boxed{}\,\frac{}{}$ = ___ r ___

$\boxed{}\,\frac{}{}$ = ___ r ___

Figure 7.17.

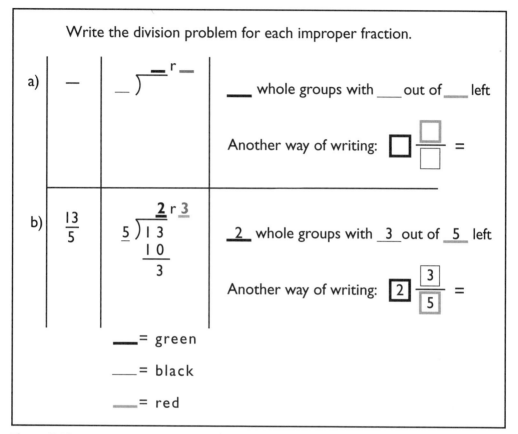

Figure 7.18.

deficits in visual perception and spatial organization; they emphasize associations that help students understand the process of changing from an improper fraction to a mixed number. As before, the objects can be divided into groups to dramatize what is said. A completed example is presented in Figure 7.18b.

6. **Tic-tac-toe.** Make a set of cards with division problems, like those shown in Figure 7.19a. Until the children are more advanced, do not include problems whose quotients require reducing when written as a mixed number. Have the children fill in tic-tac-toe boards with the mixed number for each quotient (see Figure 7.19b). After checking the boards, laminate them or cover them with clear contact paper. For practice, the students can play tic-tac-toe, alone or with a partner, by drawing a card and circling the correct mixed number if it is represented on the board. If more than one student is playing, the first person to circle three in a row wins.

Reading and Writing Decimals

Problem Areas: Difficulty interpreting written decimals in a meaningful way; difficulty appropriately attaching *tenth, hundredth,* and other decimal names to decimals.

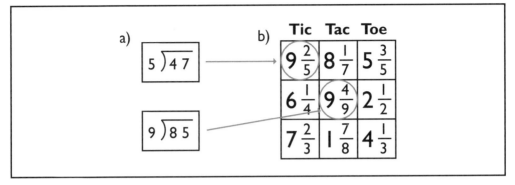

Figure 7.19.

Typical Disabilities Affecting Progress: Difficulty with abstract reasoning, auditory or visual memory, auditory discrimination, expressive language.

Background: Decimals typically are introduced using models like that of Figure 7.20a. As long as the models are present, students may be able to write and read the decimals associated with them, as in Figure 7.20b. However, the same students, particularly those with the deficits identified above, may be unable to read written decimals without visual aids. A meaningful and effective way to help students become functionally independent with written decimals is to relate them to the familiar fractional notation. Even in the symbolic form, fractions are more concrete than decimals. The 10 in the denominator of $\frac{1}{10}$, for example, cues one to say "one tenth." No similar cue for saying "tenth" is given by .1. Thus, students must simply remember what to say, and that can be difficult.

The following sequence outlines steps for helping students with learning disabilities read and write decimals by relating them to fractions. It is assumed that the students have a firm understanding of the fraction concept as equal

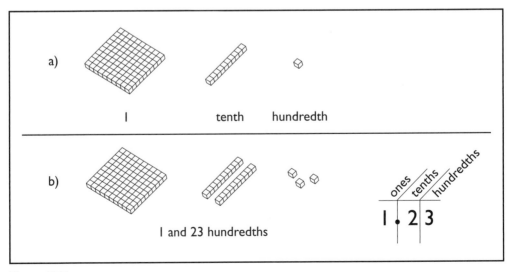

Figure 7.20.

parts of a whole. It also is necessary that they have worked with the blocks (or graph paper substitutes) to illustrate decimal numbers.

Sample Sequence of Activities

1. **Review.** Present the three blocks shown in Figure 7.21 and help students write the fraction for each. Discuss the name of each, orally emphasizing the *th.*

NOTE: *Sometimes it is necessary to color-emphasize the* th *in words for students with auditory discrimination deficits. Doing that focuses attention on the endings and on how fraction endings differ from whole-number endings.*

2. **Tell it to me.** Present pages like that in Figure 7.22. At first, cover the bottom of the page and have the children match real blocks to those appearing in the top row. Discuss the fraction written beneath each. Have the students read the fraction and note the color cueing: "One tenth has one zero, .1 (point one) has one decimal place," and so on.

3. **Write it out.** Help students complete the bottom part of the page in Figure 7.22. Here an effort is made to relate the visual model (the blocks) and the familiar fraction notation to the decimal form. Cue students to look at the number of zeros in the fraction, which tells the number of decimal places needed. "One zero (and one decimal place) for tenths; two for hundredths."

NOTE: *Omit decimal examples like .03, which require a zero in the tenths place, until children are more at ease writing other numbers with two decimal places.*

4. **Reinforce with money.** Once the concepts of decimal place value and writing decimals are established to the hundredths place, decimals can be related to money, as in Figure 7.23. Review how to write money (Figure 7.23a), but focus on the decimal part. Eventually, eliminate the dollars and just use

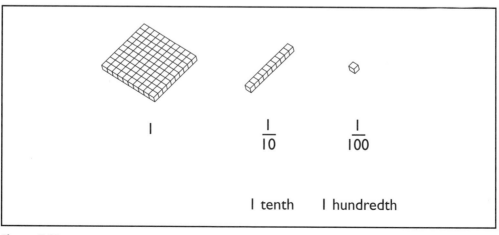

Figure 7.21.

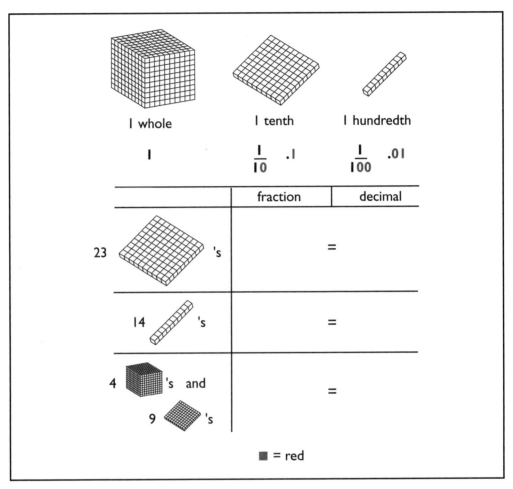

Figure 7.22.

pennies (Figure 7.23b). Now is a good time to introduce zeros in the tenths place: "$.06—that's 6 out of 100 possible pennies." Continue color-coding, if needed.

NOTE: *When abstract-reasoning skills are strong, students with expressive language or visual memory deficits may benefit from using money as a base for the introduction of decimals.*

   5. **Relate.** To make use of students' strong visual association skills, pages like that of Figure 7.24 can be provided as follow-up to the work in Activity 4 above. Pages with mixed-fraction and decimal problems also can be presented.

   6. **Phase out.** Eliminate picture cues except at the top of the page, and require students to complete exercises like those shown in Figure 7.25.

   7. **Decimal number words.** If students have auditory weaknesses but can read, have them complete exercises like that of Figure 7.26. Initially, they write the fraction form first, then the decimal. This sequence helps internalize the association between the decimal number names and the numerals them-

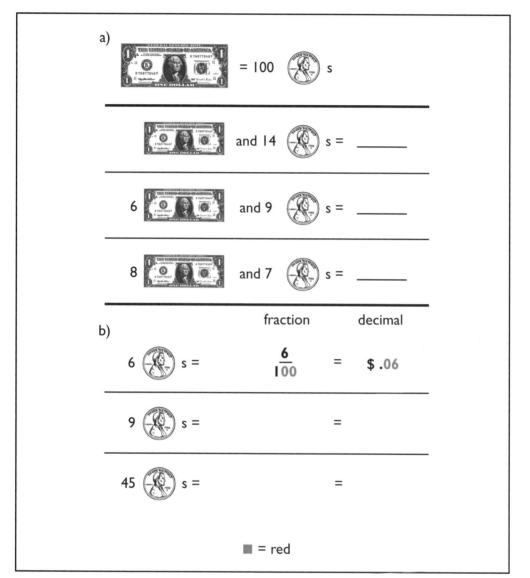

Figure 7.23.

selves. Throughout decimal work, if the students become confused when reading or writing a decimal, encourage them to think of or write the related fraction. The denominator of the fraction should help cue them to say "tenths" or "hundredths" and also indicate the appropriate number of decimal digits.

8. **Punch it in** (a practice activity for two players). As a follow-up to Activity 7 above, provide a hand calculator for each of two students and a deck of cards, such as those in Figure 7.27. The children mix the cards and spread them face up. Then, taking turns, each draws a card. After each player punches the number on his or her card into a calculator, they compare the visual displays. Then they turn the cards over to check. Players earn one tally point for each correct entry.

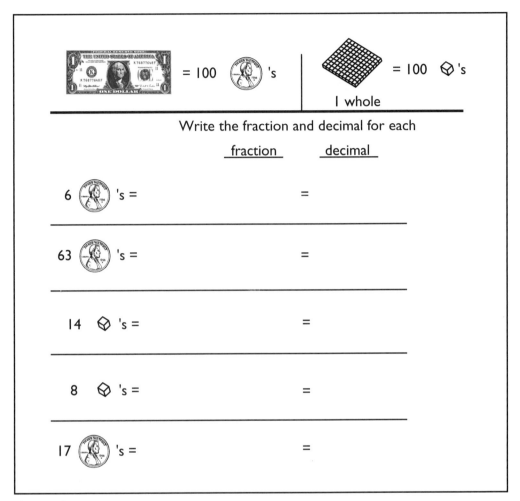

Figure 7.24.

- *Variation* (to build auditory memory and association skills): Ahead of time, read (or have the child read) the numbers on the cards into a cassette tape recorder. The child then listens to the tape, punches in the number heard, and uses the card deck to check the answer. If the tape does not allow sufficient pause between entries, instruct the child to push the "stop" button after each number.

EQUIVALENT NUMBERS

Problem Area: Difficulty identifying equivalent numbers.

Typical Disabilities Affecting Progress: Difficulty with closure, visual memory, integrative processing, abstract reasoning, retrieval, visual figure-ground.

Background: Understanding the conceptual base for rational numbers involves a clear understanding of the meaning of the word *equivalent.* Students

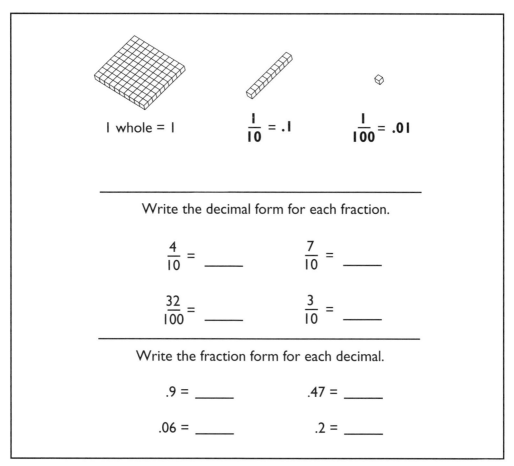

Figure 7.25.

use this idea daily, often without even realizing it, in activities such as sharing items by ensuring that "my friend has something of the same value that I do" even if they look different. Teachers use the idea by scheduling the day so that equivalent time is spent on activities of equal or similar importance. Often, however, relating this idea to the concept of numerical equivalence is more complicated. Although the concept itself is readily illustrated with physical models, the application of the concept requires several discrete subskills, including:

- knowing when it is appropriate to find an equivalent number;
- knowing what type of equivalent number is needed; and
- knowing how to find the equivalent number.

The following are some ideas that have been used successfully to teach students the underlying concept of equivalence and to enable them to apply their knowledge in a variety of situations. The section begins with ideas to help foster understanding of equivalent fractions, then equivalent decimals, and then equivalence of all kinds. This is not necessarily the only sequence to follow, but

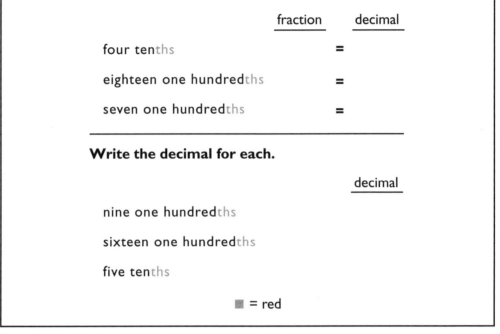

$$\frac{6}{100} = \text{six one hundredths} = .06$$

$$\frac{9}{10} = \text{nine tenths} = .9$$

Write the fraction and the decimal for each.

	fraction	decimal
four tenths		=
eighteen one hundredths		=
seven one hundredths		=

Write the decimal for each.

	decimal
nine one hundredths	
sixteen one hundredths	
five tenths	

■ = red

Figure 7.26.

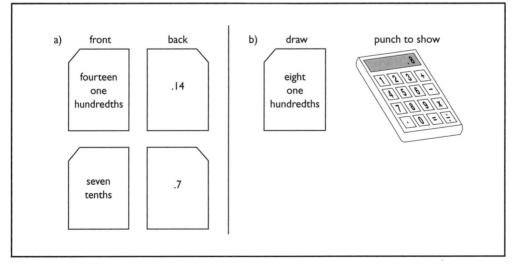

a) front   back

fourteen one hundredths   .14

seven tenths   .7

b) draw   punch to show

eight one hundredths

Figure 7.27.

it is one that is often preferable since overlearning in one area helps students apply their knowledge more confidently in other areas.

Finding Equivalent Fractions

During early developmental work with equivalent fractions, when the emphasis is on understanding the concept, physical and pictorial models must be used to dramatize the concept of equivalence. Typically, students are asked to compare shaded parts of regions, as in Figure 7.28. Children with abstract-reasoning, figure-ground, or spatial deficits may not readily recognize that an equal amount of space is colored in both drawings. The added lines in Figure 7.28b can be very confusing and prevent children from making the comparison visually.

Though specialized techniques like those that follow can help establish a conceptual basis for equivalence, other difficulties related to finding equivalent fractions also must be resolved. Some children can write a "family" of equivalent fractions by multiplying a given fraction first by $\frac{2}{2}$, then by $\frac{3}{3}$, $\frac{4}{4}$, and so on. These same children, especially those with memory, sequencing, or closure difficulties, may have difficulty finding the numerator for a given denominator, as in Figure 7.29. Consider what is involved in determining a fraction equivalent to $\frac{3}{4}$ with a denominator of 24. The student must:

- find the missing factor for the equation $4 \times \underline{\quad} = 24$;
- switch the thought process to a more standard form of an equation;
- find the product of 3×6; and
- determine the numerator.

Students *can* learn to deal with these problems. To this end, they must be actively involved in a learning program that is carefully tailored to meet their special learning needs. Suggestions for how to plan such a program for early work with equivalence are outlined below. The emphasis is on developing strong visual images with language and kinesthetic reinforcement, keeping the step size small and, equally important, making provisions for overlearning.

Sample Sequence of Activities

1. **Matchups.** Give students a construction-paper rectangle like that in Figure 7.30a. Have them state the name of the fractional part that is colored.

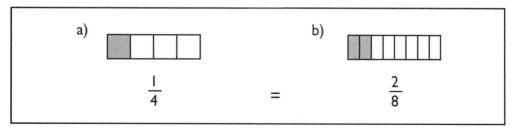

Figure 7.28.

$$\frac{3}{4} = \frac{\square}{24}$$

Figure 7.29.

If the children are strong tactual learners, texturize the shaded part. Glue pieces of felt, or spread glue and sprinkle salt or sand over the region; then glue string or straws over the lines that partition the shape. Have the students close their eyes, feel, and then name the fraction represented by the texturized area.

Repeat the procedure with the rectangle in Figure 7.30b. Encourage students to use their eyes and their hands to see and feel that the second rectangle is the same shape and size as the first. For an additional check, they can place the two shapes on top of each other.

2. **Pictures now.** Because many children cannot readily recognize equivalence when comparing two pictures they cannot move (see Figure 7.28), it often is helpful for them to use only one picture. In Figure 7.31, the students are first presented with the rectangle divided into thirds. Have them tell you, then write, that two thirds of it is colored. Next, direct them to connect the hatch marks with a ruler and write the fraction that describes the colored part. Several problems of this sort, in which the student actually uses the same space but changes the fractional name, help build up the equivalence idea without relying totally on visual perception.

3. **Plastic overlays.** Using a permanent marker and clear plastic overlays, draw rectangular shapes as shown in Figure 7.32a. Provide predrawn worksheets (see Figure 7.32b) that contain shapes congruent to those on the overlays, as shown. In the first part of the assignment, the children color in a designated fractional part of each shape on the worksheet (see Figure 7.32c). To determine equivalence, they then match the plastic overlays with the rectangles they colored. When they think they have a matching shape, they can use a grease pencil to outline the shaded area as a means of checking for accuracy. The fractions represented by the colored regions of the two rectangles are written below the worksheet shape, as in Figure 7.32d.

4. **Dot it.** Figure 7.33 illustrates another technique that helps eliminate visual confusion and focuses attention correctly. Matching shapes are aligned one above the other on worksheets, and a dotted line is used to help students recognize the equivalence being demonstrated. It also helps to have the children draw around the colored (or uncolored) area of both figures to get a better feel for the congruence in size.

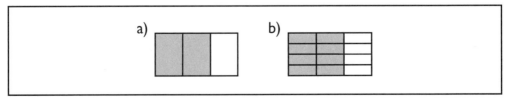

Figure 7.30.

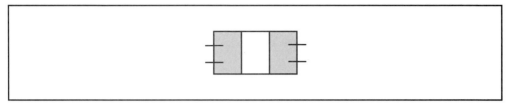

Figure 7.31.

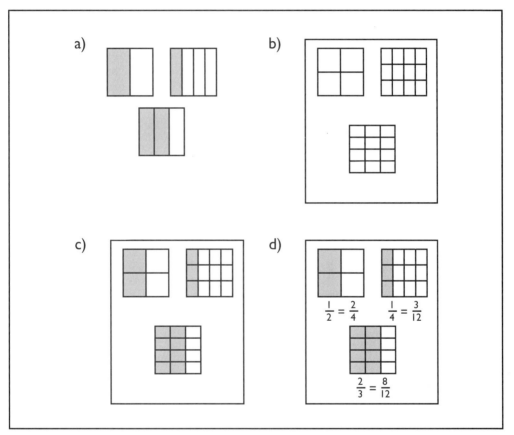

Figure 7.32.

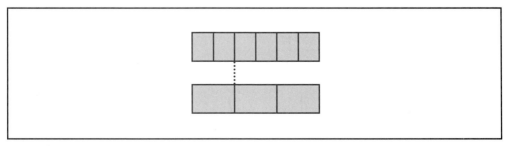

Figure 7.33.

5. **Talk about it.** Set aside time to analyze the equivalence demonstrated by picture pairs. The following dialogue, based on the example in Figure 7.34, suggests how a discussion might proceed.

TEACHER: "You said that $\frac{2}{5}$ of this figure is colored. Into how many equal parts is the rectangle divided?"

STUDENT: "Five."

TEACHER: "Correct. In the second rectangle, the same amount of space is colored, but we divided it up differently. How many total parts are there in the second rectangle?"

STUDENT: "Ten."

TEACHER: "Yes, we could also say the second rectangle has *two times as many* total parts as the first. Compared to the first, how many times as many colored pieces are in the second rectangle?"

STUDENT: "Two times as many."

TEACHER: "That's right, we colored in four parts of that rectangle, which is *two times as many* as were colored in the first one."

NOTE 1: *Make sure students understand the expression "two times as many." Sometimes it is necessary to review this idea even though students understand the concept of multiplication. They may not automatically relate the phrase to the concept of equivalence.*

NOTE 2: *Tenths were used for this activity and should be used along with halves, thirds, fourths, and other commonly used fractions during early developmental work. The way will then be paved for an earlier introduction to and use of decimals.*

NOTE 3: *Encourage students to understand that a similar comparison can be made using the expression "half as many." Be sure they understand that using the word "half" means the same as "dividing by 2." Much work in this area will help children develop a broader understanding of the concept of equivalence.*

6. **The general idea: multiply and divide.** When children are comfortable with discussions like that in Activity 5 above, introduce the idea of forming equivalent "families" by multiplying and dividing. Have children use fraction strips for $\frac{1}{3}$ and $\frac{2}{6}$. If necessary, lay them on paper and draw a dotted line between them, as in Figure 7.33. Students should verbalize the different ways

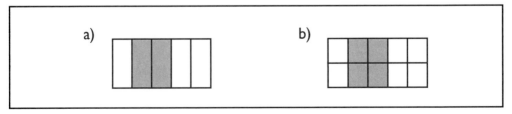

Figure 7.34.

of comparing. Compared to the strip for $\frac{1}{3}$, the strip for $\frac{2}{6}$ has two times as many colored parts and two times as many total parts. ("We can also say that the strip for $\frac{1}{3}$ has half as many colored parts and half as many total parts.") Using numbers, help students see that $\frac{2}{2} \times \frac{1}{3} = \frac{2}{6}$ and $\frac{2}{6} \div \frac{2}{2} = \frac{1}{3}$. Lead children to see how a whole family of equivalent fractions can be formed by multiplying or dividing both numerator and denominator by 2, or by 3, and so on. In early work, children should use fraction strips to verify their multiplication and division. Three or four strips can be placed under each other (on paper, using dotted lines to connect families that have been formed).

7. **Talented "1."** Gradually, strips or pictures are eliminated, and the children use the multiplication and division technique to find fractions equivalent to a given fraction. One final point should be made before pictures are laid aside entirely. Use the technique in Figure 7.35 to color-emphasize that you really multiply or divide by $\frac{2}{2}$, $\frac{3}{3}$, $\frac{4}{4}$, and so forth when finding equivalent fractions. That is the same as multiplying or dividing by 1, so the area you end with is the same as the area with which you start. All you actually change are the size and number of pieces on the strip. The colored space stays the same size.

8. **Find the numerator.** Difficulty finding a new numerator for a given denominator is often the result of an inability to retrieve the missing factor. Many students need specific training before they can retrieve the factor, as well

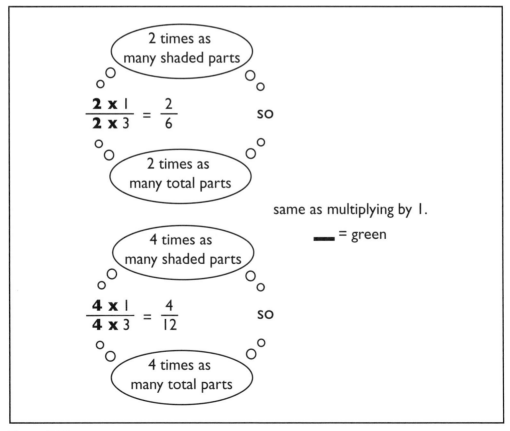

Figure 7.35.

as a controlled fact program like that described in Chapter 6. Initially, the equivalent fractions used on work pages would involve only basic facts the children have worked on, as in the examples in Figure 7.36. The examples represent three different formats, each gradually eliminating cues related to finding equivalent fractions but retaining the "help box" at the top for the facts. By the time Example 3 is used, students extend the fraction line themselves and write in the multiplication facts. This way, students who are having trouble memorizing their facts can still progress conceptually.

NOTE: *It generally is preferable not to encourage dividing the new denominator by the old one in order to determine the missing factor. This practice adds an extra step to the already complicated thought process. Although the correct missing factor may be obtained using this technique, the division step often interferes with what should be done in the numerator. The visual cueing of Figure 7.36 prompts children to "think multiplication" instead.*

9. **Turn over** (a practice activity for two players). Make a game board and an answer sheet for missing numerators as started in Figure 7.37. Also make two sets of 20 small circles to be used as the missing numerators, each set a different color. Number the circles 1 through 20 and give each child a set of circles. To begin, all circles are placed upside down. Children take turns turning over one of their circles to expose a number and placing the circle on the board so that an equivalent pair of fractions is formed. One player can challenge the other if he or she thinks that a circle has been placed in error. If the player challenged cannot correctly state what to multiply the numerator and denominator by, that circle must be removed. The answer sheet, or a calculator,

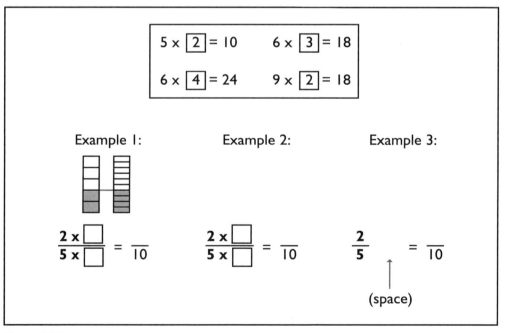

Figure 7.36.

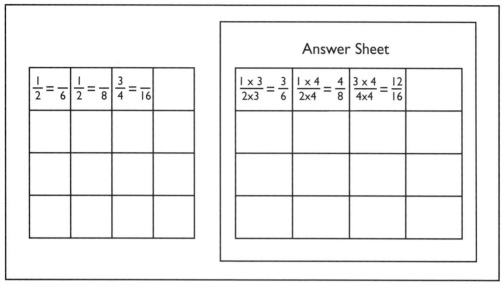

Figure 7.37.

can be used to resolve differences. The winner is the first to form five pairs of equivalent fractions.

Finding Equivalent Decimals

As noted in previous sections, an understanding of fractions is often a prerequisite to an understanding of decimals. Students should be encouraged to write the fraction equivalent for the decimal and convert that to equivalent fractions. The final step would be converting back to a decimal. Many of the activities in the previous section can be adapted to help students understand and apply the equivalence of decimals.

Sample Sequence of Activities

1. **Decimal equivalents.** The ability to find decimal equivalents for given fractions is an important skill. It generally is necessary to convert fractions to decimals in order to compute with a calculator. Some fractions, like those in Figure 7.38, are equivalent to fractions that have 10 or 100 in the denominator. When the exercises in this section are extended to help students deal with those fractions, the changeover to decimals is relatively simple for those who can read and write decimals (e.g., $\frac{5}{10} = .5$; $\frac{75}{100} = .75$).

2. **Divide to find.** Sometimes children find it easier to divide, as in Figure 7.39, in order to find the decimal equivalent of a fraction. The "divide numerator by denominator" rule is simple enough, and a calculator can be used to carry out the division. Some children can understand why the division works. The focus, of course, is on the denominator, which tells the number of parts into

$$\frac{\boxed{5} \times 1}{\boxed{5} \times 2} = \frac{5}{10}$$

$$\frac{\boxed{2} \times 3}{\boxed{2} \times 5} = \frac{6}{10}$$

Figure 7.38.

which the whole is divided. For the fraction in Figure 7.39a, the whole is divided into fourths (.25) and we have one of those parts—.25 of the whole. In Figure 7.39b the whole also is divided into fourths, but we have three of them, or .75 of the whole. Instead of dividing into fourths and then multiplying by 3, we combine steps when we divide 3 by 4—numerator by denominator.

Finding Equivalent Numbers

Once students fully understand the idea of equivalence, teachers can help them see the relationship between a variety of types of numbers. In addition, students should begin to develop a sense for the changing nature of equivalence. Figure 7.40 shows the equivalence between fourths and eighths. By using the

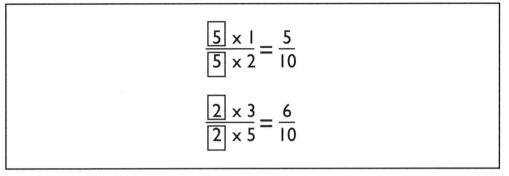

	Fraction Form →	Divide numerator by denominator →	Decimal Form
a)	$\frac{1}{4}$	$4\overline{)1.00}$ → .25	.25
b)	$\frac{3}{4}$	$4\overline{)3.00}$ → .75	.75
c)	$\frac{8}{5}$	$5\overline{)8.00}$ → 1.6	1.6
d)	$\frac{2}{7}$	$7\overline{)2.00}$ → $.3\overline{3}$	$.3\overline{3}$

Figure 7.39.

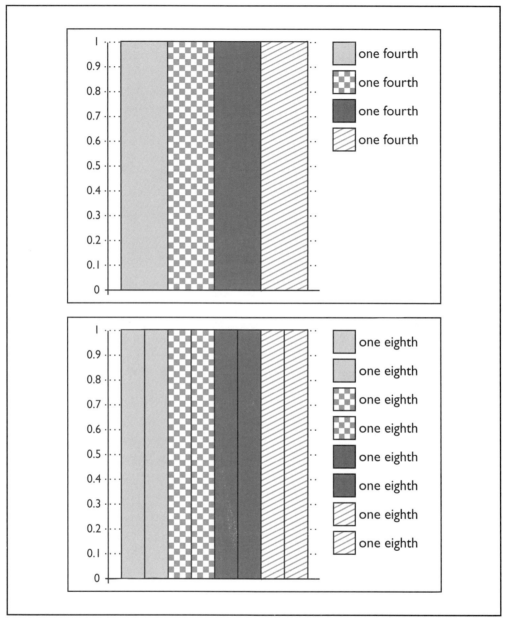

Figure 7.40.

spreadsheet and changing numbers or measurements on the graph, students will be able to see, for example, how what was initially equivalent is no longer equivalent. Although the size of the large rectangles remains the same, the size of the parts has changed. What is equivalent in one situation is not equivalent in another. A fourth of a pie means that each of four people eating the pie get the same-size piece; it does not mean that every pie divided into four parts has slices of the same size or that every pie divided into pieces of the same size is divided into fourths.

Younger children can also begin to be introduced to this changing idea of equivalence—"Look. This picture has 12 dots, for us to connect. When we have connected all 12 dots, we will have made *one whole* picture. But look, we also made *one whole* picture here when we only connected 7 dots."

NOTE: *Verbally and visually emphasize the italicized phrases at this level so that, at an early age students become familiar with hearing and applying those and other phrases such as one-third, one-fourth, etc., in a variety of contexts.*

SELECTED REAL-LIFE APPLICATIONS

Using an Inch Ruler

Problem Area: Difficulty reading fractional parts of an inch ruler.

Typical Disabilities Affecting Progress: Difficulty with abstract reasoning, visual perception, visual motor coordination.

Background: To date, the United States still has not made giant strides toward "going metric." As a result, students must continue to use inch rulers even as they learn to use centimeter rulers (see "Using a Centimeter Ruler" below). Visually the inch ruler causes more problems than the centimeter ruler. Besides being able to associate a specific number with a specific line, the student must be able to:

- differentiate visually among different lengths of segments on a linear ruler;
- associate the length of each segment with its equivalent fraction; and
- read or write a symbol (e.g., $\frac{1}{4}$) that is visually, spatially, and auditorially difficult to sequence.

When using an inch ruler to draw a line, students must know where to place the ruler in relation to the object to be measured. Visual motor coordination problems often interfere. This section will not deal with those problems except to say that, if the goal is accurate measuring, the instructor should give students guidelines to follow, as in Figure 7.41, or allow them to use lined

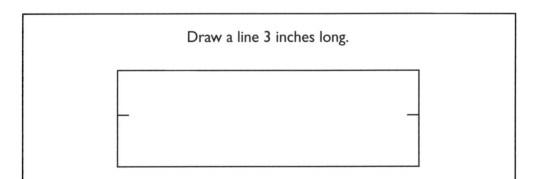

Figure 7.41.

paper. For children with figure-ground deficits, however, the latter alternative can be more difficult than using guidelines.

The basic approach to teaching students how to use a ruler involves measuring many objects. In addition, some children may require more specialized instruction, such as that outlined below.

✏ Sample Sequence of Activities

1. **Simplified rulers.** Younger children and children with learning disabilities usually start out with simplified rulers that show only quarter, half, and whole inches. Even then, they may have trouble perceiving size differences for the various parts of an inch. Colors are often helpful. Properly used, colors can focus student attention and make size differences more obvious. Figure 7.42a shows an example of a homemade ruler that can be made as a template on a disk, kept on file, and printed when needed. As children become ready, this paper ruler can be cut, glued to cardboard, and marked as in Figure 7.42b. Covering rulers with clear contact paper makes them more durable.

NOTE: *For students who are color blind, use bold, dotted, and regular line markings.*

2. **Measure.** To help children use the ruler in Activity 1 above, provide opportunities for them to measure many objects. Structure these experiences as follows: Attach masking-tape strips to several items, as shown in Figure 7.43a. At first, make sure the measurement is an exact number of inches. Later, the tape mark can be slightly longer or slightly shorter so children can learn how to measure to the nearest inch.

Gradually introduce half- and quarter-inch lengths. If the measurement is to be made to the nearest inch, the colored line segment on the tape should be

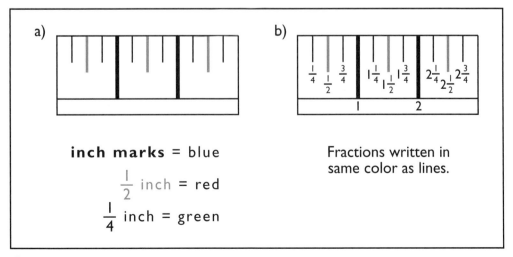

a)

inch marks = blue

$\frac{1}{2}$ inch = red

$\frac{1}{4}$ inch = green

b)

Fractions written in same color as lines.

Figure 7.42.

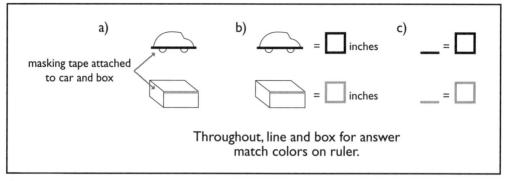

Figure 7.43.

blue to match the inch marks on the ruler (in Figure 7.42a). Similarly, the tape markers should be red when half-inch measurements are to be made and green when quarter-inch measurements are to be made.

This color-cueing technique draws the child's attention to the appropriate ruler mark needed for a given measurement. Having the numbers on the ruler is especially important for students who require overlearning or have difficulty with retrieval. After an object is measured, the measurement can be recorded on worksheets that picture the object. (See Figure 7.43b.)

■ *Extension:* As a follow-up to work with objects, have the children find and record the measurements of line segments drawn on paper. Figure 7.43c shows a sample exercise. Figure 7.44 shows another type of page that is helpful for students who have spatial deficits that make it difficult to write proper fractions and mixed numbers, or for children who have retrieval or expressive language deficits and, therefore, need visual cues. The color-coding scheme, introduced earlier, can be used as long as it seems helpful.

3. **Draw a line.** The color-coding of Activity 2 above also can be used to help students draw a line of a specific length. A sample exercise is presented in Figure 7.45a. Children use their rulers to draw over a given line then draw another line of the same length under it. Gradually, still using color to specify the length (see Figure 7.45b), instruct students to draw the segment indicated. This latter exercise still provides some guidance because the color used for the written direction draws attention to the appropriate marks on the ruler. Even nonreaders quickly pick up the color cueing and learn to perform the measurements accurately.

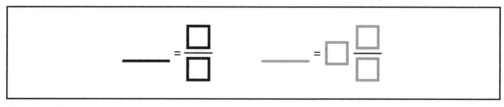

Figure 7.44.

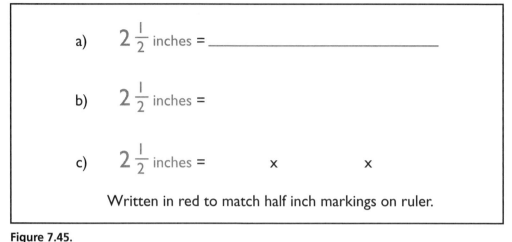

Figure 7.45.

NOTE: *Some students may require the additional guidance of start and stop marks (see Figure 7.45c) as a transition between exercises like those shown in Figure 7.45a and 7.45b.*

Using a Centimeter Ruler

Problem Area: Difficulty interpreting or writing centimeter measures.

Typical Disabilities Affecting Progress: Difficulty with abstract reasoning, visual perception, visual motor coordination.

Background: Centimeter rulers are considerably easier for children to use than inch rulers, which are based on fractions. Visually, centimeter rulers are less confusing. Each line on the ruler can be associated more readily with a verbal expression. Even if students have trouble retrieving the correct decimal number name, there is a more direct, one-to-one association between the ruler markings and words than on a linear ruler. One can associate 1.3, for example, with one large line and the three smaller ones that follow it on a metric ruler.

✎ Sample Sequence of Activities

1. **Simplified ruler.** Younger children with learning disabilities should use centimeter rulers with a midline between each two centimeters. As with inch rulers, different colors can be used for the centimeter line and the midline.

2. **Overhead rulers.** Enlarge a ruler and create a transparency (see Figure 7.46) so students can more easily examine the subdivisions. Project the picture onto a wall and let children run a finger from the left ("start") edge to the first midline.

A fraction bar, as in Figure 7.46, can be used to illustrate that the distance from the end covers 5 out of 10, or $\frac{5}{10}$ (.5) of the total distance to the centimeter mark. Continue to read other measures as the children, each time, run a finger

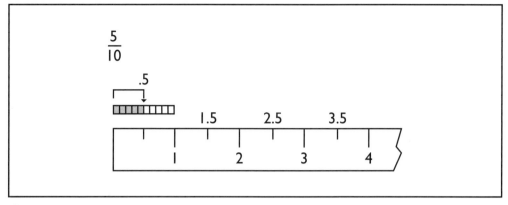

Figure 7.46.

from the left edge of the ruler: 1 cm, 1.5 cm, and so on. Later, have students write what is read. Accept responses that use fraction answers, such as "one and a half," even though technically it may not be appropriate to use the fraction instead of the decimal notation.

Estimating

Problem Areas: Difficulty remembering the sequence of steps; difficulty retaining information.

Typical Disabilities Affecting Progress: Difficulty with abstract reasoning, closure, memory sequencing, nonverbal learning disabilities.

Background: Estimation is an essential component of a strong mathematics program and is often a more important area than the ability to use computation. Increasingly, as technology becomes more exact and less expensive, using calculators and computers makes more sense than using paper and pencil for longer calculations. Students with learning disabilities often have difficulty in this area, however, and need additional practice in related areas, such as rounding fractions and decimals, which others may be able to do intuitively.

The following activities are suggested for helping students develop and improve their ability to estimate. Rather than being taught as an isolated skill, as it has been in the past, rounding should be thought of as a tool to help students process and use language as they apply estimation.

Sample Sequence of Activities

1. **Review.** Most students fairly readily understand that 38 is about the same as 40. Many even rather easily intuitively understand that $3\frac{1}{3}$ is closer to 3 than to 4. Applying this concept to decimals is a little more difficult, since there are often fewer visual and auditory cues. Practicing with a number line, as in Figure 7.47, helps students develop a mental image that makes it easier for them to develop some automaticity.

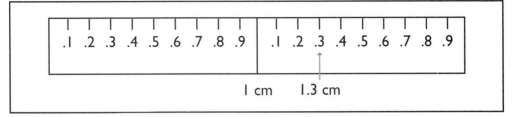

Figure 7.47.

NOTE 1: *Initially, the use of the terms* backward *and* forward *may help students more readily visualize the procedure. Later, they can be taught more commonly used synonyms.*

NOTE 2: *If students are strong tactual learners, texturize the number line or make it longer to encourage more gross-motor involvement. Have students close their eyes as they slide their fingers to either end of the line. Later, extend to other number lines that involve more choices, as in Figure 7.48b.*

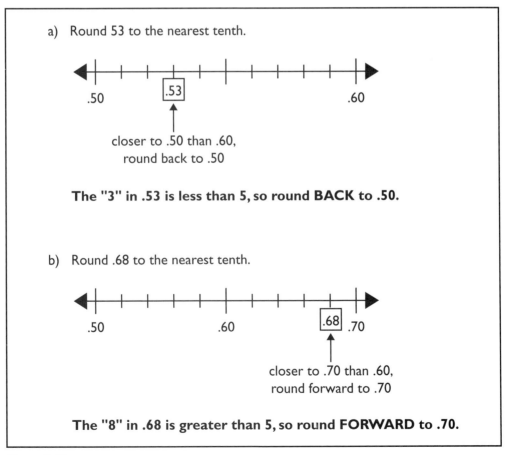

a) Round 53 to the nearest tenth.

.50   .53   .60

closer to .50 than .60,
round back to .50

The "3" in .53 is less than 5, so round BACK to .50.

b) Round .68 to the nearest tenth.

.50   .60   .68 .70

closer to .70 than .60,
round forward to .70

The "8" in .68 is greater than 5, so round FORWARD to .70.

Figure 7.48.

2. **A fast dime.** Provide two decks of cards: a "banker's deck" and a "fast-dime" deck (see Figure 7.49). Place the banker's deck in a bank box along with extra dimes and pennies. This deck contains one card for each multiple of $.10 (to $.90), whereas the fast-dime deck contains cards that list amounts between $.11 and $.89 (no multiples of $.10 included). Until students understand the activity, remove all money amounts ending in 5 from the fast-dime deck.

Shuffle the fast-dime deck and place the cards face down between the players. Students take turns drawing the top card from the deck and placing it face up in the playing area. They then use dimes (as many as possible) and extra pennies to show the amount on the card.

The banker selects the two cards from the banker's deck that are closest in value to the amount displayed (see Figure 7.50). The child in this example must then decide how a "fast dime" can be made. Is $.34 closer to $.30 or to $.40? The child must either add pennies to the $.34 pile or take some away to indicate the choice made; either 6 pennies must be added (to make $.40) or 4 pennies taken away (leaving $.30). The latter decision earns the child one point, since it involves the least number of coin moves. When students are comfortable with this activity, return the money amounts ending in 5 to the deck. Introduce the "banker's rule" that for these cards the fast dime is always the greater $.10 value.

- *Variation:* Play the same game but now use a deck in which all dollar signs have been eliminated. If the students hesitate, ask them to find a matching fast-dime card. Seeing the card usually triggers the correct idea. If necessary, allow the students to use dimes and pennies to determine "closeness to." ("Yes, 34 hundredths is closer to 30 hundredths than to 40 hundredths.")

3. **Color cue.** Help students focus attention on the "thinking" digit (the number after the number to be rounded) by color-highlighting that digit, as in Figure 7.51.

- *Extension 1:* For students who are strong in money concepts and skills, Figure 7.51b suggests one way to use money to build or reinforce rounding skills for decimals. In the example illustrated, green represents the thinking number, while red indicates the number of digits in the final answer.

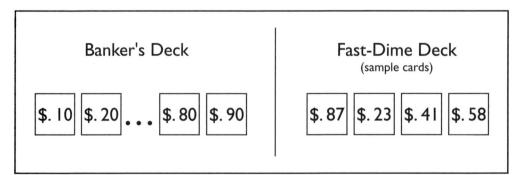

Figure 7.49.

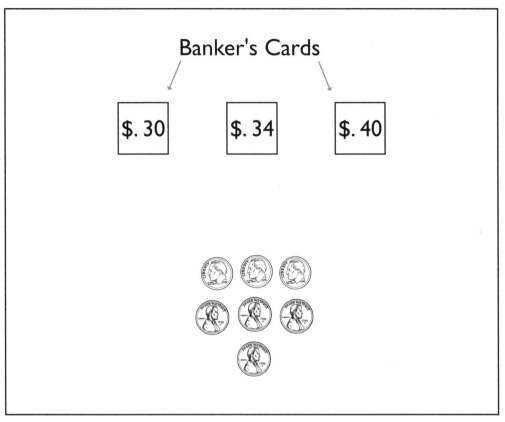

Figure 7.50.

- *Extension 2:* A natural progression from the example in Figure 7.51b consists of introducing students to rounding off using a calculator. Provide a calculator and worksheets or index cards as in Figure 7.52.

  Highlight as needed. Prerequisites: (a) determine the child's visual perceptual skills and (b) provide appropriate practice with a calculator.

- *Follow-Up Practice Game: Rounding War* (for two players): The students mix and deal out all the cards of a two-digit decimal deck. Each player turns over the top card and rounds it to the nearest tenth. The player with the greatest tenth captures both cards. Ties are resolved in the traditional "war" fashion. The winner is the first to capture all cards.

4. **What's the weather like?** People laugh all the time at weather predictions, perhaps because they rely so heavily on estimation. Children often enjoy trying to "outwit" the weatherman, and a good way to start that is to understand how the terms *partly cloudy, mostly cloudy, sunny,* etc., are applied. Figure 7.53 shows how the sky can be looked at or perhaps photographed on a clear day. Using this concrete representation students can use their knowledge of fractions and decimals to decide what the chances are of rain, sun, clouds, and so on.

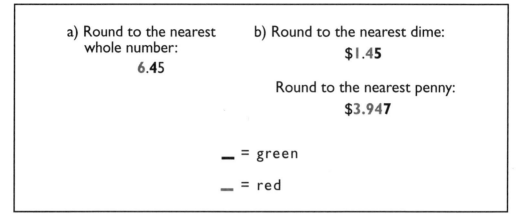

a) Round to the nearest whole number:

6.45

b) Round to the nearest dime:

$1.45

Round to the nearest penny:

$3.947

— = green

— = red

Figure 7.51.

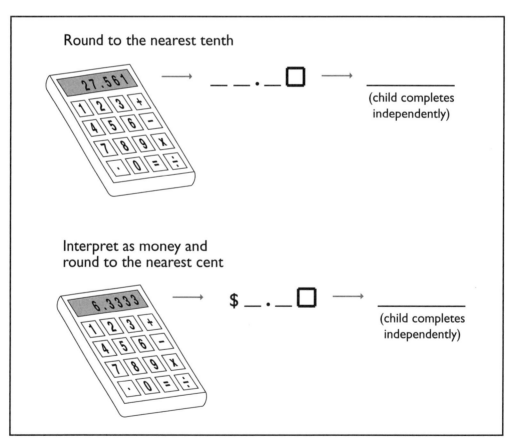

Round to the nearest tenth

 ⟶ _ _ . _ □ ⟶ _____
(child completes independently)

Interpret as money and round to the nearest cent

 ⟶ $ _ . _ □ ⟶ _____
(child completes independently)

Figure 7.52.

Look at each one of the rectangles in the grid. Some of them are completely covered by clouds and some are partly covered by clouds. If you count each rectangle that is covered at least halfway by clouds, you come up with four. Which fraction below describes the cloud cover?

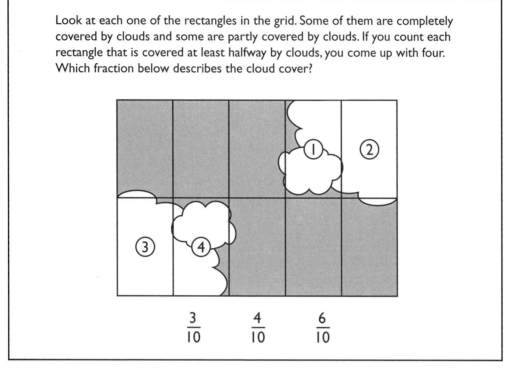

$$\frac{3}{10} \qquad \frac{4}{10} \qquad \frac{6}{10}$$

Figure 7.53. The image in this figure is a screen shot from the Internet site http://www.planemath.com/activities/sky/sky_9.html.

Chapter 8

◆ ◆ ◆ ◆ ◆ ◆ ◆ ◆ ◆ ◆ ◆ ◆ ◆ ◆ ◆ ◆ ◆ ◆ ◆

Extending Understanding and Application of Fractions and Decimals

In the typical school curriculum, early work with fractions precedes and, as suggested in the previous chapter, can be integrated with decimal topics to help children with learning disabilities develop understandings and skills for successfully using rational numbers. Generally, however, beyond that introduction, different patterns emerge. Because computation with decimals is generally easier and more closely related to whole-number computation, this topic is often treated *before* fraction computation. On the other hand, because tedious paper-and-pencil computations for rational numbers are being abandoned in favor of estimation or calculator approaches in which fractions, decimals, and even percents may be used interchangeably, these topics may need to be *integrated* during instruction.

A tricky fraction computation, for example, might be *translated to decimal form* before being computed by hand or on a calculator. In other instances (e.g., when multiplying decimals), some students might gain better intuition about a general procedure when decimals are *translated to fractions* as part of the initial development. Because of their interface in practical use and instruction, both fraction and decimal computation are treated in this chapter.

Whenever possible, as with whole numbers, it is suggested that the computational work be embedded in *applied settings* or in interesting or relevant *problem contexts*. The students themselves should be invited to suggest problem contexts for fractions. In other words, computation should arise from students' need to do or know, not merely as an end in itself. Nurturing good understanding of and proficiency with *simple* paper-pencil fraction and decimal computations is an appropriate instructional goal, but the need for involved computations and work with any but the more commonly used fractions or decimals is obsolete.

In other words, computation with fractions should involve only simple denominators that can be modeled using fraction strips or fraction circles. Similarly, decimals used in computation should be those that can be readily illustrated by "real-life" situations or modeled using money or base-10 pieces. Consequently, computations involving numbers written in thousandths or beyond and division with decimal divisors is of limited value.

The general perspective taken in the following sections is that, throughout work involving fraction and decimal computation, number sense and the practical usefulness of rational numbers should be nurtured. On a consistent basis, instruction should focus on helping children (a) select the correct operation for solving a problem; (b) decide on the most efficient method of arriving at a workable answer (i.e., mental calculation or estimation, calculator, paper and pencil); (c) explore or respect different correct solution paths; and (d) explain and justify their solution approaches.

PERSPECTIVES ON STUDENTS WITH LEARNING DISABILITIES

Even with a strong conceptual understanding of fractions and decimals, many students with learning disabilities still have trouble, especially as they begin to compute. Manipulative experiences help give meaning to the written work. Eventually, however, the use of physical objects becomes cumbersome and it is necessary to rely on pictures. For most children the use of pictures is not a problem; they make the transition from object to pictures easily. However, some children have real trouble with textbook illustrations. Techniques for handling this and other problem areas of fraction and decimal computation that typically are troublesome for students with learning disabilities are discussed in the five major sections of this chapter:

1. General Areas of Difficulty
2. Comparing Rational Numbers
3. Simplifying Fractions
4. Developing Computation Sense for Fractions and Decimals
5. Written Computation for Fractions and Decimals

Calculator work, integrated throughout the suggestions of this chapter, is also addressed in a concluding "Using Technology" section. This final section includes computer software suggestions related to fraction and decimal computation. The instructional ideas of this chapter assume that *prerequisite* understandings of rational numbers, addressed in Chapter 7, are intact as the basis for the computation program selected for an individual child.

GENERAL AREAS OF DIFFICULTY

Because of their level of involvement, individuals with learning disabilities may have great difficulty extending or applying even stable understandings to computation. General areas of difficulty related to disabilities may be due to either of two aspects of computation in which students may be involved when working with fractions and decimals, including:

- estimation and mental calculation, and
- paper-and-pencil computation.

These difficulties tend to be idiosyncratic to each student, depending on the nature and severity of the disability, as well as on the kind of compensatory techniques the student has adopted. This section addresses each of those two areas of difficulty.

General Difficulties for Estimation and Mental Calculation

Even when students have strong concepts for fractions and decimals, estimation and mental computation may be very difficult. The major difficulty underlying the success of many students with learning disabilities in these areas is parallel to that highlighted in their work with whole numbers: their inability to retain information while simultaneously processing other information. This difficulty is often accompanied by related problems. For example, the student may reverse digits while attempting to retain information, and then proceed to process the wrong data. Or, a student may know but, for language reasons, be unable to express an estimation or mental calculation.

As has been suggested in Chapter 6, in the "Mental Computation and Estimation" section, many of these students should be encouraged to use a modified mental procedure in which intermediate data is written for later reference. This has proved to be an effective approach, one that some students will need to use throughout life. Students with expressive language difficulties may need to write down the resulting estimate or mental calculation for triggering their own speaking or for displaying their result as a means of conveying it to others.

General Difficulties with Written Computation

Figure-Ground

As was pointed out in Chapter 7, children may be unable, visually, to interpret shaded fraction or decimal pictures as intended. Suppose the task is adding fractions with unlike denominators, such as $\frac{3}{4} + \frac{1}{3}$. The children may understand and enjoy representing each fraction with its fraction strip, then trading the $\frac{3}{4}$ for a $\frac{9}{12}$ strip and the $\frac{1}{3}$ for a $\frac{4}{12}$ strip, and adding the twelfths. These same children, however, may have difficulty sorting out the steps from textbook pictures that accompany the explanation of finding common denominators. They may even have difficulty interpreting pictures for simpler problems, such as the addition in Figure 8.1a.

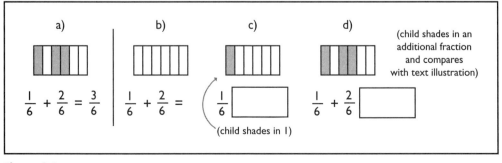

Figure 8.1.

For textbook illustrations like this, it is necessary to provide children with pictures similar to those of the textbook but unshaded, as in Figure 8.1b. Placing a card over all but the first addend in the equation, as in Figure 8.1c, the student can color $\frac{1}{6}$ of the figure. Moving the card so that the next addend is exposed (Figure 8.1d), the child next colors in an additional $\frac{2}{6}$ of the rectangle. The card is then removed and the answer written down. Finally, a comparison is made of the worksheet and textbook pages.

Patterning

Patterning requires that students be able to draw conclusions, a skill specifically taught in reading but not always in mathematics. Making the transition from concrete aids to symbolic understanding requires a strong ability to recognize number patterns. Generally, however, specific work on recognizing patterns is limited to kindergarten and first grade. At about fourth or fifth grade a high degree of abstraction is required as explanations begin to deal more with numbers than with either concrete aids or pictures. As the children begin to use symbols, their ability to recognize patterns, both obvious and implied, is important.

The fractions in Figure 8.2a, for example, illustrate an often unnoticed need for pattern recognition. The primary goal involved in changing mixed numbers to improper numbers is to understand conceptually what is happening. Ultimately, however, students remember what to do because they know they must "multiply the 4 and 3 and then add 2." In order to determine and retain the pattern, it helps students to see what the numbers do.

To help students to see and "hear" what the numbers do as they conceptualize what is actually happening (Figure 8.2b), "think" bubbles, tape recordings to match problems, and teacher verbalizations are effective.

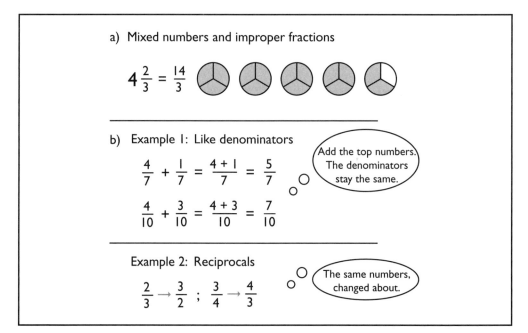

Figure 8.2.

Spatial Organization

Generally, we write letters or numbers in one direction, horizontally left to right. With fractions, however, that organization is different. Students are required to switch between horizontal and vertical alignment. Many students, especially younger ones, cannot clearly discriminate that difference. It is not unusual to see children writing fractions or mixed numbers as in Figure 8.3. As children mature, they usually develop an ability to handle these distinctions unless specific learning disabilities interfere.

Figure 8.4 presents ideas for types of preformatted pages that can be kept on file and used for this purpose. Example 1 in the figure is useful when teaching children to add or subtract mixed numbers. (The signs can be added when the numbers are filled in, allowing the teacher to decide at the time whether to use one operation on a page or to use a page of mixed operations.) With the boxes already there, the children need not be as concerned about number placement. Attention can be focused, instead, on the major goal: that of deciding whether to find a common denominator. The page is set up in two columns to help children in the decision-making process. The child writes in the first column when it is not necessary to find a common denominator, and in the second column when it *is* necessary. Example 2 illustrates a similar page of ideas for multiplication of fractions, while Example 3 suggests a format that can be adapted to division of fractions.

In relation to decimals, many students, particularly those with abstract-reasoning, motor, or visual perception deficits, have difficulty aligning digits for computing. For example, when problems like 6 − 2.4 or .8 + 2.34 are presented in vertical form, these students might fail to align "like units." Visual cues can be used to guide correct writing or placement of the decimals and fractions as they learn the various computational processes.

The items in Figure 8.4 reinforce reasoning as well, since the maximum number of spaces is presented. The student must decide whether it is necessary to use all the spaces. Figure 8.5, for example, shows a problem that does not require the student to use all the spaces provided.

Another simple yet important practice that helps to spatially organize the writing of fractions deals with the fraction bar separating numerator and denominator. Encourage children to draw this line *horizontally* ($\frac{3}{5}$), not diagonally (3/5). With the horizontal bar, there is less tendency to read a fraction as a whole number (35 or 315 for 3/5) or to confuse mixed numbers 15/8 for 1 5/8).

A final suggestion, helpful to children who must copy fraction problems from a textbook, is to provide a stencil, as in Figure 8.6. The stencil should be

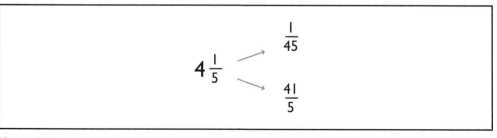

Figure 8.3.

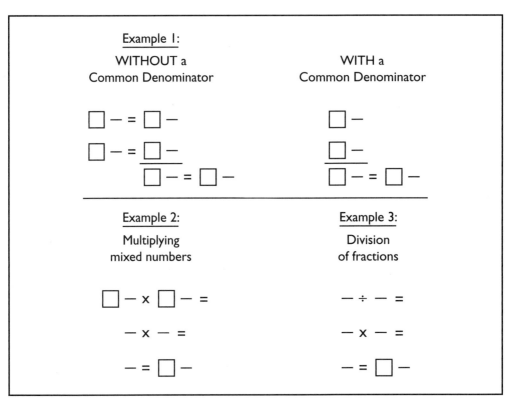

Figure 8.4.

made of clear plastic so that the entire problem can be viewed. The framing helps the students focus on just one fraction at a time. As a result the children tend to make fewer errors in copying.

Sequencing

Aside from spatial organization, sequencing is probably the next greatest problem and particularly influences a student's success with the more complex and less familiar fraction algorithms. As computational processes become more involved, what appears to be a single step may actually be two or three. Con-

$$\frac{2}{3} = \frac{16}{24}$$

$$+ \frac{1}{8} = \frac{3}{24}$$

$$\frac{19}{24}$$

Figure 8.5.

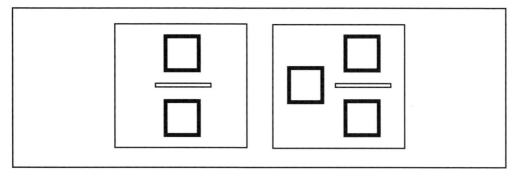

Figure 8.6.

sider the problem of Figure 8.5, where the student is required to add two proper fractions with unlike denominators. What generally is considered the first step, that of finding the common denominator, is actually three steps:

1. deciding whether a common denominator is required;
2. deciding what the common denominator should be; and
3. deciding what each numerator should be.

Children who have trouble retaining the isolated steps of a sequence often benefit from performing one step at a time until the sequence becomes automatic. For example, if the children fail to check whether a common denominator is needed, have them focus on that one step before introducing additional steps. The practice page ideas presented in Figure 8.7a may help. Instruct the students to copy problems from the book onto the pages, as in Figure 8.7b. The green circles in the denominators will help draw their attention to what the first step should be: check for common denominators. For those who have difficulty copying problems from a text, keep workbooks or textbooks in which the denominators have already been circled green. This could be done in advance, even at the beginning of the year.

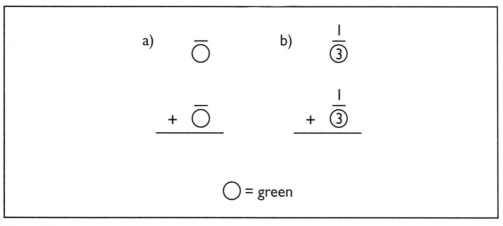

Figure 8.7.

After children have mastered individual steps and must put them all together, pages with the format of Figure 8.8 are helpful. This example is set up to show the maximum number of steps needed for adding or subtracting fractions. Encourage decision making. Remind the students that not all problems require all steps. If needed, a sample problem can be placed at the top of the page or on a 5×8 index card.

COMPARING RATIONAL NUMBERS

Problem Area: Tendency to focus on the numerals rather than the place value (for decimals) or the size of the unit and number of those units represented (for fractions); that is, in examples like .48 and .6, calling .48 the greater or in examples like $\frac{3}{4}$ and $\frac{3}{8}$, calling $\frac{3}{8}$ the greater.

Typical Disabilities Affecting Progress: Difficulty with abstract reasoning, spatial organization, auditory memory.

Background: Even students with no disabilities tend to have trouble comparing rational numbers. For those students with abstract-reasoning deficits, the difficulty is compounded. It often is necessary to teach those students a *procedure* for comparing; then, when they feel comfortable with that procedure, use visuals to demonstrate that it is a reasonable one. For students with spatial organization difficulties, the standard sequence of objects or pictures first in developmental work is appropriate, given that care is taken to avoid number lines or other aids that rely on accurate size perception.

We propose that comparison skills be grounded in ongoing problems that have meaning for students. The storyline of these problems might be presented orally while pertinent numbers and simple illustrations to help retain the storyline are provided on a transparency, card, or classroom chalkboard. Alternately, the full text of the problem might be provided and read or given to students working individually or in small groups to read and solve. By carefully selecting the problem types and the numbers used in these problems, students can

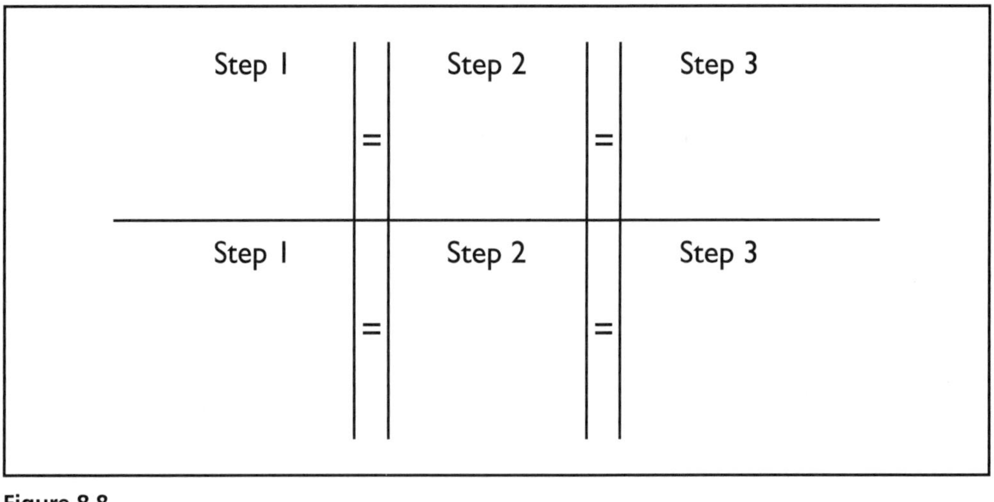

Figure 8.8.

gradually be involved in making more difficult comparisons. By varying the theme or numbers used for each problem type, students also can be led to make important generalizations about comparing the numbers. Three examples for fractions follow. Similar approaches can be used for developing and extending comparisons for decimals.

- "At [name of a child in the class]'s birthday party, 6 children were sitting at one table and 4 children were sitting at another. Both tables had the same-size chocolate chip cookie cake. At each table the cake was shared equally among all the children so that each child at that table got the same-size piece. Who got more chocolate chip cookie cake—the children at the table with 6 children or those at the table with 4 children?"

- "[Name of child in the class] had an overnight and invited many friends. Two tables were set up for lunch, one with 4 children and one with 3 children. Each table was given two pizzas, each the same size, to be shared equally among the children at the table. If all children took what was served to them, who got more pizza—the children at the table with 4 children or those at the table with 3 children?"

- "At [name of child in the class]'s birthday party, the children were seated at two tables for ice cream and cake. Mom had prepared many small cakes, each the same size. At one table, 6 children shared 3 cakes. At another table, 6 children shared 4 cakes. Who got more cake?"

As children work, some flexibility in personal choice of materials for assisting or demonstrating ideas might be allowed, depending on individual needs and learning styles. Always, students should be expected to explain their thinking. If more than one student is involved in the instructional group, listening to others' solutions and seeing how different students record their solution steps often broadens individual perspectives.

To meet individual learning needs, special techniques may need to be used in conjunction with problem-solving work. With the exception of Activity 3, the first section that follows on comparing decimals has been used effectively with students who have spatial organization deficits. The same sequence has been successfully modified for students who have abstract-reasoning deficits. Instruction for such students has begun with Activities 4 (saving the "prove" step till later), 5, 6, and then 1 below, *in that order.* Other children with learning disabilities, including those with visual perception and visual- or auditory-memory difficulties, have been helped by the suggestions, generally retaining the sequence presented. Ideas for helping students compare fractions are then presented in a separate sequence of activities and may be modified in a similar manner to meet the special learning needs of individual students.

Sample Sequence of Activities

▶ **Comparing Decimals**

1. **Shade in.** Assigning them a pair of decimals, have students shade hundredths squares as in Figure 8.9 to see which is greater.

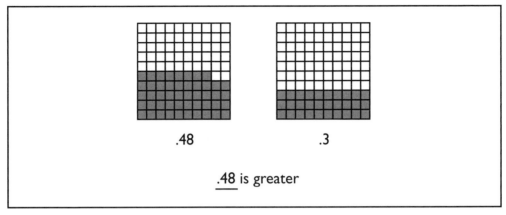

Figure 8.9.

2. **Use money** (if money concepts and skills are strong). Figure 8.10 suggests how dimes and pennies can be used to compare decimals to hundredths.

3. **On the line.** Many school textbooks suggest that students position decimals on a number line as an aid to comparing and ordering decimals (Figure 8.11). (This approach is inappropriate for students with spatial organization deficits.) "Walk-on" number line segments on which students walk from the lesser to the greater number help children who benefit from kinesthetic or motor involvement.

4. **Line them up.** Typically, it is effective to have students align decimal points to compare decimals, as in Figure 8.12. Then, digit by digit, they can

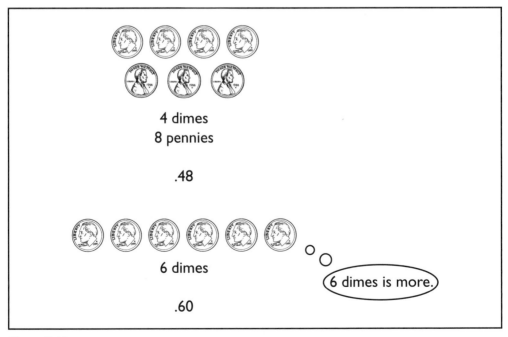

Figure 8.10.

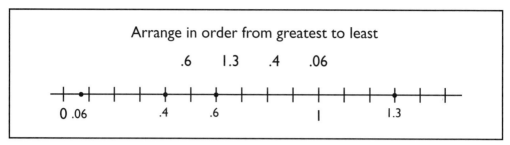

Figure 8.11.

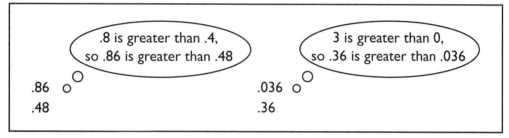

Figure 8.12.

"read" left to right to compare the numbers. (This procedure is similar to placing words in alphabetical order.) As soon as the child finds a difference in a column, the number with the greater digit has the greater value. If students require kinesthetic involvement, have them finger-trace digit pairs, stopping when they find a difference. Using ideas from Activities 1, 2, or 3, helps students "prove" that this procedure always works.

5. **Color cue.** Figure 8.13 illustrates how color-coding can be used to draw attention to critical digits in the comparison. This technique is especially helpful during early developmental work for students with figure-ground or other perceptual deficits. Eventually, students themselves can learn to color-highlight critical digits as a way of internalizing the comparison.

6. **Add zeros.** Whenever the number of decimal places in two given numbers differs, many students find it easier to compare them when extra zeros are added, as in Figure 8.14a. Evening out the number of decimal digits as shown makes the comparison more obvious, particularly when decimal points are aligned, as previously suggested. In this case, 360 thousandths is clearly greater

86   .036
48   .36

▬ = green

Figure 8.13.

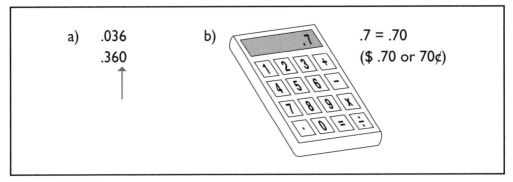

Figure 8.14.

than 36 thousandths: "We have 360 of the thousand it takes to make one whole, which is much more than having just 36 of the thousand needed."

NOTE: *Adding zeros frequently is helpful when interpreting calculator displays as money, as in Figure 8.14b. Shading, as in Figure 8.9, can be used to illustrate that two decimals, such as .7 and .70, are equivalent.*

Sample Sequence of Activities

▶ Comparing Fractions

1. **Show and write.** Students with learning disabilities generally have little difficulty at the concrete level in using physical models to compare fractions. When a storyline provides a context for using the models, as suggested in the introduction to this section, so much the better. Some students who need more structured assistance can be encouraged to use fraction pieces on workmats like those in Figure 8.15a. Loose pieces laid on the workmat can be compared visually or tactually to the unit as well as to each other.

It is better if the students themselves can discuss the fraction pieces and then fold and cut the pieces on premarked division lines. The strips and pieces can be used on the workmat during early work to illustrate certain specific fractions and to help students see, for example, that $\frac{4}{4}$, as well as $\frac{2}{2}$ and $\frac{3}{3}$, equals one whole unit. To compare fractions, students can again use the workmat as a base and, for example, lay a $\frac{1}{2}$ piece on top of two $\frac{1}{3}$ pieces to see that $\frac{2}{3}$ is more. Alternately, using preshaded bars, they might compare shaded parts of fraction strips, as in Figure 8.15a. Getting students themselves to write the fraction represented by each set of fraction pieces and to verbalize the result of the comparison is necessary to enable them to form important connections.

NOTE: *Problem storylines can be created to provide progressively more difficult comparisons. The following list suggests one such sequence, in which the last two examples are particularly difficult: $1\frac{1}{2}$ cakes and $1\frac{1}{3}$ cakes; $\frac{1}{3}$ of a cake and $\frac{5}{12}$ of a cake; $\frac{3}{4}$ of a cake and $\frac{9}{12}$ of a cake; $\frac{3}{4}$ of a cake and $\frac{8}{12}$ of a cake; $\frac{6}{8}$ of a cake and $\frac{9}{12}$ of a cake; $\frac{2}{3}$ of a cake and $\frac{3}{5}$ of a cake.*

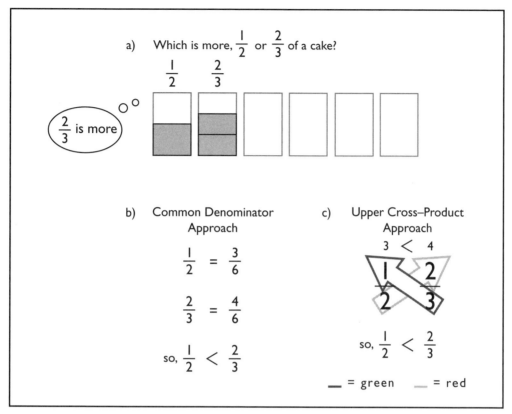

Figure 8.15.

2. **Special cases.** Students with perceptual deficits might experience some difficulty when asked to compare preshaded fraction bars or pictures of shaded regions on worksheets or textbook pages. (Ideas from the "Plastic Overlays" and "Dot It" activities on page 304 help these students.)

NOTE: *The real difficulty arises when students are asked to compare fractions using either the Common Denominator or the Upper Cross-Products Method illustrated in Figures 8.15b and 8.15c, respectively. (See Activity 3 below.) Of these two approaches, the more popular one for early work involves changing each fraction to an equivalent fraction with a common denominator.*

3. **Cross products.** Teachers interested in developing the Upper Cross-Products Method in Figure 8.16 with students can use fraction strips as shown to validate results. The upper cross products are really the numerators of fractions equivalent to the original. The common denominator is the product of the denominators in the original fraction (6 in Figure 8.16c).

4. **Color cue.** Students can cross multiply and chart several examples of each type of comparison shown to develop or verify the general pattern: the fractions compare the same way their upper cross products compare. The color-cueing illustrated in Figure 8.16 is helpful to many students: green first, then red when finding upper cross products.

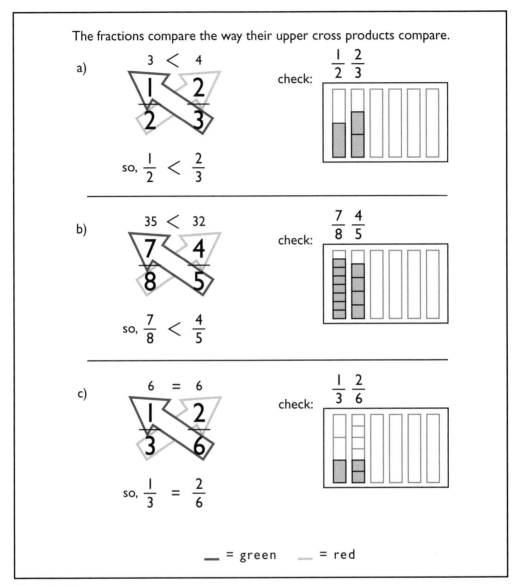

The fractions compare the way their upper cross products compare.

Figure 8.16.

SIMPLIFYING FRACTIONS

Problem Area: Difficulty writing fractions in simple form.

Typical Disabilities Affecting Progress: Difficulty with visual memory, sequencing, abstract reasoning, expressive language.

Background: When children compute, we generally ask that they express all answers in the simplest form. The ability to simplify fractions, however, involves more than understanding what to do. Actually, the easiest part is dividing the numerator and the denominator by the same number. The difficulty arises because children either:

- do not know which divisor to use for numerator and denominator in order to simplify a fraction; or

- fail to recognize the need to simplify further.

Initially, to help students concentrate on each step of the sequence, do not require the final step of simplifying an answer when teaching them to add or subtract fractions. That way, students are not forced to learn to do the following two new things simultaneously:

- add or subtract in the new context of fractions; and
- simplify in the new context of computation.

In early work with equivalent fractions, it also is important to examine equivalences like those of $\frac{4}{6} = \frac{2}{3}$ and $\frac{6}{8} = \frac{3}{4}$. This will provide the children with a background for *dividing* numerator and denominator by the same number. All too often this emphasis is slighted, since most examples are those in which one *multiplies* to find an equivalent fraction.

Deal directly with the problems children encounter when reducing fractions to simple form. The following ideas have proven helpful with students who have learning disabilities. The focus is on:

- recognizing the correct divisor for numerator and denominator, and
- knowing when to reduce.

✎ Sample Sequence of Activities

1. **Number strip.** Prepare a strip listing the numbers 2 through 9, as in Figure 8.17. Tape the strip along the chalkboard or have students glue strips to individual index cards they can keep for personal reference. As the children begin reducing, they can use the strip to assist thinking as they answer the following questions:

- *What's the greatest number or "factor" that will divide both numerator and denominator?* If the given fraction is $\frac{6}{8}$, then the greatest factor is 2 (see Figure 8.18a). For $\frac{12}{18}$ (see Figure 8.18b), one could divide by 2 and then by 3; but the greatest factor, 6, makes it necessary to divide by just one number rather than two.

- This done, look once more. *Can I divide both numerator and denominator by any other number?* Because fraction computation is more limited in focus, size

2, 3, 4, 5, 6, 7, 8, 9

Figure 8.17.

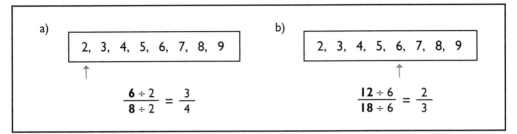

Figure 8.18.

of number used, and quantity of problems listed in exercises, the typical answer to this question will be no. Using this process, occasionally, as in Figure 8.19, fractions may require two divisions.

DEVELOPING COMPUTATION SENSE FOR FRACTIONS AND DECIMALS

Problem Areas: Difficulty recognizing and using number relationships for decimals and fractions, making mental estimations or calculations, meaningfully interpreting written equations and algorithms, selecting and using appropriate computation procedures.

Typical Disabilities Affecting Progress: Difficulty with abstract reasoning, sequential memory, visual perception, expressive language.

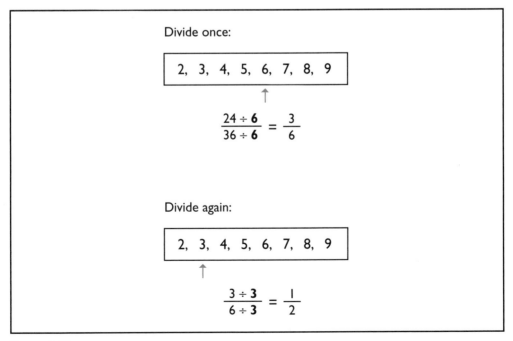

Figure 8.19.

Background: Computation sense for fractions and decimals is demonstrated by students' abilities (a) to interpret written number sentences as well as mental and written computational procedures in meaningful ways; (b) to choose appropriate calculation methods for given situations; and (c) to be able to judge whether computational results are reasonable. These abilities imply strong conceptual understandings for the numbers and operations involved and the ability to reason critically.

Besides the demands on decoding and processing skills, being "good" in any one of these areas requires time and frequent opportunities to carry out related activities. To nurture better *thinking,* less computation of exact answers is sometimes preferable. At other times, written work can be reused in different ways, as suggested in several of the activities in this section.

Just as important, however, is a positive, supportive environment and good role modeling that emphasizes common-sense estimation with fractions and decimals. Hearing teachers and other students "think aloud" as they compute to solve problems, to summarize or defend the procedure(s) used, often provides a new perspective for individual students.

If common-sense thinking about fractions and decimals is an important goal, suggestions like the following may be in order. Emphasis on appropriate use of physical models and invented, personally meaningful algorithms, as well as on mental techniques and calculator experiences should occur *before* formal paper-and-pencil procedures for computation (if any) are introduced or reviewed within a school year.

Interpreting Written Equations and Computational Procedures

Computation needs to be taught and learned meaningfully. Many students, sadly, have no intuition about what $\frac{3}{4} \div \frac{1}{2}$ or $4.2 \times .51$ means. For the first example, they may be unable to tell whether the result is more or less than 1 (more, for there are more than just one $\frac{1}{2}$-sized piece in $\frac{3}{4}$). For the second example, they may be unable to recognize that the result is very close to $\frac{1}{2}$ of 4 (because .51 is very close to .5 or $\frac{1}{2}$ of 4.2) and conclude that the answer is very close to 2.

Good beginnings toward nurturing this kind of thinking require careful attention to underlying concepts and number relationships. A problem-centered, conceptual approach to computation is suggested, which precludes many of the difficulties children otherwise typically experience in learning to compute and also reduces the amount of instructional time that must be devoted to it.

Consistent with this suggestion, one successful approach for developing good intuitions about written number sentences and computational algorithms includes:

- basing computation instruction for fractions and decimals on problem situations that have meaning for students;

- allowing students to select personally meaningful ways to solve these problems—including their choice of any manipulative or teaching aid that may be personally helpful in working out a solution;

- allowing, even encouraging, students to record their solution steps in *personally meaningful* ways—including writing any intermediate notes that may be needed to assist in decoding or processing information;

- expecting and encouraging different solution approaches; and

- expecting students to justify their thinking and explain their recording methods (if any).

As part of this approach, students are eventually expected to use their own language to interpret or describe number sentences and computational procedures. They also should be expected to collaborate with others or independently write their own "story problems" that provide realistic contexts for the numbers being used. For example, one child wrote the following story for $1\frac{1}{2} + 2\frac{1}{2} = $ _____ .

> Mom made cookies. She put $1\frac{1}{2}$ cups of flour into the bowl, then added another $2\frac{1}{2}$ cups. How much flour did she use for the cookies?

The child then used paper strips for the cups of flour (halves and whole strips), and illustrated how it was decided that *4* cups were used. Being able to freely translate from:

- the problem in numbers (the equation or computational exercise),
- the problem in words, and
- the problem illustrated with some physical model

is a powerful indicator of good number sense and can be nurtured through varied and rich problem-solving experiences. As students report on their solution strategies, different models and mental strategies typically emerge. The overall result of this approach, nurtured by a risk-free classroom environment and supported by frequent "think aloud" exchanges between the teacher and the student(s), is greater flexibility in thinking about rational numbers and more accurate intuitions for interpreting written aspects of computation.

Choosing the Calculation Method

As mentioned previously, technology has drastically changed the methods by which we compute. We have inexpensive, readily available calculators that perform routine computations with fractions or decimals. This fact broadens our concept of *meaningful approaches to computation,* which includes being able to easily compute problems we would previously have regarded as complicated. Students should be encouraged to choose and use the method that is most appropriate in a given situation. This should be especially true when working with rational numbers. Sometimes it is far preferable, for example, to estimate when computing with rational numbers and then use the calculator or paper and pencil to compare the estimate with the exact answer. The following list describes two relevant situations:

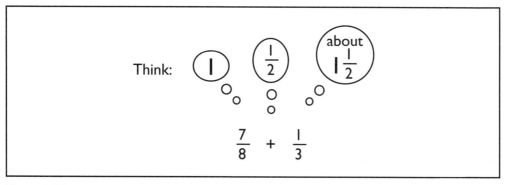

Figure 8.20.

• *Use mental calculation first.* For example: 30.15 + 26.14 is about the same as 30 + 26, or about 56. Similarly, $25\frac{5}{8} + 15\frac{1}{3}$ is about the same as 26 + 15 or close to 41. Then try paper and pencil or a calculator to confirm.

• *Let's estimate.* Figure 8.20 suggests how, when working with fractions, students might think about individual addends to estimate sums. It is also useful for students to think about whether estimates they have made are over or under the actual answer. In Figure 8.20, for example, each addend is less than the number used in the estimate, so the estimate given is an overestimate. In Figure 8.21, the estimate calculated is an underestimate. Students need to realize that in many practical situations, such as buying material needed to make a dress or deciding how much money to have with you, it is better to be over than under.

Allow for alternate responses to encourage those students who are timid or insecure. For example, in Figure 8.21, some students might round $19 up to $21 and decide that a reasonable answer is "about $7 off." In early stages, it makes more sense to accept a broader range of estimates and to help students explain their thinking than to concentrate on close estimates. Help them understand what kinds of estimates are best in what types of situations.

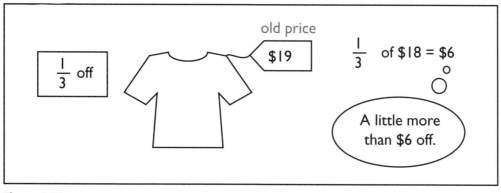

Figure 8.21.

When considering the computation $3\frac{5}{8} \div 1\frac{1}{4} =$ _____ for the problem "How many costumes requiring $1\frac{1}{4}$ yard of fabric can be cut from $3\frac{5}{8}$ yards of material?" some students think of the problem as $3 \div 1$ and estimate 3. Others may mentally compute: "$1\frac{1}{4} + 1\frac{1}{4}$—that's $2\frac{1}{2}$. So another $1\frac{1}{4}$ makes $3\frac{3}{4}$. There is enough material for 3 costumes." For similar problems, responses like the following can be accepted:

- more than 1 for $3\frac{1}{4} \div 2\frac{1}{2}$
- about 2 for $5\frac{1}{4} \div 2\frac{1}{8}$

WRITTEN COMPUTATION FOR FRACTIONS AND DECIMALS

Problem Area: Difficulty carrying out written computations with fractions or decimal numbers.

Typical Disabilities Affecting Progress: Difficulty with closure, visual figure-ground, spatial organization, sequential or long-term memory, visual perception, visual memory.

Background: An earlier section of this chapter, "Developing Computation Sense for Fractions and Decimals," highlighted students' needs to:

- initially learn and consistently apply computation in problem-solving settings;
- be allowed to use solution approaches that make sense to them, record their solution steps, and explain their thinking in personally meaningful ways; and
- develop appropriate mental calculation, estimation, and calculator techniques before or at least at the same time as formal work with written computation is addressed.

As the result of a rich, problem-centered introduction to computation like that suggested above, some students may develop personally meaningful computational approaches that preclude the need to teach more standard algorithms. Other students will require direct intervention because approaches attempted have been inaccurate or grossly inefficient. Many students will require special intervention to overcome difficulties arising from a specific disability.

As we observe, listen to, and monitor what students do and say, decisions about intervention emerge. Clearly, because of calculators, there is no need to focus on learning tedious or complex written computations, or on requiring students to spend an inordinate amount of time learning a written algorithm when an estimate is just as appropriate. Further, if the level of a student's disability is profound and the student is able to use a calculator effectively, it is better to spend precious instructional time exploiting the full use of the calculator, with an emphasis on developing the student's abilities to think mathematically in problem-solving situations. Following the suggestions of Chapter 7, this may include translating fractions to decimals before computing, or using a calculator that accommodates numbers in fractional form. This approach should free instructional time for pursuing other rich areas of mathematics like data analysis and probability or computer explorations in geometry and algebra.

The reader is referred to the preceding section, "Developing Computation Sense for Fractions and Decimals," for suggestions for treating difficulties with mental techniques or calculator use. The following ideas provide a reference for accommodating special areas of difficulty related to written computation. Although not specifically addressed, an area that often interferes with successfully using fraction and decimal skills is the increased vocabulary and the need to apply new meanings to old words. Teachers need to be aware of this situation and consider previewing vocabulary whenever needed.

Fraction Computation

Adding or Subtracting Fractions

Given the current deemphasis on fraction computation and the rare need to add or subtract fractions in daily living, many teachers seek to balance the amount of time students spend on involved paper-and-pencil computations in relation to other more important areas of mathematics. As suggested in the previous section, sometimes an estimate is sufficient.

Given that some paper-and-pencil calculation with familiar fractions is needed if (a) that type of calculation is still part of the curriculum, or (b) a calculator is not available, it typically is helpful to emphasize two "big ideas" that apply to fractions as well as to whole-number and decimal computation:

For addition:

1. Add like units.
2. If there are enough of a kind to trade up (regroup), do so.

For subtraction:

1. Subtract like units.
2. If there are not enough to take what is needed, trade down.

The first big idea—adding or subtracting like units—is directly related to finding a like denominator when a computation involves fractions with different denominators. Good number sense for fractions includes the recognition that, when the sum or difference of two unlike fractions is needed, as for $\frac{1}{3} + \frac{1}{4}$, a common label for both fractions must first be found. (See Figure 8.22a.) If fractions equivalent to each of those in the original problem are found, as in Figure 8.22b, completing the computation makes sense.

Beyond recognizing *why* and *when* like (common) denominators are needed, perhaps the most difficult aspect of hand-calculating the sum or difference of unlike fractions involves finding like denominators.

Locating equivalent fractions when the new denominator is already given and determining the common denominator for two given fractions are two completely different skills. The former requires far less abstract thinking because

We bought 2 large pizzas— $\frac{1}{3}$ of the first, and $\frac{1}{4}$ of the second were left. Altogether, how much pizza was left?

a) 1 third $\xrightarrow{\text{but}}$ b) $\frac{1}{3} = \frac{4}{12}$ c) 4 twelfths
   + 1 fourth $+ \frac{1}{4} = \frac{3}{12}$ + 3 twelfths
                                                                              7 twelfths

Figure 8.22.

much of the final answer is already in sight. The latter skill, on the other hand, requires a great deal of visual association, overlearning, working memory, and quick retrieval. Students must master this latter skill in order to be successful with addition and subtraction of unlike fractions.

Finding the Lowest Common Denominator. In line with the desire to balance the amount of time spent on fraction computation in relation to other more important mathematical topics, many teachers have adopted the following approach to finding a common denominator:

1. Check: *Is one denominator a multiple of the other? If so, that number is the lowest common multiple.*
Let students use multiple strips (see Figures 8.23 and 8.24) to help determine the answer to the question. In the $\frac{1}{2} + \frac{3}{4}$ example of Figure 8.23a, strips involving multiples of 2 and 4 are used. Four is on both strips, so 4 is the lowest common multiple of both numbers. It is called the lowest (least) common denominator and can be used as the new denominator for the two fractions.

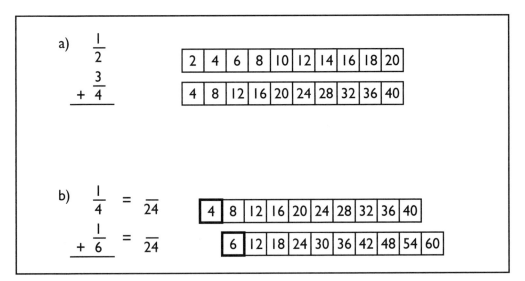

Figure 8.23.

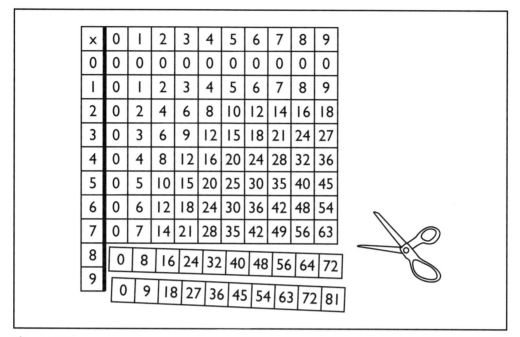

×	0	1	2	3	4	5	6	7	8	9
0	0	0	0	0	0	0	0	0	0	0
1	0	1	2	3	4	5	6	7	8	9
2	0	2	4	6	8	10	12	14	16	18
3	0	3	6	9	12	15	18	21	24	27
4	0	4	8	12	16	20	24	28	32	36
5	0	5	10	15	20	25	30	35	40	45
6	0	6	12	18	24	30	36	42	48	54
7	0	7	14	21	28	35	42	49	56	63
8	0	8	16	24	32	40	48	56	64	72
9	0	9	18	27	36	45	54	63	72	81

Figure 8.24.

2. *If one denominator is not a multiple of the other, multiply the two denominator numbers to find a common denominator.*

This step does not always provide the *lowest* common denominator. On the other hand, it very quickly provides a denominator that works and allows students to move on to more important mathematics topics.

Teachers who consider it desirable for students always to find the lowest common denominator when comparing, adding, or subtracting fractions can select from two alternate approaches:

1. Use individual multiple strips (Figure 8.23b) to locate the least common multiple as the new denominator. (This is the approach typically presented first in mathematics textbooks.) Help students slide one strip under the other (stationary) one until the least common multiple is found.

2. Find the prime factors of each denominator and multiply, being careful to use as factors only the minimum number of primes needed to make the product a multiple of each denominator number.

Both of these methods can be cumbersome and difficult. In our experience, the first approach has proven to be easier, given that the goal is always to find the *lowest* common denominator. Listing the multiples also reinforces the basic multiplication facts for children who still need practice. If necessary, provide individual cross-out sheets for unknown facts, as suggested in Chapter 7.

When dealing with more frequently used denominators, it is desirable that students automatically recognize the lowest common multiple. Though some children may find it difficult at first, it generally comes with practice for more common pairings. In the interim, ideas follow for helping students become familiar with the "listing multiples" procedure for determining the lowest common denominator of two fractions.

✏️ Sample Sequence of Activities

Teachers interested in students always using the lowest common denominator may use the following activities:

1. **Multiple strips.** Use heavy tagboard to make a personal set of multiple strips for each student (see Figure 8.23a). If the children are familiar with multiplication charts, have them cut apart the rows, as in Figure 8.24, and glue them onto tagboard. If possible, laminate the strips or cover them with contact paper. Check that students understand that the meaning of *multiples* is "answers you get when you multiply."

2. **Find it** (developmental activity for individuals or small groups). Make two decks of cards. The first deck should contain a card for each of the commonly used denominator numbers: 2, 3, 4, 5, 6, 8, and 10. Make the second deck a different color and include two cards for each number between 2 and 50. Arrange the cards *sequentially* to make it easier to locate specific cards.

Also make a pocket chart like that in Figure 8.25a, or use masking tape on the floor or desk to partition a space into three columns. The chart should be labeled as shown. The children take turns drawing two cards from the first deck. In the example in Figure 8.25a, the cards 6 and 8 were drawn. After the cards are placed in the chart, the children work together, using multiple strips if needed, to take multiples of 6 and 8 from the second deck. These cards are placed in the appropriate multiples column of the chart. The children then examine the chart to find any numbers that appear in both multiples columns. Those numbers are moved to the "Common Multiples" section of the chart (see Figure 8.25b). Finally, the lowest or smallest common multiple is moved to the "Lowest Common Multiple" section. Replace the cards in the decks and draw again to continue.

3. **Just the denominator.** Give the students a work page of about 10 addition or subtraction problems with unlike denominators. Allow them to use their multiple strips (to build visual memory) and find just the *lowest common denominator* of the two fractions. Given the problem of Figure 8.26a, for example, the students may find it helpful to circle common multiples on the laminated strips, match up the strips as in Figure 8.26b, and then write the smallest of the common multiples (24) as the new denominator for the problem (see Figure 8.26c).

Do not require the children to finish the problems at this time. The sheets can be collected, checked, and redistributed at a later date so that the problems can be completed.

NOTE: *If the multiple strips are not laminated, show the students how to place them under a clear plastic sheet so they can circle common multiples (see Figure 8.27a). Alternatively, for children with severe motor, figure-ground, or discrimination problems, glue the multiple strips to longer pieces of paper for use in a homemade tachistoscope. Children pull the strips through the tachistoscope*

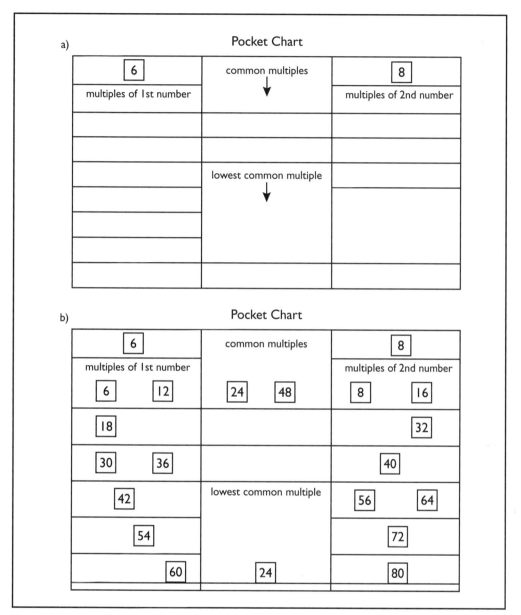

Figure 8.25.

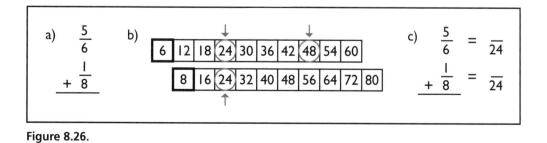

Figure 8.26.

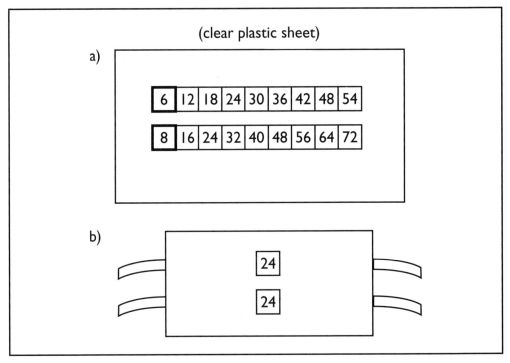

Figure 8.27.

and stop when one number appears on both strips—that will be the lowest common multiple (Figure 8.27b).

4. **Color cue.** Some students need to write out the multiples of each denominator to be able to identify the least common multiple. To help students organize their work space when listing the multiples, set up pages as shown in Figure 8.28. Highlighting the space where the common multiple will fall helps children with perseveration or figure-ground deficits know when to stop.

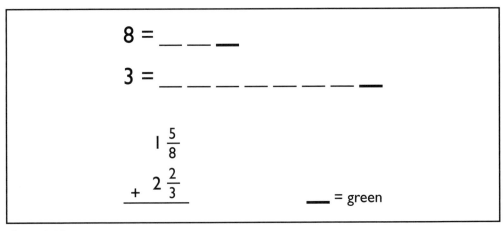

Figure 8.28.

5. **Say aloud.** Some students benefit from hearing themselves count the multiples in order to memorize them. Oral skip-counting practice is necessary.

6. **Transition.** As the students become more proficient at finding multiples, a simpler cueing system, as suggested by Figure 8.29, can be used. Instead of listing all the multiples, the child skip-counts until the circle is reached and then writes the number in that circle. This method has proven particularly effective with students who need help organizing their work for computation.

7. **Concentration** (a practice activity for two players). Students enjoy Concentration, a game that helps build retrieval and visual memory. The game requires two sets of cards. The cards of one set each show two numbers from the commonly used denominator numbers: 2, 3, 4, 5, 6, 8, and 10. The cards of the second set show the least common multiple for each pair in the first deck. Shuffle the decks and place them face down. Players take turns turning over one card from the first deck and trying to select its match from the other set of cards. Concentration game rules are followed. The winner is the one with the most pairs of cards at the end.

- *Variation:* As an independent activity, have the students time how long it takes them to pair cards from the two sets. Encourage them to keep a log of their times and gradually try to improve their records.

Regrouping in Subtraction. Students may realize *when* they must regroup and even *why* they need to do so. However, the same students may not know *how* to regroup. The error in the problem in Figure 8.30 is typical. The student confused the regrouping with the familiar whole-number procedure: 1 less ten, 10 more ones. Having completed the subtraction, the child reduced to lowest terms, unaware that anything was wrong.

Anticipating difficulties like this during early developmental work, many teachers dramatize the regrouping. Thus, trading activities often are used. In the example of Figure 8.31a, the children use materials to model $3\frac{1}{8}$. They trade 1 whole for 8 eighths and record the total number of eighths (9 eighths). Repeated experiences with fair-trade activities of this type for different fractions help most children see what is happening. This enables them to correctly apply the regrouping procedure to subtraction problems like that of Figure 8.31b. The

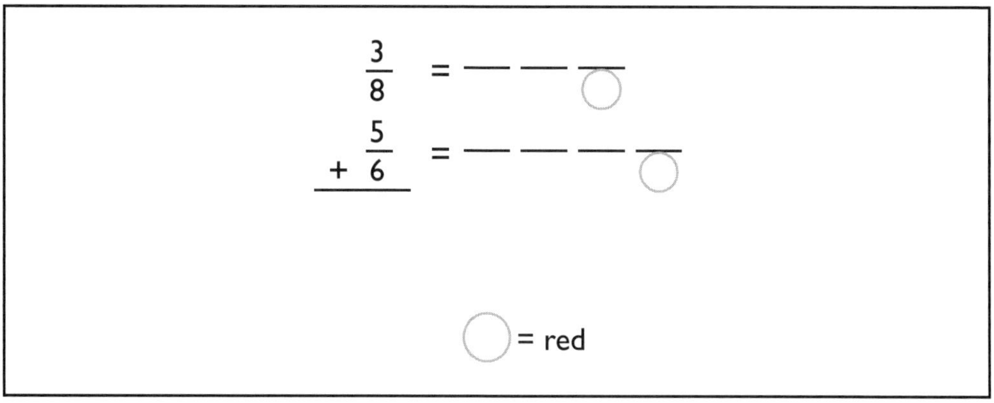

$$
\begin{array}{r}
\dfrac{3}{8} \\
+\ \dfrac{5}{6}
\end{array}
\quad
\begin{array}{l}
= \underline{\ }\ \underline{\ }\ \overline{\bigcirc} \\[4pt]
= \underline{\ }\ \underline{\ }\ \underline{\ }\ \overline{\bigcirc}
\end{array}
$$

$\bigcirc$ = red

Figure 8.29.

Mom had $3\frac{1}{8}$ yd of cloth and used $1\frac{5}{8}$ yard.
How much did she have then?

$$\begin{array}{r} \overset{2}{\cancel{3}}\overset{11}{\cancel{\frac{1}{8}}} \\ -\ 1\frac{5}{8} \\ \hline 1\frac{6}{8} = 1\frac{3}{4} \end{array}$$

Figure 8.30.

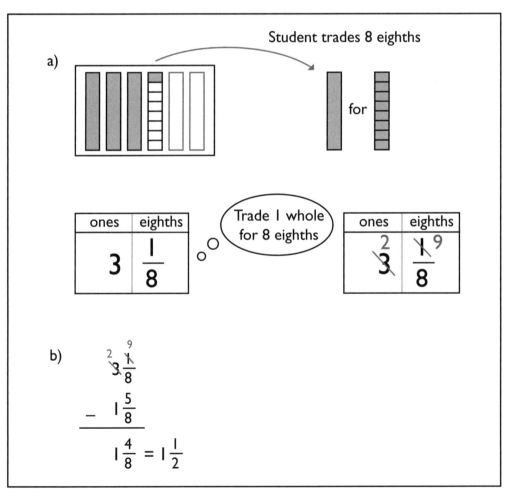

Figure 8.31.

similarity between the record-keeping format of Figure 8.31a and the regrouping shown in Figure 8.31b helps children transfer the regrouping skill to computation with fractions.

Some students do not make the transfer, however. Despite any care taken in early developmental work, specific learning disabilities cause them to fail at the symbolic level. For example, abstract-reasoning difficulties may inhibit the meaningful transition of the procedure to paper-and-pencil computation, or memory sequencing deficiencies may make it difficult to remember all the isolated steps of the regrouping process.

Given subtraction problems requiring regrouping, these children may refuse even to attempt the work, or they may revert to the more familiar procedure of always adding 10 when regrouping is necessary. For these students, more specialized cueing techniques, such as those illustrated in the following sequence, are necessary.

✎ Sample Sequence of Activities

1. **Regroup.** Before turning to regrouping within subtraction, focus on just renaming numbers that might appear in the minuend of subtraction problems. Figure 8.32a presents the format for a color-coded page that can be kept on file and used as needed. This type of page has proven helpful with children who have visual, sequential, or abstract-reasoning difficulties. Figure 8.32b presents a completed example of the problem. If the children recognize the need for regrouping, the colors remind them what to do by ordering the steps and increasing reasoning. Experience has shown that, because the students notice

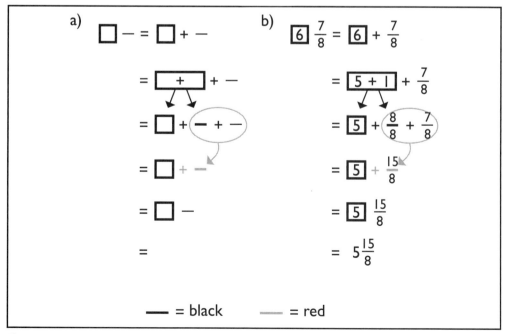

Figure 8.32.

the different colors, they tend to recall more readily the reason the steps are carried out.

2. **Talk about a shorter way.** After practicing the preceding isolated step, most students begin to notice the regrouping pattern. Some, however, will need extra help to eliminate the longer procedure. Make a chart of problems that have been solved previously through the longer procedure (Activity 1 above), but this time write only the original number and the regrouped one, as in Figure 8.33. If the students have figure-ground deficits and cannot readily sort out the numbers, use the colors as shown. The denominator of the second fraction is green to indicate a starting point. Most students quickly will notice that the denominators in both pairs are the same. The discussion can then focus on the pairs of black numbers and finally on the red ones.

The basis of discussion for the sample problem in Figure 8.33 is the idea that 1 whole, or 3 thirds, is taken from the 8 and added to the $\frac{1}{3}$, resulting in 7 wholes and 4 thirds. Similar discussions would take place for other number pairs. If helpful, materials could be used to show that the regrouping is correct. After analyzing the chart numbers in this manner, the students should be given other problems for which they independently carry out the regrouping.

3. **A middle step.** To help children retain the sequence while going to the standard format for regrouping, the intermediate step shown in Figure 8.34 is often useful.

4. **Now subtract.** Next, present subtraction problems like that in Figure 8.35. Once the children recognize the need to regroup, allow them to use a card, if necessary, to block out all but the minuend number until the regrouping is complete.

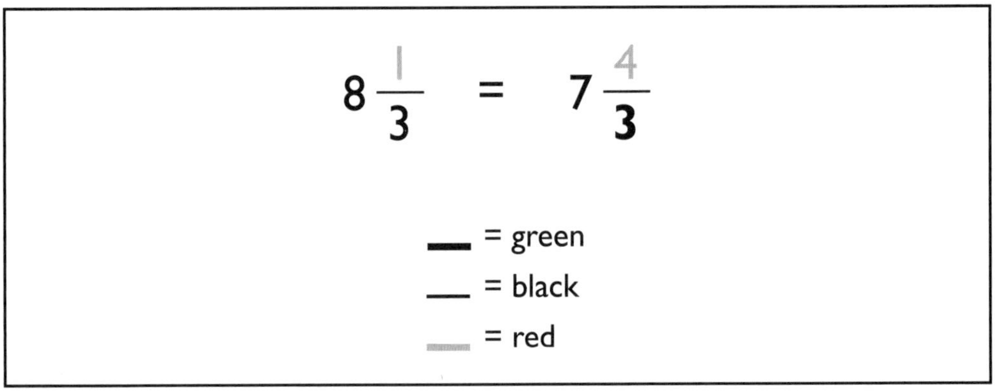

$$8\,\frac{1}{3} \;=\; 7\,\frac{4}{3}$$

▬ = green
▬ = black
▬ = red

Figure 8.33.

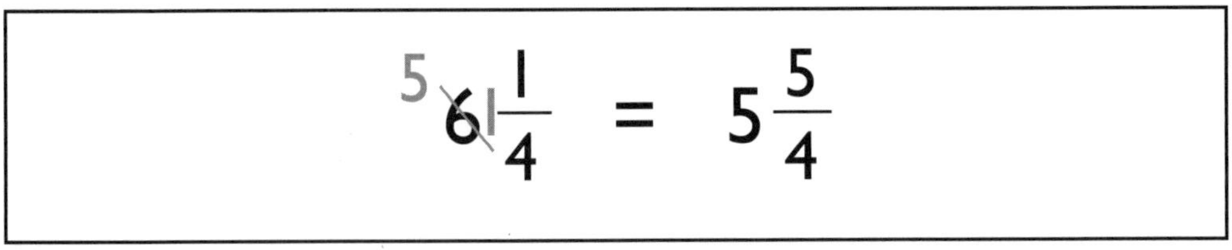

$$\overset{5}{6\!\!\!/}\,\frac{1}{4} \;=\; 5\,\frac{5}{4}$$

Figure 8.34.

$$6\frac{1}{4}$$

$$-\ 2\frac{3}{4}$$

Figure 8.35.

NOTE: *If the students have difficulty recognizing whether regrouping is needed, adapt suggestions from Chapter 7 on whole-number subtraction to work with fractions; then proceed with the ideas just outlined.*

Multiplying Fractions

In daily situations, we rarely need to carry out paper-and-pencil calculations involving multiplication of fractions. Yet sometimes the skill is useful for converting recipes, buying material, or deciding how much carpet is needed to cover a room. If necessary, however, one can convert fractions to decimals and use a hand calculator to derive the answers needed.

On the other hand, the skill must be taught to those who can learn it because multiplication of fractions (a) is still part of the modern mathematics curriculum and (b) is sometimes easier if no calculator is available or if a student has trouble retaining the conversions. Finally, it is a prerequisite for students who plan to take algebra in high school, since the procedures for handling rational algebraic expressions have their basis in the simpler computations with fractions.

Multiplication of fractions is relatively easy to teach. Some teachers, particularly those planning upper-grade review sessions, prefer to present multiplication as the first area of computation with fractions. Because there are no common denominators to be found, most students have greater success with multiplication than with addition or subtraction. Therefore, the goal is to build in many success experiences by dealing with multiplication early in the computational sequence.

The suggestions that follow have been used successfully with students who have learning disabilities. The format includes a basic sequence as well as alternative techniques that have been helpful in meeting special needs. Regardless of whether the multiplication topic is approached first or introduced after addition and subtraction, the ideas should prove useful.

Sample Sequence of Activities

1. **Shaded discs.** Using discs or construction paper circles, shade $\frac{1}{2}$ of 2, $\frac{1}{3}$ of 6, $\frac{2}{5}$ of 10, $\frac{2}{3}$ of 9, and so on. Help the students write equations to describe the shaded parts. Example: $\frac{1}{2}$ of 2 = 1; $\frac{1}{3}$ of 6 = 2.

2. **Picture it on paper.** Provide worksheets that contain geometric regions like that of Figure 8.36. Have the students use pencil or crayons to color $\frac{1}{2}$ of 2,

Figure 8.36.

$\frac{2}{3}$ of 6, $\frac{2}{3}$ of 9, and so on. As in Activity 1 above, have the students write equations to describe the shaded parts.

3. **Look for patterns.** Have the students note that answers could be found simply by multiplying numerators and multiplying denominators (or, alternately, multiplying numerators then dividing by the denominators). To reinforce the idea that *of* means *times* or *multiply,* rewrite each equation to use the multiplication symbol (×) instead of the word *of.* Examples: $\frac{3}{4}$ of 8 means $\frac{3}{4}$ × 8 means $\frac{24}{4} = 6$.

4. **Different strokes.** Some students may suggest the pattern of dividing first, then multiplying. Example: $\frac{2}{3}$ of 63. First, divide 63 into 3 equal groups (21 in each group). Then take 2 of the groups, or 42.

This approach may be the best one for students who have trouble sequencing. Figure 8.37 illustrates how color-coding can be used to support this thinking. Because the vocabulary is simple, reading generally causes no difficulty.

Figure 8.38a presents a variation of color-cueing for factors other than unit fractions. In this example, a child's attention is focused first on the number of equal groups into which 16 is divided (8), and then on the number of groups to be used (5). To help students picture this multiplication, give them a sheet like that of Figure 8.38b and a set of geometric-shaped chips. The children place chips on the sheet to illustrate the problem (see Figure 8.38c).

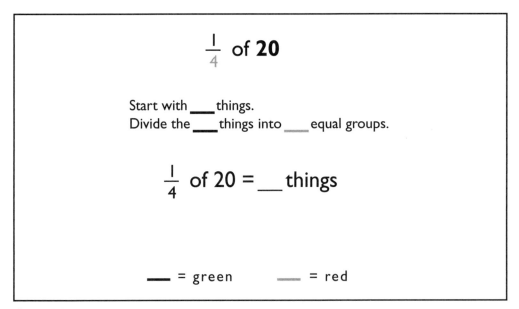

Figure 8.37.

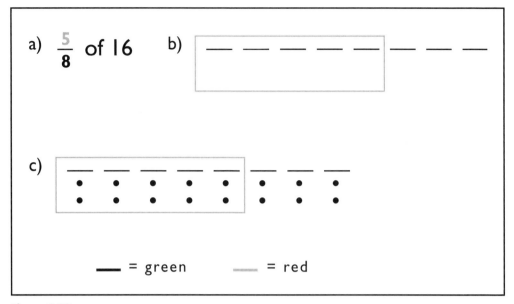

Figure 8.38.

For this example, the children take 16 chips and place them, one by one, on the sheets until all 16 are distributed. They then note that 10 of the 16 are inside the red frame. When they are ready to eliminate visual or manipulative aids like this, color-coding digits as in Figure 8.38a can serve to remind them of what was done previously with shapes and chips. As before, help the students see that there is a pattern in what the numbers do.

NOTE: *Placing chips in the shapes requires one-to-one matching. Some students may need specific help with or review of this skill.*

5. **Whole number x fraction.** Use construction paper fraction strips (all the same size). Subdivide some into halves, thirds, fourths, and so on. Have the students label the pieces and cut them apart on the subdivision lines. (Strips and pieces are illustrated in Figure 8.39.) Ask the students to place the pieces into the workmat (see Figure 8.39): 2 of the $\frac{1}{2}$ pieces, 6 of the $\frac{1}{3}$ pieces, 10 of the $\frac{2}{5}$ pieces, and so on. They should write equations to describe the finished picture each time. Example: $2 \times \frac{1}{2} = 1$; $6 \times \frac{1}{3} = \frac{6}{3}$, or 2; $10 \times \frac{2}{5} = \frac{20}{5}$, or 4.

6. **Both factors a fraction.** Repeat Activities 1 to 3 above, asking students to show $\frac{1}{2}$ of $\frac{1}{8}$, $\frac{1}{4}$ of $\frac{1}{3}$, $\frac{1}{3}$ of $\frac{1}{2}$, and so on. Have them verbalize the pattern for multiplying fractions: multiply numerators, multiply denominators. Ask students to check each equation to see if it follows the pattern.

7. **Alternative approach.** Some students have difficulty changing a mixed number to an improper fraction in order to carry out the computation. Given a problem like $4 \times 2\frac{3}{5}$, they may multiply the whole number 4 by both the numerator and the denominator of $\frac{3}{5}$. To eliminate confusion while allowing this alternate procedure, it is helpful at times to teach students to multiply a whole number by a mixed number using the distributive property. (Figure 8.40 presents an example of that approach.)

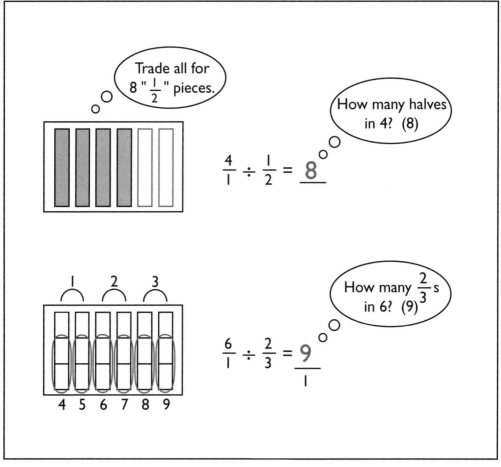

Figure 8.39.

$$4 \times 2\frac{3}{5} = 4 \times \left(2 + \frac{3}{5}\right)$$

$$= (4 \times 2) + \left(4 \times \frac{3}{5}\right)$$

$$= 8 + \frac{12}{5}$$

$$= 8 + 2\frac{2}{5}$$

$$= 10\frac{2}{5}$$

Figure 8.40.

Dividing Fractions

Many students, not just those with learning disabilities, lack good intuitions for division of fractions. For that reason they are often unaware that their answers are unreasonable when they make common mistakes like inverting the dividend rather than the divisor when computing. The activities of the following sequence have proved helpful in addressing these problems.

✎ Sample Sequence of Activities

1. **Use fraction strips and pieces.** Present problems like those of Figure 8.41 (whole numbers divided by a unit fraction). Students fold and cut unit strips (or trade fraction pieces for unit strips) to find the number of divisor-size pieces that can be had. Show students that the same result can be found by multiplying by the reciprocal of the divisor: "invert and multiply." (Confine numbers to those that can be checked using strips and pieces.)

NOTE: *The National Council of Teachers of Mathematics does not recommend a heavy emphasis on division of fractions beyond what can be modeled. Should district policy or student interest proceed beyond this point, the following suggestions may be helpful.*

2. **Color highlight.** To divide fractions, invert the divisor and multiply. When students understand this notion, color-underscore the divisor in each of several problems to emphasize which fraction should be inverted.
3. **Box it.** As a follow-up, provide a sheet with several fraction division problems. Instruct the students to box or finger-trace the divisor (the number to be inverted) for each problem on the sheet.
4. **Do just one step.** Have the students perform just the one step of writing the first equation toward solving each problem on the sheet (see Figure 8.41).

$$\text{given} \longrightarrow \frac{6}{1} \div \frac{2}{3} = \underline{\quad}$$

$$\text{child writes} \longrightarrow \frac{6}{1} \times \frac{3}{2} = \underline{\quad}$$

Figure 8.41.

Decimal Computation

Procedures for whole-number computation are so "like" those for decimal computation that they typically provide the foundation for success in decimal calculations. Despite experiences like those outlined in Chapter 7, some students with abstract-reasoning, memory, or receptive language difficulties may still find it difficult to relate to decimals because, in written form, they do not have a visual stimulus for "reading" the entire number. For 0.3, for example, there is a visual stimulus to say "three" but not to say "tenths." In fraction form, however, the written $\frac{3}{10}$ triggers saying both "three" *and* "tenths." Students who experience this difficulty may find it easier to learn fraction computation first, then use fractions to help with decimal computation. Pivotal examples incorporating fractions are included in the discussion and illustrations of this section.

Adding or Subtracting Decimals

It is common for students to make mistakes like those illustrated in Figure 8.42a. In Joey's work, digits rather than decimal points were aligned. Ann mistakenly added the 4 to the 5 as the first step of her computation. In the last step, she also skipped columns and added the whole number 8 to 2 before completing the addition.

In Figure 8.42b the child started by bringing down the 3, then continued the subtraction. In Figure 8.42c, the decimal part, then the whole-number part was added. Both subsums were recorded independently. Although mistakes like these are sometimes careless ones, they can stem from specific disabilities, particularly those identified at the beginning of this chapter. Children forget what to do, find it difficult to relate meaningfully to numbers (and then make all kinds of errors), or have problems sorting out all the numbers within the computation. Ideas for how to deal with problems such as these, in relation to decimal addition and subtraction, are outlined on the following pages.

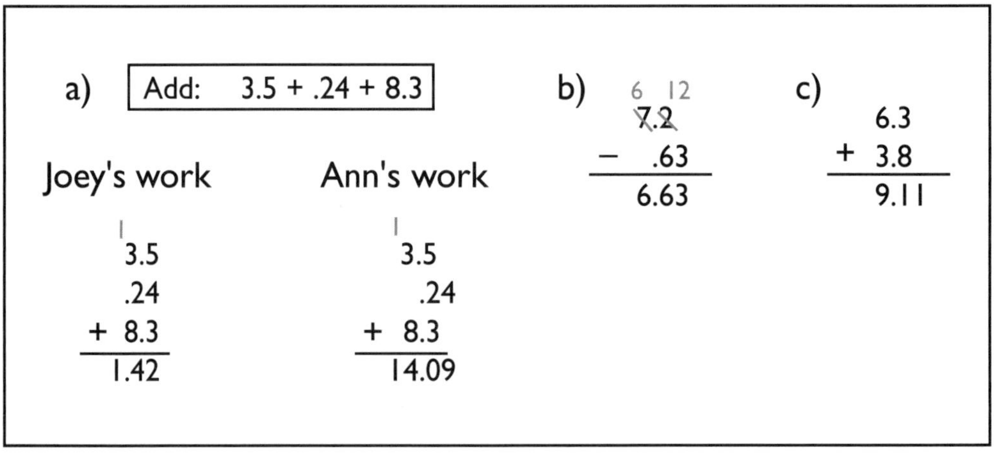

Figure 8.42.

✎ Sample Sequence of Activities

1. **Use base-10 blocks** (or graph paper pieces) to help children understand when decimals need to be aligned. Have students use blocks to picture written problems, then physically move the materials to carry out the indicated operation. At each step, the student or teacher should record what is being done in the problem itself. This step is often essential for students with learning disabilities who do not readily transfer concepts based on concrete aids to the written task. Doing this now will make it easier, at a later stage, for students to check their work with or without blocks.

2. **Use auditory cueing.** Encourage the students themselves to verbalize what they are doing. If necessary, review the first "big idea" of addition (or subtraction) of decimals: add (or subtract) like units (see Figure 8.43). Help the students recognize that doing that helps align decimal points.

NOTE: *If the students have abstract-reasoning difficulties, use the idea of auditory cueing first until they feel comfortable with a procedure they can follow. Then help them recognize that the procedure makes sense by using the idea in Activity 1 above.*

3. **Line them up.** If the students have visual perception difficulties, encourage them to do the following:

• Add extra zeros to right-justify problems like that of Figure 8.42a (Ann's) and Figure 8.42b. Use shading as in Figure 8.9 to illustrate, for example, that 3.5 = 3.50 (i.e., adding the zero does not change the value of the decimal).

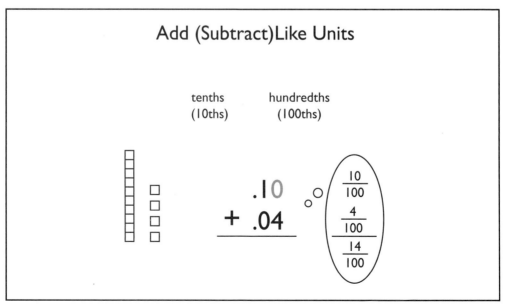

Figure 8.43.

• Use a highlighter, pen, or pencil to mark vertically all digits in a column before adding or subtracting.

• Use square centimeter paper and write one digit per space. Show the students how to place decimal points on a line.

• Turn lined paper 90 degrees and use the lines as a vertical guide to column alignment.

• Make the decimal point a bright color, as in Figure 8.44. This helps the students notice it when they recopy the problems to compute. For special cases, color-highlight the decimal point for the students and, during early work, also align the points in vertical form as shown in Figure 8.44b. Children with spatial or figure-ground deficits may require such additional assistance until they have learned to deal with the decimal point.

NOTE 1: *If children are strong tactual learners, it helps if they are allowed to finger-trace all numbers in a column (all like units) before adding or subtracting.*

NOTE 2: *Since learning to use spreadsheets is so much more a part of the mathematics curriculum, be sure to clarify for students that, although "we line up the decimals to add and subtract when we use paper and pencil, the spreadsheet does that internally. We don't always see them lined up on the screen."*

Multiplying Decimals

Students who have mastered written whole-number multiplication have a good start toward learning to multiply with decimals. The focus now is on learning to place the decimal point in the product. For many students with learning disabilities, this can be difficult. One of the most common errors made by students, including those with specific disabilities, is illustrated in Figure 8.45. Although the problem may stem from confusion over the familiar procedure for addition and subtraction, other reasons, including those linked to the preceding disabilities, also may contribute to mistakes in this area. Assuming that skills for multiplying whole numbers are strong, the following suggestions have proven effective for helping students avoid decimal multiplication errors.

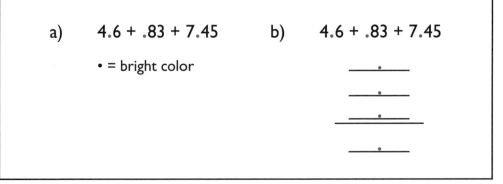

a)   4.6 + .83 + 7.45   b)   4.6 + .83 + 7.45

• = bright color

Figure 8.44.

$$
\begin{array}{r}
1.2 \\
\times .4 \\
\hline
4.8
\end{array}
$$

Figure 8.45.

✏ Sample Sequence of Activities

Prerequisite skills: The most critical prerequisite for decimal multiplication is the student's ability to handle whole-number multiplication. Another prerequisite—one that is often overlooked—is the ability to locate and count the digits of a given number. Students may have trouble interpreting and following instructions because of difficulty related to understanding and applying the meaning of *number* and *digit*. Keep pages like that in Figure 8.46 on hand and fill in the first blank before giving them to students. The color cueing and verbal patterning help focus students properly so they can differentiate between the meaning of *number* and *digit*.

Later, when the students recognize the distinction, they can independently copy given numbers into the circles before rewriting the digits. In exercises

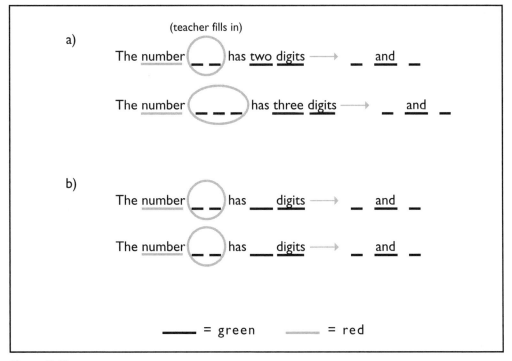

Figure 8.46.

patterned after Figure 8.46b, numbers are given for which students indicate the number of digits involved before writing them in the spaces provided.

1. **Find and chart.** Students with sequencing or memory problems and/or abstract-reasoning deficits may benefit from the approaches that follow. Make a chart of all completed problems. (See Activity 2 below, "Study the chart.")

• *Use fractions.* If students can multiply fractions well and have no difficulty changing from decimal to fraction form (and vice versa), have them solve decimal multiplications as illustrated in Figure 8.47. Choose problems that can be readily calculated mentally (though the student is required to change to fractions, compute, and rewrite as directed).

NOTE: *Encourage students to think ahead about the answer. ("Where will the decimal point go?") Some children may be helped if asked to write down their "think ahead" answer.*

• *Estimate.* (Prerequisite: Understanding the language involved—e.g., ".5 times [a number]" means the same thing as "$\frac{1}{2}$ of [a number].") Present problems like those of Figure 8.48a, where .5 (one-half) and .9 (almost 1) are used as factors. (Notice that the products are complete except for placing the decimal points.) Help students estimate placing the point correctly in the product. Suggestions for how to do that are illustrated in Figure 8.48b.

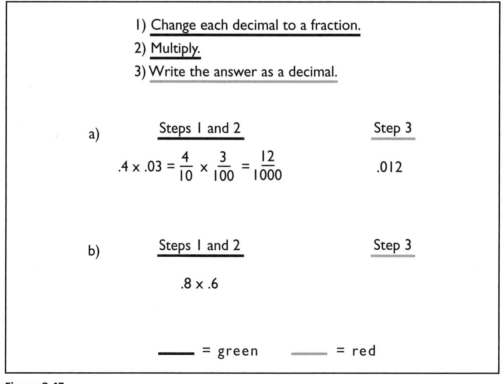

Figure 8.47.

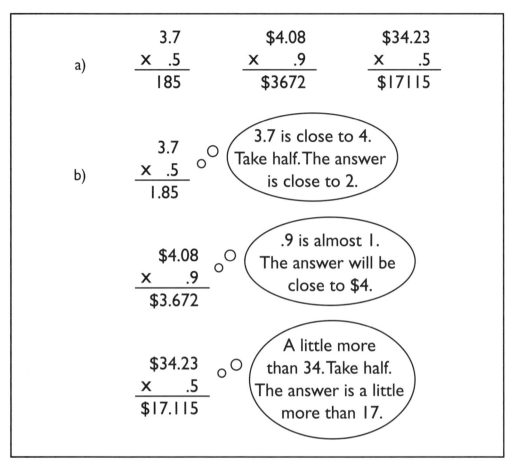

Figure 8.48.

• *Use a calculator.* A final alternative for students who can read a calculator accurately is to allow them to use a calculator to obtain decimal products for given problems.

2. **Study the chart.** (Prerequisite: Ability to readily associate numbers [number parts] with the words *problem, digit,* and *product.*) When decimal products are determined and charted using one of the approaches outlined in Activity 1 above, help students study the chart and note the recurring pattern (see Figure 8.49a). Color coding as in Figure 8.49b helps the students with self-discovery, a skill that frequently is difficult to develop. Leading questions also help: "Two decimal digits in the problem [circle the problem part]. How many are in the product?"

3. **Carry through.** Assign problems like that of Figure 8.50, using either a horizontal or a vertical format. The color scheme, the same as that used earlier, outlines the sequence to be followed. The green box and digits cue the first step: "Multiply given digits." Red indicates the last step: "Count digits and place the decimal point."

4. **The one step.** To reinforce the pattern for decimal point placement in products, gradually eliminate colors and present problems like those of

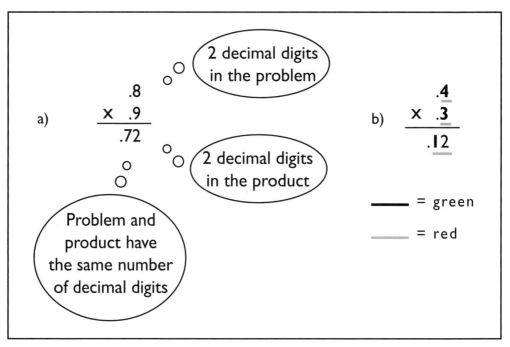

Figure 8.49.

Figure 8.51. The students complete just the one last step of each problem: that of placing the decimal point in the product.

5. **Different from +, −.** To reinforce the decimal multiplication procedure, present exercises like those of Figure 8.52. Pages like that shown can be prepared in advance and kept on file. The teacher (and later the students themselves) fills in addition, subtraction, and multiplication problems involving decimals down the left edge of the sheet. The children recopy in the appropriate column. The two-column arrangement highlights, procedurally, the basic distinction between addition or subtraction and multiplication. The column headings serve as backup in case the students forget or confuse the sequence for adding, subtracting, and multiplying. When the work is checked, get the students themselves to read or verbalize independently the procedures summarized in the column headings.

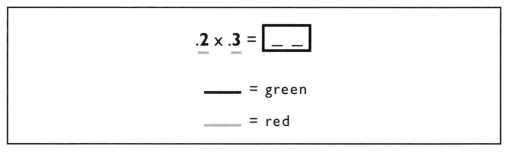

Figure 8.50.

$$
\begin{array}{r}
7.2 \\
\times \quad .6 \\
\hline
432
\end{array}
\qquad
\begin{array}{r}
9.6 \\
\times \quad 3 \\
\hline
288
\end{array}
\qquad
\begin{array}{r}
5.41 \\
\times \quad 4 \\
\hline
2164
\end{array}
$$

Figure 8.51.

Dividing Decimals

In our society the major use of division involving decimals is in practical situations involving money. In this day-to-day context, we typically deal with situations involving only whole-number divisors. Suggestions for helping students with specific learning needs to manually calculate in this context or in similar one-digit divisor situations involving decimals are outlined below. Other computation involving division of decimals is more appropriately carried out using a calculator.

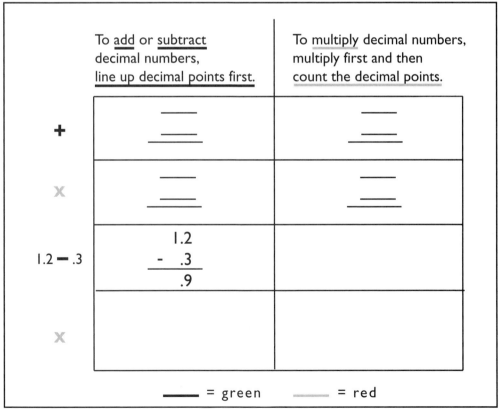

Figure 8.52.

✎ Sample Sequence of Activities

1. **Color highlight.** School textbooks typically begin decimal division with easy problems first: those with counting numbers as divisors. Since the need to divide money amounts is a common occurrence in daily life, problems like that illustrated in Figure 8.53 often are posed. Some textbooks may include problems like that of Figure 8.54. In either case, cueing can be used as illustrated in Figure 8.55 to help students focus on the decimal placement in the quotient of an "easy" problem: right above that of the dividend.

2. **Use fractions.** If students have difficulty interpreting decimals or have special strengths with fractions, they may find it easier to approach decimal division by (a) rewriting as a fraction and dividing; (b) writing the answer as a

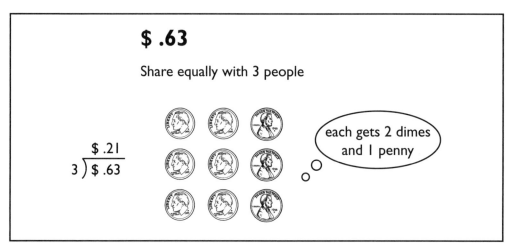

Figure 8.53.

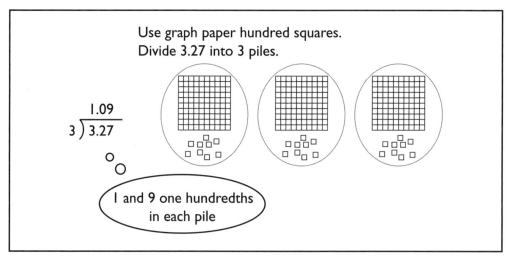

Figure 8.54.

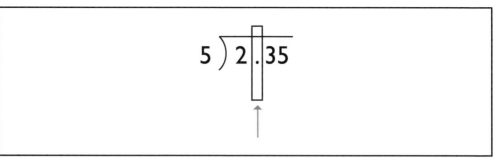

Figure 8.55.

mixed number; or (c) rewriting, finally, as a decimal. Figure 8.56 illustrates the format of a color-coded worksheet that can be used to help students with memory, sequencing, and perceptual or spatial organization deficits.

   3. **Use a calculator.** Allow students to use a calculator for decimal problems involving decimal or two-digit divisors.

USING TECHNOLOGY

Suggestions for using the calculator to both accommodate and compensate for specific disabilities have been provided throughout this chapter. Many recommendations from previous chapters specifically apply or can be readily adapted to students' work with fractions and decimals. Some of the more important of these suggestions include:

- the use of a printing model for students with motor or memory difficulties, so they can refer to the printed tape to check what has been keyed;

- the use of headphones and a calculator model with a voice synthesizer for students who need or benefit from auditory input; and

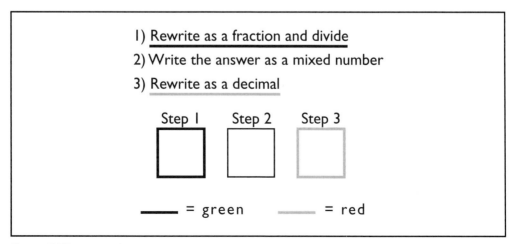

Figure 8.56.

- the use of a larger, desk-size calculator model for students with motor or visual perception deficits, so they can more easily see the keys and read the visual display.

Several calculator models are commercially available that allow fractions to be keyed, processed, and displayed. Because many of these models use a modified version of the standard fraction form, some students may find it too frustrating to use them. There are newer models now, however, that show the fraction in standard form. Aware of students' learning styles and strengths, teachers will need to work with students to determine how calculators are best used for fraction computation. Regarding their use for decimals, students who otherwise can use calculators typically have difficulty only in decimal calculations involving terminal zeros, as in Figure 8.14. Activity 6 of "Comparing Decimals," page 334, addresses this problem.

An increasing number of computer software programs are being made available for school mathematics. Examples of programs that include an emphasis on fraction or decimal computation include:

Program	Publisher/Distributor
Operation Neptune	KnowledgeAdventure
Math Keys: Fractions and Decimals	KnowledgeAdventure
Odyssey of Discovery: Fractions	Pierian Spring/National School Products
Fraction Operations	Sunburst
Mighty Math Calculating Crew	Edmark
Fractions and Decimals	Optimum Resource
Action Fraction Fun House*	Orange Cherry New Media/ National School Products
Decimal and Fraction Maze	Great Wave
Math Skillbuilders: Fractions	Gamco
Understanding Fractions Deluxe	Neufeld Learning Systems
Math Trek (Grades 7–9)	Nectar Foundation

---

*This program can be found at Educational Resources (see Appendix).

Chapter 9

♦ ♦ ♦ ♦ ♦ ♦ ♦ ♦ ♦ ♦ ♦ ♦ ♦ ♦ ♦ ♦ ♦ ♦

The Four Operations: Learning and Using the Basic Facts

Most teachers recognize that mastering basic math facts is important and useful—both in school and in life out of school. All paper-pencil calculations involve basic fact knowledge, as do estimation and mental math. Not knowing the basic addition, subtraction, multiplication, and division facts becomes a stumbling block to success in each of these areas, inviting frustration because computational work cannot be completed accurately. Lacking this knowledge makes it impossible and unnecessarily time consuming to judge whether calculated results "make sense."

Problems learning the basic facts are common among students with many different types of learning disabilities. There is little consensus, however, about what instructional practices help most to allow these students to achieve that degree of success with fact learning that lies within their specific abilities.

The traditional approach to number fact learning—which emphasizes rote drill, "fast facts," and timed tests—has serious disadvantages. We can assess fact proficiency through daily interaction with students. Daily, even weekly or monthly timed tests are unnecessary and, in fact, are counterproductive. Requiring speed and on-the-spot, fast recall is quite problematic for many students who require extra time to process not only incoming information but to recall and apply a strategy for dealing with that information or conveying their response.

For assessment purposes, an inventory assessment—in an oral, written, or other appropriate format—might be carried out on basic facts *about the third week of school each year after there has been some time for reviewing number fact learning from the previous year.* This assessment need not be timed, for in timed situations students will be less likely to explore or use those strategies necessary to make progress. Rather, teachers might sort facts into two piles as students answer: "confident about these" and "not confident." Such an initial assessment encourages reflection, establishes a baseline for measuring progress, and provides information for planning instruction. After the initial assesment, informal assessments may suffice when there is adequate one-on-one or small group time with a student each day. If direct interaction time is more limited, then some repetition of the initial assessment could be made—perhaps using a computer program that tracks answers. A balanced approach to assessment—work samples, some observations, some interviews, and some short, more formal evaluations—gives the teacher, the student, and the parent a more complete portrait of a child's fact knowledge and the progress being made. Along with assessment, routine practice—even to the point of overlearning—is still an important part of learning number facts. The suggestion is to provide short, daily opportunities for students to think about, use, and apply number facts without *undue* emphasis on immediate recall or speed.

These issues of number fact practice and assessment are particularly relevant for students who have memory, closure, discrimination, or expressive language difficulties. Some of these students also have specific language difficulties, which are addressed in the first section below: "Interpreting Language: Printed, Oral, and Symbolic." The general approach taken in the rest of this chapter, consistent with the remarks made in the opening paragraphs of Chapter 6, is that a "strategies" approach for number fact learning should be used since it allows students with learning disabilities to draw on their informal knowledge—especially their knowledge of counting and of part-whole relationships—and capitalize on their specific learning strengths.

This strategies approach can take into account any difficulties a student may have with language and can utilize the *tracking* technique that is detailed in the second section of this chapter. The remaining sections of the chapter outline how the strategies approach is applied, in turn, to help students master addition, subtraction, multiplication, and division facts. A final technology section highlights the role of calculator use for students with unusually severe learning impediments and presents samples of computer programs that may reinforce number fact learning. In order, the chapter sections appear as follows:

1. Interpreting Language: Printed, Oral, and Symbolic
2. Strategy learning for basic facts
3. Strategies for learning addition facts
4. Strategies for learning subtraction facts
5. Strategies for learning multiplication facts
6. Strategies for learning division facts
7. Using technology

Sometimes students get bogged down in higher-level computation because they do not know the basic facts or because they do not recognize *known* facts within multidigit problems. Specific ideas for handling these difficulties were outlined in the first sections of Chapter 6. As background for planning a basic number fact program for students with learning disabilities, it may be useful to review those suggestions as you consider the suggestions that follow.

Relating basic fact work in school to common daily settings is essential. Many students with learning disabilities need a structured program that emphasizes practical applications of the mathematics they are learning. Otherwise, they do not make the transfer and hence fall short when it comes to using math where it counts—in day-to-day living. With respect to basic facts, for example, children might be asked to circle one problem on a practice sheet and then be asked to describe a situation outside the classroom that might involve that number fact. For 2 + 5, for example, a child might suggest: "2 red flowers and 5 yellow flowers are outside our front door—7 in all." Be flexible: Some students, particularly those with expressive language problems, may be able to describe a situation better by drawing a picture. The goal has still been achieved.

INTERPRETING LANGUAGE: PRINTED, ORAL, AND SYMBOLIC

Problem Area: Failure to associate the correct process with the operation sign or with the written or oral direction to add, subtract, multiply, or divide.

Typical Disabilities Affecting Progress: Difficulty with closure, expressive or receptive language, visual discrimination.

Background: This section deals with two related difficulties. The first involves the printed symbol for each operation. For example, despite solid conceptual understandings, some students with learning disabilities either misperceive or misinterpret the written operation signs. A second difficulty involves not knowing what to do when presented with written or oral directions to add, subtract, multiply, or divide. Without the signs as a guide, some children are at a loss as to how to proceed. Some mathematics textbooks present skill pages of the type shown in Figure 9.1. Or teachers may simply dictate pairs of two-digit numbers with the directive to "add." Within a structured program, those types of experiences are useful for building skills when there are not language deficits. Initially, however, children with receptive language difficulties may not be able to succeed independently with exercises of that type. A chart, such as that of Figure 1.18, can be especially helpful to these students.

The following activities and exercises include other techniques for dealing with each of the difficulties summarized in the preceding paragraph. The suggestions assume that students possess a well-established conceptual understanding of each operation. If that is not the case, before proceeding, return to working with physical materials as outlined in "Building Concepts for the Four Operations" in Chapter 6.

Add

48	76	48	795
53	29	73	36

Multiply

37	42	62	82
29	27	45	24

Figure 9.1.

✎ Sample Sequence of Activities

▶ Interpreting the Operation Sign

1. **Circle.** Visual discrimination deficits may make it difficult to associate ideas properly. Use textbooks in which the operation signs have been circled, or ask the child to circle each sign on the page before solving the problem. In this way, attention is drawn more directly to the operation sign.

2. **What is the sign?** Use texture cues or color-coding, or allow the students to finger-trace before solving. Finger-tracing a sign before solving is particularly useful on pages with mixed problem types (e.g., pages of addition and subtraction problems). Sometimes a verbal reminder or visual cue to "Stop! Look at the sign" (Figure 9.2) is helpful. In severe cases, require a student to circle all addition problems and work those before turning to the subtraction examples.

▶ Interpreting the Sign or Word for Each Operation

1. **Chart it.** Figure 9.3 shows one type of supplemental page that can be prepared at the beginning of the school year and kept on file or saved as a template on a disk for future use. Each symbol on the page should be the same color as the word that denotes the operation. If the chart shown in Figure 1.18 is present in the room, the colors on the exercise pages should match those of the chart. The teacher writes problems in the left column. The child recopies and solves them in the appropriate box as shown. For some, this might be a 2-day assignment. On the first day, students would merely copy each problem into the appropriate space. After the teacher has checked the paper, the students would solve the problems.

If a child has difficulty interpreting the operation sign, focus on internalizing its meaning. Finger-tracing, matching games, and flash cards are all ways to help students overlearn so they can apply meaning to the sign.

If a child has difficulty interpreting the written words (*add, subtract, multiply, divide*), focus on building vocabulary by association with numeric examples that use the operation sign. Similar sheets can be used to help children build associations for *sum, difference, product,* and *quotient.*

NOTE: *For many students, an operation sign is readily associated with the correct word and process when the numbers used are basic facts. However, when*

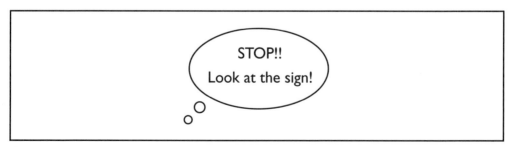

Figure 9.2.

	Add	Subtract	Multiply	Divide
48 × 6			48 × 6	
54 - 19		54 - 19		
36 + 8				

Figure 9.3.

multidigit numbers are used in computation, these same children may experience difficulty with the association. For this reason, it is important that two- or higher-digit numbers be used in the problems in the left-hand column of Figure 9.3.

2. **Page assignment sheets.** Many children perseverate and need continued help to associate the correct process with given words or symbols. Assign textbook pages or problems on a given page in random order as described in Chapter 1. Figure 9.4a shows an example of a page that can be kept on file and used as an assignment sheet for such children. The child first writes the symbol

a) Operation Problem #   b) Operation Problem #

Add ☐   Add ☐

Multiply ☐   Multiply ☐

Subtract ☐   Subtract ⊟   2, 5, 6

Figure 9.4.

beside the word and then writes the appropriate problem number(s) in the right-hand column of the sheet (Figure 9.4b). If necessary, the operation word can be underlined to match the color used for the word on the wall chart.

▶ Interpreting Vocabulary for Each Operation

1. **Circle to match.** At the beginning of the school year, go through the text and find pages such as those illustrated in Figure 9.1. Circle direction words in the appropriate color to match the wall chart. Instruct the student to place the correct sign beside the word before solving the problems.

2. **Look to the chart.** When the words *sum, product, quotient,* and *difference* are introduced, use a chart such as the one shown in Figure 9.5. Color the chart to match the coding scheme of Figure 1.18. A small copy of the chart can be pasted to the top of a child's worksheet and/or included in the vocabulary book described in Chapter 2. If the student needs more specific practice, use pages like that of Figure 9.6. The children can "X" (cross out) inappropriate problems, then work the correct ones. The color scheme adopted for the charts of Figures 1.18 and 9.5 should be carried through on pages of this type. In the example of Figure 9.6, if *sum* and + are green, then − could be black, × red, and ⌐ blue.

3. **Listen.** If students with receptive language deficits have difficulty following oral directions involving vocabulary for the four operations, initially allow them to use the Figure 9.5 card to complete worksheets like those of Figure 9.7. Prepare a tape with worksheet directions like: "In section 1, find the *sum* of each. Fill in the correct sign for each problem before you start." (Child turns off tape to work.)

Repeat, but ask for the *product* in section 2 and the *difference* in section 3. In the final section, ask students to divide first, then write the matching number sentence.

NOTE: *As overlearning occurs, students can be asked to respond to the directions first and then look at the card.*

STRATEGY LEARNING FOR BASIC FACTS

Problem Area: Difficulty memorizing the basic facts.

Typical Disabilities Affecting Progress: Difficulties with visual, auditory, or long-term memory; visual or auditory discrimination, expressive language, working memory.

Sum ⟶	+ answer
Difference ⟶	− answer
Product ⟶	× answer
Quotient ⟶	÷ answer

Figure 9.5.

Find the **sum** of 29 and 19.

$$
\begin{array}{cccc}
29 & 29 & 29 & \\
\underline{+\ 19} & \underline{-\ 19} & \underline{\times\ 19} & 19\ \vdots\ 29
\end{array}
$$

────── = green

────── = red

────── = black

.... =blue

Figure 9.6.

Background: Children who have been involved in a rich, ongoing problem-solving program as suggested in "Building Concepts for the Four Operations" (Chapter 6) will learn many number facts just from frequent exposure to them. It is important to realize, however, that basic facts are learned at a recall level over a much longer period of time than previously has been assumed, and that even for regular-class students, school mathematics textbooks rarely include enough or the appropriate type of work to promote real mastery.

This problem is aggravated for learning disabled children. Memory, discrimination, or expressive language deficits may interfere to make learning and retaining the facts very difficult. Many teachers find that children can be successful when they specifically intervene to teach recall strategies such as those suggested in the remaining sections of this chapter. For students with learning

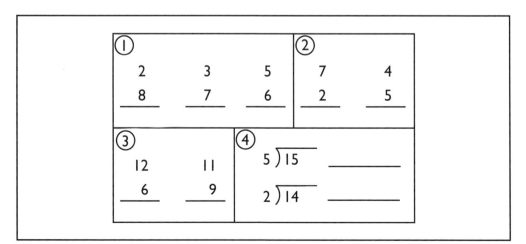

Figure 9.7.

disabilities, it will be necessary to carefully select numbers used in word problems to correspond to the small set of number facts currently being studied. A further critical part of this process is promoting the desired mastery by tracking as described and illustrated in the following sequence.

Tracking basically involves presenting only a few carefully chosen facts at a time. Much as a hunter would track a deer in the woods, children track or look for a small set of facts that are mixed in with others. Figure 9.8 shows a sample page with selected doubles at the top of the page. The technique (a) forces children to focus on given facts; (b) builds visual memory; (c) assists with expressive language difficulties; and (d) provides structure to aid working memory. Students follows the directions below the line. Short, frequent practice of this type helps them learn the facts faster and retain them longer.

Tracking is not a cure-all. Rather, it is a general approach that has proven especially useful in early fact work where the goal is to help children memorize the facts. Tracking can be applied to fact learning for all four operations as part of or as an alternative to a *strategy approach* for teaching basic facts, in which the following five phases serve as a guide:

1. *Teach retrieval strategies* such as "Start with the greater number and count on" or "Think of the picture to help with the double" or "See × 5?—Think of the clock to help." These and other strategies are presented below and in the remaining sections of this chapter.

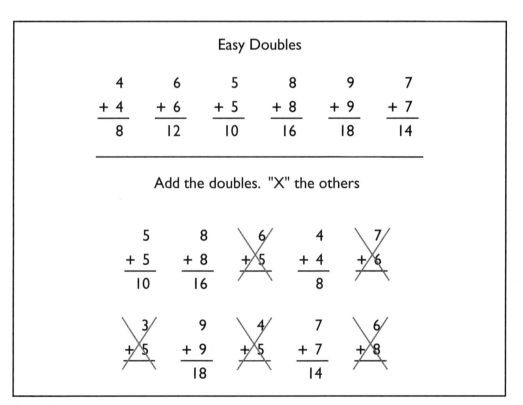

Figure 9.8.

2. *Help children use the strategy*—with emphasis on accuracy, not speed of response.

3. *Help children choose when the strategy "fits."* This is an aspect of tracking.

4. *Provide practice to speed up response* so facts are answered quickly as well as accurately. Carry through to the point of overlearning, so *consistency* and *retention over time* are promoted.

5. *Check up* (see Activities 10 and 11 in the following "Sample Sequence of Activities").

Elements of this framework, highlighting the tracking technique, are emphasized in the following sequence. Since fact mastery implies giving accurate answers quickly and being consistent in performance over time, follow-up exercises are necessary. Activities such as those described near the end of the following sequence are useful for this purpose.

Sample Sequence of Activities

1. **Preassessment.** Determine each child's level of fact mastery. Avoid timed written tests, as suggested at the beginning of this chapter. Individual assessment is best. Start by observing, over time, how individual children solve verbal problems—whether they (a) rely on use of objects, (b) finger-count, or (c) are able to count on or back for easier facts. Can they use easier facts to derive answers to other unknown facts? Some children, for example, may recognize that because $5 + 5 = 10$, then $5 + 6$ is "1 more" (11).

Sort facts into "confident about these" and "not confident about these," as described at the beginning of this chapter. Create a checklist of those facts in the "not confident" pile.

2. **Cluster.** Group facts into clusters for easier learning. Examples for addition include:

- facts with addends of 1, 2, or 3, commonly called "count ons" because children can find the answer by *counting on* from the larger number;

- 10 sums; and

- doubles.

3. **Model it.** Continue the practice of carefully selecting numbers for oral problems. Supplement this focus by using special manipulatives to dramatize finding answers for facts within a cluster, as in the examples that follow:

- *Example 1* (10 sums): Use chips (two colors) and a 10-frame made by stapling half-pint milk cartons together (see Figure 9.9). Have the children: (a) count the cartons in the frame (10); (b) place a chip (all one color) in each of 8 cartons. Then ask, "How many more chips are needed to fill the 10-frame?" (2); (c) place 2 chips (second color) in the

10 – frame

Figure 9.9.

10-frame to fill it up; (d) pick out the flash card that describes this situation and tape it to the board or chart (Figure 9.10a). Picture the 10-frame as a visual cue with the chart. Repeat, using different combinations for 10.

■ *Example 2* (addition doubles): Use the suggestions of Activity 5 below ("See and Write"). Picture the cues on a chart (Figure 9.10b).

4. **Circle it.** Provide tracking pages on which the children find and circle, from among distractors, facts in a given cluster. Children can refer to the board or wall chart, or even use the model(s) if necessary.

5. **See and write.** Plan short sessions during which flash cards for selected facts in a cluster are presented one at a time. As the cards are flashed, the child says the problem, gives the answer, and writes it on a line of a worksheet such as that of Figure 9.11a or 9.11b. At first, present only a small number of facts, those easiest or already known by the child. Then, gradually, one at a time, introduce harder facts in the cluster.

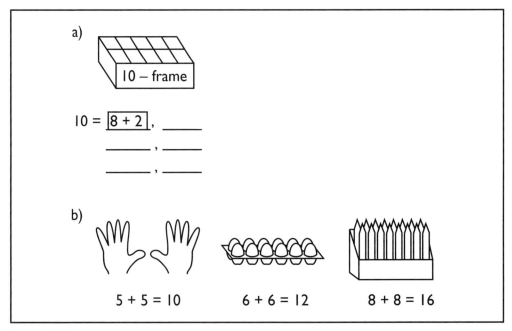

Figure 9.10.

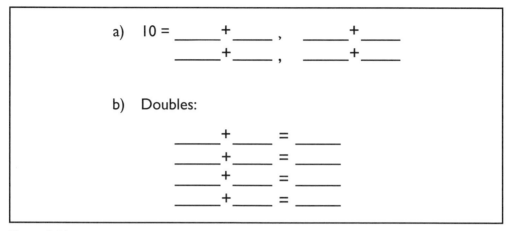

Figure 9.11.

6. **Match.** Provide worksheets such as those shown in Figure 9.12. As a form of visual training, the children study the top part of each page before completing the tracking exercise at the bottom.

7. **Find it.** Provide tracking pages like that illustrated in Figure 9.13. Have the children find and write answers *only to those facts in a given cluster.* Include about 20 problems from the cluster.

▪ *Variation:* Have the children give answers orally to facts in the given cluster.

8. **Hear and write.** For each cluster, have the children read facts—problem and answer—into a tape recorder. Later they can listen to the playback for extra reinforcement.

9. **Trace and write.** Use the answer side of flash cards. Have children finger-trace facts within a cluster, problem and answer, as they read it aloud.

a) 10 sums

8 + 2   6 + 4   3 + 7
_____
Add all 10 sums.
"X" all others.

3 + 6 = ___   3 + 7 = 10
8 + 2 = 10   2 + 7 = ___
5 + 6 = ___   6 + 4 = 10

b) × 9

4 x 9 = 36   7 x 9 = 63
6 x 9 = 54   8 x 9 = 72
_____
Multiply all 9s.
"X" all others

3 x 7 = ___   7 x 9 = 63
4 x 9 = 36   8 x 9 = 72
2 x 6 = ___   3 x 5 = ___

Figure 9.12.

What's 10?

6 + 4 = 10   3̶ ̶+̶ ̶3̶=̶ ___

8̶ ̶+̶ ̶9̶ ̶= ___   3 + 7 = 10

2 + 8 = 10   5̶ ̶+̶ ̶6̶ ̶= ___

8̶ ̶+̶ ̶6̶ ̶= ___   5 + 5 = 10

Figure 9.13.

Then have them close their eyes as they say the problem and answer quietly to themselves. Finally, ask the children to turn the flash card over, read the problem, and give the answer. If they forget, finger-tracing the problem may trigger the response. Some teachers have found it helpful to trace over flash card answers with glue. When dry, the raised surface adds an extra stimulus to the finger-tracing.

10. **Quiz.** Timed basic fact tests are very stressful for most children with learning disabilities and rarely provide information the teacher does not already have from daily observations of students. In an atmosphere where learning the facts is important, reasonable goals for mastery can be set and monitored through the use of checklists discussed later in this chapter.

11. **Review.** Systematically review facts from a cluster as other new facts are studied. Motivating games and activities are appropriate at this stage.

STRATEGIES FOR LEARNING ADDITION FACTS

Problem Area: Difficulty mastering the basic addition facts.

Typical Disabilities Affecting Progress: Difficulties with visual, auditory, or long-term memory; visual or auditory discrimination; expressive language.

Background: The activities of this section focus on strategies and models for learning the basic addition facts, which can be nurtured and monitored as children solve problems that are part of their daily program. Five major clusters of facts, encompassing all the 100 basic addition facts except zeros, are emphasized:

- count-ons
- 10-frame facts
- doubles
- doubles +/− 1
- make 10, add extra facts

Children who are good at memorizing may not need to rely on such approaches. Children with learning disabilities, however, who have memory or other difficulties such as those previously identified, may profit from more specific and structured ideas like those outlined in the following activities. The basic approach is to help students master easy facts first. More difficult facts are mastered by relating them to the easier, known facts. Models, color-coding, finger-tracing, and other visual, auditory, kinesthetic, or tactile techniques are used to help children learn the facts. What helps one child may not prove effective with another. The teacher's role becomes one of suggesting relationships, models, or strategies while remaining open to children's ideas and being sensitive to individual learning styles.

One word of caution: Keep instruction for children with learning disabilities *very simple.* If presented with too many "tricks" for remembering facts, some cannot sort out one from another. Others, however, can handle a variety of strategies during fact learning. Teachers may draw on the following suggestions, as needed, to plan a tracking sequence for individual or small groups of students. Ideas for adapting the basic sequence to meet remedial needs are included.

Basic Sequence

✎ Sample Sequence of Activities

▶ **Easy Facts First**

1. **Count-ons.** Ideas in the "Extending Early Counting Skills" section of Chapter 5 for developing counting skills are *critical* for helping students potentially learn 45 of the 100 addition facts—those having 1, 2, or 3 as an addend. Answers to those facts can be readily found by *counting on* from the greater addend rather than starting from 1 each time.

Those students who have engaged in frequent, short routines in which they counted on from midsequence (as in Figure 5.3) and have become comfortable with this method of counting will be more successful in early number fact work.

The transition from rote counting or counting dots to finding answers to the 45 addition count-ons may need to be presented step by step. The initial attempt should be to have students make the transition as in Figure 9.14a. Use numerous examples to help students make the association between counting on with dots and counting on with numbers—with the student gradually being more active in the process. Over time, fade out the initial prompt with dots and use a tracking exercise similar to that shown in Figure 9.8 in which students identify and answer count-ons that have been mixed with other facts.

If students require more specific assistance: have them take out 3 extra cubes to lay beside the problem as in Figure 9.14b, point to "6," then count on using the cubes as a visual or kinesthetic-tactile prompt. Starting with the greater addend and using 1, 2, or 3 cubes to determine answers for these smaller facts is an interim step, one students tend to drop more readily than placing dots beside the fact problem or touching points on the numeral. (The cubes require more effort to take out and place!) "Easy as 1,2,3": the goal for children who have difficulty memorizing is to think of counting on when they see 1, 2, or 3 in a problem and to *internalize* that count. That way students don't really have 45 different facts to learn—they have *one* big idea: Start with the

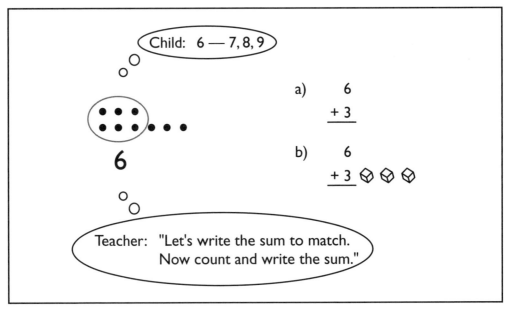

Figure 9.14.

greater number and count on. The answer is so readily produced by short counts that, in a sense, memorizing nearly half the addition facts is unnecessary.

NOTE 1: *The relationship of a fact to its commutative should be stressed from the beginning. Use simple models like a card with dots or clothespins (Figure 9.15) to help students recognize that, for any given addition fact, its "turnaround" (commutative) has the same answer: "When you know one, you know the other, too."*

NOTE 2: *Teachers may want to take time out at this point to help children note the "+ 0" pattern—"Add 0—what happens? There's no change." (The answer is what you started with.)*

    2. **10-frame facts.** Use chips and the 10-frame model of Figure 9.9 or simply draw a 10-frame on cardboard or paper (Figure 9.16) to model 10 sums

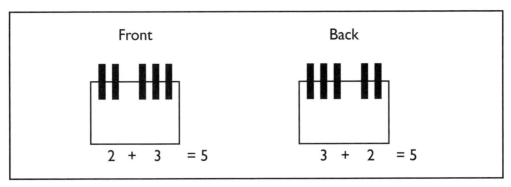

Figure 9.15.

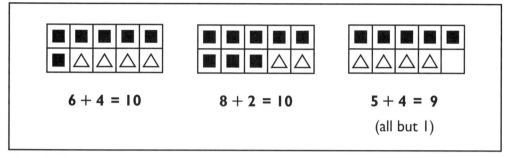

Figure 9.16.

and 5 + 4 (all but 1 in the 10-frame: 9). Have the students themselves write the number sentences to describe each situation dramatized. Practice until children can track for 10 sums as in Figure 9.8, then use the 10-frame to check.

3. **Doubles.** Use models such as those of Figure 9.17 to help children memorize addition doubles. Among other activities, involve the children in:

- writing, saying, or dictating number sentences to match cue cards;

- reading cue and associated number sentences into a tape recorder and listening to the playback (e.g., "6 + 6 is the 'dozen eggs' fact; 6 + 6 = 12";

- finger-tracing a cue card and then writing the double that it illustrates;

- tracking exercises, as in Figure 9.8;

- practice activities in which children match number sentences with associated cue cards. A variation on the card game Old Maid is good for this purpose (see Figure 9.18);

- crossing off facts as they are mastered. A chart such as that illustrated in Figure 9.19 might be useful.

▶ **Harder Teen Sums**

1. **One more than.** The "one more than" strategy is a powerful tool. Mastering a difficult fact is just "one step away." The strategy has a mushroom effect. As facts are mastered, they can be used to help learn others. Follow-up tracking is usually necessary.

- *Example 1:* Some facts are "close to" a double. This can be illustrated with models suggested by Figure 9.17—adding an extra egg, for example, to show that 6 + 6 = 12 (eggs), so 6 + 7 = 13 (eggs). Color-coding, as in Figure 9.20, may help students who are weak in making associations.

- *Example 2:* Some facts are "close to" some other known fact. Relationships referred to in the phrase "1 more than an easy fact you know" can be modeled with objects. Discrimination tasks and color-coding, as suggested by Figures 9.21 and 9.22, are also useful.

Double	Visual Cue	Auditory Cue
2 + 2		The car fact: 2 front tires, 2 back tires
3 + 3		The grasshopper fact: 3 legs on each side
4 + 4		The spider fact: 4 legs on each side
5 + 5		The fingers fact: 10 fingers
6 + 6		The egg carton fact: 6 in each half
7 + 7		The 2-week fact: 14 days
8 + 8		The crayon fact: 8 in each row
9 + 9		The double-9 domino fact: totals 18

Figure 9.17.

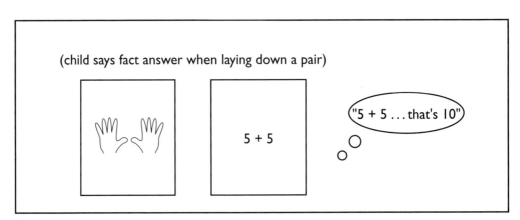

(child says fact answer when laying down a pair)

"5 + 5 ... that's 10"

Figure 9.18.

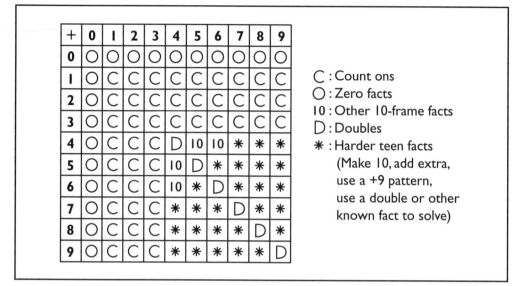

Figure 9.19.

NOTE 1: *Color-coding is sometimes useful to help students with auditory closure difficulties (which may prevent them from internally processing the emphasis placed on the stressed number) or generally to help students focus. Color-coding also helps those who do not automatically relate, for example, 5 and 6 in an addition problem.*

NOTE 2: *Many students, especially those with expressive language, working memory or executive functioning deficits, may have trouble thinking of an easy, known fact to help them with a fact they do not know. A visual cue can help. Plan activities like the following with flash cards:*

- Present a fact the student has not yet memorized (e.g., 4 + 7, as in Figure 9.21a).

- Ask students to select the easy "helping fact" from two flash cards.

- Have the children turn over the card that does not help and use the other card to give an answer ("3 + 7 = 10, so 4 + 7 = 11.") Follow-up worksheets, which direct the children to select the helper from two given facts may also be used (see Figure 9.21b).

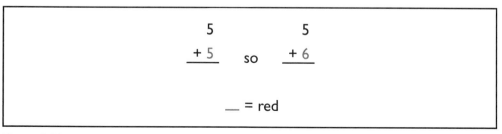

Figure 9.20.

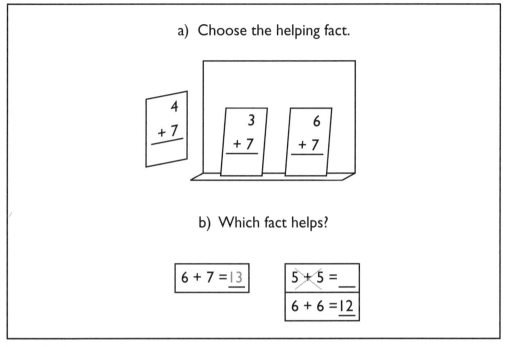

Figure 9.21.

NOTE 3: *Parallel ideas may help students who find a "one less than" strategy useful, as in the following example: 7 + 7 = 14, so the answer to 7 + 6 is 1 less (13).*

2. **Make 10, add extra.** Most of these facts have addends of 6, 7, 8, or 9. Prerequisite skill: Ability to add 10 to a one-digit number. Visual color-cueing, as in Figure 9.23, or auditory cueing through sound emphasis should be used if either seems helpful. The ones digit of the sum and of the digit added to 10 could also be texturized for finger-tracing.

- *Example:* Use the answer side of a flash card (10 + 4 = 14) with both 4s texturized. Trace each 4 with glue. When the glue dries, it leaves a raised imprint of the digits. Ask the child to "Read the number sentence." The child reads, "10 + 4 = 14." Then say, "Now close your eyes and trace over the 4s as I read the number sentence. . . . Now put your

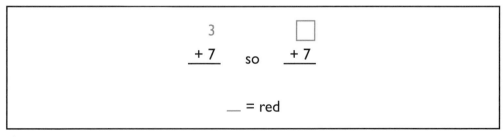

Figure 9.22.

$$
\begin{array}{r}
10 \\
+\ 3 \\
\hline
13
\end{array}
\qquad
\begin{array}{r}
10 \\
+\ 6 \\
\hline
16
\end{array}
\qquad
\begin{array}{r}
10 \\
+\ 4 \\
\hline
14
\end{array}
$$

__ = green

Figure 9.23.

hands in your lap. . . . Say the answer to this problem: 10 + 4 = 14."
Next ask the child, with eyes open, to read the front side of the flash
card problem and give the correct answer.

Basic "Make 10, add extra" strategy: As the fact is modeled, the goal is to
relate to the written fact and useful thinking:

- Using a 10-frame and chips, present a "harder teen" fact as in
  Figure 9.24a.

- Have the student "take a good look"—then cover the model.

- Referring to the written numbers, say, "Inside the frame are 8, and
  how many of these 5 outside the frame will make 10?" Ask the student
  to predict, then uncover the 10-frame and move chips to check, as in
  Figure 9.24b.

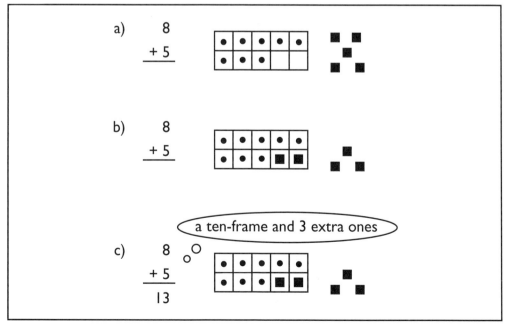

Figure 9.24.

With some students, it is useful to repeat this step until the student is comfortable with the idea:

- Have the student "take a good look"—then cover the model again.

- Referring to the written numbers, say, "You used 8 and 2 of these 5 to make 10. How many extra are still outside the frame?" Ask the student to predict, then uncover to check.

- Ask the student to tell, then write what he or she sees: "A 10-frame and 3 extra ones: 13."

NOTE: *Students who can verbalize the idea independently have internalized the process.*

3. **9s are special.** Patterns for 9s, like that highlighted in Figure 9.25, are very helpful to some individuals—"For +9, the answer ends with 1 *less* than what's added." This pattern can, of course, be illustrated using a 10-frame, as above: The answer digit is always 1 less *because* after moving a counter into the frame to "make 10," there is 1 less counter outside the frame.

NOTE: *It is important to share strategy ideas with students. It is equally important to allow students to use any strategy that is helpful to them, as long as it shows correct thinking.*

Remedial Sequence

Many older children know most of the easier addition facts, including many doubles. Their greatest difficulty is often with more difficult teen sums. The three most common strategies used by students suggest approaches that might be included in a remedial sequence:

- using a pattern for 9s;

- thinking "1 more or 1 less" than a known fact; and

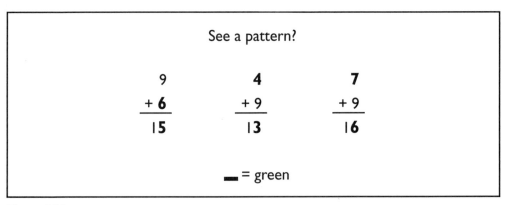

Figure 9.25.

- "using 10 as a bridge." This single strategy could in fact be used to help with *all* the more difficult teen facts.

See the ideas outlined in Activities 1–3 above.

STRATEGIES FOR LEARNING SUBTRACTION FACTS

Problem Area: Difficulty remembering subtraction facts, particularly those with teen minuends. Heavy reliance on counting.

Typical Disabilities Affecting Progress: Difficulty with visual, auditory, or long-term memory; visual or auditory discrimination; expressive language, working memory.

Background: Virtually without exception, subtraction facts are more difficult than addition for all children to master and *especially those with learning disabilities.* In early work, very few children with learning disabilities can think of and use related addition facts to help. Most children will count. Unfortunately, many students continue to count even when larger numbers and longer counts are involved.

Example: "13 – 6 = 7 because 7 + 6 = 13." A large number of students with learning disabilities do (among other things) the following:

- Count back: "13 – 6—that's 13—12, 11, 10, 9, 8, 7, 6." (The children finger-count as they say the numbers.) "That's 7."

- Count up: "13 – 6—that's 6—7, 8, 9, 10, 11, 12, 13."

- Finger-count everything: The children raise fingers to represent the minuend, lower (take away) fingers to represent the subtrahend, and then count and tell the number left. These students face real trouble when having to work with teen minuends.

By observing children during problem solving and other computational work, it is possible to determine whether they are relying unduly on counters or becoming frustrated because subtraction facts are not mastered. The challenge, then, is to lead these students through a more structured program to use the most efficient strategy they are capable of learning to answer unknown facts. And, just as children grow from year to year, it is hoped that the kind of retrieval strategies they employ also might grow. For example, students may at first *always* count back or count up, as illustrated above, to answer unknown facts. Hopefully, if awareness of the addition–subtraction relationship is mastered, these same students later may use known addition facts or some other more efficient strategy instead of always counting to derive answers to facts they do not know.

The instructional sequence below emphasizes counting only when *short counts* are involved. Visual cues are introduced to help students with subtraction doubles and 10-minuend facts. Throughout this work with easier facts, adding to check work is recommended. This approach nurtures an understanding of the addition–subtraction relationship and increases the possibility that children will use addition to help, especially when answering more difficult, teen-minuend facts.

Toward this end, we suggest that subtraction be delayed until students have mastered a modest group of addition facts. It also is better not to teach addition and related subtraction facts in back-to-back units of instruction. Students cannot use addition to check or to answer subtraction facts unless they first know related addition facts well. Delaying subtraction allows time for the necessary consolidation and the possibility that children will use addition as a retrieval strategy in subtraction number fact work. For students who continue to experience difficulty doing that, a method of using "10 as a bridge" is presented to help with more difficult, teen-minuend facts (see Activity 7 in the sequence that follows).

NOTE: *In extreme cases, such as those students with severe short-term or working-memory deficits, it may be necessary to move on to multiplication before going to subtraction. Although this may seem fairly radical, in some instances it provides the overlearning and visual feedback that students need. Since multiplication is repeated addition, there is additional time to reinforce (overlearn) the basic addition facts.*

Sample Sequence of Activities

Prerequisite skills:

- ability to recognize when two or three numbers have been said;
- ability to count on (from any number, 4 to 9);
- ability to count back (from any number, 4 to 12);
- mastery of related addition facts.

NOTE: *Refer to "Extending Early Counting Skills," in Chapter 5, for help with the first three prerequisites.*

Instructional overview:

- 27 count backs: $(10, 9, 8, 7, 6, 5, 4, 3, 2) -1$; $(11, 10, 9, 8, 7, 6, 5, 4, 3)$ -2; $(12, 11, 10, 9, 8, 7, 6, 5, 4) -3$.

- 19 zeros: $n - 0$ and $n - n$ (n = any number, 0 to 9).

- 6 new doubles: $(8 - 4, 10 - 5, 12 - 6, 14 - 7, 16 - 8, 18 - 9)$.

- 7 10-frame facts: $10- (9, 8, 7, 6, 4)$; also $9 - 5, 9 - 4$ (see Figure 9.26).

- 15 count-ups: $(12, 11) -9$; $(11, 9) -8$; $(9, 8) -7$; $(9, 8, 7) -6$; $(8, 7, 6) -5$; $(7, 6, 5) -4$.

- 26 harder facts: $(17, 16, 15, 14, 13) -9$; $(17, 15, 14, 13, 12) -8$; $(16, 15, 13, 12, 11) -7$; $(15, 14, 13, 11) -6$; $(14, 13, 12, 11) -5$; $(13, 12, 11) -4$.

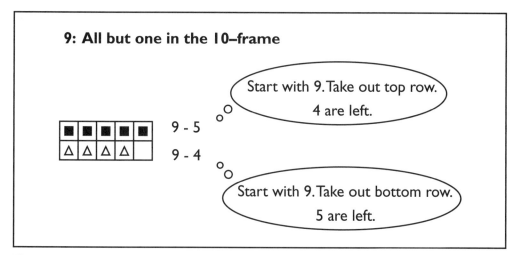

Figure 9.26.

▶ **Basic Sequence**

1. **Count back.** Let children use interlocking cubes. For each count-back fact you select, students form a train with the cubes and count back as they break off cubes to model the subtraction. For example, students start with a train of 12 cubes and count back as, one by one, they break off 3 cubes. Initially, using cubes helps avoid counting pitfalls of beginning the "count back" with the highest numbers, leaving a child one off in the backwards count. Follow with tracking exercises as in Figure 9.8. Language emphasis: "See –1? –2? –3?" (Say "Take away 1, take away 2, take away 3.") "Start big and count back."

2. **Add to check.** As soon as students can use a strategy accurately and efficiently to solve a group of unknown subtraction facts, provide "add to check" activities. These *should not* be introduced on the same day as a new strategy.

   - *Example 1:* **Take a cube.** For 7 – 2, children make a train of 7 cubes, break off 2, and write or tell (for the teacher to write) the subtraction sentence that models what was done (7 – 2 = 5). They then put the parts back together and *add to check:* "7 – 2 = 5 *because* 2 + 5 = 7." Repeat for other facts.

   - *Example 2:* **My favorites.** On a regular basis, invite students to circle two or three favorite problems on a worksheet and write the add-to-check fact beside each. Afterward, select one number fact pair on a page and ask the child to use counters to prove that what is written makes sense.

3. **Show with objects.** Introduce subtraction zero facts. Be sure students can use objects to illustrate number sentences involving zero.

4. **Use a picture to help.** Familiar pictures from addition can be used to help children with subtraction doubles (see Figure 9.17). For example: 10 fingers,

remove 5: *say* 5 are left. Or 12 eggs, remove 6: *say* 6 are left. Integrate tracking suggestions as in Figure 9.8, until children can *write* an answer, and then use the picture to check. Later, emphasize add-to-check activities, as in Activity 2 above.

NOTE: *As students master each new group of subtraction facts, cross them off a "not yet confident" list.*

5. **Use the 10-frame to help.** Provide counters and individual 10-frames. Starting with a full frame, students can take out some to model the subtraction (see Figure 9.27). Integrate tracking (as suggested by Figure 9.8) until students can write an answer and then use a 10-frame to check. Later, emphasize add-to-check activities, as in Activity 2 above.

6. **Model the counting up.** When children do not know a fact and do not recognize it as a *count back* (a –1, –2, or –3 fact), a double, or a 10-minuend fact, it often is easiest for them to count up. Start with counters, as suggested in Figure 9.28, use color-coding to help students recognize and start with the known part. When using count-up cards, as in Figure 9.28b, alternate with the child as follows:

TEACHER: (showing the card) "Say the part you know."

CHILD: "7."

TEACHER: (continues the count) "8, 9. How many numbers did I say?"

CHILD: "Two."

TEACHER: "Yes, so the answer is 2."

Repeat immediately for other count-ups. At a later time, teacher and child can switch roles—the teacher can say the known part; the child can count on and say the answer. Alternating roles helps avoid counting pitfalls that leave students one off in the count. Integrate tracking suggestions (see page 376) until children can *write* an answer and use the count-up cards or counters only to check. Later emphasize add-to-check activities as in Activity 2 above.

NOTE: *If add-to-check work has been carried out consistently in earlier work, some students may be able to use known addition instead of counting out answers.*

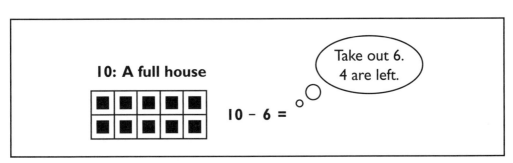

Figure 9.27.

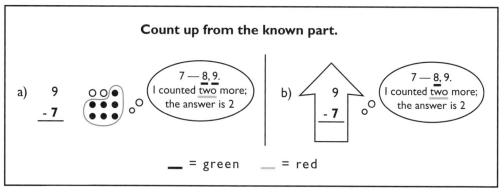

Figure 9.28.

7. **Go to 10 and on.** A basic, helpful strategy covering *all* the "hard" teen minuend facts is to "use 10 as a bridge."

Prerequisite skills: Firm mastery of teen minuend facts and recognition that teen numbers are 10 and ___ more.

• It is critical to ensure that students are consistently accurate when subtracting from 10 before proceeding.

• Help students recognize how fact pairs like those of Figure 9.29 differ. Color-coding, as illustrated, may also help. Students should note that 13 is 3 more than 10. Model, if necessary, using a 10-frame: place 3 counters outside a full frame. Comment that the answer to 13 – 6, then, is just 3 more than that of 10 – 6. Repeat for other number pairs. For the moment, do not focus on answers at all. Continue until children are aware of the pattern. Then tell them that you will show them how to find answers to difficult problems like this (point to 13 – 6) by first thinking of the easy 10 problem (point to 10 – 6).

Basic "Go to 10 and on" strategy: The goal is to relate the "counting up" strategy of Activity 6 above to larger numbers but to help children "see" how they can shorten the count because they can subtract from 10.

Bold digits are green.

1**0**	1**3**	1**0**	1**4**
− 6	− 6	− 8	− 8
1**0**	1**2**	1**0**	1**3**
− 3	− 3	− 4	− 4

Figure 9.29.

- Help students identify their *zero finger*—"You'll need a zero finger to help you think of the easy '10' fact." Have children examine the index fingers of their right hands. Help them to notice how the fingernail resembles a zero. Write a "0" on the nail or put a hole reinforcer on it: "This is your zero finger."

- Show students how to use their zero finger (refer to Figure 9.30):

  - Ask how to find the answer to a problem. If children use an efficient strategy, select a different fact.

  - If they count, tell them there's a shortcut for counting: Have them cover the ones digit of the minuend with their zero finger to form 10 – 6 (Figure 9.30a).

  - Then say, "Go to 10 (state the 10-minuend answer) and on (lift finger)—3 more" (see Figure 9.30b).

  - Illustrate with the stairstep drawing of Figure 9.30c. You start on 6 and go to 13. Instead of counting on by ones, you can go to 10 (that's **4** steps) and on **3** more to 13—that makes **7** steps.

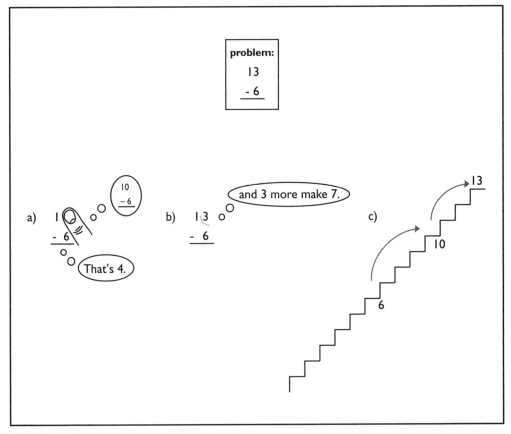

Figure 9.30.

STRATEGIES FOR LEARNING MULTIPLICATION FACTS

Problem Area: Difficulty memorizing the basic multiplication facts. Use of wild guessing or inefficient counting techniques.

Typical Disabilities Affecting Progress: Difficulty with visual or auditory long-term memory; visual or auditory discrimination; expressive language.

Background: Two things for teachers to consider when planning a more structured program for helping students with learning disabilities are the following:

1. the techniques children use to figure out unknown facts—these can be assessed by observing and listening to children solve problems and explain their solutions;

2. the sequence in which unknown facts are clustered for study.

Children who have not yet mastered the multiplication facts often use wrong or inefficient techniques for arriving at answers to given fact problems. Sometimes, particularly when their concept of multiplication is weak, children tend to guess at answers and often miss. Or they may resort to some form of counting. Some, given a problem like 7×5, very tediously lay out counters or use tally marks to show seven groups of five, and then count by fives to determine the total number. Some children do not rely on objects but skip-count mentally to find simple products.

Skip-counting by twos and fives is relatively easy and enables a child to figure out answers to multiplication fact answers. Otherwise, skip-counting is difficult for children and, in general, slower than other techniques and models, such as those that follow. If the disability is so severe that children cannot learn to apply the more efficient approaches to memorizing the facts, serious thought should be given to using a hand calculator for multiplication and division.

The extent to which children succeed in fact mastery is tempered by the sequence in which facts are presented for study. Thus, traditional textbook sequences must often be replaced by a program of study that maximizes success and minimizes frustration in early sessions with facts. The sequence below has proven highly effective in this regard.

The basic plan in the suggested sequence is "easy facts first." Motivated by success at learning "so many facts so fast" (relatively speaking), students are encouraged to "study hard the few that remain." First twos and fives, then nines—since, with the following approaches, these are the easiest to learn. (It is assumed that the commutatives of facts are studied at each step throughout the sequence.) Thus, if children also know zeros and ones, there are only 15 other facts to be studied. Ideas for helping children master these last facts are included in the activities that follow.

NOTE: *Sometimes it is preferable that children begin memorizing their multiplication facts after they have learned the addition facts. Traditionally, however, addition and subtraction facts are presented first, then multiplication and,* *finally, division. For some students, especially those who require overlearning and are weak in abstract reasoning, a more reasonable sequence involves learning the multiplication facts before the subtraction facts. (The assumption of this alternative sequence is that the concept of multiplication is addressed first, even if only at a very concrete level.)*

Sample Sequence of Activities

The following ideas are intended to be used in early sessions for each cluster of facts, with tracking pages and reinforcing practice activities carried out systematically during later sessions.

1. **Twos and addition doubles.** Children who know addition doubles usually have little difficulty with multiplication twos. Use the models for doubles in Figure 9.17 to help with multiplication twos.

- *Example:* $2 \times 6 = 12$ (egg carton model): "Two rows of six, or 2 *times* 6—that's 12." After the ×2 facts are established, children study the commutative facts. Model the commutative idea. For example, use the egg carton model or dots on cards to illustrate that 2 rows of 6 and 6 rows of 2 give the same total number: 12. Cueing exercises such as those suggested by Figure 9.31 can be used, if necessary. If additional auditory reinforcement is needed, have the children read matching pairs into a tape recorder or Language Master and listen to the playback.

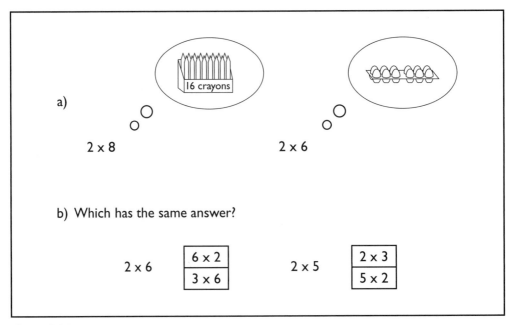

Figure 9.31.

NOTE: *It is assumed that the commutatives ("turnarounds") of facts are studied throughout the sequence.*

- *Example:* The child reads into a tape recorder: "2 × 8. That's 16, the crayon fact" or "2 × 6. That's 12, the egg carton fact." Matching pairs could also be colored or texturized alike on charts or cards for ready reference.

NOTE: *Techniques similar to those just presented are used to reinforce the learning of other multiplication facts.*

2. **Fives and clock times.** If children can tell time, use that skill to help them memorize multiplication fives. (For special help in teaching times, refer to Chapter 4.) The half-hour time should cue the answer to 6 × 5 and 5 × 6 (30). For 9 × 5 and 5 × 9, the children should think of a time like 2:45 (big hand on the 9). For 7 × 5 and 5 × 7, children can think of the big hand on the 7 (2:35). If they cannot recall the minute time right away, cue them to think of the minute hand moving from the 6 to the 7: 5 × 6 = 30 (the half-hour fact), so 5 × 7 is 5 more (35). Similarly, if 3 × 5 and 9 × 5, facts associated with quarter-hour times, are learned first, then other more difficult facts can be related to them.

- *Example:* 3 × 5 = 15, so 4 × 5 = 20 (5 more); 9 × 5 = 45, so 5 × 8 = 40 (5 less). It usually helps to use a geared clock during instruction to illustrate answers to flash card problems. Visual, auditory, and kinesthetic cueing should also be used, as needed, to teach to the strengths of individual students. Ideas suggested in Activity 1 or in Figure 9.32 can be used for this purpose. Follow through with tracking, as suggested in Figure 9.8.

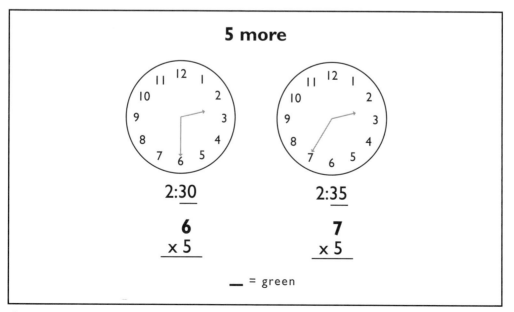

Figure 9.32.

3. **Nines patterns or finger cues.** Many patterns can be derived from the nines tables (refer to Figure 9.33). For example, the sum of the answer digits is always 9; the first digit of the product is always 1 less than the factor being multiplied by 9. Some students with learning disabilities can learn to recognize and use these patterns as a help in fact recall. Most cannot, however—there are too many separate patterns to be integrated and remembered. But students can use their hands for multiplication nines. To do so, they first "number" their fingers, left to right, from 1 to 10, as in Figure 9.34a. Then, to multiply 9 × 3 (or 3 × 9), students fold down their third finger (Figure 9.34b) and read the product from their fingers: 2 fingers to the left and 7 to the right of the folded finger: 27. For 7 × 9 or 9 × 7, they fold down their seventh finger: 6 fingers to the left and 3 to the right of the folded finger: 63. Whether nines are approached through patterns or finger cues, reinforcement, as noted elsewhere in this chapter, should be provided, along with tracking pages as in Figure 9.8.

4. **About zeros and ones.** If students do not already know multiplication of zeros and ones, these facts could be introduced now. It is common for students to be confused over fact answers to problems containing zero. Students with learning disabilities are no exception. Often the problem does not show itself right away in addition and subtraction. After students have been introduced to multiplication, however, the difficulty quickly emerges. When *multiplying,* the product for facts containing zero as a factor is always zero. When adding zero to any addend, the nonzero digit is the sum. Children become confused about when to write zero for a fact answer. The following ideas may help when such difficulties appear:

• *Act it out.* Introduce zero facts dramatically. For example, have the students act out number facts containing zero. For example, for 3 × 0, use a bag filled with candy. Dramatize reaching into the bag *three times* and, each time, bringing out no candy. "How much candy did I pull out of the bag?" ("None.")

× 9	
1	9
2	18
3	27
4	36
5	45
6	54
7	63
8	72
9	81

Figure 9.33.

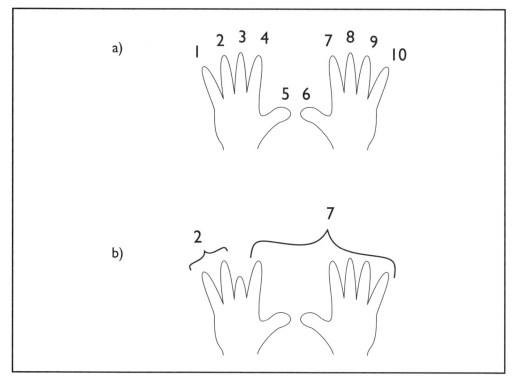

Figure 9.34.

- *Provide auditory cueing.* In the above activity and on other occasions when a ×0 fact appears, use an auditory cue to reinforce (prompt) the correct answer. For example, "×0 is a wipeout. You get nothing at all."

- *Have students "sort out" facts that have zero as an answer.* Provide a mix of addition, subtraction, and multiplication cards with zeros to be sorted into two piles: "zero answer" and "not-a-zero answer" piles.

NOTE 1: *While they are not technically "basic" facts, some students may enjoy studying tens and elevens before turning to harder facts. Since they probably can already skip count by tens, the multiplication pattern for tens is easy to learn. Permit students to use a hand calculator to discover the patterning for elevens.*

NOTE 2: *Take stock at this point. Because the sequence so far has emphasized the easier facts, it is assumed that students will have developed a certain confidence for learning facts. Use this time to help students determine what number facts they have learned and what remains to be studied. Charts like those of Figures 9.35 and 9.36 can be used for this purpose.*

5. **15 to go.** Some students with learning disabilities will need to rely solely on tracking pages (see Figure 9.8) and practice activities to master the 15 remaining facts. As suggested in the opening discussion to the section, one or two of these facts might be learned (possibly as the "fact for the week") while easier fact clusters are being studied. Several of the following strategies, such

Figure 9.35.

as "twice as much" and "add on," require a higher level of reasoning but are beneficial to students who need a more language-based approach.

• *Break apart: Easier facts.* The concept of the distributive property can be applied to "slicing down" harder facts for easier study. The basic idea is to use two easier facts to figure out a harder one.

  ■ *Example:* For 7 × 8, first remind students, "7 × 8 means 7 eights." The child can add as in Figure 9.37. Still, writing out everything is confusing to many students. You may want to keep the presentation oral, perhaps writing just "16 + 40 = 56."

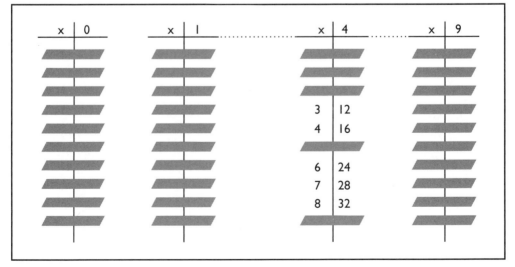

Figure 9.36.

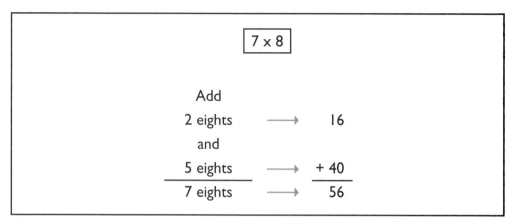

Figure 9.37.

- *Half as much.* "Figure out half, then double it." Approximately half the remaining 15 facts can be learned using this approach.

  - *Example:* "4 × 6. Think of half. 2 × 6 = 12. Now double it: 4 × 6 = 24." Twice as many cards, pictured in Figure 9.38, can be used to illustrate the point.

- *Add on.* An example of this familiar notion will serve to emphasize the idea: 5 × 8 = 40, so 6 × 8 = 48 (8 more). Children build from known facts. Encourage them to think: "5 eights. Now we have 6 eights. What do we add?" ("Eight.")

  - *Variation:* Subtract from (a known fact): 5 × 4 = 20, so 4 × 4 = 16 (4 less). "5 fours. Now 4 fours. So 4 less."

- *It's a square.* Five of the remaining facts are perfect squares and can be shown as in Figure 9.39. Children with strong visual memories might be cued by thinking of the squares.

- *Other cues.* Children themselves have suggested the following cues: (a) 6s rhyme: 6 × 4, 24; 6 × 6, 36; 6 × 8, 48; (b) the "grade school" facts: in order, grades 1, 2, 3, and 4 (12 = 3 × 4); 5, 6, 7, and 8 (56 = 7 × 8). Sharing ideas like these sometimes helps children create their own.

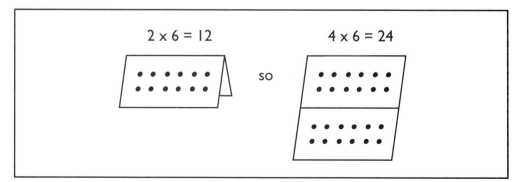

Figure 9.38.

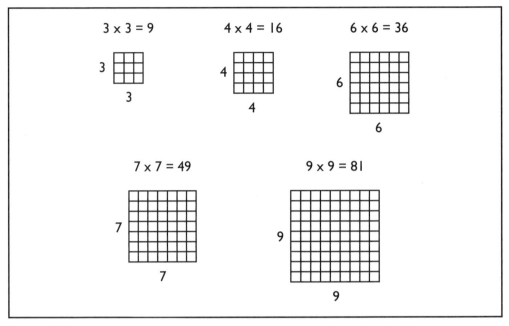

Figure 9.39.

STRATEGIES FOR LEARNING DIVISION FACTS

Problem Area: Difficulty memorizing division facts.

Typical Disabilities Affecting Progress: Difficulty with visual, auditory, or long-term memory; visual or auditory discrimination; expressive language.

Background: Even with numerous problem-solving experiences, students with learning disabilities may find it difficult to master division facts for two major reasons: (1) they do not know related multiplication facts, so using them to derive or check answers to related division facts is not possible; and (2) specific disabilities stand in the way. The suggestions that follow are based on the assumption that at least the first difficulty can largely be removed when division is delayed until a reasonable number of multiplication facts are mastered. The suggestions otherwise are based on structured cueing and tracking strategies that have helped many of our students.

✏ Sample Sequence of Activities

▶ **Easy Facts: ÷2s, ÷5s, ÷9s**

1. **Teach a way to work out answers fast.** If students do not know ÷2s, ÷5s, or ÷9s, they can use retrieval strategies parallel to those for multiplication of 2s, 5s, and 9s to help. *Language emphasis:*

- *"See ÷2? What's the picture?"* (For 14 ÷ 2, for example: 14 days ÷ 2 weeks = 7 days in each week.)

- *"See ÷5? Think minutes after. Where's the minute hand?"* (For example, 35 ÷ 5: think 35 minutes after the hour—the minute hand is on the answer digit, 7.)

- *"See ÷9? What's the pattern?"* (Refer to the suggestions of Figure 9.40.)

In addition to the auditory language emphasis, visual cues including color-coding can be used to promote more rapid recall of unknown facts.

2. **Multiply to check.** No matter how the subtraction or division answer is obtained, follow through, when possible, with feedback like the following: "Yes, 15 ÷ 5 is 3 because 5 × 3 = 15." Use materials to illustrate the relationship between a pair of facts: 15 objects shared among 3; each gets 5. And (returning to the original position) 3 fives = 15.

  ▪ *Variation:* Have the children write answers to a small set of division facts and listen to a tape recorder to check. The taped message should give not only the answer but the related fact each time.

3. **Find it.** Provide exercises like that of Figure 9.41, in which children cross out the wrong helping fact and answer the related helping fact along with the division fact given. Follow through with tracking as described on page 376. Include flash cards that prompt children to answer a given division fact, then flip over to the side with the related multiplication fact to check. Use color cueing as in Figure 9.42 if that seems helpful.

4. **Circle favorites.** On a regular basis, invite students to circle two or three favorite division problems on a worksheet and write the multiply-to-check fact beside each. Afterward select one number fact pair on a page and ask the child to use counters to show that what is written makes sense.

5. **Helpers.** Place multiplication facts that the children know at the top of a worksheet. Suggest that they use them to help answer the division fact problems on the page. Students may even write the helper fact beside the fact given.

6. **Throughout.** Encourage finger-tracing (of textured number sentences) or use color-coding throughout the preceding activities as necessary. Such cues are systematically withdrawn until the children can independently recall related multiplication facts to help with division problems.

7. **Teach related division facts.** For example, when students know 35 ÷ 5 = 7, they can use that fact to learn 35 ÷ 7 = 5. If they know 36 ÷ 9 = 4, they can use that fact to learn 36 ÷ 4 = 9. Follow the previous suggestions including tracking, as described on page 376.

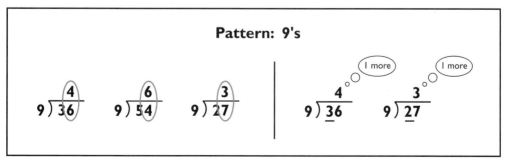

Figure 9.40.

$$35 \div 5 = \underline{\hspace{1cm}}$$

$$5 \times 6 = \underline{\hspace{1cm}}$$
$$5 \times 7 = \underline{\hspace{1cm}}$$

Figure 9.41.

8. **Consolidate learning by finding fact "families."** Provide an opportunity for students to sort flash cards into families like $35 \div 5 = 7$, $7 \times 5 = 35$. Related facts could be color-coded alike in early sessions. Alternatively, the backs of cards containing related facts could be keyed alike (e.g., all carry a red dot).

- *Variation:* Provide puzzles of familiar objects with related facts written on the pieces of each puzzle (Figure 9.43).

Special Facts

Use objects and storylines to help illustrate ideas. For example, $0 \div 5$ can be interpreted as having nothing to share—so each of the five gets zero things. Carry out sorts in which students mark only those fact problems having an answer of 0 (or 1).

Harder Facts

If multiply-to-check work has been carried out systematically, as suggested before, many students with learning disabilities will be able to use that technique to derive answers to the remaining, more difficult division facts. If not, use tracking suggestions as in Figure 9.8. Consolidate learning by emphasizing fact families.

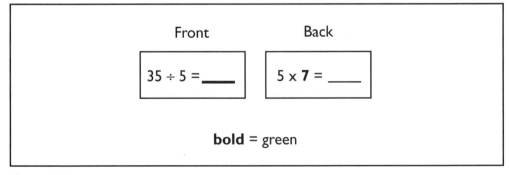

Front   Back

$$35 \div 5 = \underline{\hspace{1cm}}$$ $$5 \times 7 = \underline{\hspace{1cm}}$$

bold = green

Figure 9.42.

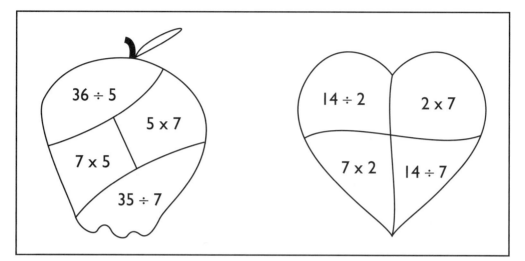

Figure 9.43.

USING TECHNOLOGY

Properly used, calculators are a valid tool for reinforcing concepts and basic fact skills. For students with severe learning impediments, they may become the major device that makes work involving number facts possible. Some of these students may need calculators for all four operations; others may rely on them only for multiplication and division. Suggestions in previous chapters, like using calculators with a voice synthesizer or printed tape, may be necessary to make calculator use possible. The chart below identifies two useful calculators:

Calculator	Advantages
Sharp EL300	Steps a student through the operations; saves steps in memory; shows steps as they are typed (e.g., 56 + 24 = 80 shows up exactly like that on the screen).
Casio Fraction Mate fx55	Large screen; keys are color-coded by type: number keys, operation keys; 4 separate memory keys

Several suggestions for using a calculator to build basic fact skills for the four operations follow:

• **Punch the sign.** Give the students sheets like the one shown in Figure 9.44. The children fill in the correct operation sign and punch out the problem on their calculators to see if they are correct.

• **Turnarounds.** To review or reinforce the idea of commutatives, give the children sheets like that of Figure 9.45. They can use the calculator to check if both facts of a pair have the same answer.

$$
\begin{array}{r} 3 \\ 5 \\ \hline 8 \end{array} \qquad \begin{array}{r} 10 \\ 3 \\ \hline 7 \end{array} \qquad \begin{array}{r} 6 \\ 4 \\ \hline 10 \end{array}
$$

Figure 9.44.

• **Beat the calculator.** Have students compare times for completing a practice sheet of facts—some memorized and some not memorized—with and without a calculator. They should find that sometimes they can work faster without a calculator.

• **Pick the helper** (subtraction or division facts). Give the students a sheet like that in Figure 9.46. Have them circle the helper fact, then punch it into the calculator. If they get the green minuend (quotient) number as the answer, they know their response is correct.

• **Computer software.** A number of microcomputer programs are available through commercial sources for reinforcing number fact learning. Examples include:

Program	Publisher/Distributor
Math Blaster (older version better allows for control of facts presented and pacing)	KnowledgeAdventure
Math Keys	KnowledgeAdventure
Gold Medal Math	EdVenture/Cambridge Development Laboratory
Turbo Math	Forest Technologies/Nordic Software
Turbo Math Maniacs	Forest Technologies/Nordic Software

3 + 7 = ____

7 + 3 = ____

_____

5 + 4 = ____

4 + 5 = ____

Figure 9.45.

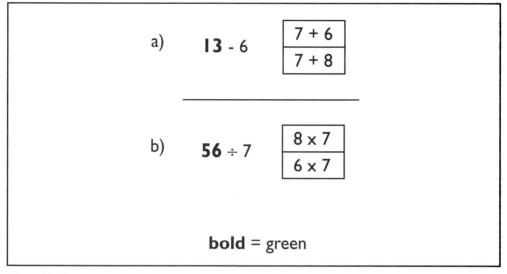

Figure 9.46.

Chapter 10

◆ ◆

Hard-To-Learn Upper-Grade Topics

Some of the topics that this chapter deals with have previously been introduced and developed in the upper elementary and junior high grades. In today's mathematics education, however, it is hoped that, at the concrete level, much of that introduction and development would take place *prior to* upper elementary school so that instruction at that level would involve expanding and applying the basic understanding. The emphasis in this chapter is on (a) ensuring that students with learning disabilities are able to apply their previous knowledge and understanding of these topics and (b) developing students' real-life awareness of their application to daily situations. The following topics are addressed:

- ratios
- proportions
- percents
- integers
- exponents
- spreadsheets

Each of these topics involves the transfer of lower-level concepts to new contexts. For students with learning disabilities this transition might not be made easily. Many students can, for example, master simpler concepts or computations related to ratio, proportion, and percent; they may be able to solve a proportion problem by filling in a missing numerator or denominator but be unable to set up the correct proportion in a given situation. Students may be able to describe the shaded part of a 10×10 grid using percents yet be unable to make a graph to explain what percent of monthly income is used for a variety of expenses. In general, they often can perform the operations when presented as computation but have trouble applying that skill to daily situations.

In some instances, students may not have mastered prerequisite concepts and procedures, hence they cannot make important associations. At other times, difficulty with long-term memory, sequencing, receptive or expressive language, or executive functioning or nonverbal learning disabilities may interfere with retrieval and application of previously learned materials. It is important to remember, though, when evaluating what is making a concept or procedure difficult for a student, that although learning disabilities may be interfering or inhibiting progress, many students are only beginning to develop their executive functioning skills, a stage that does not become fully functional until a child approaches the age of 12 or 13. Whether the problems encountered are directly related to learning disabilities may depend on a child's developmental stage of thinking. Regardless of the exact cause of the difficulty, however, understanding the impact of language as a learning *tool* or as a learning *disability* is important and can play a vital role in helping students to handle these higher-level thinking skills more successfully.

As integers and exponents are introduced and applied to order of operations, other difficulties emerge. Visual perception problems, for example, are at the root of many errors in this area. The exponent is easily misperceived; some students even interpret a number written in exponential form as a whole number (see Figure 10.1). Students who encounter difficulty with abstract reasoning, receptive language, executive functioning, or language processing may have trouble learning what could be perceived as a new "language"—new words or familiar words in a new context. (See Figure 10.2). Success with integers requires good visual memory and visual discrimination as well as memory sequencing. A strong language base also helps, as does a solid ability to use working memory effectively. Difficulties like those identified in the preceding paragraph, as well as the fact that the context is new, leave many students with learning disabilities unsuccessful with mental and paper-and-pencil computations.

An effort has been made to deal with several of the hard-to-learn, upper-grade topics from the point of view of how learning disabilities affect understanding, retention, and application. In some instances, in order to achieve that goal, the suggested sequence differs from that commonly used. Generally, however, the emphasis is on directly relating new material, visually and aurally, to previously learned concepts and skills. The approaches outlined are among those that have proven effective in our own work with learning disabled students.

RATIOS

Problem Area: Difficulty with language and symbolism of ratio.

Typical Disabilities Affecting Progress: Difficulty with receptive or expressive language, abstract reasoning, visual perception, executive functioning.

Background: Ratios involve comparing the number of one group to that of another. Typically, the comparison is between dissimilar but situationally related units; balls to bats, cups to spoons, etc., as in Figure 10.3a. However, ratios also can involve similar units, as in Figure 10.3b (balls to balls).

Although a ratio is not a fraction, the fraction form often is used to represent a ratio (see Figure 10.4). Conceptually, this can be very confusing to students who are used to thinking of $\frac{7}{4}$ as illustrated in Figure 10.5. When introduced to ratios, students must learn to see a familiar symbol in a new context

$$5^3 \longrightarrow 53$$

Figure 10.1.

$$5^3 \longrightarrow \text{five to the third power}$$

Figure 10.2.

and to give that symbol a different interpretation. What used to be thought of as a fraction, although *visually* the same, means something different. The language of ratio is abstract, and that adds to the difficulty. The ratio $\frac{7}{4}$ is often read as "7 to 4." This statement itself is confusing. A longer but more meaningful statement would be: For every 7 (cups of flour), we need 4 (cups of milk). This type of expression makes the necessary language association far easier.

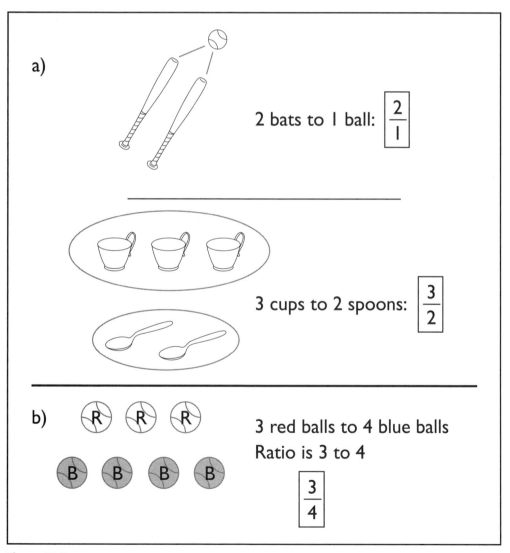

a)

2 bats to 1 ball: $\dfrac{2}{1}$

3 cups to 2 spoons: $\dfrac{3}{2}$

b)

3 red balls to 4 blue balls
Ratio is 3 to 4

$\dfrac{3}{4}$

Figure 10.3.

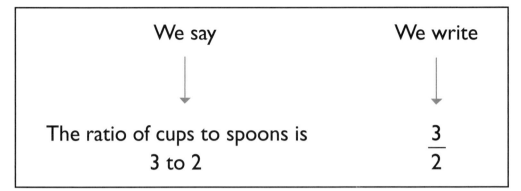

Figure 10.4.

Setting up a ratio from a simple one-step problem like that of Figure 10.6a generally is easy for students. The word *ratio* triggers the general idea, and the problem presents the numbers in the correct order for writing the ratio. Difficulty arises when the word *ratio* is not used and/or when the numbers are not presented in the same order as needed to solve the problem, as in Figure 10.6b. The suggestions that follow focus on the needs of students with learning disabilities and on ways to supplement standard approaches for introducing ratios to meet those needs.

 ## Sample Sequence of Activities

1. **Practice.** Using manipulatives and real-life materials, encourage children to develop their own ratios based on experience. For example, young children enjoy building; help them see the relationship between the concept of ratio (even if the word is not used) and the materials they are using to build. (Legos are a good, concrete visual aid to use with young children in order to foster the beginning concepts of ratio and proportion. A related software program is Bricks by Gryphon Software.)

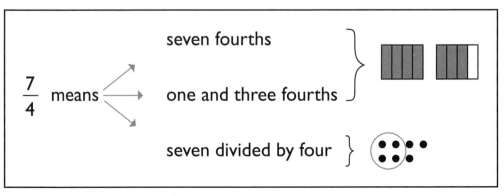

Figure 10.5.

a)   A man solves 8 puzzles in 4 hours.
      What is the ratio of the number
      of puzzles he can solve to the time
      it takes him to put them together?

b)   A man solves 8 puzzles in 4 hours.
      About how many puzzles can he
      solve in 1 hour?

Figure 10.6.

2. **Focus.** Figure 10.6 presents a typical introductory ratio problem. When asked to find the ratio of 8 to 4, students commonly say 2. To help them focus on the idea of comparing one thing to another, have students underline related parts of the problem using the same color. Figure 10.7 illustrates this technique.

NOTE: *Although, initially it might be best for the teacher to underline the related parts ahead of time, a follow-up discussion should be included to insure that students understand the thought process. Gradually, a prerequisite to solving the problem would be having students underline the related parts themselves, have their work checked by the teacher before solving the problem and expressing the answer in a complete sentence (e.g., "The ratio of boys to girls is 3 boys for every 2 girls."), and then draw a picture to show clarification.*

3. **Match.** It is often necessary to practice determining the proper ratios for given situations. Even if students understand that a ratio is written in the form of a fraction, deciding where to place the numbers may be difficult. A combination card game and puzzle can be fun and helpful at this point. Use large index cards (8×12) and make puzzle shapes as shown in Figure 10.8. The word-problem half of the card is placed in a central draw pile, and each player is dealt five ratio cards. The remaining ratio cards are placed face down in a second pile.

There are <u>9 boys</u> and <u>6 girls</u> in a classroom.
What is the ration of <u>girls</u> to <u>boys</u>?

━━ = green   ▁▁ = red

Figure 10.7.

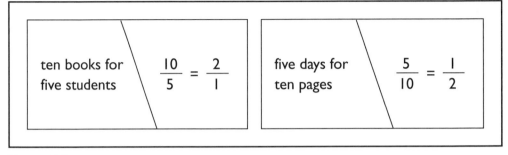

Figure 10.8.

The first player turns over a problem card. If the player already has the correct ratio on a card, a match is made and placed on the board. If not, the player calls for the ratio card. If another player has the requested card, he or she gives it to the caller. Otherwise, the caller draws one ratio card from the pile. When a match is made, the caller puts the pair of cards down on the board. Should an incorrect ratio be requested (the puzzles act as a check), the caller keeps that ratio card and draws another from the pile. The winner is the first person to run out of cards.

4. **Write it out.** Encourage children to write the words as well as the numbers when setting up a ratio. Seeing and saying the words help give the numbers more meaning (see Figure 10.9).

NOTE: *At this point, it is unnecessary to simplify (reduce) the ratio. The primary goal is to understand and set up a ratio.*

5. **Three ways.** To help students recognize and use the three ways of writing a ratio, post a chart like that shown in Figure 10.10 for students to refer to. The chart is especially helpful to children with language or visual memory difficulties.

6. **Color-code.** Similarity involves ratio; thus, it is often helpful to use colors to focus attention. Keep a set of pages, as in Figure 10.11, with color-coding as shown. To aid the transition to noncolor-coded presentations, have students color-code the figures to match statements. In written work, it may help at first to color-code statements to match the figures. For children who have trouble

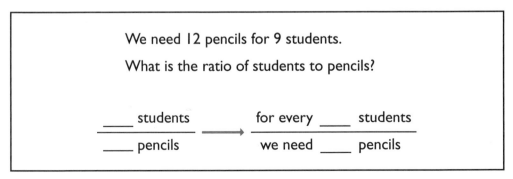

Figure 10.9.

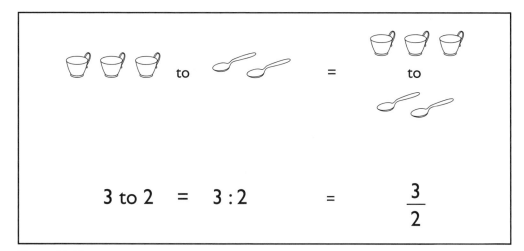

3 to 2 = 3 : 2 = $\dfrac{3}{2}$

Figure 10.10.

processing what they read, this approach helps break the steps down to a manageable size. The focus here, of course, is on recognizing ratios in an applied setting rather than on setting up or solving proportions.

PROPORTIONS

Problem Area: Difficulty setting up proportions for given situations.
  Typical Disabilities Affecting Progress: Difficulty with receptive language, sequencing, abstract reasoning, executive functioning.

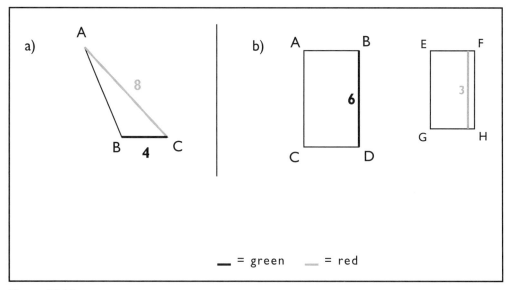

Figure 10.11.

Background: Once students have a solid understanding of equivalence and are able to solve equations, most have little difficulty solving proportions that have already been set up. (Figure 10.12 illustrates typical approaches students might use.)

Problems may arise, however, when students find it hard to draw conclusions; determine patterns; or retrieve, retain, and apply previously learned information. (Solving a basic problem, as shown in Figure 10.12, requires a strong ability to use those tools.) Similarly, when students must independently determine the proportion that applies to a given situation, as in Figure 10.13, they may also have trouble. Many students with learning disabilities can solve fairly complicated proportion problems when they are provided with some visual and/or verbal cues. The suggestions that follow may prove helpful in this regard.

 ## Sample Sequence of Activities

▶ **Language Help**

1. **Construct a chart.** Posting a chart, like that in Figure 10.14, can help *all* students organize their thinking by providing them with a visual cue to

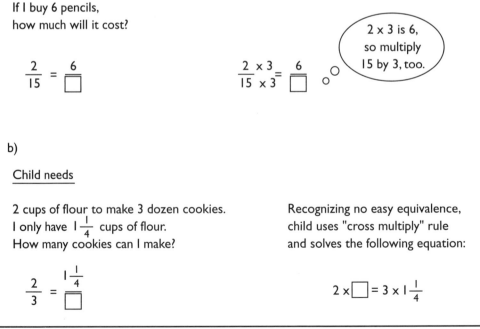

a)

Child is given

2 pencils for 15¢.
If I buy 6 pencils,
how much will it cost?

$$\frac{2}{15} = \frac{6}{\Box}$$

Child uses idea of equivalent fractions and thinks:

$$\frac{2 \times 3}{15 \times 3} = \frac{6}{\Box}$$

○ *2 × 3 is 6, so multiply 15 by 3, too.*

b)

Child needs

2 cups of flour to make 3 dozen cookies.
I only have $1\frac{1}{4}$ cups of flour.
How many cookies can I make?

$$\frac{2}{3} = \frac{1\frac{1}{4}}{\Box}$$

Recognizing no easy equivalence, child uses "cross multiply" rule and solves the following equation:

$$2 \times \Box = 3 \times 1\frac{1}{4}$$

Figure 10.12.

A recipe for 3 dozen cookies uses 2 cups of flour.
How many cookies can you make with only
$1\frac{1}{4}$ cups of flour?

Figure 10.13.

associate numbers and words. By keeping such a chart in the classroom, on the wall and/or available in a smaller version, those students who need it can unobtrusively use it. The sample chart is based on the following problem: "On the map 1 cm equals 80 km. If the distance from Santa Barbara to Los Angeles is about 144 km, how far apart are the two cities?"

2. **Recognize alternatives.** It is important to present alternate methods to help students solve problems. For example, although proportions can be used to compare prices at a grocery store, many students find it easier to use unit pricing, as in Figure 10.15.

NOTE: *When helping children understand the relationship between the more traditional ratio setup and the use of unit pricing, include learning to read labels on merchandise and perhaps take a field trip to different grocery stores to look at how unit price is displayed and determined.*

▶ **Expanding Number Sense**

1. **Establish benchmarks.** As a first step, help children sort ratios as "close to 0," "close to $\frac{1}{2}$," and "close to 1." For example, in $\frac{80}{144}$ (see Figure 10.14), the numerator is about half the denominator, so the ratio would be close to $\frac{1}{2}$. If a numerator is very small in comparison, as in $\frac{2}{40}$, the ratio is close to 0. Numerators that are comparatively large in relation to the denominator, as in $\frac{87}{90}$, characterize a ratio that is close to 1.

2. **Does my answer make sense?** Encourage students to plug computed elements of a proportion back into the original problem to check whether the result makes sense. To develop this skill, present computed elements—some correct and some way off. Students plug the number back into the problem and, using ideas from Activity 1 above, examine whether the ratios in the proportion

distance in km	=	distance in cm
80 km	=	1 cm
144 km	=	____ cm

Figure 10.14.

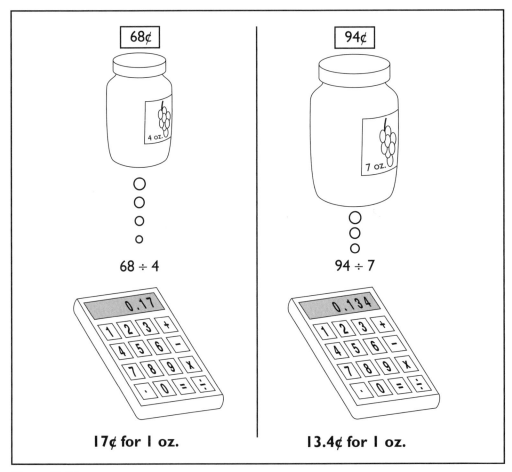

Figure 10.15.

are similar—$\frac{88}{144} \sim \frac{1}{20}$, for example, makes no sense. The first ratio is a little more than $\frac{1}{2}$. The second is closer to 0.

PERCENTS

Number Sense for Percents

Problem Area: Difficulty efficiently estimating percents in practical situations.

Typical Disabilities Affecting Progress: Difficulty with abstract reasoning; receptive or expressive language; short-term, working, or sequential memory.

Background: Using estimation skills in most daily and practical situations often involves mental computation and efficient use of a calculator more than long computations. In addition, the ability to draw conclusions and inferences is important, as students must be able to supply implied facts (e.g., "10% unemployment" really means that *of everyone counted for the survey* 10% are unemployed). In most day-to-day situations, people make quick estimates. When exact answers are required, they typically work out simple percent problems in their heads and use a calculator for more difficult ones. Rarely are paper-and-pencil calculations necessary.

Insights, experiences, and skills take time to develop. Encourage students to look for common occurrences of percents: orange juice—100% pure; mixed nuts—less than 50% peanuts; hamburger—at least 70% lean. Given time, sound teacher modeling, and systematic instruction based on ideas like those that follow, most students with learning disabilities will successfully learn to apply estimation skills to percent situations.

Sample Sequence of Activities

1. **Closer to.** Help students develop intuitions about the relative size of percents. For example, 3%, 12%, and 21% are each closer to 0% than to 50% or 100%. If necessary, have students close their eyes as they run a finger on a meter stick from 12 (for example) to the 0 end and then from 12 to the 100, to develop the notion of *closer to.*

NOTE: *In keeping with the changes taking place in math education today, the concept of percents can and should be introduced prior to middle school. When students are learning about estimating whole numbers, they can begin to learn the concept of percents based on 100 (without reference to the percent of any other number). These students frequently hear the use of the word* percent *in their daily lives and, when the idea is presented at the concrete level, using cubes and place-value blocks, they can begin to develop an intuitive understanding of estimating percents—"There are 100 blocks in this pile. If I give Toshia 48 of them, she would have* almost *50% or half of them. I would still have more than her, though."*

2. **Nice numbers are easier.** When converting between fractions, decimals, and percents, certain "nice" numbers are good benchmarks or points of reference. For example, 1%, 50%, and 100% are good benchmarks, as is the fact $\frac{1}{2} = 50\%$. Seven out of 15 is pretty close to 7 out of 14, which is about $\frac{1}{2}$ or 50%. Similarly, a fraction with a very small numerator as compared to the denominator, such as $\frac{2}{87}$, is closer to 1% than a fraction with a numerator that is very close to the denominator ($\frac{49}{53}$ is closer to 100%).

NOTE: *In earlier grades the groundwork for this skill can be laid as students learn to estimate with whole numbers. For example, give groups of students 100 Lego pieces and have them build a car:*

- "using most of the pieces, almost 100%";
- "using close to but less than 50 pieces, nearly 50%";
- "using close to but a little more than 50 pieces, over 50%."

Discussions could follow to compare how the cars varied depending on the percent of Legos used.

3. **What is likely?** Students with learning disabilities need opportunities to explore and discuss questions such as the following:

- Can we have 100% attendance at school today? 200%?
- Can a price increase or decrease 40%? 100%? 200%?

4. **Start easy.** Once students understand the concept of percents, start with the ideas of 1%, 10%, and 100%, which allows for some easy, and often needed, visualization. Using place-value cubes, as shown in Figure 10.16, and also a calculator, provide enough practice so that students begin to notice the general pattern of shifting the decimal point one or two places to the left.

NOTE 1: *When students are comfortable with the pattern, relate this step to the previous one of "closer to." "The tax rate is 9.8%. That's a little less than 10%, so the tax on $456.78 would be a little less than $45.68."*

NOTE 2: *Relate the idea of 1% and 10% to multiples of those percents: "If 10% of $65.48 is $6.54, then 20% of $65.48 is twice as much. I'll use the calculator and multiply $6.54 by 2."*

5. **Lots of ways.** Flexibility is important in estimation and when finding percents. No one way is right, and students should be encouraged to recognize what method is easiest for them *in any given situation.*

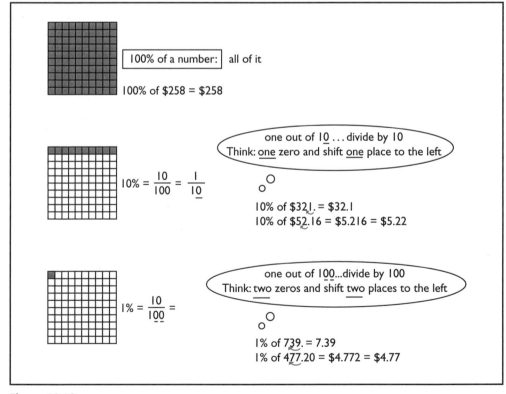

Figure 10.16.

- *Example:* 61% of 847 can be determined in any of the following ways:

    a. using a calculator and rounding the answer

    b. rounding 847 to a "nice number" (850) and breaking 61% apart:

        - 50% of 850 is 425
        - 10% of 850 is 85
        - 1% of 850 is *about* 9

        Therefore, 61% of 847 is *about* 500

    c. approximating 61% as 60% and rounding 847 to 850:

        - 10% of 850 is 85, so
        - 60% of 850 is 6(10% of 850) OR 6(85) or 510

    d. rounding 61% to the closest "nice" percent and rounding 847 to the closest "nice" number:

        - 50% of 850 is 425, so 61% of 847 is a little higher.

These types of problems should be related to real-life situations to help students understand when using nice numbers works and when it does not work. As their estimation abilities improve, children should routinely first decide whether an exact answer is needed or an estimate will do. They should decide whether the results of their estimates make sense with regard to the situation. For example, even though Step (d) in the problem above is accurate in terms of computation, using the result to buy food for a graduation party that 61% of the class will be attending might cause some problems.

Percent Equivalents

Problem Area: Changing percents to decimals or fractions.

Typical Disabilities Affecting Progress: Difficulty with sequencing, visual discrimination, long-term memory, visual memory.

Background: Generally, when teachers introduce percents, students are shown a hundreds square with part of it shaded and given the definition of percent as "per one hundred" or "out of one hundred." This type of presentation is usually understood rather easily by most students, even those with learning disabilities. The difficulty arises when students need to develop good number sense about percents so they can apply their knowledge in everyday situations (i.e., when the percent cannot easily be related to 100, such as when cereal is described as providing 40% of a daily nutrition requirement). The problem may be increased when some paper-and-pencil calculation is needed and when conversion to a fraction or decimal is required. Changing two-digit whole-number percents to fractions typically is not very hard for students. Most readily recognize what to do and remember to put the number itself over 100. However, single-digit percents are sometimes more difficult, and it is not uncommon for teachers to see the following: 6% = .6. Even harder is the conversion of fractional percents, like that in Figure 10.17, to decimals or fractions. When learning that skill, children with learning disabilities usually must think through each step to the point of overlearning. The ideas that follow should help with this and other aspects of instruction related to percent equivalents.

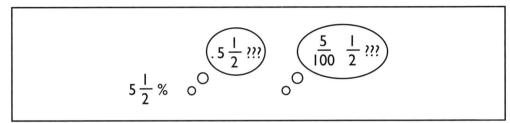

Figure 10.17.

✎ Sample Sequence of Activities

1. **Fractions first.** As noted in other parts of this book, decimals are often more meaningfully introduced when related to the familiar, less abstract fraction notation. When converting percents to decimals, it may be preferable first to change the percent to a fraction with the denominator of 100. Seeing the two zeros in the denominator often instantly reminds students where to place the decimal. This approach is particularly effective for helping students avoid the 6% = .6 error cited above. The underscoring technique shown in Figure 10.18 can be used to remind students that decimal equivalents of percents have two decimal places, even when the percent has only a single digit.

2. **One step at a time.** Given a percent like $5\frac{1}{2}\%$, students should be instructed to change the $\frac{1}{2}$ to .5 right away. This step makes it easier to change the percent to a fraction. (See Figure 10.19.)

3. **Chart it.** Using charts, as in Figure 10.20, helps students who have trouble with memory sequencing. Such a chart provides structure. For many students who enter the fifth or sixth grade with an intuitive understanding of the relationship of percents to fractions and decimals, this structure is especially important, as it helps them begin to realize how the conversions are derived.

4. **Make a book** (a practice activity for two or three players). Provide a deck of 51 cards—17 showing percents, the remainder giving the fraction or decimal equivalent of each percent. After each player has been dealt five cards, the rest of the deck is placed face down between the players. The object of the game is to make books of three cards: the percent and its fraction and decimal equivalents. If, at a player's turn, he or she has no book in hand, he or she takes the top card from the discard pile or the draw pile. The player discards one card and the next person has a turn. During a player's turn, all exposed books can be played. The winner is the one with the most books when one of the players runs out of cards.

$$6\% = \frac{60}{100} = .\underline{06}$$

Figure 10.18.

$$5\frac{1}{2}\% = 5.5\% = \frac{5.5}{100} = \frac{55}{1000} = .055$$

Figure 10.19.

Percent Form of a Fraction

Problem Area: Difficulty changing fractions to percents.

Typical Disabilities Affecting Progress: Difficulty with memory, abstract reasoning, sequencing.

Background: It is relatively easy to convert fractions to percents when the denominator is 100. The difficulty arises when the denominator is not 100. Prerequisites to successfully completing such a task include:

- understanding the concept of equivalence between fractions, decimals, and percents

- writing whole-number and fractional percents in unreduced fraction form, for example: $42.6\% = \frac{42.6}{100}$; $3.5\% = \frac{3.5}{100}$ or $\frac{3\frac{1}{2}}{100}$

- easily dividing whole numbers and decimals by 100

The general technique for teaching students to convert fractions to percents is shown in Figure 10.21: cross-multiply and solve the equation for x. Most textbooks include problems of this type in the section on proportion. For most students with good long-term memory and memory for sequencing and procedures, this approach is fine. In fact, learning-disabled students with good memory who have difficulty with abstract reasoning may also prefer this method. In general, though, when moving from converting fractions with a denominator of 100 to a percent, to converting any fraction to a percent, it is best to start with fractions that have a denominator of 10, then move to those with denominators

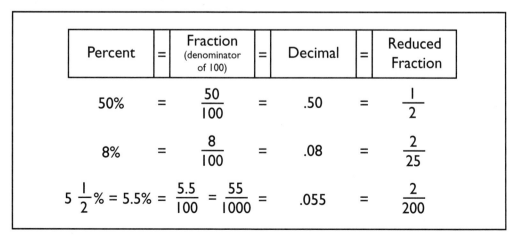

Percent	=	Fraction (denominator of 100)	=	Decimal	=	Reduced Fraction
50%	=	$\frac{50}{100}$	=	.50	=	$\frac{1}{2}$
8%	=	$\frac{8}{100}$	=	.08	=	$\frac{2}{25}$
$5\frac{1}{2}\% = 5.5\%$	=	$\frac{5.5}{100} = \frac{55}{1000}$	=	.055	=	$\frac{2}{200}$

Figure 10.20.

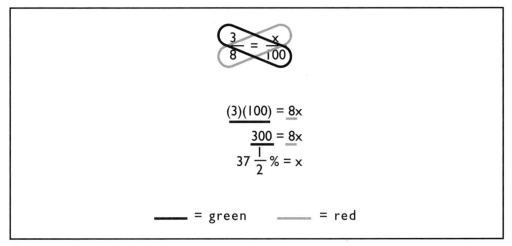

$$\frac{3}{8} = \frac{x}{100}$$

$$(3)(100) = 8x$$

$$300 = 8x$$

$$37\frac{1}{2}\% = x$$

———— = green   ———— = red

Figure 10.21.

that are factors of 100. Next, move to fractions with varying denominators. At this point, it is usually preferable to allow students to use a calculator to convert to a decimal. If the student cannot readily convert the LCD decimal display to a percent, a paper-and-pencil format, as shown in Figure 10.22, could be used. A clear page to keep in their notebooks not only assists students with recall but also provides needed language cues for those who have trouble with expressive language.

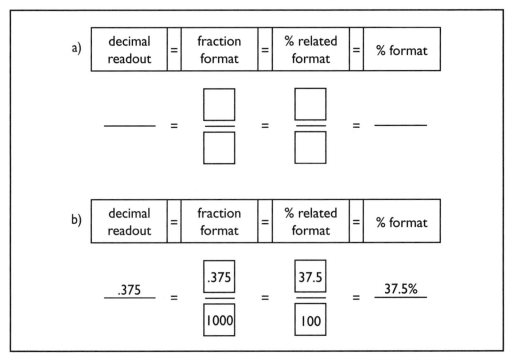

Figure 10.22.

NOTE: *Be sure students with visual perceptual difficulties use a calculator with a large enough LCD display so that they can easily see the decimal point.*

Percent in Everyday Situations

Problem Area: Difficulty using percents to solve problems.

Typical Disabilities Affecting Progress: Difficulty with abstract reasoning, sequencing, visual perception, short-term memory.

Background: Many students with learning disabilities intuitively are able to solve problems using common percents such as 50%, 10%, and, sometimes, 25% and 75%. They are able to estimate, and some students can calculate mentally with easy percents. However, as they begin to deal with other percents, things become more difficult:

- "What method should be used to solve the problem?"
- "Should a fraction or a decimal equivalent be used?"
- "Now that I've found the answer, does it need to be rounded off?"

Questions like these must be answered, and longer, more complex sequences must be employed. In addition, applying meaning to the final answer is usually difficult. Too often, a student ends up knowing only that x = 20 without being able to relate the number to the original problem. The following are ideas for helping students handle such difficulties.

✏️ Sample Sequence of Activities

1. **From problem to equation.** Determining the appropriate equation for a given word problem can be the most difficult part. It often is helpful to teach children the vocabulary related to the work and then use the color-coding techniques of Figure 10.23 to help them set up the equation. During early work, structuring problems into "one-lines," so that the equation can be written directly beneath the problem, helps students translate the verbal statement into an equation. Children learn, for example, to associate the word *of* with the × sign and *is* with the = sign.

2. **Three easy pieces.** Provide preformatted pages using the idea in Figure 10.24. Help students analyze sample problems to recognize that percent situations typically involve three pieces of information (refer to the three boxes in the figure): the part, the whole or the base, and the percent figure. A percent problem-solving exercise provides two of those pieces of information and requires that the student find the third. The format shown in Figure 10.24 can be used to solve any of the three types of percent problems:

1. the percent figure missing;
2. the "part" missing; or
3. the "whole" or base missing.

Using this approach, it becomes a matter of placing information from the verbal statement into the appropriate boxes and then solving to determine the

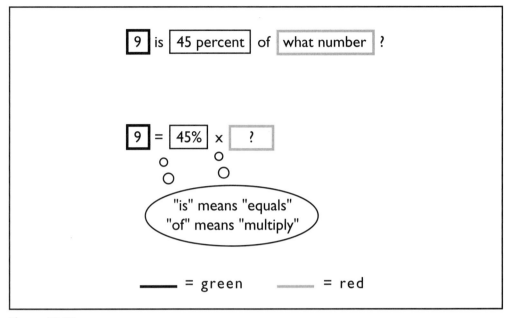

Figure 10.23.

unknown piece of information. Gradually, the students themselves learn to format their own papers, when necessary, to solve percent problems. When an answer is found, encourage students to write it above the appropriate box in the problem statement. This step is necessary for some students so they can relate the answer to the original problem.

3. **Using proportion.** Students with good sequencing, abstract reasoning, and spatial organization skills may prefer the proportion method to solve percent problems. The color-coding technique in Figure 10.25a, similar to that discussed earlier, can be used. Figure 10.25b illustrates how a page can be preformatted for this purpose and kept on file. If the proportion method is used, encourage students, as suggested in Activity 2 above, to relate the answer back to the original problem statement.

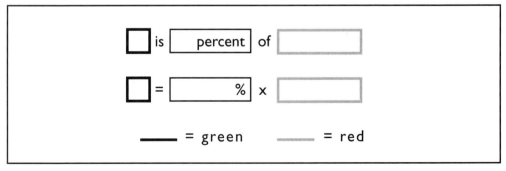

Figure 10.24.

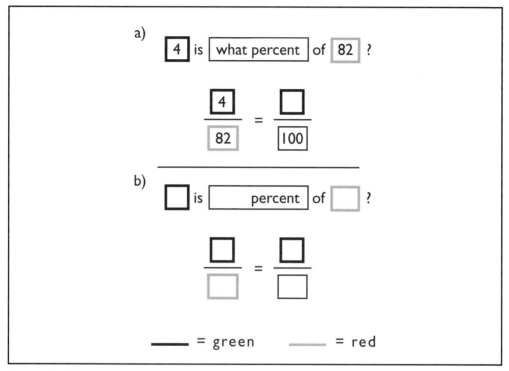

Figure 10.25.

INTEGERS

New Symbolism

Problem Area: Difficulty associating meaning with abstract representations.

Typical Disabilities Affecting Progress: Difficulty with visual and auditory association, visual perception, abstract reasoning, receptive or expressive language.

Background: We use the idea of integers (e.g., negative and positive numbers) regularly in our everyday lives. We borrow money from a friend and then we pay it back. Do we still owe money? The temperature drops 8 degrees but then climbs 9 degrees the next morning. A salary increase means that we earn more money, but then we might take a cut in salary when we switch jobs. All of these ideas are familiar to children. Even students with learning disabilities have little difficulty comprehending the meaning in context. However, when the same ideas are expressed symbolically using positive or negative integers, many children become confused. Most can readily tell you how much a friend owes them if $4 was borrowed, and they may even use the expression "I'm $4 in the hole." However, the mathematical representation is not as easily explained, although it may have the same meaning.

Poor visual or auditory association skills, coupled with poor abstract-reasoning abilities make it difficult for students to deal meaningfully with the written integer form. Students are asked to relate a *familiar* idea to *familiar* signs (+ and −) in a *new* way using *new* language. That is, they have to decide what the familiar sign now means: *add* or *positive, subtract* or *negative*. To complicate matters, new skills and new language often are presented simultaneously. Those with expressive or receptive language deficits may understand the similarity in meaning between words such as *add* and *positive* or *subtract* and *negative* but find it hard to elicit or associate the words with the correct meaning in context. These students require considerable overlearning, consistent verbal and pictorial association, and small learning increments in early work with integers.

The following are suggestions for how to deal with these difficulties during early concept development with integers. The ideas presented can be used to supplement textbook treatments that typically focus on the application of integers in real-life situations.

✎ Sample Sequence of Activities

1. **Color-code.** Children with visual discrimination difficulties or language deficits often benefit from color-coded pages like that in Figure 10.26. The colors help students to:

- associate words with symbols;

- reduce interference from visual discrimination problems;

- focus directly on the idea of "more" or "less" in a different context than that to which they are accustomed.

Using this method in real-life situations, as shown in Figure 10.26, helps students develop an automatic association of vocabulary and integers.

2. **Number line: Develop good number sense.** As children begin to use the number line, have them select examples from everyday situations to verbally describe several points on the line. Figure 10.27 presents a sample exercise.

3. **Picture it.** As a class activity, present pictures with related phrases that describe "positive" and "negative" situations. (Figure 10.26 shows sample ideas.) If possible, put the pictures and matching phrases on a card with the

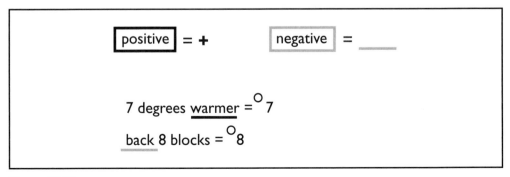

Figure 10.26.

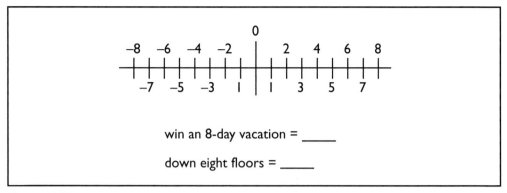

win an 8-day vacation = _____

down eight floors = _____

Figure 10.27.

guide words *positive* and *negative* at the top in two different colors. Discuss the meaning of the two terms and have students underline the key words or phrases to match the color of the guide words.

4. **Point plotting.** As students begin to plot points in all four quadrants, a color-coded grid, like that in Figure 10.28, often helps with directionality. Ordered pairs are coded according to the quadrant, as shown.

Positive and Negative Signs

Problem Area: Difficulty interpreting signs used with integers.

Typical Disabilities Affecting Progress: Difficulty with visual perception, spatial organization, closure.

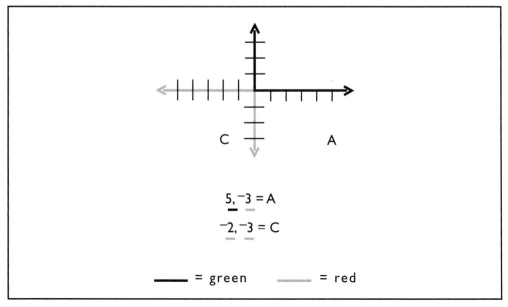

5, ⁻3 = A

⁻2, ⁻3 = C

⸺⸺ = green   ⸺ ⸺ = red

Figure 10.28.

⁻7 means "negative seven"

−6 means "subtract six"

Figure 10.29.

7 - 8

Figure 10.30.

Background: For many students, the greatest difficulty in dealing with integers is misreading or misplacing the sign. For this reason, it is essential that the teacher be consistent in the placement of those signs. When a sign is to be interpreted as negative or positive, it should be placed in a raised position, as in Figure 10.29. When used to denote an operation, the sign should be centered vertically between the two numbers that are involved. Figure 10.30 shows a typical problem that can be very confusing. Does the sign in front of the 8 mean "subtract" or "negative"? The following ideas have proven useful in dealing with problems related to sign interpretation. In our experience, they have helped make computation with integers easier for students.

NOTE: *If the school or school district allows teacher selection, choose textbooks that use the raised signs and include color-coding as part of the explanation.*

✎ Sample Sequence of Activities

1. **Circle to focus.** Preview the text and circle the raised signs in the chapter on integers. Similarly, in problems where there is no positive or negative sign (see Figure 10.31) a small circle should be placed to the left of the integer as a reminder that numbers are considered positive if there is no sign. This can be done by adult volunteers or teaching assistants. It is also a good pre-activity for students with visual discrimination difficulties. Before working on a page in the book, the assignment might be to use a highlighter or fine-point pen, depending on the size of the print, to circle the raised signs or to add circles where there are no raised signs. (As noted in other chapters, all students should be a part of the learning process, and students with learning disabilities particularly need to be aware of what they must do in order to be successful learners. This type of assignment provides for that goal.)

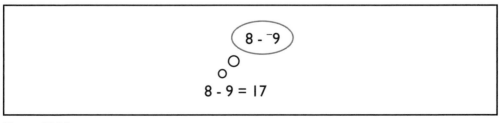

Figure 10.31.

$$9 - (^-3) + (^+4) = 9 + 3 + 4 = 16$$

Figure 10.32.

- *Variation:* An alternative is to insert parentheses within a problem, as in Figure 10.32.

2. **Use graph paper.** If students need help spatially organizing their writing of signed numbers, allow them to use graph paper. Show them how to place the signs and numbers on the lines, as in Figure 10.33. Students with severe visual perception deficits will find this activity difficult. For others, the graph paper technique simplifies the task of writing integers and computing. Graph paper with six squares to the inch works well.

- *Variation:* For students who need additional assistance to organize their writing spatially, use the format in Figure 10.34a to prepare sheets in advance. The students fill in the problem as shown in Figure 10.34b. The adaptation for vertical alignment of numbers is shown in Figure 10.35.

Computation with Integers

Problem Area: Difficulty computing with integers.

Typical Disabilities Affecting Progress: Difficulty with visual perception, sequencing, abstract reasoning, working memory, sequential memory.

Background: Computing with integers requires more sequencing and mental regrouping than previous computation involving positive integers. As with all calculations, easy problems can be completed more quickly if done mentally. For others, the ability to determine the best method is essential. In some cases, using paper and pencil may be most efficient, while in other cases using a calculator is preferable. A word of caution is in order, though, regarding using a calculator to solve integer problems. Students will need practice keying the numbers in correctly. Most calculators have a +/– key, which changes the sign of the number, but there are three other important considerations when selecting or using calculators:

1. Using a calculator requires strong use of working memory. Most people type a number in and then check the LCD readout to be sure they punched in

Figure 10.33.

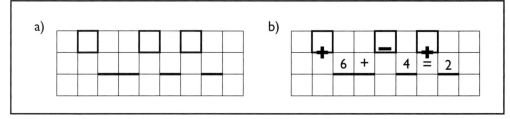

Figure 10.34.

the correct number. When solving computation problems (see Figure 10.32), there is the added step of either retaining the entire problem in one's head or looking back and forth between the keypad, the LCD readout, and the assignment.

2. Is the +/– key depressed before or after the number it is attached to?

3. When the number on the LCD readout shows a negative number, it is not raised. (The authors are not aware of any calculator that clearly differentiates between ["+" and "–"] operation signs and negative or positive.)

These three situations can be confusing for students, particularly those with memory problems or visual discrimination.

Suggestions for how to supplement or reinforce textbook treatment of integer computation for the four operations follow. Initially, require all students to proceed step by step through *all* steps. If necessary, provide problems with high numbers so that mental calculation cannot easily be done. Later, once students have mastered the thinking, present problems of varying difficulty and encourage students to decide on the best method to use: mental calculation, paper and pencil, a calculator, or some combination of the three.

 ## Sample Sequence of Activities

1. **Informal beginnings.** Most textbooks suggest activities involving chips, cards, charged particles, or walk-on number lines to introduce, infor-

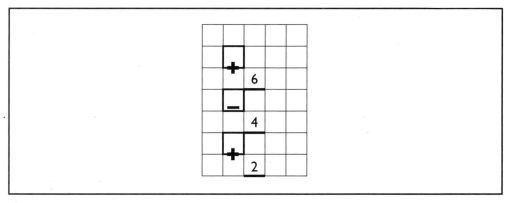

Figure 10.35.

mally, the addition of integers. It is especially important to carry out rather than omit these activities for students with learning disabilities because they help develop the mental imagery necessary to deal successfully with the addition of integers. Figure 10.36a suggests a number line activity. Alternately, the charged particle model might be used, as in Figure 10.36b.

2. **Different strokes.** Textbook treatments typically present number lines or other models in an effort to lead students to verbalize the patterns or rules for adding integers. A chart, similar to that in Figure 10.37, often helps in this area, too. For students with abstract-reasoning difficulties, expressive language difficulties, or problems with long-term memory, it generally is helpful to:

- present the chart and discuss it in conjunction with several examples, so that, procedurally, the students can use the chart to solve integer addition problems;

- have students copy the chart onto a file card or their vocabulary notebook as described in Chapter 2 for ready reference;

- have students use the rules to work out a number of problems until they become familiar with the general procedures for adding integers; and

- use a walk-on number line to verify that the sums derived in this manner actually make sense before attempting to memorize the procedural rules.

This last step usually is first in the standard sequence, but the authors' experience has been that it is more important as a tie-in to earlier informal work.

3. **For other folks.** For other students, such as those with memory or perceptual difficulties, the standard sequence is followed with additional reinforcing measures like: (a) color-coding signs to emphasize them whenever they appear in integer addition problems; (b) using the graph paper technique in Figures 10.34 and 10.35 when helpful; and (c) providing kinesthetic or motor

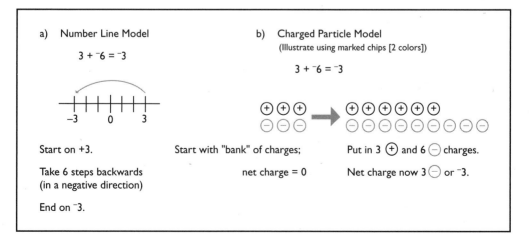

Figure 10.36.

Addition of Integers

Given Problem	What to do	Sign of sum
positive + positive	Add	**+**
negative + negative	Add	—
negative + positive	subtract to find distance between	sign of the greater addend
positive + negative		

Figure 10.37.

involvement in analyzing or certifying the procedural rules for adding integers. Additional ideas follow:

• Allow students to dramatize simple additions, as in Activity 2 above, on a walk-on number line.

• Have students think of their bodies as number lines. When both arms are spread out, the left arm can represent the negative integers, the right arm the positive ones. The body is zero. To add a negative 5 to a positive 4, for example, students must pass through 0 and on to negative 1. Doing this for several sample problems helps children internalize the action of crossing the midline when needed, as is often the case in integer addition.

■ *Variation:* An alternative to arm stretching involves taping a smaller number line from shoulder to shoulder across a child's back. The body midline is zero. As the teacher dramatizes a simple addition problem by finger movement on the child's back, the student can either (a) close his or her eyes and reverbalize the problem as it is enacted or (b) with eyes open, mimic the teacher's movements by finger walking the addition on a personal number line placed on the child's desk in front of him or her.

Subtraction of Integers

Suggestions for successful integer addition have obvious implications for integer subtraction. Informal introductory work is important. Variation of the standard subtraction sequence for students with abstract-reasoning difficulty is similar to that outlined for integer addition. Likewise, the compensatory techniques outlined in Activity 3 of the addition sequence can be reviewed and adapted to work with integer subtraction. The following ideas, based on the number line model, also deserve special emphasis. Similar activities can be carried out using the charged particle model.

Sample Sequence of Activities

1. **Act it out.** There generally is great value in having students use a walk-on or "body" number line (as in Activity 3 in the previous section). This enables the student to:

- solve simple integer subtraction problems that often involve the pattern summarized in Figure 10.38; and

- verify that given answers, or those obtained using a calculator, also can be derived by following that rule.

2. **Use the number line.** A problem like that in Figure 10.39a might be posed and the students cued to think of the related addition problem: "What must be added to $^+4$ to get $^-7$?" Starting at $^+4$ on the number line, the children find that they must take 11 steps in a negative direction to arrive at $^-7$.

The result should be charted along with others obtained in this manner. Using previously solved problems, help students notice the pattern by grouping like problems, as in Figure 10.39b. Have them verbalize that the pairs $^-7 - {}^+4$ and $^-7 + {}^-4$ have the same answer. Repeat with other similar examples to help students arrive at the conclusion: "To subtract one integer from another, the first can be added to the *opposite* of the second." Use the number line to verify the equivalence.

■ *Extension 1:* Design worksheets or card-sort activities in which students solve and then match an integer subtraction problem to an equivalent addition problem. For example:

Solve:

$^-7 - {}^+4 =$ _____ $^-8 + {}^+5 =$ _____

$3 - {}^-2 =$ _____ $^-7 + {}^+4 =$ _____

$^-8 - {}^-5 =$ _____ $^+3 + {}^+2 =$ _____

Pair:

a. $^-7 - {}^+4 =$ _____ and $^-7 + {}^+4 =$ _____

b. _____ = _____ and _____ = _____

c. _____ = _____ and _____ = _____

To subtract two integers:

Add the 1st integer to
the <u>opposite</u> of the 2nd.

Figure 10.38.

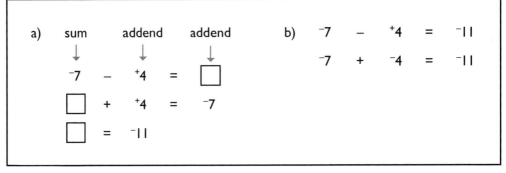

Figure 10.39.

When all matches are made, the students must use a number line to verify the equivalence of each.

- *Extension 2:* Next, give students integer subtraction problems and instruct them to carry out just the first step of each. As in Figure 10.40a, have students merely rewrite the problems without solving. After the papers are checked, the problems can be completed.

NOTE: *Most texts present integer computation horizontally; for many students with learning disabilities, however, the vertical format is easier. As shown in Figure 10.40b, it may be necessary to help the students rewrite the horizontal format.*

    3. **Different strokes.** The sequence outlined in Activity 2 above starts intuitively with number line moves, notes an equivalent method for finding answers (adding the opposites), then provides practice to understand and retain the process. Some students may have difficulty with this more sophisticated, standard method of using the additive inverse to solve integer subtraction problems. The following are suggestions for instructing these students:

- *Use number line moves* as before to introduce integer subtraction intuitively. Cue students to think of the related addition problem. Using the example in Figure 10.41a, ask students, "What must be added to a positive 4 to get a negative 7?" The students rewrite the problems, as in the second line of Figure 10.41b, to match the question. Starting at ⁺4, children move back to 0 and on to ⁻7, for a total of 11 spaces in the negative direction. This result (⁻11) is now

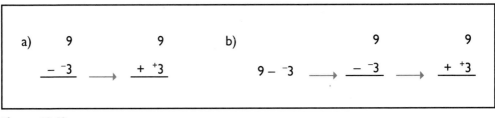

Figure 10.40.

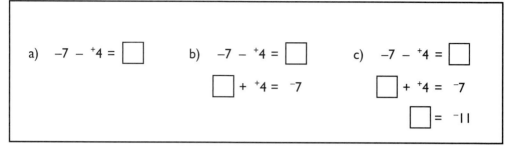

a) $-7 - {}^{+}4 = \square$ b) $-7 - {}^{+}4 = \square$ c) $-7 - {}^{+}4 = \square$

$\square + {}^{+}4 = {}^{-}7$ $\square + {}^{+}4 = {}^{-}7$

$\square = {}^{-}11$

Figure 10.41.

recorded, as in Figure 10.41c. Either the walk-on or the body number line discussed earlier can be used in this activity.

• *Write it out.* To reinforce the subtraction-addition relation and to help students internalize the procedure for subtracting, use the technique in Figure 10.42. (The subtraction sign in the problem is written in a bright color.) Write out the procedure for subtracting as shown. The students solve the problem by filling in the blanks. Later, just put an example at the top of the page as a reminder but continue to highlight the subtraction signs for all problems.

• *The whole thing.* As children begin to solve integer subtraction problems independently, encourage them to picture the number line. For the example of $8 - {}^{-}3$:

- Child writes: _____ $+ {}^{-}3 = 8$

- Child thinks: "Start at ${}^{-}3$, move forward to 0, then on to 8. That's a move of ${}^{+}11$. $8 - {}^{-}3 = 11$."

NOTE: *This method does not utilize the traditional rule for subtracting integers—that of adding the opposite (additive inverse). It is based on the addition-subtraction relationship and on developing inner language. It allows those children who respond best to concrete approaches to use that strength in their thinking. Children are encouraged to picture (or actually make) number line moves, first to zero, then on to a target number. This two-step process also can be used with two- and three-digit numbers.*

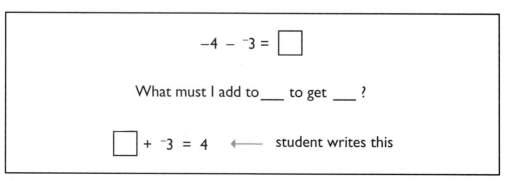

$-4 - {}^{-}3 = \square$

What must I add to ____ to get ____ ?

$\square + {}^{-}3 = 4$ ⟵ student writes this

Figure 10.42.

Multiplication and Division of Integers

Prerequisite Skills: An understanding of the concepts of multiplication as repeated addition and as commutative.

For those students who understand these concepts at the initial stages, the following activities have proved helpful in applying their comprehension to higher-level topics such as integers.

✎ Sample Sequence of Activities

1. **Products and unlike signs.** Given mastery of the prerequisites, the sign for the product of a positive and a negative can readily be identified.

- *Example:* $7 \times {}^-6$. "That's seven negative sixes." One could repeatedly add, if necessary, to obtain the ${}^-42$. Since multiplication is commutative, $7 \times {}^-6 = {}^-6 \times 7 = {}^-42$.

2. **Products and like signs.** Many students can recognize and continue the pattern to the answers in Figure 10.43a. Each product is 5 less than the one directly above it. Similarly, in Figure 10.43b, each product is 4 less than that directly above it. Further, when the answers are filled in, the students can see how, each time, the product of two negative numbers is positive. Some students, particularly those with abstract-reasoning difficulties, may not follow

a) $5 \times {}^-5 = {}^-25$ b) $5 \times {}^-4 = {}^-20$

$4 \times {}^-5 = {}^-20$ $4 \times {}^-4 = {}^-16$

$3 \times {}^-5 = {}^-15$ $3 \times {}^-4 = {}^-12$

$2 \times {}^-5 = {}^-10$ $2 \times {}^-4 = {}^-8$

$1 \times {}^-5 = \underline{\quad}$ $1 \times {}^-4 = \underline{\quad}$

$0 \times {}^-5 = \underline{\quad}$ $0 \times {}^-4 = \underline{\quad}$

${}^-1 \times {}^-5 = \underline{\quad}$ ${}^-1 \times {}^-4 = \underline{\quad}$

${}^-2 \times {}^-5 = \underline{\quad}$ ${}^-2 \times {}^-4 = \underline{\quad}$

${}^-3 \times {}^-5 = \underline{\quad}$ ${}^-3 \times {}^-4 = \underline{\quad}$

${}^-4 \times {}^-5 = \underline{\quad}$ ${}^-4 \times {}^-4 = \underline{\quad}$

Figure 10.43.

the logic of this exercise but will merely remember that, as long as the signs are the same, the product is positive.

3. **Mail time.** A table like that in Figure 10.44 also can be used as a story-line to dramatize the sign patterns for products. Since most students like to get mail, that is positive. No one likes to receive bills; that is negative.

4. **Same as multiplication.** Most students have little difficulty remembering how to handle the signs in division once they are comfortable with multiplication of integers. They are used to relating multiplication and division, so it is easy to remember (and verify) that the sign rules for quotient figures are analogous to those for products:

Divisor and Dividend	Quotient
Like signs	Positive
Unlike signs	Negative

- Example 1: $^-45 \div 5 = ^-9$ ("Yes, because $^-9 \times 5 = ^-45$.")
- Example 2: $^-63 \div ^-7 = 9$ ("Yes, because $9 \times ^-7 = ^-63$.")

EXPONENTS

Basic Concept

Problem Area: Difficulty understanding, reading, and writing exponents.

Typical Disabilities Affecting Progress: Difficulty with short-term memory, visual perception, expressive language, abstract reasoning.

Background: Students are introduced to the concept and symbolism of exponents as early as the fifth or sixth grade. At that point, the idea is dealt with basically in conjunction with factoring and primes. As students advance in mathematics, computation involving exponents becomes more common-place. Mathematical problem-solving applications in a number of fields, including medicine, science, and computer science, regularly use exponents to express both very large and very small numbers. Students with interest in those fields benefit from a firm foundation in exponents.

At the pre-algebra level, development of adequate understanding of and ability to use exponents is both important and necessary for students planning

---

If letters (+) are brought (+), that's positive (+).

If bills (−) are brought (+), that's negative (−).

If letters (+) are taken away (−), that's negative (−).

If bills (−) are taken away (−), that's positive (+).

Figure 10.44.

to continue mathematics in high school. The topic itself is not particularly difficult, except that it introduces new terminology and new notation that can be visually confusing. The following activities suggest ways of making exponents more understandable and usable, especially for those with language deficits. Previewing language and/or providing vocabulary cards may be needed for some students.

 ## Sample Sequence of Activities

1. **Helpful models.** At an intuitive level, prior to the textbook introduction of exponents, squares and cubes of various dimensions can be used, as in Figure 10.45, to acquaint students with exponential notation and language.

2. **Factors first.** Color-coding can be used in the previous activity to help students remember how to read and write exponents. Since an exponent indicates the amount of times a number is used as a factor, generally it is best to have students first write the exponential form from a list of factors (see Figure 10.46). This sequence especially seems to help students with expressive language deficits, as it reinforces the meaning of the numbers used. Figure 10.46 contains an exercise that can be kept on file or in the vocabulary notebook described in Chapter 2 and used prior to the textbook introduction of exponents. The color-coding, of course, can extend beyond the second and third powers of the base.

3. **Reverse what's given.** Once students can write the exponential form of the factored form, provide practice translating the exponential form. Again, color-coding can be used, as in Figure 10.47.

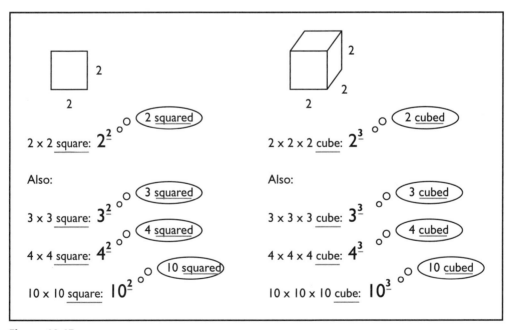

Figure 10.45.

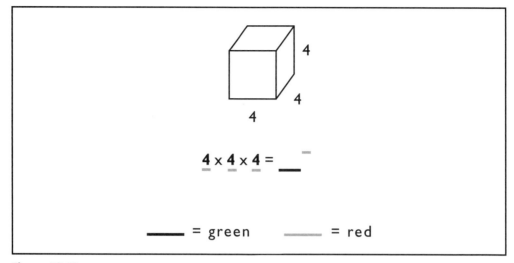

Figure 10.46.

4. **One call.** Make a deck of 52 cards. Twenty-six should show a number in exponential form, and 26 should show the same numbers in factored form, as in Figure 10.48. After each child has been dealt five cards, the rest of the deck is placed face down between the players. The game is played by making pairs of one exponential card and one with matching factors. Taking turns, players request one card from the player on their left. If that player has the requested card, he or she gives it to the caller, who can then lay a pair down. If that player does not have the card, the caller can draw one card from the pile. A game continues until no more pairs can be drawn from the pile. The first player to run out of cards wins.

5. **New terminology.** For many students, the language involved in exponents is the most difficult part of the subject. These students have trouble meaningfully associating the words, such as "six to the third power," with any visual image. To help build up the necessary language, provide language practice that is separate from computational practice. Pages such as those shown in Figure 10.49a are useful, as they present the new symbolism together with the

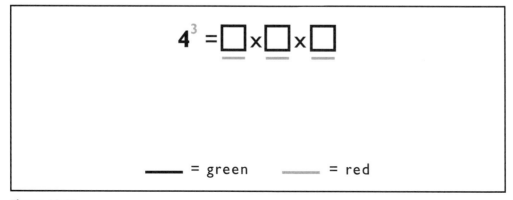

Figure 10.47.

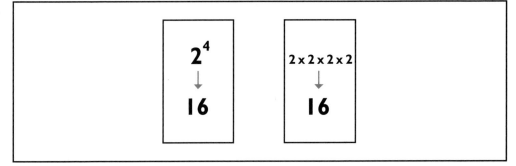

Figure 10.48.

associated language. Figure 10.49b suggests an alternate exercise that visually reinforces the fact that the exponent is raised.

Scientific Notation

Problem Area: Using exponents in scientific notation.

Typical Disabilities Affecting Progress: Visual perception, figure-ground, sequencing, closure problems.

Background: Scientific notation is used in many fields to express both very large and very small numbers. The successful conversion of numbers to (or from) scientific notation requires several major prerequisites, including:

- strong numeration concepts and skills;
- ability to multiply and divide powers of 10;
- basic understanding of and skill with exponents; and
- ability to read decimals.

Application of all these isolated understandings and skills when writing numbers in scientific notation requires good reasoning, recall, and sequencing.

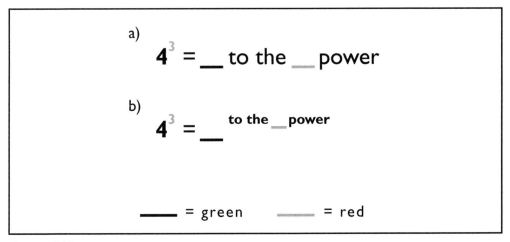

Figure 10.49.

These are typically weak areas for students with learning disabilities. In addition, closure or visual perception deficits can lead to confusion when reading the numbers. Too often, such deficits make it seem as if these students do not understand what to do, when, in fact, they may be losing the place or unable to recall information. The following suggestions offer ideas for how to handle some of the common problems children face as they deal with scientific notation.

✎ Sample Sequence of Activities

1. **Color-highlight.** During early work for students with figure-ground deficits, it sometimes helps to highlight the digits to be used. Figure 10.50 illustrates two alternatives for color-coding digits. Highlighting in this manner helps minimize the chance that students will lose their place or misperceive the numbers read.

2. **Use a mask.** Some students need to use a card, as in Figure 10.51, to block out part of the number field while counting digits. Students write the answer, digit by digit, while moving the card.

3. **Help for computation.** When multiplying with scientific notation, color-highlight, as in Figure 10.52, to help students apply the distributive law. Otherwise, the visual field can be confusing. Texts can be highlighted as in Figure 10.52a. Pages, formatted as in Figure 10.52c, can be kept on hand for students to use.

SPREADSHEETS

It is beyond the scope of this book to include a detailed discussion of using spreadsheets with learning disabled students. Nonetheless, the authors felt that a brief discussion should be included, given the increased use of technology and the need to ensure that students are proficient in this area. The

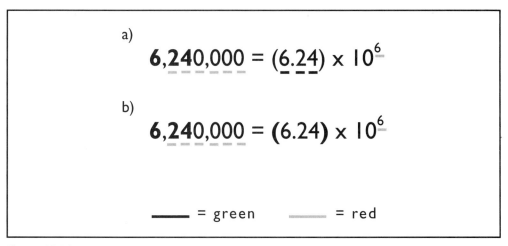

a)
$$6{,}240{,}000 = (6.24) \times 10^6$$

b)
$$6{,}240{,}000 = (6.24) \times 10^6$$

——— = green   ⋯⋯ = red

Figure 10.50.

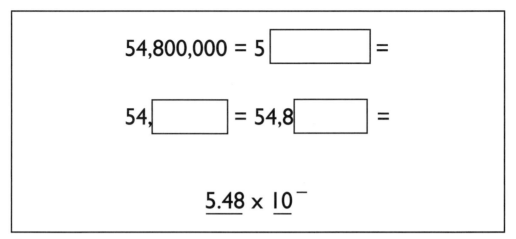

Figure 10.51.

approach taken is to provide teachers with an introduction to the possibilities of using spreadsheets to clarify concepts while simultaneously teaching students *how* spreadsheets, and other types of data, can be used. Before showing a few examples, though, it is important to address some of the prerequisites for successful use with spreadsheets. Probably the most important is the vocabulary aspect. Throughout this book the changing use of verbal and symbolic language has been addressed (e.g., the fraction bar can mean "out of," "divided by," or "is to"). To successfully use spreadsheets, one needs to be aware of still more changes. For example:

- the = sign now takes on a new meaning; it is usually an instruction to the computer that a formula is going to be entered;

- multiplication is now represented by the asterisk (*);

a) $(3.6 \times 10^{3}) \times (4.31 \times 10^{-5})$

b) $(3.6 \times 4.31) \times (10^{3} \times 10^{-5})$ student rewrites inside parentheses

c) $(\quad \times \quad) \times (\quad \times \quad)$

       ——— = green   ——— = red

Figure 10.52.

- instead of telling the computer exactly what numbers to use for computation, as when using a calculator, we now designate an operation by the cell in which the number is located; and

- alphabetizing or ordering numbers in descending or ascending order is usually represented by the word *sort*.

These represent only a few of the familiar words and practices that are now used in a different context. There are others, and there are variations among spreadsheet applications. Although exploration is exciting for students and often a very good use of time, it is important to remember the goal of any given assignment. In the context addressed here, the goal is to use the spreadsheet as a tool to assist in learning some of the higher-level skills while also developing some beginning knowledge about using a spreadsheet. The examples shown below can be made relatively easily. (These were done in Clarisworks 4.0.)

Figure 10.53 shows a spreadsheet that can be used to encourage problem-solving skills regarding percents. The student who set this spreadsheet up had little difficulty with the mechanics. It wasn't until a discussion took place, however, along with the use of tiles representing percents, that the student realized that:

- 50%, 25%, and 10% stood for portions of the large 100% section rather than portions of the area that was shaded (Figure 10.53a), and

- a portion was missing. Only 85% of the chart was filled in. Once this was realized, the mechanics of adjustment were easily handled and the student also applied some important reasoning skills with regard to percents and how they may be portrayed in charts and graphs (Figure 10.53b).

Figure 10.54 shows another type of spreadsheet that can be used to help students solve percent problems. The setup in this diagram takes into account the need for students to use language and thought processes, thus the horizontal format, which reinforces reading from left to right. If desired, the values can be imposed on the bars and the bars can be different colors to match the words on the left and above (e.g., the cost is $65.78 and the related text and bar on the graph would be green, as thinking starts there). A duplicate of this chart can be made and placed below it. Using the duplicate and adjusting the values that are put into the cells, students can watch and compare what happens as tax rates increase and decrease or as costs increase and decrease. At the same time, they are learning a little about spreadsheets, as they will see the formulas in the box whenever they go to change a value.

Figure 10.55 shows the final project of a student who needed to visualize the relationship among percents, fractions, and decimals. Only a minimal amount of working knowledge about using a spreadsheet was required since the information could be put in exactly as it was thought about. The "Make Chart" option was used, and the student was able to see the labels, language, and visual relationships. (The original of this chart was done in color, which made it even easier to make associations.) In addition, a printout could be made for the student to use for other work as the topics of percent, ratios, and proportions were addressed in more detail.

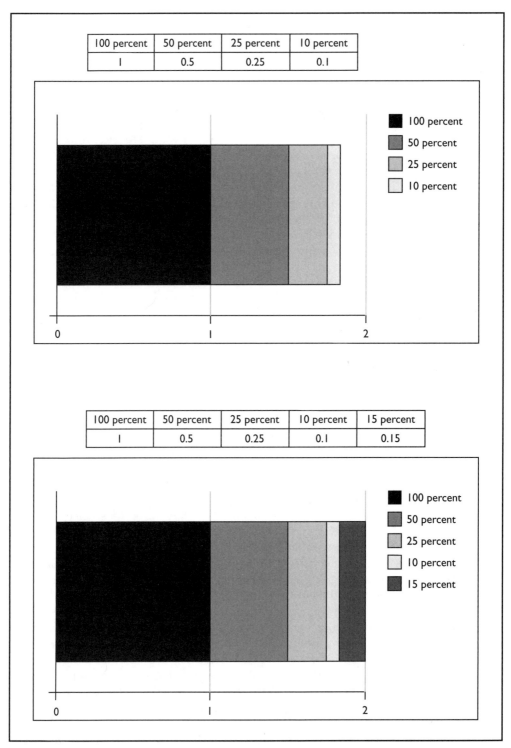

100 percent	50 percent	25 percent	10 percent
1	0.5	0.25	0.1

100 percent	50 percent	25 percent	10 percent	15 percent
1	0.5	0.25	0.1	0.15

Figure 10.53.

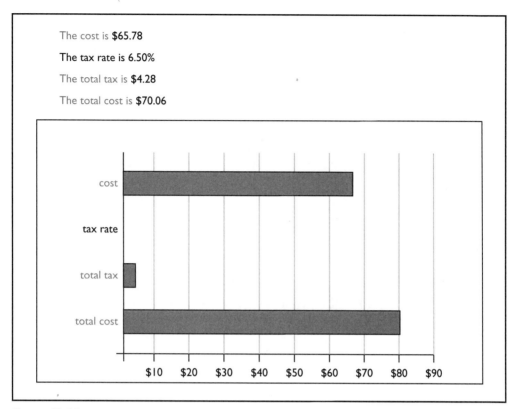

The cost is **$65.78**

The tax rate is 6.50%

The total tax is **$4.28**

The total cost is **$70.06**

Figure 10.54.

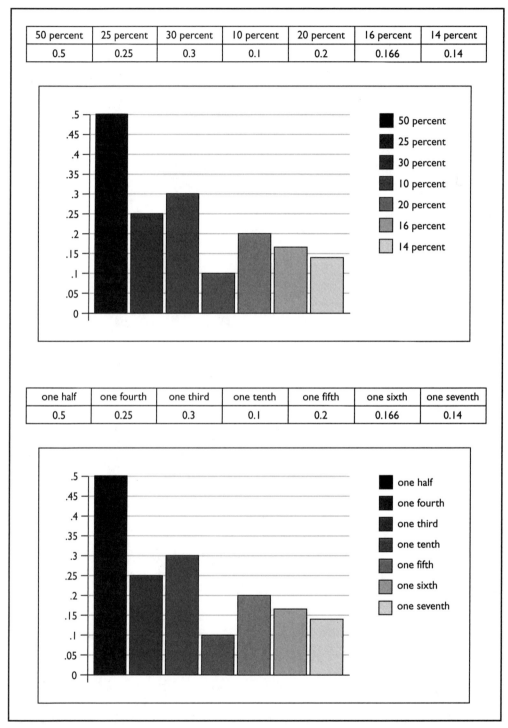

50 percent	25 percent	30 percent	10 percent	20 percent	16 percent	14 percent
0.5	0.25	0.3	0.1	0.2	0.166	0.14

one half	one fourth	one third	one tenth	one fifth	one sixth	one seventh
0.5	0.25	0.3	0.1	0.2	0.166	0.14

Figure 10.55.

♦ ♦ ♦ ♦ ♦ ♦ ♦ ♦ ♦ ♦ ♦ ♦ ♦ ♦ ♦ ♦ ♦ ♦

Commercial Software Distributors

Cambridge Development Laboratory
86 West Street
Waltham, MA 02451
800-637-0047
http://www.edumatch.com

Educational Resources
P.O. Box 1900
Elgin, IL 60121-1900
Western region: 800-624-2926
http://edresources.com

Forest Technologies
765 Industrial Drive
Cary, IL 60013
847-516-8280
http://foresttech.com

Learning Services
P.O. Box 10636
Eugene, OR 97440-2636
800-877-9378 (west)
800-877-3278 (east)
http://learnserv.com

National School Products
101 East Broadway
Maryville, TN 37804
800-627-9393

Commercial Software Publishers

Attainment Company
P.O. Box 930160
Verona, WI 53593-0160
http://www.attainment-inc.com

Don Johnston
P.O. Box 639
Wauconda, IL 60084-0639
800-999-4660
http://www.donjohnston.com

Edmark
P.O. Box 97021
Redmond, WA 98073-9721
800-691-2986
http://www.edmark.com

EdVenture Software
203-852-9246
http://www.edven.com

**EIKI International, Inc.
    (Language Master)**
26794 Vista Terrace Drive
Lake Forest, CA 92630-8113

Gamco
Siboney Learning Group
8135 Forsyth Boulevard, Suite 212
Clayton, MO 63105
888-726-8100
http://www.gamco.com

Great Wave Software
5353 Scotts Valley Drive
Scotts Valley, CA 95066
800-253-5469
http://www.greatwave.com

Intellitools, Inc.
55 Leveroni Court, Suite 9
Novato, CA 94949
800-899-6687
http://www.intellitools.com

KnowledgeAdventure
4100 West 190th Street
Torrance, CA 90504
800-545-7677
http://www.knowledgeadventure.com

MathTek/WBGU-TV
245 Troup Street
Bowling Green, OH 43403

Micrograms Software
9934 North Alpine Road, #108
Machesney Park, IL 61115-8240
800-338-4726
http://www.micrograms.com

Mindplay
160 West Fort Lowell Road
Tucson, AZ 85705
520-888-1800
http://www.mindplay.com

Nectar Foundation
10 Bowhill Avenue
Nepean, Ontario K236S7
Canada
http://www.nectar.on.ca

Neufeld Learning Systems
7 Connifer Crescent
London, Ontario N6K2V3
Canada
http://www.neufeldmath.com

Nordic Software
P.O. Box 83499
Lincoln, NE 68501
800-306-6502
http://www.nordicsoftware.com

Optimum Resources
18 Hunger Road
Hilton Head Island, SC 29926
888-784-2592
http://www.stickybear.com

Pierian Spring
5200 SW Macadam, Suite 570
Portland, OR 97201
800-472-8578
http://www.pierian.com

Sunburst
101 Castleton Street
P.O. Box 100
Pleasantville, NY 10570
800-321-7511
http://www.sunburst.com

Tom Snyder Productions
80 Coolidge Hill Road
Watertown, MA 02472-5003
800-342-0236
http://www.tomsnyder.com

Ventura Educational Systems
910 Ramona Avenue, Suite E
P.O. Box 425
Grover Beach, CA 93483
800-336-1022
http://venturaes.com/about.html

Shareware Sites

Ambrosia Software, Inc.
P.O. Box 23140
Rochester, NY 14692
716-325-1910; fax 716-325-3665
http://www.AmbrosiaSW.com

Brochu Software
http://sitelink.net/jbrochu

Crossword Express
http://www.adam.com.au/johnstev/

John V. Holder Software
http://www.cc.northcoast.com/~jvholder/

Kevin's Polyominoes Home Page
http://kevingong.com/Polyominoes

Kids Domain
http://www.kidsdomain.com

**LittleFish Software for Primary
   Schools**
http://members.aol.com/weefishes

Math Dittoes2
http://www.mathdittos2.com/index.html

**SCET Software/Scottish Council for
   Educational Technology**
74 Victoria Crescent Road
Glasgow, Scotland G12 9JN
http://www.scet.com

Script Software (CopyPaste)
http://www.scriptsoftware.com

References

Badian, N. A. (1992). Nonverbal learning disability, school behavior, and dyslexia. *Annals of Dyslexia, 42,* 160.

Capps, L. R., & Pickreign, J. (1993). Language connections in mathematics: A critical part of mathematics instruction. *Arithmetic Teacher, 41*(1), 8–12.

Denckla, M. B. (1991). Academic and extracurricular aspects of nonverbal learning disabilities. *Psychiatric Annals, 1*(21), 717–724.

Denckla, M. B. (1994). Measurement of executive function. In G. Reid Lyon (Ed.), *Frames of reference for the assessment of learning disabilities: New views on measurement issues* (pp. 117–142). Baltimore: Brookes.

Fennema, E., Carpenter, T. P., Levi, L., Franke, M. L., & Empson, S. (1997). *Cognitively guided instruction: Professional development in primary mathematics.* Madison, WI: Wisconsin Center for Education Research.

Foss, J. M. (1991). Nonverbal learning disabilities and remedial interventions. *Annals of Dyslexia, 41,* 129–133.

Garnett, K. (1999). Math learning disabilities. [On-line]. Available: http://www.ldonline.org/ld_indepth/math_skills/garnett.html.

Hotz, R. L. (1999, May 11). Numbers and our divided brain. *New York Times,* p. B2.

Johnston, D. (1997). Access to Math (verson 1.0) [Computer software]. Wauconda, IL: Don Johnston Incorporated.

Kamii, C., & Lewis, B. (1990). Constructivist learning and teaching. *Arithmetic Teacher, 38*(1), 34–35.

Kulak, A. G. (1993). Parallels between math and reading disability: Common issues and approaches. *Journal of Learning Disabilities, 26,* 666–673.

Matte, R. R., & Bolaski, J. A. (1998). Nonverbal learning disabilities: An overview. *Intervention in School and Clinic, 34,* 40.

National Council of Teachers of Mathematics. (1995). *Assessment standards for school mathematics.* Reston, VA: Author.

National Council of Teachers of Mathematics. (2000). *Principles and standards for school mathematics.* Reston, VA: Author.

Rourke, Byron P. (1993). Arithmetic disabilities, specific and otherwise: A neuropsychological perspective. *Journal of Learning Disabilities, 26*(4), 214–226.

Russell, S. N., & Dunlap, W. P. (1977). *An interdisciplinary approach to reading and mathematics.* San Rafael, CA: Academic Therapy Publications.

Zentall, S. S., & Ferkis, M. A. (1993). Mathematical problem solving for youth with ADHD, with and without learning disabilities. *Learning Disability Quarterly, 1,* 16.

Index

About the Authors

◆ ◆

Nancy S. Bley is academic coordinator at Park Century School in Los Angeles, California, where she has been on the faculty since 1976. Park Century is an independent day school that specializes in teaching students with learning disabilities. In addition to her work at Park Century, she maintains a private practice, working with learning disabled students who need help with various academic areas, the use of technology, and study skills. Ms. Bley has also taught Diagnosis and Remediation of Mathematical Difficulties to Students with Learning Disabilities at UCLA Extension. Prior to working at Park Century, she taught math to elementary and high school students at the Francis W. Parker School in Chicago. Ms. Bley was co-editor, with Carol A. Thornton, of *Windows of Opportunity: Mathematics for Students with Special Needs,* published by the National Council of Teachers of Mathematics. She has presented at numerous conferences including the Learning Disabilities Association of America, the Council for Learning Disabilities, Computer Using Educators, National Educational Computing Conferences (NECC), International Dyslexia Association, International Reading Association, Association of Educational Therapists, and the Research Council for Diagnostic and Prescriptive Mathematics. Ms. Bley has published articles in various areas of learning disabilities and is particularly interested in ways of using computers with students with learning disabilities.

Carol A. Thornton is a distinguished professor in the Department of Mathematics at Illinois State University–Normal, where she teaches graduate and undergraduate mathematics education courses. Thornton has 10 years' teaching experience in public schools, has started and directed a clinic for children with severe learning difficulties in mathematics, and currently spends 3 to 4 days each week with teachers and their students. An elementary school mathematics textbook author, Thornton has published numerous books and articles targeted for special education teachers. Primary among her publications are teacher resource or instructional materials related to basic fact mastery and compensatory strategies for helping children learn mathematics in problem-centered contexts. She has been a speaker and workshop leader at numerous state, regional, and national meetings, and throughout her professional life she has directed teacher enhancement grants for special and regular education teachers that have focused on strategies for improving mathematics instruction among students with special learning needs.